THE HOLY SWORD

THE
HOLY SWORD

THE STORY OF ISLAM FROM
MUHAMMAD TO THE PRESENT

ROBERT PAYNE

*The moment of mystery
is as the flashing of a sword in the air*
Jalalu'l-Din Rumi

ROBERT HALE LIMITED
63 Old Brompton Road
London, S.W.7

PRINTED IN GREAT BRITAIN BY RICHARD CLAY AND COMPANY LTD.,
BUNGAY, SUFFOLK

FOR MY FATHER

CONTENTS

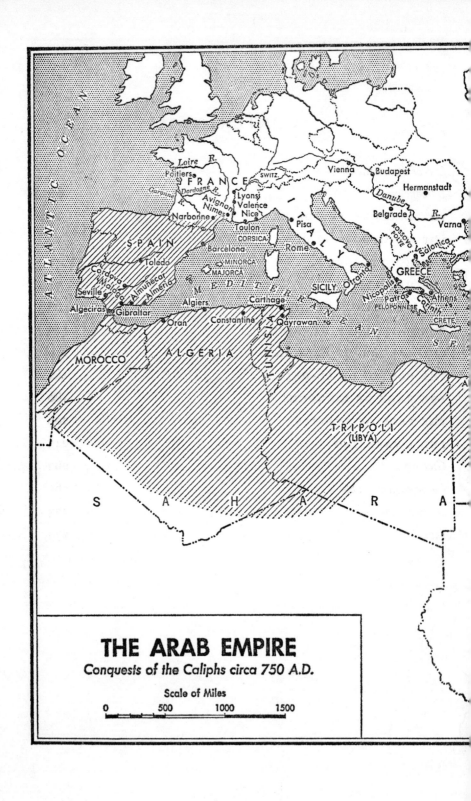

THE ARAB EMPIRE

Conquests of the Caliphs circa 750 A.D.

Scale of Miles

0   500   1000   1500

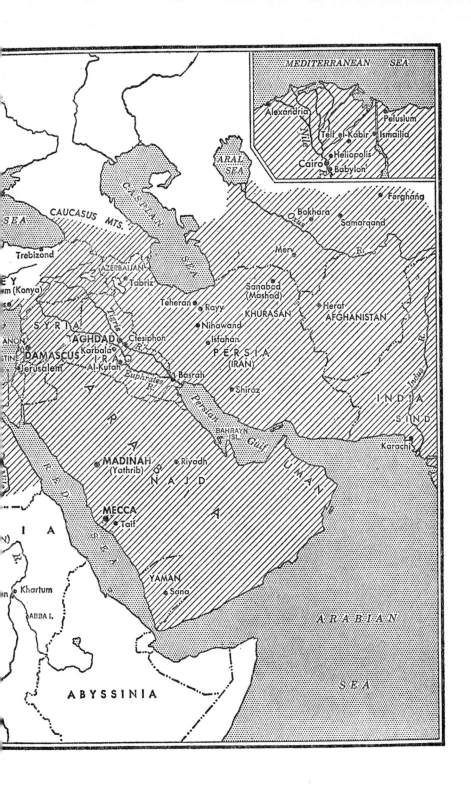

MEDITERRANEAN SEA

Alexandria
Pelusium
Tell el-Kabir
Ismailia
Heliopolis
Cairo
Babylon

ARAL
SEA

Ferghana

CASPIAN

CAUCASUS MTS.

Bokhara
Oxus
Samarqand

SEA

Trebizond

Mery

AZERBAIJAN

Tabriz

Sanabad
(Mashad)

Herat
AFGHANISTAN

Teheran
Rayy

KHURASAN

Indus R.

SYRIA

Tigris

m (Konya)

Nihawand

BAGHDAD
Ctesiphon
Isfahan

PERSIA
(IRAN)

DAMASCUS
Karbala
Al-Kufah
IRAQ

Jerusalem

Basrah

Euphrates
R.

Shiraz

INDIA

SIND

Persian

ANON
STINE

A
R
A
B
I
A

RED
SEA

Gulf

BAHRAYN
ISL.

Karachi

MADINAH
(Yathrib)

Riyadh

NAJD

OMAN

MECCA
Taif

I A

Khartum

ABBA I.

YAMAN
Sana

ARABIAN

ABYSSINIA

SEA

LIST OF ILLUSTRATIONS

ACKNOWLEDGEMENTS

The copyright of the above illustrations is held by the following: the British Museum, no. 1; the Mansell Collection, nos. 2, 12 and 16; the Metropolitan Museum of Art (Rogers Fund), New York, no. 3; the *Radio Times* Hulton Picture Library, nos. 4, 5, 6, 7 and 13; the Iraq Petroleum Company, nos. 8, 9, 10 and 11; the Persian Embassy, no. 14; the Government of India Tourist Office, nos. 15, 17 and 18; the Victoria and Albert Museum, nos. 19, 20 and 21.

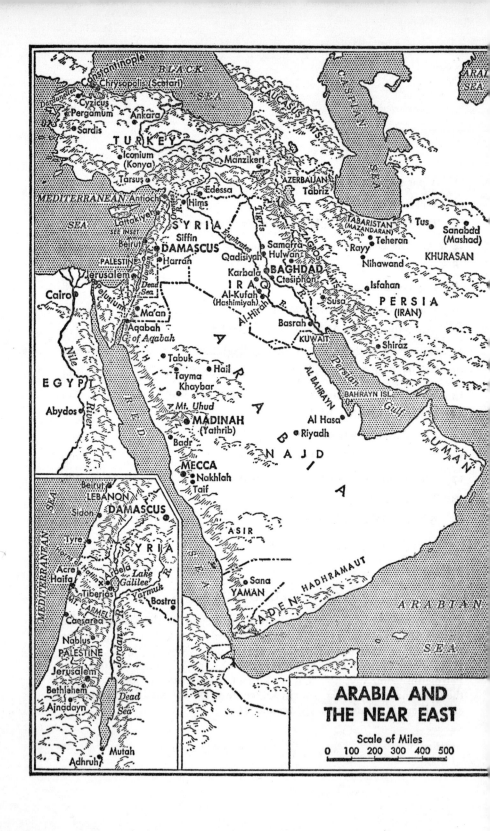

ARABIA AND
THE NEAR EAST

Scale of Miles
0   100   200   300   400   500

INTRODUCTION

I REMEMBER coming in the evening through the high fortress gates of the city of Rhodes, and while the fountains played and the shadows swirled I wandered through the Street of the Knights and out into the Turkish quarter where the minarets stood against the sunset. It was very quiet that evening, though the starlings were racing like black clouds across the sky. I do not know how I found myself in the Turkish cemetery in the shadow of a mosque, the grass overgrowing the stone turbans on the tombs of long-dead governors and civil servants, who once ruled the island by order of the Sultan in Constantinople. If it was quiet in the streets, it was still quieter in the cemetery. Soon an *imam* appeared, wearing the green turban of a *hajji* and a shapeless white gown, an old man bent by age, with a face of remarkable sweetness and dignity. We spoke in French for a while, and when I was leaving and it was very dark, he said, shaking his head: 'Every inch of this island has its drop of blood, and now the wars are over—they were all unnecessary!' Then he waved his hands towards the assembled ghosts of the conquerors, and we went out into the streets laden with incense, and he gave me a small blue tile from a ruined fountain, and said: 'Peace be upon you.'

I remember the nobility of the *hajji*, the look of settled composure on his face. He was like the Arabs I had imagined in my childhood. In my day there were no histories of the Arab conquests: one learned by bits and pieces; the child made up his own history. There was Baghdad in flames, the horsemen riding over the desert sands, the endless wars across the length and breadth of Asia—the Veiled Prophet, Shah Jehan, Akbar, the Alhambra, the dhows laden with slaves, and always the mosques in the setting sun. I thought all Arabs were dark-featured, bearded and of beautiful carriage, the most enviable of mortals; and I still think they are enviable. I was sixteen when I saw real Muhammadans for the first time. They were not peaceful—they were hacking at themselves with swords.

In those days I lived in the naval base at Simonstown in South Africa, overlooking the blue waters of False Bay and the golden hills of the Hottentot Hollands. Some Malay workmen invited me to attend the *kalifah* ceremony in the local school hall. For weeks they had prepared for the ceremony. As they sat about the stage there was nothing to suggest that anything extraordinary was about to happen. Someone was beating on a metal drum. Someone else was pouring incense in the flames. I knew these men well, and they invited me on the stage, so I sat with them in the smoke of incense, listening to the drumbeats, admiring the strange medley of weapons they had brought with them—curving swords, knives, daggers, skewers, even steel knitting needles. I asked Ibrahim about the heavy sword he was cradling in his arms. 'It is a holy sword,' he said, grasping it by the handle. 'It is many hundreds of years old.' And in truth the sword quivering in his hand looked holy: so old and grey and mottled; and I knew it was razor-sharp, because I drew my finger along the blade.

So perhaps half an hour passed, until they fell into a trance, their eyes closed, their lips moving. Suddenly Ibrahim threw off his coat and stood there naked to the waist, a strange smile of contentment on his lips. Then the sword flashed above his head and he brought it with a sickening crash against his outstretched left arm. The sword shivered, as though it had struck iron; but there was no wound. Later, with the same force, he stabbed himself in the stomach with the sword and the blade penetrated about four inches, and once again there was no blood. He inserted the sword between his ribs and drove it right into his chest; and he did not die. He was smiling when he drew the blade out again. Then he handed the sword to me—there was no trace of blood on it—and said 'Strike! It will not harm you! We shall see that no harm comes to you!' But I did not take the sword.

For the rest of the evening the Malays stabbed, hacked and cut themselves, drove spikes and knitting needles through their tongues, necks and cheeks, and came to no harm. There was no blood, or only a little trickle. Swords flashed, drums were beating, the sweet-smelling incense made us all drowsy, but not so drowsy that we were unable to recognize that something miraculous was happening. Swords went through them as through butter. What was astonishing above everything else was the strength employed to drive the swords home and the way the flesh opened to the sword-points. 'You have to say the name of God over and over again,' Ibrahim said later. 'Then everything is possible.'

I saw all the workmen again the next day; they were working in the naval base as though nothing had happened. They joked about the *khalifah*, and some of them had small wounds which they painted with mercurochrome.

Never before or since have I witnessed such command of spirit over matter. I have seen men walking through fire, but this was a small matter in comparison with the great driving swords which tore through the flesh of these Malays and left them unscathed; and though I shall never know how such a display adds to the glory of God, I know they performed these rites in complete innocence, proving only that if a man has faith in his God, nothing is impossible to him.

Since then, wandering through Malaya, Java, Persia and India, I have envied their serenity, their delighted absorption in their prayers, their sense of the world as a place to be enjoyed. Few Muhammadans have ever committed suicide. Western man's burden of guilt is unknown to them. They are a people who have acquired happiness and a sense of community with their brethren through the ritual they perform five times daily; and if the validity of a religion can be measured by the contentment it brings to men, then Muhammadanism possesses a validity above the ordinary. Yet the contentment of the Muhammadan arises from the precarious balance of forces. Like Christianity, Muhammadanism is dogged by a vast series of unresolved theological problems, and like the Christians the Muhammadans are the willing servants of an ideal which few can ever hope to approach.

As the breach between East and West widens, we tend to think of Muhammadans as members of an opposing camp. But in fact they belong to the West. They are, whether we like it or not, indissolubly linked with our own culture; are a part of us; have roots which are the same as ours; share the same portion of the energy of God. We tend to forget that Jesus is the Messiah of the Muhammadans, as He is ours. According to a famous *hadith*, one of the traditional sayings of Muhammad was 'There is no Mahdi save Jesus son of Mary.' And at the coming of the Last Day Jesus will descend triumphantly from the skies, wage war on Antichrist and die for the second time, and His body will be buried in a tomb beside Muhammad before he rises once more to rule over a Paradise of youth and freshness.

Such promises may give little comfort to Christians, who see the world in the light of other dispensations. Muhammadanism has no priesthood, no rounded tradition of scholarship, none of those elements of sensuous ceremonial which go with Western worship. Our worship derives from the Jewish and Byzantine courts, our God an imperial figure elevated beyond all empires; theirs is the harsher God of the deserts, blazing like the sun over the abysmal lives of the desert dwellers, giving little comfort to men except the knowledge that they will enter Paradise if they obey His iron laws. Muhammadanism is a religion which is still raw, still bleeding. It is a religion without tenderness, without a Virgin, without love in the sense by which we understand love: the face of Muhammad is wholly masculine. So it has remained, and it is unthinkable that it will ever change.

But the harsh law of Muhammad, binding men with heavy fetters, has had the effect of producing another kind of freedom. In their ascent towards the Unknown, they move with a similar motion of wings; from a distance those hawks and eagles might be Christians winging their way to the blue vaults of Heaven. If the sources are remote from one another, if the fierce language of the Quran, written in letters of fire, seems remote from the gentler message of the New Testament (as rock-bound Mecca is remote from the Sea of Galilee), yet there is a meeting place of the spirit among the mystics. The Muhammadan mystic recognizes Jesus as his exemplar. The great Persian poet Jalalu'l-Din Rumi is brother to St. John of the Cross, and St. Teresa of Ávila would have understood the words which fell so simply from the lips of the saintly Rabi'a al-Adawiyya. The greatest of all Muhammadan mystics, who went by the name of al-Hallaj, 'the corder', offered himself as a sacrificial victim for the sins of men and spoke in a language so full of Christian overtones that many regarded him as a heretic. The history of Islam is a long dialogue with Christianity.

In the Middle Ages Muhammad became 'the accurst Mahound', and Dante placed him in Hell, his body split down the middle in punishment for heresy, while his adopted son Ali, as the lesser heresiarch, was punished only by having his face torn apart, and so together the two heretics were left wandering down the doleful road—*la dolente strada*. In the Middle Ages it was believed that Muhammadanism was no more than a Christian heresy; it was only later that men realized that Muhammadanism sprang from original roots. The mind of Muhammad was saturated with Jewish and Christian legends and histories, but he stripped the Old and New Testaments of all that was not native to Arabia. His heroes therefore were Adam, Abraham, Moses, Jesus, all those who could be imagined as living on Arabian soil, tribal chieftains of gaunt and commanding aspect, men who stood at the gates of revelation. He saw them against the golden sands and shuddering skies, and being transmuted into Arabs, with Arab casts of mind, they came to possess a peculiar Arab relevance. He had imagined them anew, so that they came to him with great force and vividness. In much the same way Virgil transformed the Trojans into Romans, and the Chinese transformed the grave features of the contemplative Buddha into the smiling Goddess of Mercy.

Such transformations have occurred at all periods in human history, and the effect is often surprising. There is nearly always a leap, a strangeness, the sense of a deliberate distortion. The Christian, seeing his heroes in their Muhammadan disguise, is baffled by their sudden remoteness, for they give the appearance of improvisations constructed out of a chance assembling of odd legends and scraps of history. It is only later that we become aware how deeply rooted they are in the Arab environment, possessing a perfect validity of their own. The gulf that separates the Christian from the Muhammadan is a very narrow one, but it is centuries deep; and it is too late to build a bridge across it.

From the very beginning there were differences so vast that no human mind has been able to reconcile them. It is not only that Muhammadans are incapable of understanding a God who is expressed in terms of the Trinity and cannot bring themselves to believe He was crucified in the flesh, but their normal habits of mind, their aims and preoccupations, are at variance with ours. Though schooled in Greek philosophy, Arabs have never completely accepted the fundamental tenets of Western logic: to them an inquiry into the nature of virtue and goodness is meaningless, since all virtue and all goodness come from God. As our minds move by slow progressive steps up a rational ladder, as the Chinese mind moves in great sweeping circles, so the mind of the Muhammadan moves in sudden short-paced spurts of remarkable power and energy, illuminating the darkness with a quick and blinding light, then retiring into the dark again to prepare for another explosive outburst. The greatest of Muhammadan thinkers have been freebooters and raiders of the spirit, who did not take easily to established laws, even the laws of their religion. They had the failings of guerrillas. They moved like lightning, but often found themselves in unmapped territory where they were at a loss to recognize the castles they were attacking, and so attacked all of them indiscriminately; and sometimes they hurled their most potent weapons at shadows. They were men without patience. They must know all, or give up the game. To read al-Ghazzali or Ibn Arabi is to see men making war on heaven nakedly, having thrown their weapons away as unworthy encumbrances in the contest.

Nakedness indeed was the weapon they prized above all others as being the most dependable, since it is the ultimate weapon, shared by all alike. They insisted upon giving a place to the human body and human passions; Plato's bloodless categories were therefore foreign to them, and they moved more easily in the less rarefied world of Aristotle. Only an Arab philosopher—and that the greatest—would dare to say that man comes closest to God in the embrace of a woman.

Today with the Arab world awakening at last after centuries of sleep, it is more than ever necessary to come to grips with the Arab mind. There is a sense in which they are more dangerous to our peace than the Russians. To the uncommitted nations they speak with the authority which comes from naked conquest. They speak as man to man, proudly, contemptuous of our mechanical marvels even when they enjoy them, for to them God is so much greater than all our foolish strivings that they regard the power of the bomb as insignificant in comparison with the power of God, and they have no illusions about material progress. Their strength lies in their humanness. They are ruthless and at ease in a world where we are increasingly restless and incapable of decision. Hamlet still walks our fortress walls, but an Arab Hamlet is unthinkable.

We have good reason to study the Arabs and probe into their ways of thought, for they have conquered the world before, and may do it again. The fire lit by Muhammad still burns strongly, and there is every reason to believe that the flame is unquenchable.

So I have written this book in the hope that men will look closer at Arab origins, and I have called it after the strange two-pointed sword which Muhammad won as a trophy at the battle of Badr, because the sword became the symbol of his imperial pretensions. As far as I know, it is the first attempt to write a reasonably complete cultural history of the Arab conquests from the beginnings to the present day. I have concluded the book with seven portraits of Arab leaders who lived through the last 150 years because this seemed the simpler way to present the vast changes which have brought about the Arab awakening.

I hope something of the sweep and roar and fury of Arab history has come clear through these pages. Out of Arabia there came a proud and august people who in their time conquered most of the known world, and there is still too little about them in our history books. Sooner or later we shall have to learn to live with them.

B

THE SANDS OF THE DESERT

As far as the eye can see there is only yellow sand, black pebbles, small outcrops of flinty rock and the dim footprints of the sand foxes. Under the asphalt-blue sky of noonday the rippling sand seems to quiver and change colour from bronze to gold and then to a strange yellowish purple. The heat is staggering. It seems to explode out of the earth in blinding waves; and the horizon, like a thick black line scrawled on the rim of the world, seems to dance. When the wind comes over the desert, the heat grows thicker, juicier, an intolerable uproar of heat, striking between the eyes. The never-ending desert is never silent. At noon you hear it moaning and rustling; at night when the temperature falls to zero you can hear the shattering of the desert rocks.

In the gold emptiness of the sprawling desert, life flows to a rhythm unknown to our climate. There are no cycles of vegetation. Centuries pass; there is no change except that the rocks are a little smoother. But deep below the sheets of sand a minute, secret life exists nevertheless. One rainfall, and the desert becomes a fiery carpet of purple and scarlet flowers whose frail roots, thinner than threads, lie deep in the subsoil, resting on rock. For a few days the flowers wither on their stems, till the petals turn black and shrivel and are whirled away in gust of hot wind. Then there is only sand again, and the crumbling knife-sided rocks, and the rare oases.

In all this desolation of Arabia there are only a few towns. Even today there are places where no one has ever penetrated, virgin still, though the seacoast is encumbered with names. The visitor wandering across the desert may come upon caravans such as the Romans saw, for the Arabs wear the same clothes, eat and drink from the same utensils and equip their camels with the same accoutrements as they did centuries ago. Leopards and hyenas prowl, an occasional ostrich hops across the desert sand, and fat yellow lizards with thick tails sun themselves on the rocks, and time stands still. Eternity is very close to Arabia even in this age of oil wells.

Not all of Arabia is desert: there are lava fields, and mountains nine thousand feet high in southern Asir, and fertile fields in the uplands of Najd, and rivers wind along the coastal plains. Yet the desert colours the life of the Arabs; it is inescapable. Here 'heaven is as iron and the earth is as brass', and insecurity is bred into the very roots of life.

No one knows where the Arabs come from, or whether they were there from the beginning. A stern, unyielding people, with little taste for civilization until they ventured abroad, they were and are a handsome race

with close-knit loyalties, agile, querulous, proud of their capacity to survive in an inhospitable land, sullen and secretive, quick to anger and quick
to begin a friendship, ferociously brave in battle and very sensual. They
live in the flesh, lacking the sense of guilt and shame which comes in more
temperate climates.

There is majesty in their harsh landscape, and there is majesty in
their speech. They are perfectly aware of the infinite complexities and
magnificence of their language. 'God gave three great things to the
world,' says the Arab proverb. 'The brain of the Frank, the hands of
the Chinese, and the tongue of the Arab.' In Arabic there are only
three long vowels and the consonants have all the importance; nevertheless there is a natural richness and a superb delicacy in the spoken
language. So many Arabic words have entered our own language
that even those who know no Arabic can guess at the sounds spoken in
Arabia. Here are sixty words in common use which we have taken from
them:

admiral	calibre	ginger	orange
albatross	camphor	giraffe	ream
alchemy	carmine	guitar	saffron
alcove	caraway	jasmine	satin
alfalfa	chemistry	jasper	sequin
algebra	chemise	julep	sherbet
alkali	cipher	lute	syrup
almanac	coffee	mattress	sloop
amber	cotton	mohair	sofa
arsenal	crimson	monsoon	sumac
artichoke	cupola	mufti	talc
atlas	elixir	mummy	tambour
benzine	garble	muslin	tariff
cable	ghoul	myrrh	traffic

It would be comparatively easy to compile a much longer list: altogether about 1,000 words with Arabic origins have entered the English
language. If you will recite some of these words softly, with a slight sing-
song intonation, you will have some idea of the sound of Arabic, a language
marvellously equipped to deal with the most complex aspects of philo-
sophical speculation and the most subtle poetry. In the Quran, which is
at once poetic, speculative and fiercely moralistic, the language reaches its
greatest heights. Muhammad, who detested poetry, was the greatest poet
to come out of Arabia.

Of the beginnings of this language we know almost nothing, and we
know hardly more about the early history of the Arabs. All we know
derives from travellers' tales, the reports of Roman expeditions, and the
stone relics found in the sand. Much of our knowledge derives from
Herodotus, who was rarely wrong when he reported on things he saw with
his own eyes, but who showed demonstrable ignorance when he turned

his attention to Arabia. 'It is,' he says, 'a place which exhales the most delicious perfume, being the only country in the world which produces frankincense, myrrh, cassia, cinnamon and labdanum.' He says frankincense trees were always surrounded by a swarm of winged and brightly coloured serpents. As for their religion, he says they worshipped Orotal and Alilat, the first, he explains, being Bacchus and the second Urania. In this he was wrong, for Orotal is evidently *Allah taalah*, the name by which the Arabs to this day address the Almighty, and Alilat is the goddess Allat, who was worshipped in the shape of a square stone at Taif on the edge of the plateau, not far east of Mecca. They had other gods. There was al-Uzza, the morning star, who had her cult at Nakhlah; the great explorer, Charles Doughty, saw her one night by lantern light—she was an untrimmed mass of scaly grey granite, shaped like a thighbone. There was also Manah, the goddess of destiny, who was worshipped as a black stone in Qudayd on the road between Mecca and Yathrib.

But while Herodotus tells us little about their religion, he does provide us with our first glimpse into the nature of Arab loyalties. He is describing a solemn ceremony of oath taking:

> When two men desire to swear an oath of friendship, a third stands between them, and he cuts the palms of their hands near the base of the thumb with a sharp stone; then he takes a little tuft of wool from their clothes, dips it in their blood and smears the blood on seven stones lying between them, all the while invoking the names of Bacchus and Urania.[1]

The tuft of wool, the blood, the stones, the covenant between men—we shall meet them again and again as this history unfolds.

When the Arabs made oaths, they kept them: Herodotus says there was no people on earth who respected their pledges more religiously. Because they were bred in the raw heat of the desert and were surrounded by forces which seemed determined to put an end to their lives, they regarded themselves as pathetic creatures, who must continually prove themselves. In the desert a man is stripped clean of pretensions: he is what he is. So they relied largely on their own strength, the strength which comes from the covenants they made with one another, and the power which came to them from their gods, who were represented by the strangely shaped stones they found in their wanderings.

To this day the Arabs worship stones, and so do all the followers of Muhammad. There is nothing particularly surprising in stone worship. If it is believed that a stone has fallen from the sun, the moon, a planet or a bright star, then the stone becomes the physical embodiment of the mysterious forces which move the universe; and by standing completely naked before such a stone and offering a blood sacrifice, the worshipper places

[1] *Histories*, III, 8.

himself within the circle of divine power emanating from the stone, and some portion of this power is communicated to him.

Today all the holy stones of Arabia save one have been swept away. The one remaining stone, known as the Black Stone, though it is a dark reddish-brown, was worshipped in Mecca long before the time of Muhammad. No one knows its history, and no one has ever tried to determine what kind of stone it is. In pre-Muhammadan times it was believed that the stone had fallen from the moon and was sacred to the old moon god Hubal. The stone was enclosed in a small square temple known as the Kaaba, which also contained many lesser idols and included at one time a Byzantine icon of the Virgin. Here at the time of the new moon following the summer solstice, at the hottest time of the year, the ancient pilgrims came to worship the moon god, stripping off all covering in token of their humility. Naked, they touched the stone with their right hands and then reverently kissed it, and afterwards they walked round the Kaaba seven times, making the first three circuits with quick steps and the last four more slowly, each circuit representing the procession of one of the planets. By day this office was performed in silence, and by night with clapping hands and whistling through the fingers, for the new moon was rising and they welcomed its presence.

Worship at Mecca was not limited to the sevenfold circuit of the Kaaba. Next came the drinking of the waters of Zamzam, a holy well which lay nearby, very brackish and lukewarm, followed by running seven times between the two low hills of Marwa and Al Safa, less than a thousand feet apart across the centre of Mecca. No one remembers what blessings were originally conferred on pilgrims drinking the waters, while Muhammadans declare that running between the hills recapitulates Hagar's frantic search for water for her son Ishmael, but this was evidently a later gloss; these small hills were stones representing ancient gods, and therefore to be worshipped. The pilgrimage to the holy well and the hills is known as the Lesser Pilgrimage.

There followed the Larger Pilgrimage, involving a journey of some twenty miles to a holy mountain, a granite shoulder about 200 feet high, on the plain of Arafat. From noon to sunset the pilgrims lingered on the hill in meditation, then gathered themselves with all speed to reach the neighbouring town of Muzdalifah, where they bought or picked up from the ground twenty-one small stones. Returning to Mecca, they paused at a place called Mina, where they sacrificed sheep and camels, strewing the entrails over the earth, and after praying over the stones brought from Muzdalifah and breathing on them, they threw them at three pillars representing the evil spirits. The climactic ceremony took place not at Arafat, the sacred mountain, nor at Mecca, the sacred city, but on the obscure plain of Mina in the shadow of granite mountains.

To this day no one knows why the plain of Mina was chosen as the place of sacrifice. Later Muhammadan tradition asserts that the stone pillars are located at the spot where Satan tried three times to tempt Abraham to rebel against the order of Allah to kill his own son. Of all the places which Muslims are enjoined to visit in their pilgrimage, or *Hajj*, only one is intimately connected with the Prophet; all the other places, and all the sacrifices performed at them, derive from the age when Arabs worshipped stones.

Today every Muhammadan who makes the pilgrimage to Mecca performs the sevenfold circumambulation of the Kaaba, and the Lesser and the Greater Pilgrimage. For him the drinking of the waters of Zamzam is only one, and perhaps the least important, of the many rites he must perform to obtain merit from the pilgrimage. Yet it is this spring of unpalatable water which lies closest to the mystery of Muhammad.

During a time of drought about A.D. 530 a certain Abd al-Muttalib of the powerful tribe of Quraysh decided to dig for water. He was known for his interest in legends and traditions. Among these traditions was one which spoke of a sacred well near the Kaaba which had stopped flowing three hundred years before. Abd al-Muttalib dug for the well on the traditional site, found the coping stones and cleared out the debris of centuries. He was near the bottom of the well when he discovered unexpected treasure. The treasure consisted of two golden gazelles, some swords and several complete suits of armour, forming the regalia of the last Jurhamite king, who had evidently ordered it to be thrown down the well before taking to flight.

Stunned by the discovery of so much treasure, Abd al-Muttalib kept it secret for some days. When the tribal leaders heard of the discovery, they claimed it on the grounds that they were the guardians of the sacred places and the legal inheritors of the property of the former kings. Abd al-Muttalib suggested that he possessed the treasure by right of discovery and offered to allow the moon god Hubal, whose emblems were contained in the Kaaba, to adjudicate the case. The tribal leaders agreed. Accordingly six arrows were chosen—two yellow arrows representing the claims of the Kaaba, two black ones for Abd al-Muttalib and two white ones for the Quraysh tribe. Lots were then cast with the arrows, and so it happened that the golden gazelles fell to the Kaaba, the swords and suits of armour fell to Abd al-Muttalib, and none of the treasure fell to the Quraysh.

Abd al-Muttalib possessed complete power over the treasure, to do with it as he thought fit. He decided to hammer the gazelles into golden plates to decorate the gates of the Kaaba, and some of the gold was used to make a lock and key. He hung the swords over the door to protect the holy place, and kept the armour for himself. The waters of Zamzam soon acquired a reputation for sanctity, and their discoverer, from being an obscure member of a powerful tribe, became rich and famous as the guardian of the well.

Some forty years later, when Abd al-Muttalib was an old man, the father of many children, the Abyssinian Viceroy of Yaman in south Arabia threatened to attack Mecca unless the Kaaba was destroyed by the Meccans themselves. He was a Christian, determined to raise the Cross on the sanctuary of the pagan moon god. The Meccans held fast to their beliefs, refused to destroy their most cherished possession, and sent out an expedition to meet the army of the Abyssinian Viceroy. Poorly equipped, the Meccans were no match for the Abyssinians, who advanced under cover of armoured elephants: they were the first elephants ever seen by the unhappy Meccans, who panicked and began to make overtures to the enemy, even offering to destroy the Kaaba if their lives were spared. A messenger was sent to the camp of the Viceroy, but the messenger died during the journey and his death was regarded as a sign from Heaven that the Kaaba must be preserved. Some time later, when the Abyssinians were only three days march away, the elders of Mecca, among them Abd al-Muttalib, were summoned to a parley. Once more they were threatened with extinction unless the Kaaba was destroyed. The elders offered a third of the wealth of the region of Tihama if the Viceroy would call off his crusade, but the offer was refused. Still threatening, the Viceroy sent the elders on their way. He treated them with great dignity, and when he heard that some of Abd al-Muttalib's camels had been captured by his army, he ordered them returned to their owner.

In despair the elders made their way back to Mecca and prepared to abandon the town. They made no effort to take the Kaaba with them: so holy an object belonged to its holy site, and would have lost its power once it was uprooted. According to tradition Abd al-Muttalib offered a last prayer to the moon god to preserve the Kaaba, leaning on the gates he had plated with gold. Then he hurried away to the hills.

The Meccans expected the Abyssinians to advance but Hubal had heard their prayers. Overnight an epidemic, perhaps an aggravated form of smallpox, swept through the army, which suffered so many losses that the Viceroy decided to return to Yaman. Arabic tradition pictures the Abyssinians reeling back to the Yamanite capital of Sana afflicted by plagues, floods and the treachery of their guides. Hardly a soldier survived, and the Viceroy himself died of a malignant disease shortly afterwards. No one could doubt the power of the moon god who had kept an army of elephants at bay.

For a few more years the Kaaba proclaimed the power and mercy of a pagan god, but the sacred reddish-brown stone was not immune from sacrilege, even after Muhammad had established his Kingdom. On January 12, A.D. 930, a powerful army of Qarmatians, followers of a strange mystical sect originating in Iraq, descended upon Mecca at the time of pilgrimage after a forced march across the uplands of Najd. They took the town by storm, slaughtered 30,000 pilgrims, filled the well of Zamzam with corpses and set about desecrating the holy places. One of the more daring Qarmatians tore the stone from the wall and smashed it, and the fragments were later removed to al-Hasa in the Bahrayn region of the Persian Gulf on the opposite side of Arabia, where Abu Tahir, the leader of the Qarmatians, had his headquarters. There the scattered fragments of the stone remained for twenty-two years in spite of the continual appeals of the Meccans, who offered to pay 5,000 pieces of gold for the restoration of the fragments; and when at last the Qarmatians decided to return them in obedience to an order from the Fatimid Caliph, it amused them to hint that they were returning some pebbles they had picked up at random. The Meccans, however, recognized the true stone, now broken into some fourteen or fifteen fragments. These fragments were restored to their place in the wall of the Kaaba, and there is no record of any further damage until the beginning of the eleventh century, when the half-mad Fatimid Caliph Hakim, appalled by the continued worship of a stone, sent an emissary to Mecca to destroy it. The emissary was armed with an iron bar, and succeeded in chipping off three small pieces before he was himself torn to pieces by a howling mob.

The stone remains, and millions of worshippers who owe no allegiance to the moon god Hubal have kissed and caressed it over the years. Today the fragments are embedded in pitch and held together by silver wires—there are three large fragments and perhaps eighteen smaller ones—and all of them together can be covered by the outspread fingers of one hand, for the width of the stone is no more than ten inches. Once it was milky white, a proper colour for a stone believed to have fallen from the moon, but age has discoloured it, and already it is losing its reddish lustre and turning black. In all of history there is no object of veneration which has been worshipped for so long a time.

The Kaaba too has suffered its vicissitudes. Once it was no more than a square of wall open to the sky, but it was already roofed in the time of Abd al-Muttalib. The swords which he hung over the golden gates have long since vanished, and so have the golden gates—the present gates are of hammered silver presented by a Turkish Sultan of the sixteenth century. Legend says that Abraham built the original Kaaba, and Ishmael is buried close by, but these legends seem to be comparatively recent additions to an enormous corpus of legends invented to explain the significance of the site. Today the shrine is empty. Of the Kaaba known to Abd al-Muttalib nothing remains except a shattered stone.

All of Arabia is haunted by these mysterious fragments, which are so small that a man could put them in his pocket and forget them. All over the world the influence of the stone can be felt, continually radiating like the ripples of water when a stone is flung into a pool. It speaks of a time when men lived in direct communion with the heavenly presences, when the rising of the new moon was still a mystery and each worshipper stretched out his hands for its beneficent influences. In primitive societies power belonged, not to the golden sun, but to the white moon, who tended the crops and the fruit trees and guided the rivers from their sources in the mountains.

But the power of the moon was already waning. In the year following the attack on Mecca there was born to the youngest son of Abd al-Muttalib at a place not far from the well of Zamzam a male child who was solemnly held up to the flashing gates of the Kaaba when only a few days old. It was probably Abd al-Muttalib who gave the child the name by which he was always know—Muhammad, meaning 'the praised one'.

With his coming the ancient gods were swept away, to give place to Allah, 'the supreme and only God, from whom there flows the eternal radiance, the source of all things in the universe'. And within a generation Arabia emerged from its long sleep and hurled itself upon the world.

THE MESSENGER OF GOD

MUHAMMAD IBN-ABDULLAH never knew his father, who died before he was born. His mother Amina seems to have been a beautiful and sickly woman, unable to care for her only son, who was so often ill that it was thought best to remove him from the unhealthy air of Mecca and send him to the highlands. So at the age of two he was placed in the hands of a foster mother, the wife of a poor shepherd of the Banu Sa'd living at Taif, a hill town southeast of Mecca. The boy grew up in poverty, despised by his rich relatives, his inheritance from his father being no more than five camels, a few sheep and an Abyssinian slave girl called Baraka.

The boy's first memories were of flowering orchards, for Taif then as now was a wonderfully fruitful oasis on the edge of the desert, full of apple trees, peach trees and vineyards. Gradually the boy's health improved: his cheeks took on the warm rosy-white colour which they retained to the end of his life; and though short for his age, he was stocky and well-muscled. According to a fairly authentic tradition Halima, his foster mother, observed that even as a boy he was given to fits of abstraction, and there were some who said he bore the seal of God from the beginning. When he was four or five he tended sheep. Occasionally he was brought to Mecca on visits, where he attended the pagan ceremonies at the Kaaba and knelt at the feet of his grandfather, now well past seventy and married to a young bride, a man with little time to spare for his innumerable grand-children.

Muhammad was about five years old when he suffered the first of the strange visitations which came to him at intervals throughout his life. There seems to be no doubt about the authenticity of the visitation, for similar stories are reported of many saints. He was walking in a field with one of Halima's sons when he suddenly fell down, shouting as he sprawled on the ground that two men in white garments were splitting open his belly and stirring it up. His companion could make nothing of what was happening and ran back to the shepherd's house to summon assistance. Halima and her husband came running to the field, to find Muhammad no longer sprawling on the ground, but standing up, all the blood drained from his face. Asked what had happened, he spoke of the two angels who had cut open his belly, searching for something, though he did not know what it was. The shepherd was afraid he was possessed by a devil and said he should be returned to Mecca before his malady became the talk of the town. But when Halima brought the boy to Mecca, Amina said quietly that it was something she had expected and they should pay no attention to these attacks.

For a few more months Muhammad remained at Taif, and then,

perhaps at the insistence of the shepherd, he came to live with his mother in Mecca. A year later, returning from a visit to her relatives in Madinah, she died suddenly in the village of Abwa, where she was buried. Muhammad was heartbroken. He had lost his mother, and his foster mother refused to let him live at Taif. At the age of six he was an orphan, completely destitute, his only remaining possession being the faithful Abyssinian slave girl Baraka, who took her courage in her hands and led the boy to the house of Abd al-Muttalib, who took pity on him. For two years Muhammad remained in this house overlooking the Kaaba, while the old man taught him the ceremonies attached to the worship of the moon god and told him the legends of the place. Then when Abd al-Muttalib died, Muhammad was placed in the care of his uncle, Abu Talib, a kindly man who dealt in cloths and perfumes and owned some sheepfolds in the hills. Abu Talib was concerned that children should earn their keep, and so for the second time Muhammad became a shepherd, but now there were no flowering orchards to gaze upon: only the flinty hills of Mecca flashing in the sun.

Already at the age of eight the pattern of his life was being determined—long days of contemplation, swift journeys, the sense of being abandoned, visitation of spirits, and always the dream of Paradise in the orchards of Taif. Twice he had suffered the deaths of those close to him, but perhaps the death that most affected him occurred before he was born. From the beginning he was a man in search of his father.

The restless childhood was followed by a restless youth. He was about ten when his uncle first allowed him to accompany caravans to the north, hiring him out as camelman and guard. Tradition asserts that he was travelling with his uncle in Syria at the age of twelve when he met a Nestorian monk called Bahira, who hailed him as God's messenger. What is certain is that at an early impressionable age Muhammad showed a predilection for conversing with priests and rabbis when the caravans stopped at the trading posts, and he stored these conversations in his capacious memory. He could not read or write, but he had the Arab's memory for detail and the Arab's enjoyment in fluent argument. He seems to have been constantly travelling, his journeys extending from Yaman in the south to Damascus and Bostra in the north. Syria especially pleased him, and long afterwards he said: 'Truly God has maintained guardians of the word in Syria; they are forty in number, and when one dies another takes his place; and through them the land is blessed.'

It was a time of unrest in Mecca and the surrounding districts. The death of Abd al-Muttalib had left the Quraysh without a strong leader, and there were many contenders for power among the tribesmen. There was trouble too with the Bani Hawazin, a Bedouin tribe owning great areas of land in the Najd. A war, known as the 'impious war', broke out when the Bani Hawazin violated the oath against fighting during the sacred months. The Quraysh took to arms, and Muhammad took part in an obscure skirmish with his uncle Zubayr, though he did little more than gather up the arrows shot by the enemy and hand them to his uncle, and act as shield-bearer. He was a man who had no great liking for war, and avoided it whenever possible.

The troubles within the Quraysh came to an end with a solemn declaration of friendship among the rival clans, followed by brilliant celebrations of brotherhood. It was agreed to form a confederacy to punish wrong-doing and secure justice among the different branches of the family. Muhammad was present at the celebrations, and years later he remembered them with pleasure, saying: 'I would not exchange for the choicest camel in Arabia the remembrance of being present at the oath which we took in the house of Abdullah when the Bani Hashim, Zuhra ibn Kilab and Teim ibn Murra swore that they would stand by the oppressed.' The Bani Hashim was the branch of the Quraysh to which Muhammad belonged, deriving its name from the father of Abd al-Muttalib, a man who in his time had been guardian of the Kaaba, keeper of the battle flag, mayor of the town and the most generous supporter of widows and orphans.

At the age of twenty Muhammad had little hope of being able to follow in the footsteps of his great-grandfather. He was a hired hand with no prospect of making a fortune or sitting in a place of authority. At intervals he tended his uncle's sheep and goats; for the rest he followed his uncle's caravans and sometimes sold small quantities of merchandise. Before him there stretched a life indistinguishable from the lives of countless other Arabs, and he seems to have been perfectly content.

He was about twenty-five when he attracted the attention of a forty-year-old widow, Khadija, who had lost two husbands and acquired an impressive fortune. She was a warm-hearted, handsome woman, who had heard from one of her agents of Muhammad's skill as a camel driver and manager of caravans. She asked to see him, and seems to have fallen in love with him the moment she set eyes on him. She had good reason to admire him, for he was a vigorous and handsome fellow with an air of authority about him. Her husbands had both been sickly, and this camel driver of noble descent looked as though he could manage her estates, give her many more children and satisfy all her desires.

In later years Muhammad enjoined that no portraits of people should ever be made, since every portrait was an act of worship removing the contemplation of the observer from the worship of God, but Arab chroniclers continually portrayed him in words. Of his appearance we know innumerable intimate details, and if he entered a room we would recognize him instantly. We would recognize him by the timbre of his voice, the way he walked, the way he gestured, the way he sat upon the ground, even the way he slept. Of no other founder of a great religion do we know so much; and what is strange and a little disturbing about the portrait is its very humanness. He is of the earth, earthy; only the great glowing eyes speak of Heaven and the angels.

The man who entered the household of Khadija was sturdy and thickset, of medium height, with heavy shoulders and a thick black curling beard. He was beetle-browed, and long black silken lashes, which he painted with kohl, fell over eyes which were very large, dark and piercing, and often bloodshot. His skin was rosy, 'soft as a woman's', and he had a Roman nose, thin and aristocratic, with flaring nostrils. He had dazzling white teeth, but was gap-toothed towards the end of his life. When he laughed, which was often, he opened his mouth wide, so that the gums were visible, and when he spoke, he turned his whole body, not only the head. It was a good head, with a high forehead, and a little too large for the body, and his thick hair glistened and fell in waves to his shoulders. What people remembered most was the sweetness of his expression, and the sudden opening of the enormous eyes.

The chroniclers have gone to great pains to record every detail of his physical appearance. They speak for example of his chest—'From the chest down to the navel then was drawn a thin line of hair, while the other parts of the chest and stomach were hairless, although there was hair on his blessed arms and shoulders and the upper part of his chest.' They speak of his strange lurching walk 'as if he were ascending a steep and invisible hill', and how he ate, sitting on the ground with one leg extended and the other posted, and how he slept always on his right side with the palm of his right hand under his right cheek. They speak too of the mole, the size of a pigeon's egg, which lay between his shoulders. Of his voice they say it was very low and deep, but when he shouted, it was like a blare of trumpets, frightening everyone in sight. As he grew older, he became round-shouldered, and with that strange quick walk of his he resembled more than ever a bull about to charge. His hair never turned grey, but was as thick and lustrous at the end as in his youth.

We know his likes and dislikes: he hated dogs, lizards, people with yellow teeth, painters and sculptors, costly silks and embroideries, the smell of garlic and onions. He loved children, honey, cucumbers, dates, pumpkins and every kind of perfume. He liked to go about the house mending furniture, cobbling shoes, and patching his own clothes; and he milked his own goats. He had a sweet tooth, and there was some softness in him.

He was entirely happy with Khadija, who adored him and gave him six children, four girls and two boys. The boys, Qasim and Abdallah, died in childhood: it was one of his greater griefs that in all his life he fathered no male child who grew to maturity. So he continued to live out his life in the placid backwaters, caring for his own children and Khadija's three children by a former marriage, supervising the estate, attending fairs, and sometimes engaging in earnest conversation with his wife's cousin Waraqa, a learned man, the first to translate parts of the Old and New Testaments into Arabic. There was a seed of restlessness in Waraqa, who at different times embraced Judaism and Christianity, only to return to his ancient primitive faith. It was perhaps from Waraqa that Muhammad imbibed his strange and sometimes inaccurate knowledge of the Mishna and the Talmud.

At thirty-five he was a man of substance, a good husband and a good father, handsome above the average, given to occasional fits of abstraction, remarkable only for being unremarkable. He was not a particularly good steward of Khadija's estate, and much of their wealth evaporated over the years. His friends were wealthy merchants like Abu Bakr, who shared his passion for helping widows, orphans and strangers. Abu Bakr was a cloth merchant who had grown rich through his own efforts, but he seems to have felt his wealth was a burden almost too great to be borne. He had a long thin face with sunken cheeks and deep-set eyes, and was very lean, and walked with a stoop. Muhammad had known him since they were youths together on the caravan trails, and often sought his advice.

So the years passed quietly with a growing family, a handful of friends, the faithful Khadija at his side. Every night he worshipped at the Kaaba, and every morning he attended to his business affairs. He was a man who had no need to fortify himself with ambition. Wealth had come to him effortlessly, and just as effortlessly he could end his days surrounded by his grandchildren. But it was the quiet before the storm.

The storm came suddenly one night, at the hottest time of the year, after a long period of meditating alone in a cave outside of Mecca. No one knows what brought him to the cave. It may have been the memory of the ascetic monks in the Syrian desert who also worshipped their God in caves, alone with the Alone. Or perhaps he was influenced by the wandering hermits called Hanifs, meaning 'those who have turned away from idol worship', who emerged about this time from the Najd, to proclaim the virtues of solitude and the worship of the One God. It may have been the seed of restlessness communicated to him by the old visionary Waraqa which sent him out into the desert to live for weeks on end in silent contemplation. What is certain is that the storm broke over his head, and the world was never to be the same again.

As Muhammad told the story of his first great revelation, he was lying asleep or in a trance, wrapped in his cloak, when he heard a voice saying: 'Read!' He answered: 'I cannot read.' The voice said again: 'Read!' He answered: 'I do not know how to read.' Once more, this time with terrible force, the voice said: 'Read!' He answered: 'What can I read?' The voice thundered:

> Read in the name of your Lord, the Creator,
> Who created man from a clot of blood!
> Read! Your Lord is most merciful,
> For he has taught men by the pen
> And revealed the mysteries to them!

He was shown a scroll, which seemed to be of silk with letters of fire written on it. He read the words, though he had never read before, and when he awoke, he remembered them, for they were 'as though written upon his heart'. Trembling, he went out of the cave on to the hillside, not knowing what had happened to him, and afraid he must be a *sha'ir* or possessed. Angels had come to him before, leaving him weak and dispirited, but that was long ago in his childhood. He was in such agony of mind that he thought of throwing himself off a precipice, and then he heard a voice from heaven saying: 'O Muhammad! You are Allah's messenger, and I am Gabriel!' Lifting up his eyes he saw 'about two bowshots away' the figure of an angel standing in the sky. He was rooted to the spot, dazzled by the brightness of the angelic eyes, and once more he heard the voice. He turned away, but everywhere he turned he saw the angel standing before him, until at last the angel vanished, and he was alone with the beating of his heart.

Later in the morning, terrified by the visitation, he hurried back to Mecca and told Khadija what he had seen. He was afraid he was going mad, but she reassured him. There is a tradition that she tested the genuineness of the visitation by making Muhammad sit first on her right knee, and then on her left: there was no thunderclap from heaven, and Muhammad was aware of angelic presences hovering close by. When she began to remove her garments and sit Muhammad on her lap, he thought he saw the angelic presences departing in great haste. Khadija explained that if it had been a visitation of devils they would have remained around the bed, to watch what happened. 'Rejoice,' she said, 'for truly you have seen a visitor from heaven, and no harm can come to you!' Some time later she asked Waraqa, now close to death and quite blind, about the strange meeting in a cave. The old man answered that the angel who appeared to Muhammad was the same who came to Moses, the son of Amram: there was no doubt that a revelation was at hand.

Khadija and Waraqa were his first disciples. After them came Abu Bakr, who seems to have believed in the revelations at first more out of friendship and the desire to please an old friend than because he felt there had been a true revelation; he always deferred to Muhammad. Then there was Ali, Abu Bakr's handsome ten-year-old son, who lived in Muhammad's house. Finally there was Muhammad's slave, Zayd, who was short and dark with a depressed nose, and was so much in love with his master that he refused his freedom when it was offered to him. In the beginning these were his only followers.

At first Muhammad seems to have been unsure of himself, of his power to communicate his visions. He was in an agony of apprehension, for the angel foretold the end of the world, the terrible punishments in store for those who refused to worship the One God, the blaze of eternal flame. There is a compulsive violence in those early proclamations which Muhammad heard, or said he heard, during his frequent visits to the cave. The verses move to the rhythm of hammer beats. They proclaim the end of man and the beginning of a new dispensation, in images that leap at breakneck pace from earth to Heaven and back again, and in the original Arabic they can make the hair stand on end. Here, for example, is the proclamation known as *The Overthrowing*:

> When the sun is overthrown,
> And when the stars fall,
> And when the mountains are moved,
> And when the camels big with young are left by the wayside,
> And when the wild beasts are herded together,
> And when the seas rise up,
> And when the souls and bodies come together
> And when the girl-child, buried alive,
> Asks why she has been killed,

And when the book of fate is opened wide,
And when the heavens are stripped bare,
And when Hell is set ablaze,
And when Paradise comes near,
Each soul shall know what it has done!

Oh, but I call to witness the planets,
And the stars as they rise and fall,
And the night when it closeth,
And the morning when it giveth forth breath.
Truly, this is the speech of a noble messenger,
Mighty and honoured by the Throne of the Lord,
Obeyed in heaven, and very faithful.
No, your companion is not mad,
Who saw the angel on the clear horizon!

(Sura lxxxi)

In a strict sense these verses—there are others like them—are not vision-ary. They do not, like the Book of Revelation, describe an event in Heaven or the unfolding of an Apocalypse; there is no attempt to depict the process by which the threatened dissolution of the world and all the cosmic spaces will be brought about. What Muhammad (or the Angel) was doing with tremendous effect was to declare with simple imagery that mankind was doomed, almost past hoping for, unless it followed the ways of God; and in those early days he was less concerned to demonstrate the ways of God than to insist upon doom. Doom was in the air he breathed, and he could almost feel the scorching flames on his face. Again and again he reverts to this theme, as in the chapter known as *That Which Striketh*:

That which striketh!
What is this which striketh?
Ah, who will convey to thee what the Striking is?
The day mankind shall become like scattered moths,
And the mountains like tufts of carded wool,
Then as for him whose scales are heavy,
He shall enter into Paradise;
But as for him whose scales are light,
The Abyss shall be his dwelling-place!
And who shall convey to thee what the Abyss is?
A raging fire!

(Sura ci)

What shall a man do when he knows the world is coming to an end? Muhammad was in a quandary. He listened to the Angel, remembered the words that came to him, informed his immediate family, and suffered in silence. He was like a man involved in a conspiracy, who dares tell no one except his immediate family. There seems to be no other explanation for the fact that in the early years he attempted to make no converts. He did not publicly announce his mission; he devised no rules for the followers of the One God; he did not storm the Kaaba. Tradition asserts that at the end of three years he had no more than forty followers, who may have been the members of his own household, relatives and close friends. He was not yet a missionary committed to the overthrow of the ancient gods.

But about 614 A.D., in the fourth year after the visitation in the cave, he began to assert himself, wandering through the streets of Mecca and intoning the messages he had received from the Angel. Young people,

c

strangers and slaves listened to him, and some accepted his claim to be the Apostle of God. The Meccans were amused, then angered. They had a simple punishment for heretics. They took them into the desert, stripped them naked, and left them to lie in the devouring sun until they howled for mercy. Some of Muhammad's followers recanted, while others, the hardier ones, continued to worship the One God in secret. Their meeting place was a house on the hill of Safa belonging to the convert al-Arqam, or a cave outside Mecca. The Quraysh showed no sympathy to the new faith, and when Muhammad at last spoke against idol worship before the Kaaba and was nearly strangled to death—he was rescued just in time by the faithful Abu Bakr—they realized they were dealing with a lunatic or a man determined to risk his life for his beliefs, and decided to destroy him. The number of his followers was growing. Slaves and women flocked to the secret meetings, but there was also a sprinkling of rich merchants. Among them was Uthman ibn-Affan, the friend of Abu Bakr, a rich merchant with a passion for good works and a degree of piety towards Muhammad that was sometimes galling on the nerves of the members of the secret community. Muhammad's daughter Ruqayya was married to the son of his uncle Abu Lahab, who detested the new faith and did everything he could to stamp it out. Disgusted with Muhammad, he announced that the marriage between the two young people was void. Thereupon Muhammad arranged a marriage between Ruqayya and the rich merchant. Uthman gloried in possessing the daughter of the Apostle of God, and placed his fortune and not inconsiderable knowledge of conspiracy at the service of the new faith.

Three merchants—Muhammad, Abu Bakr and Uthman—were in command of a strange conspiratorial movement against the pagan gods. They moved stealthily and silently about the town, held meetings, prayed, and waited expectantly for each new pronouncement from the One God. The Quraysh were up in arms. They could threaten Muhammad, but they could not kill him for fear of the blood vengeance of his clan. They could, however, kill his followers, and at the season of pilgrimage they posted men on all the roads to warn the pilgrims against the madman who was attempting to turn them away from the worship of Hubal. The followers of Muhammad were in no position to fight back; and like many other persecuted sects their thoughts turned to emigration. Abyssinia, a day's sail across the Red Sea, provided a haven of safety. Accordingly, a small group of the poorer converts, numbering eleven men and four women, under the leadership of Ja'far ibn Abu Talib, a cousin of Muhammad, set sail from Jiddah and took refuge in the country of the Negus. It was no more than an exploratory expedition. Others might follow in large numbers if the persecution grew more violent.

And in fact the persecution was growing so violent that Muhammad himself quailed before the power of the idol worshippers. He announced that the One God was not altogether averse to the innumerable gods of clay and stone: there was some merit in them, and worshippers who sought the intercession of Hubal were not thereby excluded from Paradise. He was prepared to compromise, if only to gain time. The Quraysh decided that Muhammad was behaving more reasonably, and for a brief while the persecution was lifted. A message was sent to the exiles in Abyssinia, recalling them to Mecca.

One of the most determined opponents of the new faith was a certain Umar ibn al-Khattab, a young giant of fearful aspect—they said of him that his scowl could kill, and his walking staff was more terrible than most men's swords. Umar was highborn, related to the most powerful families in Mecca, and like many young aristocrats he was disposed to seek easy solutions to his problems. He came to the conclusion that the best way to put an end to the new faith was by killing Muhammad. One day he decided to put his resolve into effect, and marched, sword in hand, to the house of al-Arqam, where he knew Muhammad was hiding. On the way he met a friend who asked what he was doing. 'I am going to kill Muhammad!' Umar declared, and he was a little puzzled when the friend, a secret convert, suggested that there might be better things to do, and less dangerous ones. 'Are you not afraid they will take vengeance on you?' the friend said. 'Why kill a man who is so much beloved by your favourite sister?' For the first time Umar learned that his sister had become a convert. He went straight to her house. He paused outside to listen to the chanting of one of the verses of the sacred book containing the messages received by Muhammad—it was the verse describing the miracles of Moses and the glory reserved for those who accepted the revelation of the One God—and when he could bear the sound of chanting no more, Umar burst into the house and attacked his sister and her husband with his sword. His sister's face was covered with blood, and he was about to kill her when she said: 'We are followers of Muhammad, believing in the One God and in His messenger, and you may do with us as you please!' Umar was impressed by her passionate sincerity and let the sword fall from his hand. She showed him the palm leaf on which the verses were written. He studied it with care, and asked if he could take it home with him. 'No,' said his sister. 'You are unclean from long worshipping of idols, and you may not touch it until you have been cleansed!' Umar went out and washed himself, and took the leaf home. The next day he went swordless to the house of al-Arqam and paid homage to Muhammad as the messenger of God.

The conversion of the young aristocrat alarmed the Quraysh, who now determined upon stronger measures. Disturbed and frightened, Muhammad made plans for another emigration to Abyssinia. This time he sent not a handful of poor converts, but many of his most important supporters, numbering eighty-three men and eighteen women, under the leadership of Uthman ibn-Affan, who possessed sufficient authority to guide the faithful if Muhammad should be killed. This flight to Abyssinia was a reconnaissance in strength designed to ensure that the faith should continue in the event that it was proscribed in Mecca. They were dark days, and no one knew what lay in store.

Outraged by the growth of the faith, its enemies were determined to use the sternest measures. Muhammad was hiding in a castle belonging to his uncle Abu Talib, high up in a gorge east of Mecca. They demanded his surrender. In exchange they offered Abu Talib the fairest of their young men in place of Muhammad and a vast fortune in money; all they asked was that they should be allowed to kill Muhammad and have done with him. Abu Talib refused. He was indifferent to the new faith, but his family loyalty was strong. Unable to get their hands on Muhammad, they blockaded the castle, refused to allow food to reach it, and even attacked it without success. Finally, in A.D. 617 they issued a decree of excommunication against the whole clan to which Muhammad belonged. No one belonging to this clan was allowed to marry Meccans belonging to other clans, nor were they allowed to have business dealings with them. Muhammad's followers could be attacked with impunity. The decree of excommunication, written on parchment, was solemnly hung up within the Kaaba.

There were bad days to come, but the faithful remembered these as the worst. In effect, they were outlaws with every man's hand against them. For three years Muhammad was compelled to remain in the stronghold, emerging only during the annual season of pilgrimage when all hostilities were suspended. At such times, in his defiant way, he went about the town preaching and praying, proclaiming his revelations. He could not be attacked, but he could be hindered and annoyed, and the wife of Abu Lahab, his inveterate enemy, amused herself by strewing thorn bushes in the sand where she knew he would walk barefoot. Muhammad cursed her and her husband in a *sura* of quite extraordinary vehemence:

> Cursed be the hands of Abu Lahab: he shall perish!
> His wealth and gains shall avail him nothing!
> He shall be burned in the flaming fire!
> Faggots shall be heaped on his wife,
> On her neck a rope of palm-fibre!

(Sura cxi)

The curse, however, was not immediately effective, and Abu Lahab survived for some years to wage an increasingly bitter war against his nephew. According to tradition, he died of a broken heart on receiving news of one of Muhammad's more spectacular victories.

Beleaguered in the fortress, Muhammad was a force to be reckoned with. Somehow he continued to exert his influence on his followers who were still hidden in the town; and the messages of God, which came to him with increasing frequency, were written down by scribes and distributed to the faithful. The messages told the faithful to hold on; the enemy was bound to fail; did not deliverance come to Abraham? With a wealth of imagery and a spate of rabbinical learning, he demonstrated that defeat was only the prelude to inevitable triumph. As for the idol worshippers, they were like the spider 'who taketh unto herself a house, and lo! the frailest of all houses is the spider's house, if they but knew'. His temper, always stern since the visitation in the cave, grew sterner. More and more he demanded complete surrender to the purposes of God. More and more his mind turned to the harsh antitheses: peace and abundance for the faithful, hell-fire for the enemies of God. Life itself was of no value, for 'the life of the world is but a sport and pastime, and the only true life lies in the life to come'. Everything was to be gained by dying in the faith: honour, merit in the eyes of God and the rewards of Paradise, which he painted in brilliant colours. Paradise was a garden where immortal youths and virgins attended to the comforts of the blessed spirits as they reclined in everlasting shade. Added to these comforts was the satisfaction of looking down at the contortions of sinners clothed in pitch, flames covering their faces. This simple creed, all the more effective for being simple, spurred the faithful to renewed efforts; and the enemies of the faith gradually abandoned their attempts to destroy Muhammad by decree. As for the decree itself, a not altogether reliable tradition asserts that it had been eaten away by white ants until only the words *Bismika Allahumma* ('In thy name, O Allah') remained. Muhammad is said to have seen a vindication of his mission in the penetrating action of the white ants.

Whatever the reason for this failure to strangle Muhammadanism at birth, there is no doubt that Muhammad was shaken by his long imprisonment in his fortress-stronghold. The Meccans were still sullenly opposed to any faith which interfered with the annual pilgrimage to the Kaaba and all the other holy places surrounding Mecca. They made it clear that they would continue to make Muhammad's life intolerable. For him it was doubly intolerable, for about this time he lost within a few days of one another both his beloved wife Khadija and his uncle Abu Talib, who had always aided him generously without ever believing in his mission. In a mood of resignation and despair, accompanied only by his slave Zayd, Muhammad made his way to Taif, where he had spent the happiest days of his childhood. He expected to be welcomed. Instead he was sneered at and stoned, and finally thrown out of the city. When last seen, he was being pursued by a rabble of children and slaves, and there was blood running down his legs.

Chastened, he returned to Mecca, and when the holy days came around and he was allowed to wander unharmed, he found himself among a small group of pilgrims from Yathrib, an oasis some two hundred miles north of Mecca. To them he proclaimed his mission, and he may have been a little surprised to find them listening to him attentively. Yathrib had been founded by Jews, had an abundance of date palms and goldsmiths, and was something of a commercial rival to Mecca. The rabbis in the town were continually proclaiming the coming of the Messiah, and the men from Yathrib were disposed to believe that Muhammad was indeed the promised Messiah. They were not so sure that he would be welcomed in Yathrib and asked for a year in which to prepare for his reception. Perhaps they were temporizing; perhaps they were simply wise men who knew what difficulties lay in the way of welcoming a Messiah and wanted to ensure that all Yathrib would come out and greet him. They left, promising to send twelve men with their answer the following year. For another year Muhammad was compelled to live out his shadowy life in Mecca, smarting from his wounds.

It was perhaps in this year that he received a truly terrifying visitation from the Angel. No one knows exactly what happened, for the Quran contains only a brief and passing reference to the event. According to tradition Muhammad was awakened in the depth of night by the Angel Gabriel, who thundered: 'Awake, thou sleeper!' He was dazzled by the brightness of the Angel, and by the shining of a strange winged horse which had a human face. This horse was restless, but grew calm when Muhammad mounted it. Then in a flash the winged horse soared into the heavens in the direction of Jerusalem, plunging to earth at Mount Sinai and Bethlehem, where Muhammad offered prayers, and then continuing its progress. At the Temple in Jerusalem the horse alighted, and Muhammad simply fastened it to the rings and entered into the Holy of Holies to find Abraham, Moses and Jesus praying together. He joined them for a space, but a ladder came down from Heaven and he soared again towards the Seventh Heaven and entered the house of the Creator, where the light was blinding with an indescribable glory. There he was embraced by God, whose face remained invisible in the annihilating brightness, yet he was made aware of the face as a presence, and he felt God's touch on his breast and shoulder, a touch which froze him to the heart and to the marrow of his bones. Blinded and dazzled, he stumbled from the divine presence; the celestial ladder brought him with the speed of lightning to Jerusalem, and with the same speed the winged horse returned him to the house of one of his converts in Mecca.

Such was the story he told later, and generations of Muhammadan scholars have hotly debated the meaning to be attached to the vision. They have debated whether Muhammad was transported in the body or in the spirit, and what precisely were the words spoken to him when he was embraced by God. Those who believe he was transported bodily point to the footprint in the Dome of the Rock in Jerusalem where he leaped upon his winged horse; those who believe he was transported in the spirit support their belief with the tradition derived from Ayesha, the young wife he had married after the death of Khadija, who declared that on this very night he was sleeping soundly by her side. Many disputed Muhammad's claim to have entered the Seventh Heaven, and for a while only Abu Bakr and a few intimates were completely convinced. Abu Bakr was the father of Ayesha, and he had long ago resolved to believe everything Muhammad told him.

Meanwhile the faith was fighting to survive. The horror of proscription was exchanged for the horror of indifference, as the Meccans, now accustomed to the presence of the Apostle of God in their midst, hoped that the faith would die a natural death. They had good reason to hope for the eventual disintegration of the movement, for Muhammad's account of his supernatural journey to Heaven aroused a shocked incredulity among some of the believers. The early days of martyrdom were over; and Muhammad, locked in his fortress, was far more dangerous than Muhammad walking free in the market place.

To survive, the faith needed a base of operations, preferably a city on one of the trade routes of Arabia, where Muhammad in his own person could exercise spiritual and earthly dominion. Such a base might be provided by Yathrib, and more and more his thoughts were directed to that northern city. He was overjoyed when, exactly a year following his meeting with six men of Yathrib, there arrived in Mecca five of the original six together with seven converts, who welcomed him as the appointed Messiah and at the Pass of Aqabah between Mecca and Mina swore an oath of allegiance to him. 'We shall worship only the One God,' they declared. 'We shall not steal, nor commit adultery, nor kill our children; we shall not commit acts of slander; and she shall not disobey the Apostle of God in anything that is proper.' It was a strange oath, for it left many things unsaid, and seems to have been designed as a statement of the *minimum* beliefs necessary for adherance to the Muhammadan cause. And having declared their allegiance, the twelve returned to Yathrib accompanied by a teacher selected by Muhammad. Soon, according to the chroniclers, there was not a house in Yathrib where men were not eagerly discussing the Quran.

But while Yathrib was being converted, affairs in Mecca remained stationary, and for another year Muhammad was compelled to remain in a town where he was generally detested. News of the secret oath at the Pass had got about, and the authorities were in a quandary. It was bad enough to have Muhammad in their midst, but what if he entered Yathrib in triumph? They foresaw that he might exact vengeance. With Yathrib in his power, there was nothing to prevent him from attacking Mecca and trampling down the gods.

Many efforts had been made to destroy Muhammad. They had blockaded the fortress, attempted to starve him out, killed his followers and placed a ban of interdiction on his clan. They had not dared to attack him physically. Now someone—perhaps it was Abu Lahab—suggested a wonderfully simple solution to the problem: from each clan one member should be chosen by lot to murder Muhammad, and if they all attacked him simultaneously, then the blood guilt would be on all of them, and the family of Muhammad would be incapable of taking revenge on all the clans. The suggestion, however, was not carried out, but the great historian Ibn Khaldun dates the hardening of Muhammad's heart to that bleak year when his own death seemed so close and his followers seemed about to melt before his eyes. There came to him a revelation ordering him to make war upon his enemies 'until there is no more persecution and all men follow the way of the One God'. Henceforward he would use the sword, if all else failed.

But there was no need to use the sword: only to wait patiently for the time when Yathrib would welcome him as the Messiah. Waiting was intolerable, but better than death without the fulfilment of God's word. Finally, two years after the meeting with the men of Yathrib, at the holy season, there came a second deputation from Yathrib consisting of seventy-five men and two women. It was March, A.D. 622, on a moonless night when Muhammad journeyed to the Pass to receive the final verdict

from Yathrib. He was at once the plaintiff and the defendant, the sup-
pliant and the conqueror. They told him that Yathrib was preparing to
receive him with open arms. 'Our lives,' they said, 'are at the service of
the Apostle of God.' Muhammad chanted some verses from the Quran
and might have departed immediately for Yathrib if his uncle al-Abbas,
who felt for his nephew the same kindly sympathy shown by Abu Talib,
had not interposed with a question. He asked what guarantees there were
for Muhammad's safety. Did they realize that all Arabia might arise
against the city which had chosen the messenger of God? He suggested
they should make a solemn compact to defend Muhammad. The men of
Yathrib swore to defend Muhammad and his followers to the death, and
when they asked what would be their reward if they perished in the cause,
Muhammad answered simply: 'Paradise!'

With this second oath at the Pass of Aqabah, Muhammad was free of
all the chains that bound him to Mecca. He would leave the town, and
when he returned he would come, not as some beggarly preacher in the
market-place, but as a conqueror.

He decided to act warily, for he had not yet received divine authority
for the journey, and every inch of the way must be prepared. During that
spring and early summer, 150 of his followers made their way to Yathrib.
They went by ones and twos, in secret, following rarely used pathways, so
that the authorities in Mecca should not know they were escaping. But
reports of strange movements on the roads to Yathrib kept coming in, and
one night in June guards hammered at Muhammad's house. There was
just time for Muhammad and the faithful Abu Bakr to wrap Ali in a green
mantle as he lay on a couch, and slip away. When the guards broke in,
they pounced on Ali, who was fat and heavy and could be taken for
Muhammad in the flickering light of torches. They thought they had
Muhammad in their grasp, and were enraged when Ali said he knew
nothing about the whereabouts of Muhammad. Abu Bakr's house was
then searched. His daughter Amina was asked: 'Where is your father?'
and answered quite truthfully: 'I do not know'; whereupon she was
slapped so hard that one of her ear-rings fell off.

Meanwhile Muhammad and Abu Bakr were making their way through
the streets of Mecca to the bare and flinty hills, where they had already
selected a hiding place in a cave and arranged for a guide and two fast
riding-camels. When morning came, the Quraysh were engaged in a
desperate attempt to catch up with him. They scoured the city, sent armed
guards through the gorges, and posted a reward of 100 camels to anyone
who captured Muhammad. One party even paused outside the cave
where they were hiding, and Abu Bakr in the dark interior saw them
standing about the open mouth. He warned Muhammad that they were
about to be captured, and burst out weeping at the thought of victory so
tardily stolen from their hands, but Muhammad said quietly: 'Do not
grieve, for God is with us!' The guards moved away, and at nightfall Abu
Bakr's son and daughter and his herdsman brought them food. Finally,
after three days, came the guide and the fast camels, and they set out for

Yathrib, riding mostly at night, using unfrequented pathways. Even then they were pursued. Four days out from Mecca, a troop of armed horsemen from Mecca led by an old soldier named Suraqa, famous for his iron-grey helmet of hair and the roughness of his furry arms, came up with him. Once again Abu Bakr thought all was lost, and once again Muhammad had to tell him: 'God is with us.' Suraqa's horse reared up and fell when it came near to Muhammad, and Suraqa seems to have been profoundly moved by this evidence of Muhammad's spiritual power. There was a brief conversation between the warrior and the messenger of God, and Suraqa thought it the better part of virtue to pretend there had been no meeting in the desert and returned without his prisoner to Mecca.

There were no further setbacks. At last, after a journey of a little over two hundred miles—they rode mostly at night to avoid being overtaken—they came in sight of Yathrib, which had heard of their coming and was in a state of excited expectation. Still unsure of the welcome he would receive, Muhammad decided to delay his triumphal entry and for five days stayed in the suburb of Qubah some three-quarters of a mile south of the city. There envoys came to greet him with peace offerings and the promise of full security. Then at last on September 20, A.D. 622, with thirteen years of humiliation behind him, he entered Yathrib like a king with an escort of seventy warriors.

For his followers this day marked the beginning of a new era, and during the reign of the Caliph Umar it was decreed that the Muhammadan calendar should start with the year of the triumph. In fact the Muhammadan calendar starts a little before, beginning on New Year's Day, which occurred on July 16. It was the year of the *Hijra*, which means 'the breaking of bonds'. In those days perhaps only Muhammad knew how well and truly they had been broken.

THE HOLY SWORD

IN THE first year of his reign at Yathrib, Muhammad showed himself at his best. He received revelations, issued decrees, signed treaties, but always humbly; and there was something about his manner which suggested more the dedicated devotee in the cave than the conspirator in his fortress. Quietly, confidently, he was putting his house in order. He was living modestly with his second wife Sauda, a widow whom he seems to have married out of pity, and his court consisted of his young secretary Zayd ibn Zabit, who was a native of Yathrib, his faithful black slave Bilal, and his servant Abdallah ibn Masud, 'he of the slippers, the cushions and the dunghill', a fiery thin-legged man with flaming red hair and a passion for scented garments, whose chief claim to fame was that he was the first to recite the Quran openly in the streets of Mecca. No king ever lived less ostentatiously. For seven months his palace was the lower floor of a house overlooking an ancient burial ground which he had chosen as the site of his mosque; his furniture consisted of a coarse matting of palm leaves and an earthen jug.

The mosque, too, was small and unprepossessing, no more than a rough enclosure with earthen walls, pillars made from the date palms which grew in the burial ground, and a roof of palm leaves daubed with mud. There were three doors cut in the walls, one facing Jerusalem, one for Gabriel and one in the name of mercy, which led to Muhammad's private quarters. The courtyard was used for prayer, for meetings, and for sheltering the homeless. The mosque was quickly built. Muhammad himself helped to build it, enjoying the labour and encouraging the workmen with a hymn composed in their honour. None of the amenities we are accustomed to see in mosques were present: there was no pulpit, no niche facing in the sacred direction, no hanging lamps, and instead of tiles and carpets on the floors there was only beaten earth and sand. Muhammad delivered his sermons while leaning casually against a palm trunk. In those days only one thing disturbed him: the damp climate with its poisonous exhalations, cold by night and unbearably hot during the day. Accustomed to the dry climate of Mecca, he prayed: 'O God, make Yathrib dear to us, even as Mecca is, or even dearer. Bless its produce, and banish far from us the pestilence.' Many of his followers died; many sickened; many begged to be allowed to return to Mecca. Surprisingly, Muhammad was unaffected, and seemed to grow stronger as the days passed.

All through those early months he showed an air of settled contentment. He was gentle and kind. He listened attentively to the advice of the Jewish rabbis, and resolved the quarrels of the Aus and Khazraj, the two dominant tribes of Yathrib, each possessing its own fortress. He drew up a solemn charter with the Jews, granting them equal rights of citizenship, full religious liberty and military protection on condition that they take part in the defence of the city; and he ordered that the Muhajirun (refugees from Mecca) seek the friendship of the Ansar (the helpers, people of Yathrib) by swearing oaths of loyalty to one another. Wanting to please the Jews, or to placate them, he gave instructions to his followers to pray three times daily, following Jewish practice, instead of twice daily, which had been their custom in Mecca. The faithful were ordered to be circumcised. He chose Friday as the Sabbath, differing from the Jews only in allowing his followers to continue working on this day. The Christians used wooden clappers and bells to summon the faithful to divine service; the Jews used trumpets; Muhammad decided to use the human voice. The first prayer caller was the Negro slave Bilal, whose thunderous voice echoed across the rooftops the words revealed by the Angel: '*La ilaha ill' Muhammad rasul Allah!*' ('There is no God at all but God, and Muhammad is His messenger! Come to prayer! Come to security!') Sometimes at the dawn call, Bilal would add the salutory recommendation: 'Prayer is better than sleep!' Muhammad was so pleased with his slave's addition to the divine text that he allowed it to become part of the ritual. When Bilal had summoned the city to awake, he would descend from his rooftop and hurry to Muhammad's door, saying: 'To prayer, O Messenger of God! To salvation!'

So the months passed in a strange quietness, as though Muhammad were slowly withdrawing from the world of action, settling disputes and the affairs of a small predominantly Jewish city, and receiving the homage of the tribesmen of the desert. The revelations continued, notable for their toleration and forbearance. Benignity flowed from him. He spoke often of the need for charity. 'He who is not affectionate to God's creatures,' he declared, 'that man will not receive the affection of God. Those who clothe the naked of the faith will be clothed by God in the green robes of Paradise.' The most beautiful of the traditional sermons seems to date from this time. Muhammad opened the sermon by declaring that when the world was formed, it trembled so violently that God set mountains upon it to strengthen it. He continued:

The angels asked, 'O God! Is there anything in Thy creation stronger than mountains?' God said: 'Yes, iron is stronger than mountains, for it breaketh them.' The angels said: 'O God! Is there anything in Thy creation stronger than iron?' God said: 'Yes, fire is stronger than iron, for it melteth it.' The angels said: 'O our defender! Is there anything in Thy creation stronger than fire?' God said: 'Yes, water overcometh fire: it killeth it and maketh it cold.' Then the angels said: 'O God! Is there anything in Thy creation stronger than water?' God said: 'Yes, wind overcometh water, for it putteth it in motion.' The angels said: 'O our cherisher! Is there anything in Thy creation stronger than wind?' God said: 'Yes, the children of Adam when they give alms with their right hands and conceal it from the left, they overcome all!'

There were perhaps other reasons for Muhammad's gentleness and benevolence at this time, among them his approaching marriage to Ayesha, the nine-year-old daughter of Abu Bakr, to whom he had been betrothed for some time.[1] There was also the approaching marriage of his daughter Fatima with his adopted son, Ali. Fatima was fifteen, Ali about twenty-three. Tradition asserts that Muhammad's wedding to the lively Ayesha was a model of simplicity, her dowry being only a few ounces of silver and the wedding supper consisting only of milk. The marriage between Fatima and Ali was considerably more elaborate. Dates and olives were provided for the wedding feast, and Ali, by selling a number of his best camels and coats of chain mail, provided his bride with two skirts, a headband, two silver bracelets, a leather pillow stuffed with palm leaves, a drinking cup, a hand mill, two large earthen jars and a pitcher. Ayesha was small and plump, Fatima tall and slender, sloe-eyed, with a gift for singing. She was accounted the most beautiful among Arabian women, as Ali was accounted the most handsome among Arabian men. At this time he was in the full flower of his manhood, broad-shouldered and well-muscled, with soft grey eyes, a ruddy complexion, and a thick black beard. Like his father-in-law he lived simply in one of the huts which lay beside the mosque.

As he surveyed his small kingdom Muhammad seems to have become increasingly aware of his precarious hold on the affections of men. There was still only a handful of followers; how few they were was demonstrated when he ordered the oath of brotherhood: only fifty-four refugees from Mecca responded. Perhaps a hundred Meccans joined him in Yathrib; there was a small colony in Abyssinia; a few secret sympathizers remained behind in Mecca, and there was a scattering of tribesmen prepared to obey his orders; and this was all. He maintained his power in Yathrib by virtue of his personal ascendancy. Soon the Jews who had looked upon him as the promised Messiah began to see the error of their ways. He was no Messiah; he was a man whose revelations came from a God infinitely remote from Jahweh. Quarrels arose. Muhammad hardened his heart. Quite suddenly he received the revelation that his followers should turn when they prayed not towards Jerusalem but towards Mecca. Soon there came another revelation: it was right and proper for the faithful to kill the infidels.

No one knows why Muhammad changed so abruptly from a benevolent despot, the devoted servant of the Merciful and Compassionate God, into

---

[1] Bukhari, in his collection of traditional sayings, gives Ayesha's wonderfully vivid description of her preparations for the marriage. 'I was six years old when the Prophet betrothed himself to me in Mecca,' she said. 'Three years later in Madinah, I being nine years old, had a fever and lost my hair, but it had all grown again long and thick. One day I was on a swing surrounded by children friends. My mother came and called me, I did not know what for. I went to her. I was out of breath, and she made me stop at the door until I got my breath back. She then washed my head and face with some water, and took me to a room where there were some Ansar women, who cried out: "Happiness and blessing and best fortune be upon thee!" My mother handed me over to them and they dressed me up. They had scarcely finished when the Prophet entered suddenly. They gave me over to him.'

a ruthless conqueror. Perhaps power corrupted him; perhaps he knew the faith would never survive without unsheathing the sword. What is certain is that his character changed. Where he had been soft he became hard.

It began with small raiding parties sent out to intercept the caravans driving northward from Mecca, between Yathrib and the Red Sea, to Syria. Six separate raiding parties were sent out with orders to plunder the caravans, without success, though once at least the raiders waylaid a rich caravan, only to be warned off by local tribesmen. With the coming of the holy month of Rajab in December, A.D. 623 the exasperated raiders under Muhammad's command saw their opportunity. They decided to take advantage of the general peace. Two days before the end of the holy month Muhammad sent eight raiders under sealed orders to the south in the hope of cutting off a rich Quraysh caravan known to be proceeding to Mecca. The text of the sealed orders, which has survived, reads: 'Go forward to Nakhlah in the name of the Lord, and with His blessing! Yet do not force any of the followers against his inclination. Proceed with those who accompany you willingly; and when you have arrived at the valley of Nakhlah, then lie in wait for the caravans of the Quraysh.'

By coincidence or design this strange document was opened on the last day of the holy month. By the time the first caravan came in sight, two of the raiding party had fallen back to search for a stray camel; there were therefore only six raiders preparing to attack a caravan laden with wine, raisins and leather, guarded by four Quraysh soldiers. It was an unequal combat. One of the raiders was disguised as a pilgrim, with shaven head and white linen gown. He advanced under cover of his disguise, asked some simple questions and suddenly shot an arrow at the guard he had been speaking to, who happened to be a man of Hadramaut under protection of the Quraysh. Within a few moments the treasure was in the hands of the raiders, and the caravan turned towards Yathrib. It was the first time a man had been killed at Muhammad's orders. Yet Muhammad received the news of the capture in a towering rage, upbraiding the raiders and telling them he had never commanded them to fight during the sacred month: they had in fact misinterpreted their orders. Soon afterwards he received the appropriate revelation:

> They ask you about making war in the sacred month. Say: Warfare in this month is a great offence, but to obstruct the way of God and to deny Him, to hinder men from the holy temple, and to expel his people thence, that is more grievous to God. For idolatry is worse than killing.
>
> They will not cease from fighting against you until they have made renegades from your faith, if they are able. And whosoever becometh a renegade and dieth an unbeliever, his works shall come to nothing in this world or in the world to come. Such are the rightful owners of the Fire, and they shall abide there for ever.
>
> (Sura ii)

In slightly different terms, and with different emphases, the same revelation was to be repeated at intervals, uplifting his warriors when they were weary and inciting them to ferocious acts of bravery in battle. To those who fell in battle a vast reward was promised; the martyrs would 'live in the presence of their Lord, their wants supplied, rejoicing in the bounty which God has given them'. Muhammad hinted that those who died in battle would enter the souls of green birds and feed forever on the fruits of Paradise. A late *hadith* reads: 'Know that Paradise lies beneath the shadow of swords.'

After this first obscure engagement Muhammad searched for an opportunity to make war on the Quraysh. It came in January, A.D. 624, when Abu Sufyan, a leading Meccan merchant, returned from Syria at the head of the most important caravan of the year, with 50,000 pieces of gold. His route lay through the country of Yathrib, between the mountains and the sea. When rumours of Muhammad's design reached him, he sent a camel driver to Mecca with a frantic appeal for help. The camel driver arrived at the Kaaba out of breath, sick and weary, so distraught that he was almost unintelligible. A certain Abu Jahl mounted a roof and sounded the alarm; and soon there were a thousand armed men hurrying from Mecca, most of them believing the caravan was already lost; at best they hoped to punish the raiders. This army, led by the nobility of Mecca, was the best they could put into the field; Muhammad's army numbered no more than 313 men, ill-armed and roughly equipped; most of them belonged to the Ansar.

Muhammad sent out two scouts to watch the movements of the caravan, and learned that it was approaching Badr, a small town where a famous fair was held every year on a sandy plain. His small tattered army therefore made its way cautiously towards Badr, hoping to come upon the caravan by surprise. He knew the Meccan army was approaching, but he seems to have been in no hurry. 'Go forward in good heart,' he told his men, 'for God has promised me either the caravan or the soldiers, and by God it is as though I now saw the enemy lying prostrate.' With the Meccan forces destroyed, he could drive south and occupy Mecca. Then all of Arabia would fall into his hands.

When Abu Sufyan realized that Muhammad was bent on conquest, and that the army was in danger, he sent a hurried dispatch to the Meccan forces, urging them to return to Mecca. Abu Jahl, however, was determined upon a show of force. 'We will not go back,' he exclaimed. 'We shall spend three days in Badr, slaughter camels, feast and drink wine. We shall have girls to play for us, and the Arabs will hear that we have gathered together and show respect for us.' But when the army reached Badr, there was no feasting.

Muhammad's army was in fighting trim, eager for conquest. The Ansar in particular rejoiced in the prospect of booty, and they swore to follow Muhammad even if he ordered them to plunge into the sea. When night fell, the two armies were divided only by a low chain of hills. Muhammad saw them coming down into the valley while standing before a little hut made of palm branches, where he had spent the night with Abu Bakr. He prayed to God for a quick victory, saying: 'O God, here come the

Quraysh in their vanity and pride, contending with thee and calling Thy apostle a liar! O God, grant the help Thou didst promise me! Destroy them this morning!' As usual, Muhammad's prayers were like commands uttered to the Most High, and as usual they were answered. The enemy seems to have been alarmed by the small numbers of the Muhammadans, and one of their spies is reported to have returned to the camp with the eerie knowledge that they were contending with principalities and powers. The spy was asked how many Muhammadans he had seen. He answered: 'Three hundred men, more or less, but with them are the caravans of Yathrib laden with Death. These men have no refuge except their swords!' It was a complaint to be heard many times during the days of Muhammad's climb to power.

During the night a providential rain had fallen, softening the ground where the Quraysh were forced to pass, while paradoxically hardening the ground where the Muhammadans were standing. Everything worked in favour of Muhammad. The enemy came down the hill with the sun in their eyes, and at first they could not even make out the positions of the Muhammadans, concealed among the small sandy ridges. All Arab battles opened with single combats, and in all these preliminary engagements the Muhammadans won victories. Muhammad with Abu Bakr retired to his command post, his final instructions to his army being an order not to engage immediately, but to keep the enemy at a distance by means of showers of arrows; and he hinted that angelic hosts would come to their assistance. So he remained in the hut, guarded by a single soldier with a drawn sword, praying and sometimes sleeping, while the battle continued into the morning. Among his prayers were many calling upon the Lord not to forget His promises, reminding Him that if the enemy won, there would be none left to sing His praises. Abu Bakr was afraid these constant entreaties and recriminations would only annoy the Lord, but Muhammad silenced him. 'Be of good cheer, Abu Bakr,' Muhammad said. 'I have seen Gabriel holding the rein of a horse, and there is dust on his teeth!' In the valley many of the Muhammadans believed the angelic hosts were fighting for them.

At the height of the battle a storm rose, and some thought they saw the white turbans of the angels floating above the storm. When the Muhammadans were hard pressed, Muhammad darted out of the hut, picked up a handful of small stones and threw them in the direction of the Quraysh, shouting: 'Confusion seize them!' Then he ordered a charge, and the hard-pressed Meccans fled in a disorderly rout, leaving seventy dead on the field. Among the dead was Abu Jahl, whose head was struck off by Abdallah ibn Masud, Muhammad's secretary; and when the head was presented to Muhammad, he exclaimed exultantly: 'It is more acceptable to me than the choicest camel in Arabia.' The Muhammadans who were killed in the battle were honourably buried; the enemy dead were thrown into a pit, while Muhammad addressed them, saying: 'O people of the pit, have you found that which God threatened is true?' His companions were a little surprised to see him speaking to the dead, until he said quietly: 'They know.' It had been a strange morning, with the neighing of horses heard high overhead, the storm coming just at the time when it was needed by the beleaguered Muhammadans, but nothing surprised them more than this sad colloquy with the dead.

Altogether the Muhammadans had lost fourteen dead, the majority being Ansar, and therefore expendable. About seventy of the enemy were captured. Some of the companions wanted to kill the captives, but Muhammad reminded them that there were wives and children of his followers still in Mecca, and no good would come of a general butchery. Two of the captives were killed—al-Nadr, who had ridiculed the revelations of Muhammad, saying they were a collection of Persian tales, and Uqba, who had once attacked Muhammad in the Kaaba—and the rest were ransomed. Among the most important prisoners was al-Abbas, the Apostle's uncle, destined to be the eponymous founder of a long line of reigning Caliphs, a man of towering build who was captured by a man only a little bigger than a dwarf; and to explain his capture al-Abbas liked to say he had surrendered to an angelic horseman of gigantic size.

The battle won, Muhammad returned to Yathrib to superintend the division of the spoils. Those who had fought most vigorously claimed that the greater share should go to them; they saw no reason to divide the spoils with the old men who guarded the camp or those who stood aloof from the actual fighting. A new revelation came to Muhammad, known as *The Spoils of War*. In this Gabriel made clear that the Muhammadans had not of themselves won the victory: that honour was God's alone. 'They slew them not, but God slew them; and thou [Muhammad] threwest not when thou didst throw, but God threw, that he might richly reward the faithful.' To God, too, the Archangel ascribed the sleep that fell upon Muhammad in the middle of the battle, and it was God who revealed that no mercy need be shown, for had not God said: 'I will cast terror into the hearts of the infidels! Strike off their heads, maim their fingers!' God was weary of 'the whistling and the clapping of hands' at the Kaaba; it was time the unbelievers devoted themselves to the one True God. There was to be war to the death between the faithful and the infidels, and as for the spoils, one-fifth was to be reserved for God and His messenger. The iron, which glowed white-hot during the battle, was now tempered with victory, and there was divine authority for using it ruthlessly. At Badr the holy sword was raised, to remain in Muhammad's hands until death took it away from him.

Nothing in the revelations following the battle at Badr suggested the least mercy. On the contrary, mercy was to be regarded as a sign of weakness. 'The Messenger of God may take no captives until there has been slaughter in the land,' says the Quran. 'Though you desire the lure of the world, God desires for you the Hereafter.' Martyrdom in battle was to be regarded as the highest prize, the quickest means of entering Paradise. In a little while Muhammad was to say: 'I testify that all those who are wounded for God's sake God will raise on the Day of Judgment, and

A beautifully illuminated page from a copy of the Quran executed in Persia in the sixteenth century: the beginning of Sura xix, the chapter of Mary

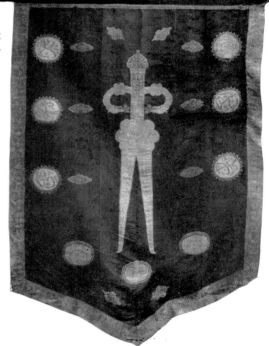

(*Above*) The Great
Mosque of Mecca con-
taining the Kaaba

(*Right*) The Holy
Sword, the two-pronged
Sword of Islam, dis-
played on a damask
Turkish banner thought
to be of the fifteenth
century

their wounds shall be resplendent as vermilion, and as odoriferous as musk.'

Meanwhile there was the booty to be attended to: a great treasure consisting of 150 camels and horses together with vast quantities of vestment and armour. A number of swords were captured, among them a strange double-pointed sword which came to be known as Dhu'l-Faqar, or 'Cleaver of Vertebrae'. Muhammad wore it during all his subsequent battles, and seems to have believed that the possession of this sword was the demonstrable sign of inevitable victory. In time the sword was inherited by Ali, and many copies were made engraved with the words 'No sword can match the Cleaver, and no young knight can compare with Ali'. Subsequently the sword became a holy relic, passing into the hands of the Abbasid Caliphs, who regarded their possession of the sword and mantle of the Apostle as proofs of their legitimacy. When the Abbasid Caliphate came to an end, the sword vanished; and there is no sign of it among the holy relics inherited by the Osmanli Turks.

Emboldened by the possession of the sword, and certain of eventual victory, Muhammad occupied the following year in consolidating his gains. He had failed to capture the caravan, which succeeded in slipping away during the fighting, but he had gained in prizes and ransom money an amount far greater than the worth of the caravan; and he had put terror in the hearts of the Quraysh. He was in no mood for half measures: he would attack when the proper time came. Better still, he would taunt the Quraysh into attacking him, far from their base, and watch their slow bloodletting at the gates of Yathrib.

A year passed before the Quraysh dared to attack in force. There had, it is true, been occasional skirmishes during the interval. Once Abu Sufyan, who had been in charge of the Meccan caravan at Badr, led two hundred of his horsemen nearly up to the walls of Yathrib. He killed two of Muhammad's followers, ravaged the fields, burned the date palms, and fled in such a hurry when Muhammad organized a sortie that he was forced to throw away the meal sack he carried over his saddle bow; and since all his followers did the same the short battle came to be known as 'the battle of the meal sacks'. There were skirmishes, brief encounters, sudden raids, but the major battle was still to come.

One day towards the end of January, A.D. 625, Muhammad was praying in the mosque when a sealed letter was handed to him. The letter contained the information that 3,000 Quraysh, including 700 warriors in armour and 200 cavalry, with a huge baggage train, were making their way slowly towards Yathrib. Muhammad continued his prayers, and then summoned a council of war. Some of his advisers urged him to stay within Yathrib, others that he should make a sortie and attack the enemy on the march. Abruptly, Muhammad made his own decision. He marched to his own house, put on his armour, announced that it would not be fitting for a Messenger of God to lay aside his armour until he had fought against his enemies, and led a thousand men out of Yathrib; of these about a third defected and decided to return home. Muhammad

D

was left with 700 men. They were no picked troops, but a rabble under arms, with only two hundred wearing armour. Mostly they were archers, and Muhammad himself was provided with a bow.

The armies met at the foot of Mount Uhud, three miles to the north of Yathrib, in a barren region of scrub and low granite hills.

Muhammad seems to have entered the battle in a mood of profound weariness, without the exhilarating knowledge that God was fighting on his side. He had grown fat and heavy; he was alarmed by the defections; he suspected treachery in the ranks; and he was certain that within Yathrib itself there were many who would regard his defeat as a blessing. At the battle of Badr he had resigned himself to God's will, never giving orders, certain that the angels would come to his assistance. This time he took an active part in the engagement, and issued three imperative orders to his troops. He ordered a detachment of some fifty archers to remain at all costs on a small foothill at the base of Mount Uhud, to protect his left— 'Do not move from this place; if you see us pursuing and plundering the enemy, do not join us; and if we are ourselves pursued, do not attempt to rescue us.' He commanded his troops to maintain their close-knit formation, and he forbade them to advance until he had given the order. He knew his men well. He was afraid the battle would develop into a wild mêlée, in which all the advantages would accrue to the enemy.

And so it happened, although at first God's favours were showered on the Muhamadans. As usual, the battle opened with individual combats, with the women in both camps urging on their favourites with taunts and the clanging of tambourines. Muhammad, wearing two coats of mail, retired to his command post. His troops were on higher ground, and the enemy came up the slope with banners flying, with Abu Sufyan leading the centre and a hundred horsemen on each wing. The Muhammadan square held firm. There were more attacks, with the Meccans attempting to carry the left wing, but there was no faltering on the part of the Muhammadans. The Meccans were recoiling from a third, or fourth, unsuccessful attempt to break the square when Muhammad gave the order for a general advance; and when the Meccan centre fled in a disorderly rout, the Muhammadans, who had been held back so long, were themselves thrown into confusion while they attempted to catch up with the enemy. Worse still, the fifty archers ordered to remain on the foothill rushed down in the plain, unable to control themselves at the sight of so much booty. The battle became a mêlée. Khalid ibn al-Walid, the slender and handsome captain of the Meccan cavalry, saw his opportunity, galloped his horsemen round the flank, occupied the foothill which Muhammad had chosen as the pivot of the battle, and fell upon the Muhammadan rear, saving the day for the Quraysh. The Muhammadans found themselves sandwiched between an enemy gradually recovering from a rout and a detachment of cavalry determined to cut them down like grass. They panicked, and might have been slaughtered to a man if it had not been for a handful of stalwarts who kept their ground.

None of the surviving accounts of the battle of Uhud reflect credit on

Muhammad's strategy. From the moment when he gave the order to charge to the moment when the Meccans abandoned the field, there seems to have been only a wild confusion. Muhammad himself was wounded. One blow struck him in the face, knocking out one of his teeth, and another drove his helmet rings into his cheek. He was not alone among the leaders in being wounded: Ali, Abu Bakr and Umar were all wounded, and for long periods reported dead. Muhammad hid in a ditch, his face covered with blood and one eye hanging out of its socket. Once, as he lay there, he looked up and saw his wife Ayesha tucking up her skirts while carrying waterskins and pouring water into the mouths of the wounded soldiers; and the sight of her anklets gleaming on that hot day gave him courage. A soldier saw him hiding and shouted: 'Take heart, the Messenger of God is alive!' Muhammad silenced him, and it was some time before he had recovered sufficiently to be moved: an old man, heavy with fat, burdened by two heavy coats of chain mail, in a roaring temper.

Meanwhile the Meccans were carrying all before them. They had killed Hamza, the Apostle's favourite uncle, and the wife of Abu Sufyan raced to the place where Hamza was lying, cut out his liver and attempted to eat it. The Meccans in their triumph amused themselves by plundering and mutilating the dead, cutting off ears and noses, and stringing them together into necklaces; and they went on to massacre the wounded. Once Abu Sufyan was heard crying out that all the leaders of the Muhammadans were dead, but Umar could not contain himself, and shouted: 'Thou liest! They are all alive, thou enemy of God, and will requite you yet!' Abu Sufyan seems to have thought the Muhammadans were boasting, and returned to Mecca with the conviction that Muhammad had been killed and the Muhammadans as a fighting force were no longer to be reckoned as serious contenders for power. At nightfall he rode off towards Mecca, leaving seventy of his dead on the field. The Muhammadans lost seventy-four dead, and most of them were mutilated.

The shock to Muhammad was such as to make him question his most profound beliefs. He was no longer the impassive leader of men, but a man humbled to the ground, who wept openly and consoled himself with the thought that defeat was meant to try his faith in himself. The Meccans had abandoned the field, when they could have attacked Yathrib and taken all before them; but he warned his followers against ascribing this to God's intervention, though he was pleased when some of the survivors spoke of seeing red-turbaned angels flying high above the battlefield. No; the fault had been in the hearts of the believers, for not believing. Too many of them had their minds on booty; too few had been aware that God was watching them. He, too, had been at fault, for not dealing sternly enough with traitors and defaulters. As one might expect, the revelation which came a few days later underscored the need for the sternest possible measures and a fierce endurance. 'Endure! Endure to the utmost! Stand firm in the faith and fear God, so that you may triumph.'

For Muhammad the triumph was still inevitable: a temporary defeat might be no more than the sign of the coming victory; and in this faith, but with haunting doubts, he looked to the future to avenge the horror at Uhud.

Now more than ever he was convinced that ultimate victory depended upon the sword. The intoxication of defeat was followed by the intoxication of vengeance; and every page of the Quran during this period is filled with oaths and maledictions against his enemies, not only in Mecca, but among the Jews and 'hypocrites' in Yathrib. Always suspicious of the Jews, he became more suspicious. The Jewish tribe of the Bani al-Nadir owned rich possessions within three miles of Yathrib. Invited to attend a feast to be held below their fortress walls, Muhammad went to visit them, accompanied by Ali, Abu Bakr and Umar. While there, he heard rumours of a plot to kill him by hurling a millstone from the top of the fortress wall on the feasters below. It was no more than a rumour, and the tribesmen indignantly denied they had ever had such an intention. Muhammad, however, was convinced that they were plotting his death and, returning to Yathrib, he summoned a large force to punish the infidels. The Jews took refuge in their fort. Muhammad attempted to attack the fort, but failed, and had to content himself with burning their date palms, on which they depended for their supplies. He had more troops than the tribesmen, and was perfectly prepared to embark on a long siege. The Jews suggested a compromise: they would abandon their village and offer it as a free offering to Muhammad provided they were allowed to leave, retaining all their property including their weapons and whatever they could carry on their camels. Muhammad agreed, and the tribesmen wandered away 'to the sound of tambourines and pipes, with singing-girls playing behind them'. It was an easy victory, and there were many more easy victories that year.

There were raids against Bedouin tribes in the south, and at least one raid against the tribesmen on the Syrian frontier, who had been plundering caravans destined for Yathrib. Most of these raids produced satisfactory booty: only one was completely unsatisfactory. This was a raid on the Ghatafan tribe in the Najd; there was no fighting because a sudden wave of panic fear seized the soldiers on both sides. Tradition relates a strange incident which occurred during the prolonged lull as the armies faced each other. A Ghatafan called Gaurath offered to kill Muhammad. Asked how he would do so, he answered that he would take Muhammad by surprise. It was very simple: he would saunter across the battle lines, ask permission to examine Muhammad's sword and then kill the Apostle with it. Gaurath had no difficulty crossing the battle lines. He found Muhammad sitting with his sword on his lap, examined the sword and asked permission to hold it. Muhammad gave it to him, whereupon Gaurath unsheathed it and brandished it over his head, saying: 'Aren't you afraid of me, Muhammad?' Muhammad answered: 'No, why should I be?' Gaurath said: 'Can't you see I am holding your sword in my hand?' Saying this, he made a gesture as though about to strike off Muhammad's head, but the sword fell from his hand when Muhammad answered calmly: 'God will protect me.' This incident is supposed to have been referred to by the Archangel in the revelation known as *The Table Spread*: 'O you who believe, remember God's favour to you when a people were minded to stretch out their hands against you, but the blow was deflected.'

Such stories, of course, were legion; and already Muhammad was assuming the stature of a living legend, a man of superhuman strength who sometimes appeared veiled so that men would not be blinded by the radiance streaming from his face. They spoke of his prowess in battle, and how he shivered and trembled at the approach of his revelations; and they collected his nail parings. To touch his garments, to hold something which once belonged to him, to be permitted into the presence—these were the signs of blessedness, the promise of Paradise. Muhammad himself appears to have been perfectly conscious of the legend he had created, and he was not averse from using it to his own advantage.

But while the public portrait suggested a man of godlike powers, he showed to his intimates all the frailties of his very human nature. It was his custom to take his favourite wife Ayesha on his campaigns. One day, returning from a campaign, they passed the night in camp not far from Yathrib. Muhammad was in a hurry to return, and the order to continue the march was given unusually early. The main body of troops had already moved off when Ayesha discovered that she had lost her favourite necklace. She decided to search for it, and after she had been searching for some time she discovered that she was alone in the desert, for her camel had moved off—the cameleer had thought she had entered the howdah and was safe behind the heavily embroidered curtains. She was not perturbed. 'I wrapped myself in my smock and then lay down where I was, knowing that if I were missed they would come back for me.' She had been lying there for only a few minutes when a soldier called Safwan ibn al-Muattal came up to her. He recognized her instantly, and offered to let her ride on his camel, and together they went in search of the army. Failing to find it, they rode to Yathrib, where Ayesha took to her bed. She was ill, and knew nothing about the frenzied rumours until some days later when Muhammad, after a conversation with Ali, openly accused her of misconduct. Ali was in favour of divorce. 'Women are plentiful,' he said. 'You can easily change her for another.' He suggested that Ayesha's conduct deserved harsh measures, adding that her slave girl would be able to throw light on the matter. But the slave girl found no fault in Ayesha except that she was sometimes neglectful when preparing dough and would fall asleep, and then her pet lambs would come and eat the dough she was kneading. Muhammad was in a dilemma. He trusted Ali's judgment, and relied heavily on the judgment of Abu Bakr, Ayesha's father. At his wit's end, he entered Ayesha's hut and begged her, if she had committed any sin, to repent, for God, had the power to accept repentance from His slaves. For days Ayesha had been weeping, but now there were no more tears. In her extremity she remembered a phrase from one of Muhammad's revelations: 'My duty is to show a comely patience.'

Muhammad was deeply moved. He began to shiver and tremble; a leather cushion was placed by his head; the moment of revelation was at hand. At last there fell from him 'as it were drops of water on a winter day', and he was heard saying: 'Good news, Ayesha! God has sent down word about your innocence!' Together with the proof of her innocence, the revelations defined the punishments to be meted to those who had slandered her. Ayesha herself was a little surprised by the divine intervention. 'I thought myself too insignificant,' she said later, 'for God to send down a special message concerning me, to be read in the mosques and used in prayers.'

So the days passed amid intrigues and recriminations, and occasional forays into the hinterland, while in Mecca preparations were continuing for a massive onslaught against Yathrib. Muhammad was forewarned. Learning that ten thousand men of the Quraysh, together with the Ghatafan, were marching on Yathrib, he held a council of war to determine how the city could be put in a state of defence. A former slave, Salman al-Farisi (the Persian), suggested that they should dig a trench on the southeastern quarter of the city, which was entirely defenceless. For six days the work of digging went on, with Muhammad himself encouraging the workmen with the hope of reward in Heaven. There was some malingering. To prevent this, Muhammad informed his followers that he had received a special revelation: 'The only true believers are those who beg the Apostle's leave before absenting themselves from work. Allah is forgiving and merciful!' Occasionally the Apostle performed small miracles, as when a heavy rock refused to budge: he spat on it, and the rock became sand. And once, when someone gave him a handful of dates, he spread them on a cloak and watched them miraculously increase until there were enough to feed all the men working on the trench.

When Abu Sufyan came up to the walls of Yathrib at the head of the tribes, his scouts reported the presence of the ditch. He was surprised. Nothing like this had ever been employed in Arabian warfare before. He sent his men against the ditch, and watched them fall back; and then sent a letter to Muhammad taunting him for using a strategem of such baffling novelty. Muhammad had his own problems. His army of three thousand men were already disaffected, trembling before the ten thousand who faced them on the other side of the ditch, knowing that the Jews in Yathrib were in secret communication with the enemy. For nearly a month of chill spring weather the armies faced each other, while Abu Sufyan pondered how to breach the ditch and the Muhammadans spoke bitterly about the course of the war. 'Muhammad promised us we would receive the treasures of Chosroes and Caesar,' they complained, glancing up at the rain of arrows and stones which fell on their camp, 'but today not one of us feels safe going to the privy.' Idleness corrupted them; so did waiting; so did the knowledge that the enemy was expecting an uprising in the city.

There were brief engagements, occasional forays and assaults, but no pitched battles. Once a small party of Quraysh horsemen, including Amr ibn Abdu Wudd, the uncle of Muhammad's first wife Khadija, discovered a place where the ditch was narrow and succeeded in leaping across to challenge the bravest of the Muhammadans. Ali fought with Amr on horseback and on foot, until they were lost in a cloud of dust; and when the dust settled, Ali was seen wiping his sword on Amr's garments.

While the siege lasted, Muhammad spent much of his time in prayer, and some part of every day was spent in attempting through spies to buy off the enemy. An attempt to buy off the Ghatafans by offering them one third of the produce of the date palms of Yathrib failed when one of Muhammad's followers asked bluntly whether he was acting on his own behalf or on behalf of the One God: whereupon Muhammad cancelled the agreement with the Ghatafans. Intrigue followed intrigue. The Jewish tribe of the Bani Quraiza, with its strongholds southeast of Yathrib, was found to be in direct communication with the enemy. Time was running out. Muhammad prayed for a miracle. One stormy night he stood at the trench, surrounded by his cold and starving men, and he was heard saying: 'Who will go and see what the enemy is doing—that man shall be my companion in Paradise.' There was no answer. No one dared to go, until at last a man called Hudhayfa decided to make the journey into enemy territory. Hudhayfa stole up to Abu Sufyan's command post, and returned with the news that the Quraysh were already preparing to raise the siege. The storm had chilled them to their marrows, upset their cooking pots and overthrown their tents; their camels and horses were being thrown into confusion; the men had no heart to continue an endless siege and they were beginning to believe that Muhammad had raised the storm by enchantment. Hudhayfa reported he had actually seen Abu Sufyan mounting his camel so hurriedly that he did not realize its foreleg was still hobbled. Muhammad received the news gratefully, throwing his mantle over Hudhayfa, and then together they bowed and prostrated themselves. Long before dawn the Quraysh were on their way back to Mecca, and in the morning Muhammad left the trench and returned to Yathrib.

There had been almost no fighting in the battle of the ditch, but there was fighting to come. On the very day the Quraysh raised the siege, Muhammad ordered an attack on the treacherous Bani Quraiza in their towers of refuge. He was in no mood to show mercy. His army had been terrified when it became known that the Bani Quraiza were in league with the enemy: something of that terror can be glimpsed in the words of the revelation received shortly after the departure of the Quraysh: 'When they came at you from above and below, and when your eyes grew wild and your hearts reached to your throats, and you thought vain things about God.' For twenty-five days the fortresses were besieged, while Muhammad debated with himself what he would do to the traitors. He would deal with them sternly and implacably, but exactly how he would deal with them was not revealed to him until the last moment.

When the starved defenders in their fortresses were seeking peace at any cost, Muhammad offered to allow them to surrender on condition that the

Aus, their supposed allies, should decide their fate. The Bani Quraiza agreed to these simple terms, and the Aus signified their willingness to make the decision, suggesting only that the final decision should be made by their chief. Everyone seemed to believe that the Bani Quraiza would share the fate of the Bani al-Nadir: they would simply be exiled, and all the property they could not carry with them would fall into the hands of Muhammad.

It did not happen like this. The chief of the Aus, a huge and corpulent man called Sa'd ibn Muadh, had been wounded by an arrow during the course of the battle of the ditch, and was being cared for in the mosque. He had become a convinced Muhammadan, believed that hell-fire awaited all traitors, and was in agony from the wound. Mounted on a donkey, and propped up with a leather cushion, he was brought to the tribunal. On the way, when asked to deal kindly with his former allies, he replied bitterly: 'I shall speak according to the will of God, and care not whether they will hate me.' When at last Sa'd saw the Jews who had agreed to abide by the judgment he pronounced, he raised his hand and said: 'I condemn the men to death, their property to be divided by the victors, their women and children to be slaves!' There was a long silence followed by a torrent of objections, and then Muhammad said: 'Truly Sa'd has declared the judgment of God from beyond the Seventh Heaven!'

The terrible judgment was carried out to the last detail, with Muhammad himself superintending the general massacre, even helping to dig the trenches in the market-place. The next morning the Jews, with their hands tied behind their backs, were taken out in batches of five or six at a time and forced to sit on the edge of the trench; then they were beheaded, and their bodies were tumbled into the trench. Among those who were beheaded was the Jewish prince Huyayy ibn Akhtab, who tore holes in his flowered ceremonial gown so that it would not be worn after him. Muhammad was watching the executions when Huyayy was led across the market-place with his hands tied to his neck by a rope. As he confronted Muhammad, the Jewish prince said proudly: 'I do not blame myself for opposing you. It appears however that a massacre has been written against the sons of Israel.' Then he sat down on the edge of the trench and his head was struck off.

Only one woman was beheaded. She was arrested and removed for safe custody to Ayesha's hut, and was talking to Ayesha when the order for her death was given. Years later Ayesha recalled how the woman had burst out laughing. 'It was very strange,' Ayesha said. 'She was in such good spirits, and she kept on laughing even though she knew she would be killed!' Ayesha was not the only one surprised by Muhammad's vindictiveness. A wave of fear ran through the ranks of the Muhammadans as well as the remaining Jews and Bedouin tribesmen as they contemplated the fury of the Apostle of God, now more determined than ever to wield power by the sword.

Imperceptibly his character was changing. He was still warm and human towards his intimates, still laughed hugely, still demonstrated a kind of gentle amusement in the world around him; but towards those of his followers who were not included within the charmed circle of his friendship, he showed a kind of defiant tolerance. They were the rabble he would hurl against his enemies. When he appeared among them, they fell into stunned silence, prostrated themselves on the ground, in terrified reverence of the man who had been lifted up to the heavens and spoken with God. Had not God ordered the massacre, and had not Muhammad carried it out without the batting of an eyelid?

For six long years Muhammad had waged war from his base at Yathrib, now renamed Madinat Nabi Allah, 'the City of the Prophet of God', in his honour, and never for a moment had he lost sight of his main object: the conquest of Mecca. Determined to use every strategem, every threat, to accomplish this purpose, he sent a stream of spies into the city to spread the terror of his name and to discover the weaknesses of its defenders, while at the same time he attempted to block the Meccan caravan routes and assumed control over them. He hoped to surround the city with enemies and to destroy it from within, and already his power extended almost to the gates of the city.

Accordingly he decided to take the city by storm, disguising his army as pilgrims. He made known to the authorities at Mecca that 1,400 pilgrims with himself at the head proposed to enter Mecca peacefully, armed only with the sheathed swords allowed to all pilgrims. He sent messages to neighbouring Bedouin tribes, asking them to accompany him, but only a handful joined the expedition. In February, A.D. 627, during the holy month when all fighting was forbidden, he set out with seventy camels. He was within ten miles of Mecca when he learned that a large number of troops were camped outside the north gate, to bar his progress. Worse still, a detachment of cavalry under the command of the brilliant Khalid ibn al-Walid was hurrying up the road, and it was reported that the Meccan soldiers were wearing leopard skins, a sure sign that they intended to offer battle. Muhammad decided to continue his progress, but to avoid giving battle as long as possible; and when a tribesman revealed to him a scarcely known track winding among the hills, he listened eagerly. It was a rough and dangerous track; the Muhammadans complained bitterly; and Muhammad was able to silence their complaints by pointing out that the Children of Israel had also travelled dangerously along unknown pathways among forbidding hills. At last he came to the oasis of Hudaibiyah, at the boundary of the holy area, and, learning that Khalid ibn al-Walid had wheeled back to help the defenders of Mecca, he decided to wait upon events. Emissaries were sent to the Quraysh, to explain his peaceful intentions. Spies came and reported that the city was not yet prepared for an uprising. The Quraysh sent ambassadors, who noted that Muhammad was treated with the reverence due to emperors: when he washed his hands, his followers rushed to gather the holy water he had touched, and when he spat they collected his spittle and treasured it. 'I have seen Chosroes and Caesar and the Negus of Abyssinia,' reported one ambassador, 'but never did I behold a sovereign so revered as Muhammad. Whatever happens, his followers will never desert him.'

The Meccans however were wary. They hinted, and sometimes said aloud, that Muhammad's purpose was conquest, and they may have known that Muhammad had announced only a few days before: 'I shall not cease from fighting until God gives me victory or I perish!' For several days negotiations continued, while Muhammad protested his innocent intentions and the Quraysh assiduously temporized, hoping to find some way of preventing his entry. At last Muhammad decided to send his son-in-law Uthman as his personal ambassador to the chiefs of the Quraysh. Uthman was an Umayyad and possessed great influence. For three days he was closeted with Abu Sufyan at a secret rendezvous inside the city. On the third day, when no news had come from him, Muhammad concluded that his son-in-law had been murdered, summoned his troops, ordered them to take 'the oath unto death' to fight until they had taken possession of the city, and prepared to attack immediately. He was on the verge of a battle which would have been the bloodiest of all.

At the last moment, when Muhammad was already preparing to attack, Uthman appeared in his camp unharmed, accompanied by the Quraysh ambassador, Suhayl ibn Amr, who was eager for a settlement but determined to prevent Muhammad from making his triumphal entry. Suhayl suggested a truce. If Muhammad would agree to abandon his entry this year, the Meccans promised in return to clear the city for three days every year so that the Muhammadans could make the pilgrimage undisturbed. Furthermore, no young Quraysh would be allowed to enter the ranks of the Muhammadans without the permission of their guardians: they must be sent back. On the other hand, turncoats from Islam would be allowed to remain in Mecca. This unequal agreement, intended to last for ten years, appalled many of Muhammad's followers, who saw in it an abject surrender to Quraysh power. Muhammad, more farseeing, saw it as the wedge which would destroy them.

When the peace treaty was being drawn up, Muhammad summoned Ali and dictated the words: 'In the name of God, the Compassionate, the Merciful——' At this point Suhayl interrupted: 'Stop! Say, as we have always said, *In thy name, O God!*' Muhammad decided not to quibble over the invocation, and continued: 'These are the conditions of peace between Muhammad, the Apostle of God, and Suhayl ibn Amr——' Once more Suhayl objected firmly, saying: 'If I believed you were the Apostle of God, I would not have fought you. Write instead your own name and the name of your father.' Thereupon, obeying Suhayl, Muhammad drew up the text of the Truce of Hudaibiyah, by which a ten-year peace was proclaimed 'without reservations or bad faith'. The document was solemnly signed and witnessed; Muhammad shaved his head and slaughtered the seventy camels he had promised, and with difficulty prevented a rebellion among his own troops who had hoped to plunder Mecca. On the return journey a strange revelation was handed down, proclaiming that Muhammad had won a great victory. It was not a victory, but defeat; yet it showed the way to victory. Soon, much sooner than most of his followers can have dared to hope, Mecca fell to them like a ripe plum.

Most of the Muhammadans were baffled by Muhammad's easy acceptance of the truce. They did not know, and could not guess, that simply by agreeing to the truce Muhammad had inevitably weakened the power of Quraysh. They had been compelled to treat with him, and he had shown himself magnanimous: throughout the proceedings he had behaved with the careless effrontery of a man who could afford to wait because he knew that power would fall into his hands. When his followers objected that in the treaty he was not recognized as the Apostle of God, he answered simply: 'God knows.'

If Mecca was not yet ripe, there remained a hundred other towns which could be raided with impunity. To provide booty for his soldiers, he decided to raid the rich Jewish colony of Khaybar, three long days' camel ride to the northeast, on the edge of the Najd. Khaybar was famous for its date palms, grazing lands and wheat fields; also for its strong fortresses. Muhammad advanced against the city at the head of 1,400 men, while the two war banners, one representing the sun and the other a black eagle, fluttered before him. The outposts were easily reduced, but the main citadel for a long time refused to submit. Trenches were dug round the powerful fortress, battering rams were brought up, and one after another the captains of the Muhammadan army led the assault, only to be hurled back. At last Muhammad decided it was time to let Ali demonstrate his prowess. Ali had held back, suffering from an inflammation of the eyes, which cleared up when Muhammad spat in them. Wearing a scarlet vest and a cuirass of steel, holding the celebrated sword Dhu'l-Faqar in one hand and a sacred banner in the other, Ali showed that he was still the first soldier of Islam, 'the Lion of God'. Arabic historians vie with one another in enlarging on his fanatical courage. Nothing daunted him. When his shield was struck from his hand, Ali wrenched the fortress gate from its hinges and used it as a buckler for the rest of the fight. Abu Rafi, one of Muhammad's slaves, said: 'He held it in his hands until God gave him victory, then he tossed it away. Afterwards with seven others I examined the gate, and none of us could turn it over.'

When the Jews surrendered Muhammad gave orders that the treasure be handed over to him. At first Kinana ibn al-Rabi, the prince of Khaybar, refused to reveal where it was hidden, but when a fire was lit on his chest and he was already dying, he revealed the secret. He was then executed. Not long afterwards his wife, the princess Safiya, was led past his headless body and presented to Muhammad, who fell in love with her and threw his mantle over her as a sign that she now belonged to him. The young and beautiful princess became one of his favourite wives and survived him by forty years.

Muhammadan historians have never attempted to minimize the cruelty of their heroes. The battle of Khaybar was fought mercilessly, and most of the leading citizens were killed in the fighting or executed out of hand in the heat of the triumph. Muhammad was appalled by the behaviour of his victorious troops, and his last order of the day condemned the soldiers who raped pregnant women, ate the flesh of donkeys and stole the booty before it was properly apportioned.

The Jews surrendered, but not all of them lost hope. One of those who went on fighting was Zainab, the wife of a Khaybar chieftain, who had lost her husband and all her male relatives. She offered to provide a meal of roast lamb for the victors, and when the offer was accepted, she made inquiries about which parts of the lamb Muhammad preferred. Learning that he particularly liked a shoulder of lamb, she prepared the roast and drenched the shoulder in poison. Muhammad bit into the shoulder and exclaimed: 'This bone tells me it is poisoned!' One of his followers named Bishr, who had swallowed some of the lamb, died in agony. There was a long silence until Muhammad summoned the woman who had served the feast and accused her of deliberately poisoning the lamb. She confessed eagerly. 'If you had been only a king,' she said, 'then you would have died of poison, but since you are the Apostle of God I knew you would be unharmed.' He was pleased with her answer, and forgave her, but to the end of his days he suffered from the effects of the poison.

Such acts of mercy occurred only rarely, and were usually reserved for beautiful young women, whom he added to his harem. Yet it was noted that he showed no desire to massacre or enslave the survivors at Khaybar, who were allowed to continue working their land on condition that they paid him the value of half their yield. The spoils were divided according to a complicated system of shares, the greater part going to the men who had accompanied him on the ill-fated expedition to Mecca. More spoils and more treasure came from the Jewish colonies in Fadak, Wadi al-Qura and Tayma, a city a hundred miles north of Madinah, which capitulated soon after the fall of Khaybar.

About this time Muhammad began to send messages to all the neighbouring princes and kings, suggesting the advantages of submission to the faith of the One God. Such messages were received by the princes of Yaman in the far south of the Arabian peninsula and by the princes of Ghassan, on the borders of Syria, and by a multitude of feudal chieftains in the outlying areas of Arabia. Another message was sent to Cyrus, the Byzantine governor of Egypt, who wanted no trouble on his eastern border and therefore returned a civil reply with some presents, including two beautiful slave girls. Muhammad presented one to his court poet Hassan ibn-Thabit, and kept the other, Mary the Copt, for himself. She was the prettiest of his concubines and the only one to give him a son, who was named Ibrahim. When the son died in childhood, Muhammad was overwhelmed with grief, sobbing bitterly until he was reminded that he often proclaimed against the outward expression of grief. Why was he sobbing when the child was so soon to enter Paradise? He answered softly: 'It eases the afflicted heart. It does no harm to the dead, and does not profit him, but it is a comfort for the living.'

At such moments Muhammad, dead for so many centuries, comes to life again. His tenderness, his cruelty, his strength and his frailties were inextricably commingled; and he seems to have been obscurely puzzled by the sharpness and range of his own emotions. Grief laid him low so often that it became a habit with him, and he was continually intoxicated with joyful knowledge of an avenging God who fought by his side. To women he was nearly always gentle, but to men, even to his intimates, he was always hard and demanding.

In the chequered career of the Apostle of God there are strange interludes, and nothing is stranger than his decision to enter Mecca peacefully, following the agreement made at Hudaibiyah. The year before he had intended to storm the city; he still intended to take it by storm; but this year, the seventh since the *Hijra*, he went through all the motions of the pilgrim determined to show his devotion to the Kaaba. With two hundred of his followers armed against treachery, and twelve hundred unarmed, he rode to Mecca to find that the Quraysh had abandoned the city to him, according to the treaty. Evidently they had no fear of him. They noted that the pilgrims were poorly dressed, probably destitute, and it was an act of mercy to allow them to make their offerings. Muhammad ran round the Kaaba, embraced the black stone and kissed it, and stood aside to watch his followers performing the same service. He was allowed to stay in Mecca for three days, but asked for a postponement on the grounds that he was about to marry for the ninth time, this time to a fifty-year-old widow, and he could not bring himself to believe the Quraysh would refuse his invitation to the wedding feast. But the Quraysh were determined to be rid of him. 'Get out!' they said harshly. 'We don't need your food!' To delay was to invite war. Accompanied by his followers he left Mecca peacefully and made his way to the oasis of Sarif, where the marriage was consummated.

Peace towards Mecca, war against the rest of the world! So in the intervals of prayer and revelation he planned his final conquests, which brought his armies almost to the Dead Sea and almost to Yaman. He was ageing rapidly, but his spirit and determination were unchanged. When he heard that a messenger he had sent to the commander of the fortress at Bostra in Transjordan had been killed, he sent an expedition under his foster-son Zayd ibn-Harithah with three thousand troops, among them Khalid ibn al-Walid, who had abandoned the worship of idols, to avenge the murder. At Ma'an, at the head of the Gulf of Aqabah, they learned that the Byzantine frontier force, amounting, according to Arab tradition, to 200,000 Greeks and tribesmen, was waiting for them. They debated for two days whether to continue the journey or to return, but finally decided to attack their vastly superior opponents when the poet Abdallah ibn-Rawaha reminded them that they were not fighting with strength of numbers but with the all-powerful strength of the One God; and victory or martyrdom was equally desirable. At the village of Mutah near the southern tip of the Dead Sea they faced a Christian army for the first time. Zayd fell before the enemy's spears, and the command of the army was then given to Ja'far, Ali's brother, who fought on until he was surrounded, holding up the standard of Muhammad with his bleeding stumps when his hands were cut off. Abdallah ibn-Rawaha was the next to command the army, and he too fell. Then it happened that Khalid ibn al-Walid, who only a year before had been a captain in the army of the Quraysh, was promoted from the ranks to command the wavering Muhammadans. Singlehanded, he had very nearly defeated the Muhammadans at Uhud. Now he turned the defeat of the Muhammadans into a half-triumph, disengaging them from the enemy, then at night attacking their out-posts, marching and counter-marching so that they were completely deceived into believing he had received reinforcements, and obtaining so much booty that when he returned to Madinah, laden with spoils, he was treated as a conqueror until the people of Madinah remembered the loss of Zayd and Ja'far, and then once more they gave way to their grief.

Muhammad was appalled by the deaths of the two leaders who had been so close to him. He wept openly, and spoke of how on the day when Ja'far died, he had seen him in a vision with a company of angels: he had two wings whose forefeathers were stained with blood. Asked why he wept, he answered: 'They are tears of yearning for the death of my brother.'

The violent deaths of those who were near to him often had the result of precipitating violent action. In despair of punishing the Greeks, Muhammad turned his attention to Mecca. A brawl between a Bedouin tribe converted to Islam and some partisans of the Quraysh gave him a suitable pretext to threaten the city. He spread the rumour that he would attack in force, and was surprised to learn that the Quraysh were visibly frightened. Ambassadors came, to remind him about the ten-year truce, which had eight more years to run. He dismissed them with the reminder that they permitted brawls and otherwise disturbed the peace. At the head of the largest army he had ever mustered—there were at least ten thousand well-armed troops—he set out for Mecca on January 1, A.D. 630. On the way he was met by his old enemy, Abu Sufyan, who came in the guise of a penitent, begging to be admitted into the presence and threaten-ing to wander abroad like a beggar to die of hunger and thirst if he was not received. Muhammad received him kindly, and accepted his conversion to Islam; and when reminded that Abu Sufyan was a man who liked to have some cause for pride, Muhammad announced that anyone who entered Abu Sufyan's house would be granted safety. To ensure that Abu Sufyan would not change his mind, Muhammad directed that he should be taken to a high place overlooking a pass, from which he could see the endless armoured columns marching towards Mecca; and to ensure that the Meccans would be suitably impressed, he commanded his followers to light watch fires on the hills overlooking the city. That night all Mecca trembled, waiting for the threatened assault, but when morning came there was no fighting except for a short skirmish at the south gate. Muham-mad's forces advanced from two sides simultaneously, and Mecca sur-rendered. Only twelve or thirteen Meccans were killed. By sabotage, by deceit, by the terror of Muhammad's name, the city had been weakened;

and it fell into his hands, as he had long ago suspected it would fall, like a ripe plum.

The sun was rising when he entered the city on camelback, a lone figure dressed in the white garments of a pilgrim. In the hush which descended on the city he was seen to ride seven times round the Kaaba and whenever he passed the black stone he touched it with his camel stick. On the previous occasion he had made the circuit on foot, running with his strange loping stride and heaving shoulders; he had fondled the black stone with his hands and kissed it with his lips. But those times were passed. Now, as Emperor of Arabia, he rode slowly, and he seems to have been a little frightened by his new eminence. When someone approached him in fear and trembling, he said: 'Why are you trembling? I am no Emperor, but the son of a Quraysh woman, who ate flesh dried in the sun!'

As the herald of the new dispensation, he knew exactly what to do. The triumph did not lie in ceremonies; it lay in the establishment of the new order. In all his life there was no more solemn moment than when he entered the Kaaba and surveyed the 365 idols standing against the walls. There was the moon god Hubal darkened with age, statues of Abraham and Ishmael with divining arrows in their hands, a wooden dove, painted angels, pictures of Jesus and the Virgin. Muhammad ordered them to be destroyed, and there is a tradition that they turned to powder when he pointed his stick at them. There is another tradition that he allowed the pictures of Jesus and the Virgin to remain.

When he had destroyed the idols, he came to the door of the Kaaba and pronounced what was at once a benediction and a summons to the new dispensation. 'There is no God but God; there is none with him,' he began. 'God has made good His promise and helped His servant. From this day every claim of privilege or blood or property is abolished by me, except the custody of the Kaaba and the watering of the pilgrims. O Quraysh, God has taken from you the pride of idols and the veneration of ancestors. Know that man springs from Adam, and Adam springs from dust. Know that God created you male and female and made you into peoples and tribes that you may know one another; the most noble of you are those who worship God most.' On that note, as of one withdrawing from the combat, he concluded his sermon, and for the rest of his two-week stay in Mecca he lived quietly and unostentatiously, spending his days in conversation with his old companions. Long ago he had received the revelation: 'Truth hath come; darkness hath vanished away.' Against all odds he had succeeded in capturing Mecca; for twenty years his life had been the wildest and most improbable of adventure stories; and now at last in a profound sense his life was over, and it was time to rest.

But there was no rest. He had hardly installed himself in Mecca when he heard that the Hawazin tribesmen of the Najd had allied themselves to the Thaqif tribe at Taif, prepared to fight to the death in defence of their idols against the conqueror of Mecca. Desperate, they had assembled an army of 30,000 near Hunayn on the western pilgrim road some two hundred miles north of Mecca and within seventy of Madinah. As Muhammad had done so often in the past, they were attempting to cut the main roads joining Mecca and Madinah. They were disciplined troops, and offered a deadly threat to the survival of Muhammadan power. There was nothing to be done except to march against them promptly. On February 1, A.D. 630, early in the morning when it was still dark, Muhammad was leading his troops down a narrow valley near Hunayn when he was ambushed. There had been no warning. The enemy lay well-hidden in the underbush and in the small paths leading along the valley. Arrows, spears and stones fell among the unsuspecting Muhammadans, who panicked and fled. Muhammad shouted: 'Where are you going? Come back! I am the Apostle of God!' No one paid any attention until the cry was carried up by the Apostle's uncle, al-Abbas, a man with a stentorian voice, whose shouts summoning the men of Hudaibiyah to form ranks around Muhammad echoed and re-echoed through the narrow valley. There was so much confusion that men on camelback had to dismount to join the close-knit square around Muhammad. Finally a hundred men gathered around the standard, fighting with the courage of despair; and when the tide turned, Muhammad was seen standing in his stirrups and gloating happily over the victory, saying: 'Now is the furnace heated!' Then he stooped from the saddle, gathered a handful of dust and flung it in the direction of the retreating enemy. 'Confusion on their faces!' he shouted. 'May the dust blind them!' The enemy fled, and for many months afterwards Muhammad remembered that a hundred men had saved the day.

With the Hawazin in full flight, Muhammad ordered his troops to press on with the attack until they had destroyed the enemy camp. An immense booty was secured, not easily, for the Hawazin fought nobly; and one of the saddest stories of Muhammad's campaigns is told about the confused fighting around the tents. An old warrior, once the leader of Hawazin, was attempting to escape, hidden behind the hangings of his howdah. A young Muhammadan named Rabi'a ibn Rufay thought a woman was hiding there and made the camel kneel, and when he saw the old man, he struck out with his sword, but the sword broke in his hand. 'Your mother,' said the old man quietly, 'has given you a poor weapon, but there is a better hanging behind my saddle. Take it, and strike me above the spine and below the head, as I once used to do, and then tell your mother you have killed Durayd ibn al-Simma, for many times have I protected the women of your tribe!' The boy took the sword and killed the old warrior. Returning home, he told his mother what he had done. 'By God,' she said, 'you have killed a man who set free three mothers and grandmothers of yours!'

Similar incidents are recorded through all these hard-fought campaigns, and there were more to come. The Thaqif tribesmen escaped to Taif, where Muhammad had spent his childhood, with the Muhammadans in hot pursuit. They shut themselves up in their strongholds, and for twenty days fought off the besiegers. For the first time Muhammad countenanced the use of Byzantine weapons—catapults, battering rams

The Dome of the Rock at the top of Mount Moriah in the Haram-es-Sherif compound of Jerusalem. The construction of the present mosque was started in A.D. 691 by the Umayyad caliph, Abd-al-Malik ibn-Marwan, on the site of the temples of Solomon and Herod. The building is a magnificent work of eighth-century architecture

The interior of the Dome of the Rock, showing the rock upon which Abraham prepared to sacrifice his son, Isaac, and the Prophet Muhammad is said to have prayed before his ascension into heaven

(*Above*) The south face of the Great Umayyad Mosque, Damascus, begun by Caliph Walid ibn-al-Malik in A.D. 707. (*Left*) The interior: the domed structure is believed to contain the head of Saint John the Baptist

and testudos. The defenders hurled molten iron from the walls, and in re-
taliation Muhammad ordered that their vineyards should be put to the
flames. Attempts to enter Taif by treachery failed; and when one night
Muhammad dreamed that a cock was pecking at a bowl of butter, he interpreted it as a sign that the venture was doomed to failure. The siege was
lifted, and the disconsolate Muhammadans returned to Madinah.

Taif was no more than an incident in a general war: Muhammad could
afford to be patient. From all over Arabia ambassadors were flocking to
his court, offering tribute, demanding to be allowed to worship the One
God. In the past he had been implacable against his enemies, and especially against the satiric poets who poured scorn on his high purpose.
When he entered Mecca in triumph he ordered the execution of two singing
girls for singing ribald songs about him; and for a long time the famous
poet Ka'b ibn Zuhayr had enjoyed the distinction of being on the list of
enemies to be killed out of hand by the faithful. One day, shortly after
Muhammad's return to Madinah, Ka'b received a message from his
brother, a convert, saying that Muhammad was inclined to be merciful to
those who sought repentance. Ka'b made his way secretly to Madinah and
slipped up to Muhammad during morning prayers. When the prayers
were over, Ka'b put his hand in Muhammad's and began to recite the
great ode for which he is chiefly remembered.

Poetry was a commonplace of Arabia, and the historians of Islam re-
late in great detail the poems which were recited in the midst of battle.
Most of these poems are lame and imitative, but Ka'b's poem, written
in despair, breathes a new fire, an astonishing freshness. Beginning with a
lament for his lost mistress, whose inconstancy saddened his heart and
whose beauty inflamed his desire, he goes on to describe with even greater
affection the she-camel that bore his mistress away:

> Her eyes, like those of the lonely white oryx, gazed across the stony wilderness,
> Her neck was heavy, her forehead high as a millstone, her flanks robust,
> Male-like, full in the cheek, no tick ever penetrated her hide,
> Foaled by a noble dam, long-necked, smooth-breasted and nimble,
> Well-bred with her eagle nose, heavy ears, muzzle like a pickaxe . . .

So he goes on, describing a legendary camel who is only Muhammad
disguised, while the mistress he laments is himself in his legendary past,
grief-stricken now because he is in the presence of the Messenger of God,
'noble as the racing camels with tawny hocks, fearful as the lions in the
thickets of Aththar'. It is heroic poetry raised to a pitch of intense excitement by the awareness of danger. The great camel fades into the glare of
noonday, and suddenly Ka'b introduces the figure of the mother bewailing
the death of her firstborn, pleading as all men plead for some surcease
against death, some light against darkness:

> But the Messenger is the torch who has lighted up the world, a brilliant fire;
> He is the sword of God for destroying ungodliness; his men have no weakness.
> Like shining camels they march and parry the deadly blows of the enemy.
> Warriors with high, straight noses, clad in coats of mail woven by David,[1]
> They do not exult when they hurl their spears against the enemy,
> And are not cast down by failure: they never shrink from the gates of death!

---

[1] In the Quran (xii, 80) David is described as a maker of coats of mail.

E

At this point Ka'b concluded his recital of the great ode known as the *Qasida-i-Banat-Su'ad*, and in the long silence that followed it was seen that Muhammad was strangely moved. Suddenly he threw his striped Yaman cloak, the *burda*, over the poet, as a sign that all his former errors were forgiven. Ka'b preserved the cloak to the end of his life, refusing all offers for it. Years later, in the time of the Caliph Muawiya, his descendants sold it to the royal treasury for 10,000 dirhems. For nearly six hundred years, until the Abbasid Caliph al-Mu'tasim was murdered by order of Hulagu during the sack of Baghdad, this cloak was worn by the Caliph in processions and solemn ceremonies. Then it vanished. It seems to have been burned to ashes during the conflagration of the city.

With the battle in the valley of Hunayn all regular warfare between the Muhammadans and pagans in Arabia came to an end. Contemplating his long series of rapid victories, Muhammad conceived the idea of a universal empire: 'One Messenger, one faith, for all the world!' Once more he sent dispatches to the countries bordering upon Arabia, requesting them to cease worshipping idols, to reverence the One God and to recognize his mission. According to the traditionist Bukhari, he wrote to the Emperor Heraclius in Byzantium:

> In the name of God, the Beneficent, the Compassionate! From Muhammad, the servant of God and His Messenger, to Heraclius, the chief of the Romans!
>
> Peace be with him who follows the guidance. I invite thee into the faith. Become a follower of Islam, and thou wilt be at peace—God will give thee a double reward. If thou turnest away, on thee will be the sin of thy subjects. O Followers of the Book, come to an equitable agreement with us. Serve none but God, associate none with Him, and take unto thyselves no other masters. Proclaim thyself followers of the faith, and all shall be well between us.

It is unlikely that Heraclius received the message, and it is still more unlikely that a similar message was ever received by Chosroes II, Emperor of Persia, who is said to have seized the letter in a rage and torn it to pieces. When the news was brought to Muhammad, he is supposed to have proclaimed prophetically: 'Even so shall God rend his empire to pieces!' But though these messages were perhaps never delivered, there was no doubt about Muhammad's intentions. As old age came over him, as he penetrated more and more deeply into the mystery of the pure and transcendent God he worshipped, and whose Messenger he proclaimed himself to be, the more certain he was of the need to carry his message to all quarters of the earth. The holy sword, raised at Madinah, would not be sheathed until the whole world had acknowledged the faith. He had always fought against the strongest. He would send his armies against Heraclius first, and then perhaps against Persia. Once more he took the field, at the head of an army of 30,000. It was the height of summer, but he had chosen the season deliberately, saying that he intended to set out in the worst season of the year on a long and arduous march against overwhelming odds: it was in this way that victories were won. To those who complained of the heat, he answered: 'Hell is hotter.' And when Ali protested at being left behind in Madinah, Muhammad answered: 'Are you not content to stand to me as Aaron stood to Moses?' Many believed that with these words he had already proclaimed his successor.

Muhammad's battles were not always victories, and the expedition against Heraclius was as inconclusive as his defeats. Reaching Tabuk, halfway between Madinah and Damascus on the frontiers of the Byzantine Empire, he seems to have realized that nothing would be gained by the venture, and after receiving tribute from a few obscure Christian tribes he decided to return. In the interval Taif had fallen. In an unusually gentle mood he pardoned the inhabitants, and asked no more of them than confession of the faith and the rejection of idols. They begged to be allowed to keep their idols for a few more weeks, so that the people would grow accustomed to worshipping without them, but Muhammad said: 'They must be destroyed now!' Then they asked that Muhammadans should do the work of destruction, because they were afraid, and Muhammad said: 'We shall do so willingly.'

In those last days the immense power which had fallen to him seemed to make him more gentle. At the time of the pilgrimage of A.D. 631 he was ill, and sent Abu Bakr as his representative. Not till the following spring did he decide to go in person, with all his wives and a great company of the faithful, said to amount altogether to 124,000 people. He rode round the Kaaba, shaved his head and distributed portions of his hair among the companions, explained the ceremonial duties of the pilgrims and then climbed Mount Arafat, where he delivered his farewell sermon. There was no trace of rancour, no cruelty, no heavy and demanding burden on the people. He asked that all his followers should be brothers, abolished usury, proclaimed the rights of women and of slaves, and put an end to blood feuds. He said:

O people! Hearken to my words, for I know not whether after this year I shall ever be among you again.

Your lives, your property and your honour are sacred and inviolable, until you appear before your Lord, as this day and month are sacred. Remember, you will soon meet your Lord, and He will call you to account for your deeds. . . .

O people! Satan despairs of ever being worshipped in your land. But should you obey him even in trifling matters, it will be a source of pleasure for him. So you must beware of him in matters of the faith. . . .

O my people! You have certain rights over your wives, and they have rights over you. You have the right that they should not defile your bed and that they should not behave with open unseemliness. If they do, God allows you to put them in separate rooms and to beat them, but not with severity. If they refrain from these things they have a right to food and clothing, given with kindness. . . .

And your slaves! See that you feed them with such food as you eat yourselves, and clothe them with what you clothe yourselves; and if they commit a crime you cannot forgive, then part from them, for they are the servants of the Lord, and are not to be harshly treated.

O people, listen to my words, and understand them! Know that all the faithful are brothers unto one another. You are all one brotherhood. It is forbidden to take from a brother save what he gives willingly: so guard yourselves from committing evil. And may those who are present tell these words to those who are absent.

Verily, I have concluded my mission! I have left among you a plain command, the Book of God, and manifest ordinances. If you hold fast to them, none of you shall go astray.

When he had finished speaking, he cried out at the top of his voice: 'O Lord! I have delivered thy message!' From all over the valley came the answering cry: 'O Lord, thou hast!' Once more Muhammad raised his eyes to heaven and said: 'O Lord, bear witness for what I have done!' Then he came down the mountain and made his way to Mecca, where he remained for three days before returning by slow stages to Madinah.

He was already ill when he reached Madinah. He was listless, with burning pains in his back, a heavy fever. On May 27, he was well enough to present a banner to Usamah, the son of his foster-son Zayd who had fallen at Mutah, and there was a small ceremony as the army went off to avenge that strange defeat. One night, accompanied only by a servant, Muhammad stole out to the cemetery on the edge of Madinah and for a long time gave himself up to melancholy reflections. Standing there, a little apart from the servant, he addressed the dead companions of his earlier days: 'Peace be unto you, O people of the graves! Happy are you, for your lot is better than ours! Trials and tribulations fall upon me like waves of darkness following one upon another, each darker than the rest.' Then he turned to his servant and said: 'The choice is given to me— either the keys and the treasuries of this world with a long life followed by Paradise, or to meet my Lord and enter Paradise at once.' The servant asked him to remain in the world, but Muhammad said he had already chosen to enter Paradise immediately.

When Muhammad returned from the cemetery, he heard Ayesha calling out: 'My head! My head!' Entering, Muhammad reproved her gently: 'Nay, Ayesha, it is *my* head thou shouldst be complaining about!' And then, because she was suffering from fever and he wanted to amuse her, he said: 'Would it distress thee if thou wert to die before me? For then, Ayesha, I would pray over thee and wrap thee in thy winding-sheet and myself commit thee to the grave!' Ayesha answered quickly: 'And then come back to my house and enjoy a new wife?' Muhammad smiled, but she saw he was ill and cared for him tenderly.

Though in great pain, he could still walk a little, and appeared at the mosque, supported by Ali, with his head bound in a towel. He prayed for the men who had fallen at Uhud, and later issued final orders for the expedition against the Syrians. His companions thought he was suffering from pleurisy and gave him the appropriate remedy: an ill-tasting mixture of Abyssinian herbs. After tasting the remedy, and learning that it was intended to cure him of pleurisy, he said angrily: 'God would never afflict me with pleurisy!' Then, to punish them for their ill-considered choice, he ordered them all to take the medicine. Ayesha asked him a little later who should take the prayers in the mosque. He said: 'Abu Bakr will superintend the prayers.' Then Ayesha reminded him that her father was a delicate man with a weak voice who always wept when he recited the Quran. 'Still, he will take the prayers,' Muhammad answered, adding that his wife was behaving like Joseph's companions. Afterwards Ayesha explained that she had wanted to spare her father the responsibility of following in Muhammad's footsteps: if everything went wrong, then the blame would fall on him.

On the morning of his death, Muhammad seemed to have recovered; and when the believers had gathered in the mosque and Abu Bakr was leading the prayers, he appeared at the door of his hut, smiling approvingly. Abu Bakr noticed that the attention of the faithful was wavering, and when he saw Muhammad, he stepped down from the *minbar* and begged Muhammad to take his place. 'No,' said Muhammad, 'lead the men in prayers.' Then he sat down on the right of Abu Bakr, and prayed. At the end of the prayer he turned for the last time to the men gathered in the mosque; and the same fears which tormented him in the cemetery returned to plague the last moments of his life. 'O men,' he said, 'the fire is kindled! Rebellions come like the darkness of the night! By God, you cannot lay these things to my charge! I allow what the Quran allows, and forbid what the Quran forbids!' Then he stumbled back to the dark hut and Ayesha's welcoming arms.

Strangely, hardly anyone thought the end was near, perhaps because when he spoke in the mosque his voice had been wonderfully resonant and clear. Abu Bakr returned to his house some miles away, and Ali visited the bedside and stayed only long enough to surmise that Muhammad was well on the road to recovery. Only al-Abbas, Muhammad's uncle, saw the look of death on the ageing face. He implored Ali to return to the hut and secure the succession. 'If you do not, you will be a slave three nights hence,' al-Abbas warned him. But Ali was too proud, or too loyal to his adopted father, or too fearful of being refused, to enter that hut again while Muhammad was living.

Towards noon, as he lay with his head against Ayesha's breast, his wandering eye fixed upon a green tooth stick. He asked for it, and Ayesha gave it to him, and was a little surprised to observe him rubbing his teeth with it more energetically than she had ever seen him rub before. Then he laid the tooth stick down, and soon she felt his head growing heavier on her breast and his hand growing limp in her own. He began to breathe very hard, but suddenly there was no more breath in him. Ayesha thought his last words were: 'The most exalted has entered Paradise.' Others thought he said: 'God forgive me, have compassion on me, and take me to the highest heavens!'

He died about noon, on June 8, A.D. 632, in a small and crowded hut,
surrounded by his servants and his wives. Muhammad himself explained
his illness by the weakness and shock which came as a result of his revelations: no man could live happily with the fire of God pouring through his
body. Others contend that he died of malaria. Muhammadan historians
proclaim that he died in blessedness and peace, confident in the knowledge that he had fulfilled his mission, but the words he uttered in the
mosque suggest that he was aware of failure. 'O men, the fire is kindled!
Rebellions come like the darkness in the night!'

There were to be many dark nights, many rebellions, much kindling of
the fires. Muhammadanism after Muhammad is the story of a decline, of
man's inability to continue in the paths of holiness proclaimed by an
authentic visionary. In the short time that was given him, Muhammad
built up a powerful religious movement directed towards the welcoming of
the Kingdom of God. He had seen the earth opening beneath him; known
shuddering awe; felt the scorching flames on his face. With pathetic certainty he came to the knowledge that the world must be changed by force
of arms, yet the ruthlessness, which he did nothing to conceal, hides a kind
of savage tenderness. Of all the great visionaries who at various times have
come to torment an evil world with visions of Paradise, he was perhaps the
most human, the most like ourselves.

With his coming the imagination of the world changed. He left an impress which cannot be argued away, if only because he spoke—not always,
but sufficiently often—with an authentic majesty. Yet to the end there was
something dreamlike in his progress through the world. Perhaps the best
of all judgments on him was spoken by the great Andalusian philosopher,
Ibn Arabi, who said: 'All of Muhammad's life passed before him like a
dream within a dream.'

THE HOLY WORD

Muhammad was dead, but the memory of the man lived on in his recorded sayings and in the obscure book of poems dictated to him by the Archangel Gabriel. Dead, he was more powerful than when he was living. The earthly man with his wives and concubines, his blazing visions and sudden bloodthirsty passions, was not forgotten; but the image which impressed itself upon his followers was of a man who lived his life strangely alone, untouched by mortal sin, possessed of excessive tenderness towards living things, powerful and robust, dominating Arabia by the force of his character and by his formidable energy, a man of impulse about whom innumerable anecdotes were told, and most of them proclaimed his essential humanity. For the Arabs Muhammad was a man like themselves, but raised above them by his visionary gifts; and they found only his tenderness strange.

The modern student of the Quran is baffled by this tenderness, which is perhaps his greatest strength. It comes when least expected, suddenly, and often on the wings of violence. He roars and splutters; the whole world is breaking asunder; the flames are already pouring out of the earth like breath from the nostrils; heaven is shuddering; and suddenly in the midst of all this upheaval, all these threats of the Last Judgment awaiting sinful man, there comes the caressing note, a sweet diapason. In place of majestic uproar there is the vision of cool gardens and fountains, the promise of eternal life.

It is worth while to pause for a moment before the quite astonishing polarity of Muhammad's mind. Violence and gentleness were at war within him. Sometimes he gives the appearance of living simultaneously in two worlds, at one and the same moment seeing the world about to be destroyed by the flames of God and in a state of divine peace; and he seems to hold these opposing visions only at the cost of an overwhelming sense of strain. Sometimes the spring snaps, and we see him gazing with a look of bafflement at the world around him, which is neither the world in flames nor the world in a state of blessedness, but the ordinary day-to-day world in which he was rarely at home.

Living in this way in a strange imaginative quarrel with himself, believing himself to be appointed by God and in communion with angels, he could hardly have acted otherwise than he did. When the judgment of God failed to visit the heathen, he determined to carve out a principality which would be obedient to God's commands. He exchanged spiritual violence for physical violence, and gloried in it, and perhaps saw very little difference between them. The sword cleaneth. And in all this he was not very far removed from Jesus, who said he came not to bring peace but the sword and whose darker sayings suggest an unfathomable knowledge of the violence of Heaven and the violence of the human soul.

We shall not understand Muhammad unless we come to grips with those extremes of temperament and imagination which he sometimes manifested simultaneously. Outwardly calm, he was a man in perpetual conflict with himself. His ideas and visions were continually changing at the mercy of events, yet strangely to the Arabs he appeared as a man of singleminded purpose, who never veered from his one announced aim of bringing all men to the worship of the One God. The Arabs saw simplicity in the vast confusion of the Quran; and being, like Muhammad, quick and intricate in establishing relations between distantly related objects, they were not perturbed by inconsistencies. They saw Muhammad plain. He had said simple things in a rich and sonorous language, and they held fast to his simplicities, leaving to the scholars the task of examining his more complex statements. He had lived and died, and at the Last Judgment he would intercede for all sinners who accepted the faith; and in this belief millions of Muhammadans were to pursue their obscure lives, certain that if they obeyed his commands they would enter Paradise. In exactly the same way millions of Christians have lived out their lives without disturbing themselves about the complex problems of Christology. There is the simple Christ and the infinitely complex Christ; in the same way there is the simple Muhammad and the infinitely complex Muhammad, who baffles the imagination and sometimes seems to vanish altogether as the scholar probes through layers of legend in search of the man beneath.

Though we have abundant testimony about Muhammad's earthly life, most of our knowledge of him comes from second or third hand: the earliest surviving biography was written nearly a hundred and fifty years after his death. But if completely authentic details of his life are often lacking, there is no doubt about the authenticity of the greater part of the Quran, which was first compiled only a few years after his death, perhaps during the reign of the Caliph Umar, who ordered that every word uttered by Muhammad by way of revelation should be collected 'whether inscribed on date-leaves, shreds of leather, shoulder-blades, stone tablets or the hearts of man'. The Quran, as it has been handed down to us, is Muhammad's testament assembled by men who knew him well and who could vouch for the accuracy of most of the revelations. There are gaps; many suras were lost; a few may have been fraudulently invented for political reasons; but it is indisputable that the Quran provides a portrait of the whole man. Dimly in the distance we see the face of God; in the middle distance stands the Archangel Gabriel; in the foreground, large as life, stands Muhammad himself, red-faced and shuddering with the excitement of the knowledge that he is indeed God's trumpeter.

It is a portrait unlike any portrait painted before or since, composed like a mosaic of thousands of small pieces of fusing together. The Quran impresses for the same reason that the prophetical books of the Old Testament impress: the violence of the imagery, the sense of tremendous battles being fought within the soul, the intimations of impending doom. There is no continuous story, nothing comparable with the Gospels, nor even with the Book of Revelations, where the visions appear in their inevitable and natural sequence. Here everything is fragmentary, bursting like hot shrapnel. Ideas, visions, laws, opinions, fragments of myth and legend, follow one another pell-mell. Everywhere there are confusions, inconsistencies, improvisations, passages where the meaning seems to be deliberately obscured and others where the sentences are left in mid-air. There are interminable passages of dull dialogue in which God relates His own speech and the tiresome replies. Scraps of myth and legend are introduced, only to be abandoned before their relevance has become clear, while Muhammad or the Archangel run after wilder hares. Carlyle's statement: 'It is as toilsome reading as I ever undertook, a wearisome confused jumble, crude, incondite' puts succinctly what readers often feel on their first reading, but many, like Carlyle himself, have learned to change their mind on a second and a third reading. Crude and incondite it is, but it blazes with life and passion. The very incoherence of so many passages gives stature to the passages where there is a blinding clarity. There are not many of these passages, but they have the effect of holding the inchoate mass together, of giving form to the formless. These passages are like beacons which light up the surrounding deserts.

No single idea runs through the Quran except the terrible majesty of the One God. Again and again, until the mind reels at the constant repetition, Muhammad insists upon the one essential cornerstone of his belief: God uncreated, undivided, immanent in all things, Light of Lights, the eternal Creator to whom all things in time will return. So in the sura known as The Cow, amid brief disquisitions on a multitude of subjects, including pilgrimages, divorce, menstruation, the rights of women, proposals of marriage and the need for killing the adversaries of Islam, there appears quite unexpectedly the Throne Verse:

> There is no God save Him, the Living, the Eternal.
> Slumber overtaketh Him not, nor doth sleep weary Him.
> Unto Him belongeth all things in Heaven and on the earth.
> Who shall intercede with Him save by His will?
> He knoweth what is before and what cometh after,
> And no man can comprehend whatsoever save by His will.
> His Throne is as vast as the Heavens and the earth,
> And the keeping of them wearieth Him not.
> He is the exalted, the Mighty One.

(Sura ii)

So again after a long and complicated rendition of the story of Moses, his early struggles and ultimate triumphs, the Quran declares: 'Call not upon any other god but Him, for there is no other God. All things shall perish save His face.' The decrees of God are inescapable: He is everpresent, watching all things, and 'closer to man than his neck-vein'. He is a stern and unyielding God, but at the same time filled with gentleness and loving-kindness, disposed to reward those who are faithful to Him. He has neither height nor weight nor any kind of form: He is the power of the Heavens and the power that moves the seed in the womb, and He is the lamp guiding the wayfarer. In the most magical of all the verses in the Quran, He is compared to a small lamp set in a niche, lighted with the oil from the blessed tree on Mount Sinai:

> God is the Light of the Heavens and the earth.
> The similitude of His Light is as a niche wherein is a lamp,
> And the lamp is within a glass,
> And the glass as it were a pearly star.
> This lamp is lit from a blessed tree,
> An olive neither of the East nor of the West:
> Almost this oil would shine, though no fire touched it.
> Light upon Light, God guideth whom He will to His Light.
> And He speaketh in parables to men, for He knoweth all things.
> This Light is revealed in the temples
> Which God hath permitted to be raised in His name:
> Therefore men praise Him in the morning and in the evening,
> Whom neither trade nor traffic divert from the remembrance of His name,
> As they offer prayers and make payment of alms
> Through fear of the day when hearts and eyeballs shall roll,
> In hope of reward for their most excellent deeds.
> God giveth His blessings without stint to whom He pleaseth.
> As for the unbelievers, their works are like a mirage in the desert,
> And the thirsty dream of water, but find nothing there.
> But God is present. He payeth them their due with swift reckoning:
> Or like the darkness of the ocean in a time of tempest,
> Wave riding upon wave, the clouds hovering over them:
> Layer upon layer of darkness,
> So that a man putting forth his hand scarcely sees it:
> For him there is no light when God refuses His Light.
> Hast thou not seen how all things in Heaven and Earth praise Him?
> The very birds as they spread their wings praise Him:
> Every creature knoweth the worship and the praise,
> And God knoweth all their deeds.
> To God belongeth the Kingdom of Heaven and the Earth,
> And unto Him all things shall return.
>
> (Sura xxiv)

There is nothing in the whole Quran to equal this long passage uttered with the full breath and with an overwhelming sense of assurance. Terror lurks in the Quran, but here terror is kept at bay, and the passion is spent. One imagines him in old age glancing up and seeing the lamps being lit, and then very quietly composing this hymn in honour of the Light of Lights. To these verses and especially the beautiful opening verse the Muhammadan mystics returned again and again, never tiring of that mysterious lamp whose rays bathed the whole universe.

Muhammad did not often talk in similitudes: there are few moments when the voice is not urgent and demanding. Even when he is describing the fruitfulness of the earth, the vision fades into the terror of harvest when all the gold fields are shorn by the sickle of God:

> The similitude of the earth is as a golden robe
> Such as the earth wears when watered by the rain,
> And the harvest ripens for men and beast together:
> Beautiful is the earth with her adornments!
> Woefully do men believe themselves her master:
> Then cometh Our commandment stealthily in the night,
> Or in broad daylight We utter the command,
> And make her barren, laying her waste,
> As though she had never blossomed in her day.
>
> (Sura x)

He portrays, then, a stern and unrelenting God, suspicious of men, an all-knowing and all-powered Arbiter, demanding the absolute submission of men and only occasionally tempering His justice with mercy. Submission (*islam*), under its various aspects, is the continual study of Muhammad. Before a God so majestic only the most perfect submission is worthy of man; and for those who despair of God's mercy he has only contempt. It is a contempt which sometimes flares into a strained and murderous violence, but it is still contempt.

Nearly always when Muhammad contemplates 'the submissive man', he finds himself inevitably contemplating the patriarchal figure of Abraham, on whom he had modelled himself. For him Abraham is the archetype, the vast and portentous figure standing in the sun, throwing his long shadow over the whole of Arabia. As Muhammad developed, so too did his portrait of Abraham. In the earlier revelations Abraham is an apostle of God, whose task is to admonish the people and lead them into the way of righteousness. In those early suras he stands alone, with neither Ishmael nor Isaac to comfort him. In the suras written at Madinah, perhaps under the influence of the Jewish rabbis, the portrait takes on depth and colour. Suddenly Abraham appears as the founder of the Kaaba, led there by a heavenly light, building on the place chosen for him and hearing a voice from the clouds, saying: 'Surrender!' In the story of Isaac, as retold by Muhammad, we meet 'the submissive man' in his most exemplary form.

Muhammad does not follow the classic account of the *Akedah*, as told in Genesis xxii. Significantly there is no painting of the scenery, no Mount Moriah, no journeying to the altar of sacrifice and no angelic voice to interrupt the sacrifice at the last moment. 'Take now thy son, thine only son Isaac, whom thou lovest, and get thee into the land of Moriah, and offer him there for a burnt offering upon one of the mountains that I shall tell thee of.' All this is absent. Instead Muhammad tells the story in a kind of shorthand, as though he were too moved altogether to describe the event in detail, and so he provides only a bare recital of what happened. Here is the story of the *Akedah* as told by Muhammad:

> When the boy had reached the age when they could walk together, Abraham said: 'My son, I have seen in a vision that I must sacrifice thee! What thinkest thou?'
>
> The boy answered: 'My father, do what thou art commanded. God willing, thou shalt find me patient.'
>
> They both surrendered to God's will, and the boy was flung down on his face.
>
> God said: 'Abraham, the vision is fulfilled. In this way we reward the righteous, when they are put to a bitter test. Thy son shall be ransomed with a noble sacrifice and he will be praised by all generations to come.'
>
> (Sura xxxvii)

That is all; and it is enough. Arabic tradition has embroidered on the

bare outline, telling how Abraham went up the mountain with a knife and
a rope, and how a ram appeared, the very same ram whose horns for
centuries decorated the Kaaba. But here tradition is unconvincing.
Muhammad portrayed the incident in the starkest possible terms—'the
boy was flung down on his face'—and beyond that it was impossible for
him to go.

But the figure of Abraham was still incomplete. At some later date
Muhammad concluded that his mission was to revive the forgotten religion
of Abraham, to give it strength and purpose, and so he placed in the mouth
of Abraham the prayer which contains in embryo the whole thesis of
Muhammadanism:

> O Lord, accept our service!
> For Thou hearest all and knowest all.
> Make us submissive unto Thee,
> And make our seed submissive unto Thee.
> Show us the ways of worship and turn to us in mercy:
> For Thou art forgiving and merciful.
> And raise up in our midst a Messenger
> Who shall declare unto us Thy revelations,
> And shall instruct us in the Scriptures,
> And in wisdom and in purification from sin,
> For Thou art wise and mighty beyond all others.
> Who but the foolish would forsake the religion of Abraham?
> We surely have chosen him in the world,
> And in the hereafter he is among the upright.
> When the Lord said unto him: 'Surrender,'
> He answered: 'I have surrendered unto the Lord of the Worlds.'
> He enjoined this faith on his children, and so did Jacob, saying:
> 'My children, God has chosen this faith for you.
> Therefore submit yourselves to the Lord before you die.'

(Sura ii)

Long after Muhammad's death a *hadith* puts into his mouth the words:
'Die before you die.' Initiates in the Sufi mystical orders, according to the
philosopher al-Ghazzali, are supposed to have obeyed the injunction: 'Be
like the corpse in the hands of the washer.'[1] But at no time did Muhammad encourage a deathly submission. He asked that men should submit
to God's will and prostrate themselves in the full knowledge of God's glory
as living and sentient beings, conscious of the beauty of the earth and its
impermanence.

While the portrait of God as the Creator and Sustainer of the universe,
demanding from men their perfect submission, is rounded out in a pro-
fusion of utterances, the Quran is less successful in depicting man and his
place in the universe. Once again there are hesitations and ambiguities.
Men are God's creatures, and only by living in terror of His power will
they escape 'the fire whose fuel is flesh and stones'. Nevertheless all of
creation was made for the enjoyment of man, who stands higher than the

---

[1] According to the Jesuit theologian Alphonsus Rodriguez (1526–1616), the injunction:
'Submit like a corpse' goes back through St. Francis of Assisi and the early Fathers of the
Church to its source in St. Paul (Col. iii. 3), who saw in Abraham's blind obedience to
God in the sacrifice of Isaac the model of the Christian's submission to Divine Providence
(Rodriguez, *Christian and Religious Perfection*, II, v, 6).

angels.[1] Of all the creations of God man is supreme, for he alone possesses the knowledge of God's infinite blessedness; and though the Quran nowhere explicitly states that man was created in the image of God, it constantly hints at the majesty of man even when insisting upon his abject dependence on God. Man is a humble slave, but he is also God's viceregent on earth, and the angels bow down before him:

> The Lord said to the angels: 'I am placing on earth one who shall rule as my viceregent,' and the angels answered: 'Wilt Thou put one who will do evil and shed blood, while we have for so long sung Thy praises and sanctified Thy name?'
>
> The Lord said: 'I know what you do not know.'
>
> Then He taught Adam all the names of things, and showed them to the angels, saying: 'Tell me the names of these things, if you are truthful.'
>
> The angels answered: 'Great is Thy glory! We have no knowledge save that which Thou hast taught us. Thou alone art wise and all-knowing.'
>
> Then the Lord said to Adam: 'Tell them their names!' And when Adam named them, He said: 'Did I not tell you I know the secrets of Heaven and earth? And I know what you reveal and what you hide.'
>
> The Lord spoke to the angels: 'Prostrate yourselves before Adam,' and they all prostrated themselves save Iblis alone, who refused from pride and joined the ranks of the unbelievers.
>
> (Sura ii)

For Muhammad the angels are divine messengers, guardians of Heaven and of men, whose service is to sing the praises of God. They are winged, and terrible to look upon. The greatest of them is Gabriel, who spoke to Muhammad 'on the uppermost horizon at a distance of two bows' lengths or even nearer' and who is evidently not included among those who bowed down to men. He is 'the terrible one', whose eyes flash fire and who can descend in an hour from Heaven, overturning a mountain with a single feather. According to a tradition reported by Ayesha, Muhammad said: 'The angels are formed of light, and the *jinn* of fire.' In time a vast collection of *hadiths* concerning angels was put together, and one of the most firmly held beliefs of the Muhammadans proclaims that there are seventy curtains of light, shadow and fire separating the angels from the Throne of God. Though Muhammad enjoyed the idea of the angels bowing before men so much that he repeated the story five times in as many suras, he gave no precise description of them, perhaps because he had encountered an angel and felt an understandable reluctance to remember Gabriel's appearance.

[1] The Eastern Church long believed, and then forgot, that man is higher than the angels. 'Man is more valuable than all creatures, and I dare to say that he is more valuable than any creature, visible or invisible, more valuable than the ministering angels,' wrote St. Macarius (*Fifty Spiritual Homilies*, XV, 22). This concept, long dormant, was revived by St. Gregory Palamas in the fourteenth century.

But if there is little about angels, there is much about the joys of Paradise and the pains of Hell. For Muhammad, Hell (*Jahannam*) is an abyss filled with fiery flames. Here there are hot and evil-smelling salt wells, which the thirsty drink without comfort. There are torture chambers with neck irons and chains manipulated by nineteen infernal guards under the command of treacherous superiors. There is a tree Zaqqum 'which springeth up from the bottom of hell and its fruit is as it were the heads of devils'. There is no explanation as to why this tree should be particularly frightening, nor does Muhammad explain why Hell should have seven gates with each gate 'having its own portion'. His clearest and most revealing statements come when he speaks of Hell as something portable. 'Bring hell!' God says on the last day: thereupon the angels will form ranks and 'Hell shall be brought nigh'. One imagines a flaming cart being wheeled into position, but it is possible that he intended to suggest the presence of some gigantic beast with gaping jaws which would be let loose among the sinners, scorching them with its incandescent breath.

For Muhammad, Hell is all fire and flame and the anguish of repentance. 'Hell,' he says in one place, 'almost bursts with fury':

> When they are flung into this burning,
> Surely they shall hear the roaring of the flames,
> Hell almost bursting with fury.
> And whensoever anyone is cast among the flames,
> The wardens shall say: 'Where you not warned?'
> They reply: 'Yea, but we rejected the warner.
> God has revealed nothing: you are in error.'
> And they will say further: 'If only we had listened,
> We would not be burning.' So they confess their sins.
> Far from God's mercy are the dwellers in the flames,
> But those who fear God without seeing Him,
> To them shall come forgiveness and great rewards.
>
> (Sura lxvii)

How great were those rewards we see when Muhammad comes to discuss the joys of Paradise, which he conceives as an oasis on the cool uplands far from the burning heat of the desert. It is a very practical Paradise. The blessed sit on cushions, robed in green silk with silver buckles, drinking spring water mingled with spices or great draughts of wine sprinkled with musk. They sit in the shade of trees, in rows facing one another, enjoying the company of the *huris*, 'the white ones', who gaze at them with retiring glances; neither man nor *jinn* has touched them; they have the purity of pearls or jacinths.

These paradisaical joys are purely masculine: there is never a hint about the joys reserved for women, though they were promised entry into the garden. In Paradise women are freed from the infirmities of their sex. It is never made clear whether they join their husbands, who are ministered to by the *huris*, 'the fair ones, close-guarded in pavilions'. There are no angels in Paradise. There is only the infinite afternoon of dalliance beside the heavenly streams, the endless sweetmeats offered on trays of gold, and the eternal pouring of wine. Muhammad failed like many other religious leaders to describe a credible Paradise.

His genius lay in other directions. When he speaks of Hell and Paradise, we are made aware of his own wrath against the infidels and his own anxiety for the peace he had known in the oases of the Arabian uplands. But when he speaks of the practical regulation of the religious life on earth, he speaks with the authority of one who understands the forces which move men and give them comfort. He laid down very simple rules to enable men to live at peace with themselves. These rules changed during the course of his life, for he approached them experimentally, testing them against the endurance of his followers, never satisfied with them until those last days when he addressed the faithful on Mount Arafat and saw that his work was accomplished.

There are five rules, each with its distinct purpose: the profession of faith, prayer, alms, fasting and pilgrimage. The profession of faith involves no complex creed; to be included among the Muhammadan community a man has only to repeat the simple creed: 'I testify there is no god but God, and Muhammad is His messenger.' Prayer is more complicated. Five times a day—just after dawn, just after noon, in the mid-afternoon, just after sunset and at nightfall—the believer recites the appropriate prayers and performs the appropriate prostrations, which are strictly regulated. The order of prayers invariably follows a pattern which derives from the earliest days of Islam, and has continued unchanged to the present day. The prayer opens with the words 'Allahu Akbar—God is greater than all'. There follows a short recitation in praise of God: 'Glory to Thee, O God, and Thine be the praise, blessed be Thy name, exalted be Thy majesty, and there is none to be worshipped save thee. I seek refuge in Thee from the cursed Shaitan.' Then the believer utters the fatihah ('the opener'), the first and most popular sura in the Quran, which seems to have been written towards the end of Muhammad's life:

> In the name of God, the Merciful, the Compassionate.
> Glory be to God, Lord of the worlds, king of the Judgment Day.
> Thee only do we worship: to Thee we cry for help.
> Guide us on the right path,
> The path of those on whom Thou hast bestowed favours,
> Not those who incur Thy wrath nor those who have gone astray.[1]

After this verse the believer says: 'Amin' ('So be it'), and recites one of the short chapters of the Quran. At this point he lowers his head and lets the palms of his hands reach down to his knees and says: 'Glory to the great Lord', only to resume the upright position when he says:

> God listens to him who praises Him.
> O Lord, to Thee is due all praise!

Here comes the act of complete submission with the believer prostrating himself, toes, knees, hands and forehead touching the ground. In this position he says: 'God is the greatest of all. Glory to my Lord, the Highest.' The last words are uttered at least three times. For a moment the

[1] According to tradition, 'those who incur Thy wrath' refers to the Jews, and 'those who have gone astray' to the Christians.

prostration is over. The believer sits up with his hands resting on his knees, and utters a concluding prayer:

> O God, grant me Thy protection,
> Guide me to safety and grant me sustenance,
> Set my affairs in order and exalt me!

One *rak'a*, or cycle, is over: the prayer then begins afresh. There are two *rak'as* at dawn, four at noon, four in mid-afternoon, three at sunset and four at nightfall. Gestures are prescribed at every point of the ritual, and they can never be changed. Throughout the prayer there comes the solemn repetition of the name of God, joined to a complicated ritual of gesture and posture, which is like a dance around a single point. In the mosques the worship remains strangely individual. Each man removes his shoes as he enters the mosque, spreads his prayer rug, turns towards Mecca and is ready for prayer.

Muhammad said that he favoured two of the rules especially: the rule of prayer, and the rule of alms. These alms are in fact a tax levied on the Muhammadan to be spent either for humanitarian purposes—the redemption of slaves, aid to members of the community, debtors and travellers—or for those whom, in conformity with the Quran, it is important to win over. After the conquest of Mecca, money from the alms fund was given to important members of the Umayyad family as a bribe; to those who objected, Muhammad answered that the money was being spent 'for God's purposes'. Alms money may also be used in preparation for a *jihad*, or 'holy war'.

The fourth rule, fasting, applies only to the month of Ramadan. Fasting is observed every day from sunrise to sunset, beginning as soon as a white thread can be distinguished from a black one. The believer must abstain from food, drink, perfumes, tobacco and conjugal relations during the day, and must hear or recite the whole Quran at least once during the month. During Ramadan the faithful spend as much time as possible in the mosque, 'glorifying God for His goodness'. Lanterns are hung from the tops of the minarets and lamps inside the mosques are lit for the evening prayers.

At least once in his lifetime the believer is enjoined to take part in the *Hajj*, or pilgrimage, which includes the circumambulation of the Kaaba, the course between Al Safa and Marwa, and halts at the outlying sanctuaries at Mount Arafat, Muzdalifah and the valley of Mina. The pilgrim wears the proscribed dress known as *ihram* (mortification), consisting of two lengths of towelling, one round the waist, the other over the back, leaving the right arm exposed. For the pilgrim the Quran prescribes: 'Let him have neither commerce with women, nor fornication, nor a quarrel on the pilgrimage.' He must not destroy plant or animal life, except the five nuisances—a crow, a kite, a rat, a scorpion and a biting dog. He must abstain from perfumes, oils, dyes and cosmetics, the paring of nails, the cutting or plucking of hair, and the tying of knots in his garments. Each infraction of these rules requires the sacrifice of a sheep or a goat.

The pilgrimage is a survival of the ancient Arabian pilgrimages to the holy stones. Almost none of the customs attendant upon the pilgrimage derive from Muhammad's time. Even the wearing of the *ihram* is known to derive from the costume worn by the ancient Arabs when visiting holy places and consulting oracles. Muhammad changed the sevenfold *tawaf* or circumambulation of the Kaaba only in one respect: before his time it was performed naked. Mount Arafat was a holy mountain before Muhammad spoke from it, Muzdalifah was the seat of the thunder god, and the seven idols in the valley of Mina are said by the historian Masudi to have represented the seven planets. Muhammad called on the faithful to perform the pilgrimage but never explained why; and many of his followers doubted its efficacy. The Caliph Umar is reported to have expressed himself on the Black Stone: 'I know that thou art a stone, that neither helps nor hurts, and if the Messenger of God had not kissed thee, I would not kiss thee.' But the Caliph did kiss the stone, and he seems to have felt, like countless Muhammadans who came after him, that a kind of divinity reposed in it for being worshipped so long.

Above all, the Kaaba and the stone, like a jewel set on a tabernacle, serve as objects of devout contemplation, intimately connected with Muhammad if only because he ordered that the ancient tradition be continued. If the Kaaba was the House of God, then the stone illuminated it, like a lamp or a gateway: the worshipper was nearest to God when he touched the stone. The ritual circumambulation of the Kaaba often produces a state of trance, and many devout Muhammadans have spoken about the overwhelming sense of reverence which accompanies them as they perform the traditional ceremony. 'The heads are lowered, the tongue is humbled, and the voices are raised in prayer,' says al-Batanuni. 'Those who confront the Kaaba find themselves weeping, and their hearts are weeping also, and they are filled with pure thoughts of intercession.' No one else explained the secret of the Kaaba so well as the great Sufi philosopher Bayazid when he said: 'On my first pilgrimage I saw only the Kaaba; on my second pilgrimage I saw the Kaaba and God; the third time I saw God alone.' Since in Muhammadan art it is not permissible to reproduce the features of any living man or living god, we can assume that the Kaaba is an abstract portrait of the god worshipped by Muhammadans. The Kaaba and the Black Stone correspond, as objects of worship and adoration, to the crucifixes in the western churches.

To the Muhammadan the crucified Christ inspires loathing and terror. It is inconceivable to the Muhammadan imagination that God should become flesh, and give His beloved Son to the world to be crucified. Muhammad knew, and was deeply impressed by, the story of Jesus, whom he calls 'the word of God', but he could not accept that God was crucified. Again and again he returns to the study of Jesus, like someone fascinated by an insoluble riddle. He tells many anecdotes about Jesus, based upon his reading of the Apocryphal Gospels. He teaches that Jesus is the greatest of prophets, but still only a prophet, and he eliminates the Trinity altogether, because it is inconceivable to him that God should

F

share His glory with His Son or with the Holy Ghost. 'He who ascribes partners unto God, that man is as though fallen from the sky and the birds have snatched him away and he is blown by the wind to a far-off place.' Muhammad came to the belief that there was indeed a crucifixion, but at the last moment another body was substituted for Jesus, or perhaps it was only a ghostly body. 'They did not slay Jesus, nor crucify him, only a likeness of it appeared to them.' The Quran describes at length the birth, the annunciation and the making of clay birds, but it never depicts a Jesus recognizable to Christians. We are made aware of reservations, ambiguities, a sense of bemused perplexity. He tells more about Jesus than about any other religious figure, but to little advantage, for the portrait is dim and the pieces do not fit together.

In the early suras Muhammad describes Jesus as a miracle worker, who could raise the dead and who was beloved by God. Jesus was a Messenger, one of those brought near to God, a sign, a mercy, even a *nabi* or prophet, which Muhammad himself, though universally called the Prophet, rarely claimed to be. Towards the end Muhammad seems to have regarded him as an angel of vast and unlimited powers, who for a brief while wore a human dress. He possessed great reverence for Jesus, but seems to have been puzzled by a figure so remote from the Arabs. It is inconceivable that Muhammad would ever have said: 'Learn of me, for I am lowly in heart.'

Muhammad showed the same baffled incomprehension towards Christians. There are moments when he rages against them. There are other moments when he says they are the closest of all to Muhammadans: "The nearest in affection are those who say: 'We are Christians.' That is because there are priests and monks among them, and because they are free from pride." He disliked monkery and proclaimed that there should be no monks in Islam, but he seems to have been profoundly affected by the real humility of the Nestorian monks and anchorites he met in his travels. To the Christian the most astonishing of his statements on Jesus is one reported in Muhammad ibn-Ishaq's vast *Life of the Messenger of God*. One day Muhammad was asked about the appearance of Abraham, Moses and Jesus, whom he had seen during his ascent to heaven. Muhammad replied that there was no man more like himself than Abraham, while Moses was ruddy-faced, tall, curly-haired, with a hooked nose. Jesus had a reddish colouring, was of medium height, and his face was covered with freckles, but the most extraordinary thing about him was that his hair hung lank 'as though dripping with water, but there was no water on it'.

Many descriptions of Jesus as visualized by the early Muhammadans have survived. Some of them can be traced to the Apocryphal Gospels, and others may have been based on surviving legends. The most perturbing, because the most complete and rounded, is given by ath-Thalabi in his *Stories of the Prophets*:

Jesus, son of Mary, was a ruddy man, inclined to white. He did not have long hair, and he never anointed his head. Jesus used to walk barefoot, and he took no house, or adornment, or goods, or clothes, or provisions except for his day's food. Wherever the sun set he arranged his feet in prayer till the morning came. He was curing the blind from birth and the leper and raising the dead by God's permission and was telling his people what they were eating in their houses and what they were storing up for the morrow. He was walking on the surface of the water in the sea. His head was dishevelled, and his face was small. He was an ascetic in the world, longing for the next world and eager for the worship of God. He was a pilgrim on the earth until the Jews sought him and desired to kill him. Then God raised him up to heaven; and God knows best.[1]

There briefly, but with astonishing clarity and detail, is Jesus as seen by the Muhammadan imagination. They were fascinated by him, wrote about him continually, and invented a host of stories about him, many of which are included among the *hadiths* or collected sayings of Muhammad. Nearly all of them are coloured by purely Muhammadan preoccupations, and only a very few preserve a recognizable Christian spirit. Here is a brief selection of stories and sayings attributed to Jesus:

The world is a bridge; therefore pass over it lightly, and do not pause on the way.

Be like the dove concerning God: for when the two young are removed from its nest and killed, she returns to the same place and brings forth others.

Though you should worship Me like the people of the heavens and the earth and have not love in God and hate in God, it will avail you nothing.

It is related that Jesus in his wanderings came upon a man fast asleep, wrapped in his cloak. Then Jesus wakened him and said: 'O sleeper, arise and glorify God.' Then the man said: 'What do you want of me? I have abandoned the world to its own people.' And Jesus said: 'Sleep on, my friend.'

Jesus and the disciples came upon the carcase of a dog. The disciples said: 'What a stench it makes!' Jesus answered: 'How white are its teeth!'

There came to Jesus some unbelievers who said: 'You have raised people who died recently, and perhaps they were not dead; so raise for us one who died in the earliest times.' He said to them: 'Choose whom you will.' They said: 'Raise for us Shem, son of Noah.' Then he came to his grave and prayed two *rak'as* and called on God, and God raised Shem, son of Noah, and lo! his head and beard had become quite white. But someone said: 'What is this? There were no white hairs in

---

[1] James Robson, *Christ in Islam* (New York: E. P. Dutton & Co., 1930), p. 29.

your day.' He replied: 'I heard the summons, and I thought the Resurrection had come, so the hair of my beard and head became white with terror.' Someone asked: 'How long have you been dead?' He replied: 'For four thousand years, but the agony of death has not left me yet.'[1]

What is remarkable about these sayings is how deeply they affected the Muhammadan imagination while remaining outside the normal *ambiance* of the Muhammadan mind. There is something foreign in them. They do not correspond to any of the apocryphal sayings of Jesus, yet they have an authentically Christian flavour, sharpened a little by the sands of the desert and the intense brilliance of an Arabian sky. Jesus has become an Arab. The most familiar to Muhammadans is the first saying, which the Emperor Akbar inscribed on the gateway of the palace at Fatehpur Sikri which he abandoned soon after building it. The most beautiful, and the most mysterious, is the second, with its insistence upon the supreme virtue of sacrifice, an idea which has no place in Muhammadan theology except in the sense that a devout Muhammadan should sacrifice himself in war against the infidel.

The Sufis, of course, accepted Jesus as one of themselves, and whenever they read in the Quran the words 'sword' and 'holy war' they accepted them in a metaphorical sense. Like Ibn Arabi, they regarded Jesus as the last and greatest of the saints. 'Surely,' says Ibn Arabi, 'the seal of the saints is a Messenger; and in the world He has no equal. He is the Spirit and the Son of the Spirit, and Mary is His mother.' In one of his poems Jalalu'l-Din Rumi tells the story of the parrot who pretended to be dead, and was accordingly thrown out of its cage and flew away into freedom. The poet points the moral: 'The parrot died into self-abasement. Therefore make thyself dead in prayer and poverty of spirit that the breath of Jesus may revive thee and make thee fair and blessed as His breath.' But though Jalalu'l-Din Rumi could speak in praise of Jesus, he could also speak in contempt of Christians. He laughed at them for confessing their sins to priests, and he could not understand why they should pray to the Crucified for protection, when He could not protect Himself from the Jews. Of all the differences which divided Muhammadans from Christians, the greatest is their different attitudes towards the Crucifixion.

Though Christians have rarely shown a remarkable talent for behaving peaceably, they have never doubted that peacemakers are blessed. Muhammad never doubted that war was a blessed thing when fought on behalf of the faith. Again and again in the Quran he urges his followers to implacable war:

> Slay them wherever you find them, and drive them out of the places they drove you from. Idolatry is worse than war. But do not fight them within the precincts of the Mosque unless they first attack you there; but if they attack you there, then slay them. Such is the reward of unbelievers.

[1] James Robson, *Christ in Islam* (New York: E. P. Dutton & Co., 1930), pp. 71, 57, 78, 71, 45, 109.

If they mend their ways, know that God is forgiving and merciful.
Fight them until idolatry is no more, and God's religion is supreme.

(Sura ii)

Such brutal encouragements to war are repeated *ad nauseam* in the
Quran, and there is not the least doubt that he meant exactly what he
said. By precept and example he sanctified the sword. No other religious
leader of comparable stature has ever urged such unpitying wars against
his enemies. The saying attributed to Muhammad, 'Know that paradise
lies under the shadow of swords,' is one which Muhammadans have always
taken to heart. To this argument the classic Christian reply in our day was
given by Pope Pius XII in 1951 in *Ingruentium malorum* ('The Advancing
Evils'), when he offered the Catholic doctine in the struggle against the
Church's enemies:

> Strong, like David with his sling shot, the Church will face fearlessly
> the infernal enemy, repeating against him the words of the young
> shepherd: 'Thou comest to me with a sword, and with a spear, and with
> a shield. But I come to thee in the name of the Lord of hosts, the God
> of the armies . . . and all this assembly shall know that the Lord saveth
> not with sword and spear' (I *Samuel* xvii. 45–7).

For the Muhammadan the *jihad*, or 'holy war', has become an essential
element of the faith; all of Islam would have to be turned upside down if
the doctrine were eliminated. It only just escaped becoming one of the
five rules: not that Muhammadans have ever doubted that the command-
ment was given by Muhammad, but they have sometimes doubted the
need to broadcast warlike purposes. We shall see, as this history advances,
how often and with what appalling lust for loot they have embarked on
wars against the infidels and the faithful alike. When Timurlane led his
armies into India, he announced that his purpose was to give booty to his
soldiers and bring all Indians under the Muhammadan yoke; but among
the great heaps of skulls which decorated his triumph at Delhi were many
Muhammadan skulls. Again and again we shall find Muhammadans
mercilessly destroying the living descendants of Muhammad.

Yet Muhammad could be gentle on occasion with a disarming gentleness. Among his recorded sayings are many which testify to his almost
feminine sensibility. Passionately fond of women and children, he forbade
his followers to treat their wives brutally and he insisted that slaves should
be treated humanely. According to one of his traditional sayings:
'Heaven lieth at the feet of mothers.' According to another he said:
'Whoever doeth good to girls, it will be a curtain to him from hell-fire.'
Still another *hadith* declares: 'God is gentle and loveth gentleness.'

After Muhammad's death, when the memory of the man was still fresh,
and for centuries afterwards, his remembered sayings were written down
and collected and assembled. To these there was appended the names of
the companions who reputedly heard them from Muhammad's lips and
the names of all those who had handed down the tradition. Six great

collections of these sayings were compiled, the most important being one by Ahmad ibn-Hanbal (780–855) which was edited by his son. It contains nearly 30,000 sayings grouped under the names of 700 companions of Muhammad. These traditions are of varying worth, and by far the greater number of them are patently worthless, having been written down by inventors who hoped to profit by their inventions. But occasionally amid so much dross the authentic words can be heard, as we hear them in the Quran, winging through space and time as though they had just left his lips. Here are a few of his traditional sayings:

Verily my heart is veiled with melancholy and sadness for my followers; and verily I ask pardon of God one hundred times daily.

One hour's meditation on the work of the Creator is better than seventy years of prayer.

The world is sweet to the heart, and green to the eye; and verily God hath brought you, after those that went before you. Therefore look to your actions, and abstain from the world and its wickedness.

What business have I with the world? I am like a man on horseback, who standeth under the shade of a tree, then leaveth it.

God hath treasuries beneath the Throne, the keys whereof are the tongues of poets.

Go in quest of knowledge even unto China.

Acquire knowledge. It enableth its possessor to distinguish right from wrong; it lighteth the way to Heaven; it is our friend in the desert, our society in solitude, our companion when friendless; it guideth us to happiness; it sustaineth us in misery; it is an ornament among friends, and an armour against enemies.

Paradise is nearer to you than the thongs of your sandals; and the Fire likewise.

God said: I was a hidden treasure and desired to be known; and therefore I made the Creation that I might be known.[1]

Such were the words of a man who spoke sometimes with a fierce compassion about the evils of the world. The strong, stark outline of Islam as we know it now was absent in its founder; and like the rocky deserts with red pinnacles among which he lived, he changed with the changing colours of the sky. His service was ascetic, his aim was to conquer the world; and between asceticism and conquest his mind, filled with brilliant contradictions, moved helplessly from pole to pole. He despised the world as 'play, and idle talk, and pageantry', and at the same time he was so much a creature of the world that his love for it, and the people in it, is manifest in his works. He saw God as the absolute transcendent power, as white-

[1] Allama Sir Abdullah Al-Mamun al-Suhrawardy, *The Sayings of Muhammad* (London: John Murray, 1949), pp. 98, 94, 50, 100, 94, 92, 94, 85, 82.

hot majesty and omnipotence; and like a man who has stared long at the sun, he seemed to be blinded by what he had seen, and almost his spirit evaporates in the burning heat of God. There was about him none of the angelic quality he saw in Jesus. He saw himself as a new Abraham or a new Moses, but he resembled most of all Jacob, who wrestled with an angel and saw the angels ascending and descending, and marked the place with a stone, which he called the House of God.

THE ARABIAN CALIPHS

ON THAT hot summer afternoon when the body of Muhammad lay in the arms of Ayesha and the wives were lamenting and the companions were preparing to wash the body and clothe it in a shroud, the ferocious old warrior Umar ibn-Khattab blundered into the hut. He took one look at Muhammad, so still and calm in death, and refused to believe what he saw. He was heard muttering: 'Verily, by the Lord, he shall return!' and then he ran off to the nearby mosque and began shouting that Muhammad was not dead, he would return accompanied by his angels, and was even now preparing to take his place in the mosque. He was dead, but in the twinkling of an eye he would arise again! Saying this, Umar unsheathed his sword, prepared to drive it into the heart of the first believer who refused to believe in the immortality of the Messenger of God. And while he spoke he heard the lamenting of the women.

So the afternoon went on until another visitor entered the hut, a man who was prematurely old and himself close to death. This was Abu Bakr, the closest after Ali of all the friends of Muhammad. He had been told, probably by Ayesha, that Muhammad was recovering, and he obtained permission to retire to his house in the country until he was summoned by his daughter to see the body of the man he loved most in the world. He was trembling when he saw the body. Gently removing the coverlet, he stooped down and kissed his friend on the forehead, murmuring: 'Sweet wert thou in life and sweet art thou in death. Yea, thou art dead! Alas, my friend, my chosen one!' Then he kissed the face for a second time and stumbled out into the bright sunlight and hurried to the mosque, where the worshippers were waiting expectantly for the Second Coming. At the sight of Abu Bakr they fell silent. Abu Bakr told them what he had seen. Never again would anyone set eyes on the Messenger of God walking among them as of old. 'Those of you who worshipped Muhammad,' he declared, 'know that he is dead; and those of you that worship God, know that the Lord liveth forever and never dieth.' He went on to quote the words of the Quran: 'Muhammad is no more than a messenger: all messengers before him have passed away. If he dieth or is slain, will ye turn back on your heels? He who turneth back will do no harm to God, but God rewards those who are grateful.' Long afterwards Umar ibn-Khattab recalled this moment. 'By the Lord,' he said, 'it was so, that when I heard Abu Bakr recite these verses, I was horror-stricken, my limbs trembled, I dropped down, and I knew of a certainty that Muhammad was dead!'

For the rest of the afternoon the women prepared the body for the grave, while the stunned followers of Muhammad gave themselves to their grief, milling about aimlessly in the mosque. No one knew what the future would bring. Almost alone and singlehanded Muhammad had brought the Islamic state into being, and as far as anyone knew he had made no recommendation for a successor. He had announced the law on all manner of subjects relating to daily life, but there was no law which related how the state should be ruled after his death, or how he should be buried, or what honours should be paid to him. In this crisis Abu Bakr remembered that Muhammad had once told him: 'A prophet should be laid in the earth in the place where he dies.' And so it was arranged to bury him in Ayesha's hut, and all that night the gravediggers were heard digging the hard flinty earth with pickaxes. The next day the mourners came to look for the last time on the beloved face, which was strangely white and already withered. Then at night the red mantle he wore in battle was lowered into the deep grave, and his body, wrapped in three shrouds, two of white linen and a third of striped Yaman cloth, was laid on the mantle. Over him they built an arch of unbaked brick, and then the earth was shovelled over the tomb. There, below Ayesha's hut, he has remained ever since.

If Muhammad had not died in the hut of his favourite wife, the history of Islam might have been very different. Many of his followers believed Ali would be elected to the vacant kingship, for Ali was his adopted son, married to his daughter Fatima, proud and handsome and possessed of demonic energy when aroused, but careless of his great gifts. He seems to have been more than usually careless on the day of Muhammad's death. Ayesha detested him, and her father distrusted him. Accordingly, when Abu Bakr and Umar were still in the mosque and there came a rumour that the Ansar were already congregating in the council hall at Madinah to discuss the election of a new king, they hurried to the meeting place and by virtue of their closeness to Muhammad they were able to dominate the proceedings. Only a few of the Companions were present. Abu Bakr took Umar and Abu Ubaydah by the hands and suggested that one of them be raised to the kingship. Both refused the honour, and Umar declared that the kingship belonged properly to Abu Bakr, 'the second of the two when they were in the cave alone'. Was he not the man whom Muhammad loved most? Was he not wise above the generations of men, and did he not belong to the tribe of the Quraysh, which held the sacred Kaaba in its possession? Muhammad, too, had belonged to the Quraysh, and it was unthinkable that Arabians would swear allegiance to anyone from other tribes. At last, late in the evening, Abu Bakr was elected king by acclamation and granted the title of *Kalifa*, or 'Successor', becoming the first of the four Caliphs who ruled from Madinah. The next morning he took his seat at the *minbar* in the mosque, occupying the place so long occupied by Muhammad. Umar called for the oath of allegiance to Abu Bakr. The Ansar protested, but they were outnumbered and overawed, and Ali took what comfort he could in silence. It was six months before he took the oath of allegiance to the Caliph.

Abu Bakr was a man of genuine humility and strength of character, and started his reign auspiciously by declaring that he derived his power from the people and expected to be removed from office if he disobeyed the laws of God. His famous inaugural sermon suggests the quality of the man:

Verily I have become the chief among you, though I am not the best among you. If I do well, help me; set me right, if I am in the wrong. You shall show faithfulness to me by telling me the truth—to conceal the truth from me is treachery. The weak and oppressed among you shall be strong in my eyes, until I have vindicated their just rights, if the Lord wills; and the strong among you shall be weak in my eyes, until I have made them fulfill the obligations due from them. Now hearken to me: when the people abandoneth the fight [*jihad*] in the ways of the Lord, He casteth them away in disgrace. Know also that wickedness never aboundeth in any nation, but the Lord visiteth it with calamity. As I obey God and His Messenger, obey me; but if I neglect the laws of God and His Messenger, then refuse me obedience. Arise to prayer, and the Lord have mercy on you!

So, very calmly, Abu Bakr started his reign, conscious of his own power and determined to extend the sway of Islam by whatever means were available. He needed to be calm, for the country was in revolt. From south, north and east came information that the tribes which had accepted Islam from the hands of Muhammad were refusing to accept it from the hands of his successor, and they were refusing to pay taxes. False prophets were arising, among them a certain Musaylimah of the Bani Hanifah, who composed a book of prophesies modelled on the Quran, and a Christian woman called Sajah, who later led an army from the Persian frontier almost to the gates of Madinah. As if this were not enough, Abu Bakr was plagued with the problem of what to do with the army led by Usamah, which Muhammad had ordered dispatched to the Syrian frontier a few days before his death, to avenge the Byzantine victory at Mutah. The best troops of Madinah were in the army, which was encamped outside the city. Usamah was a young man, only twenty years old, and Abu Bakr's advisers were suggesting that the army be retained for the defence of the city and placed in the hands of a more experienced man. Abu Bakr decided otherwise. Muhammad himself had ordered the advance, and who was he to delay it? 'Madinah may stand or fall,' he declared. 'The Caliph may live or die, but the words of Muhammad must be fulfilled.' When the army set out, he walked for some miles beside Usamah, who was on horseback, as a sign of his faith in the missionary powers of the army.

Madinah was now without its best soldiers, but Islam was never so powerful as when it was defenceless. Less than two months later an insurgent army appeared at the gates of the city. Abu Bakr ordered a night attack with all available men under arms. The insurgents were repulsed, and there was a short breathing space, until Usamah returned from the Syrian frontier, having accomplished little except to confirm the Caliph's advisers in his inexperience. Command of the army was placed in the hands of Khalid ibn al-Walid, the victor of Uhud.

Khalid was a born guerrilla leader, highly-strung, shrewd, ruthless, possessing the fanaticism of the convert. He was one of those generals who glory in the greatest risks and by their very recklessness turn defeat into victory. Inevitably, when the tribespeople revolted, Khalid employed strong measures. 'The taste of blood is pleasant on my mouth,' he said once, and all through the campaigns against the tribes which filled the first year of Abu Bakr's reign Khalid was in the forefront, whetting his appetite for blood.

The hardest fought of these campaigns ended in the ancient city of Yamamah in the southern Najd, where Musaylimah with an army of 60,000 was solidly entrenched. At the head of three flying columns Khalid rushed against the enemy, only to be hurled back under the impact of his first violent charge. As usual he had underestimated the strength of the enemy. He regrouped quickly, stung by the taunts they flung at him. He charged again and again with a reckless disregard of his own safety and the safety of his men. Arabic historians never tired of telling stories of the courage of the Muhammadans in this battle. They tell of Qais ibn Thabit, whose leg was hacked off by a sword: in his last moments he hurled the leg at the enemy. Then there was the heroic Bara' ibn Malik whose brother had been a servant in Muhammad's household and who was known for the strange shivering fits which he suffered on the eve of battle. At last the shivering fits would come to an end, and he would hurl himself with the speed of an arrow at the enemy, having generated so much strength and speed that he was well-nigh invulnerable. When Musaylimah's followers retreated behind the walls of a vast orchard, Bara' ibn Malik begged his companions to toss him over the wall. They refused, fearing he would be killed immediately. He insisted on being allowed the privilege of dying for the faith. Lifted on top of the wall, he jumped down into the orchard, fought his way against all odds to the gate and flung it wide open, and then the Muhammadans poured in. There was such a massacre in the orchard that forever afterwards it was called 'the Garden of Death'. Musaylimah, a small parchment-faced man with a long nose, suffered the indignity of being killed by an Abyssinian slave called Wahshi, a convert to the faith, famous as the killer of Muhammad's uncle Hamza at the battle of Uhud— he slew Musaylimah with the same javelin with which he slew Hamza. Khalid disliked half measures. With Musaylimah slain, he ordered his men to continue killing. The historian Tabari says that more than 10,000 infidels were killed that day, for the loss of 700 Muhammadans, including a large number of those who had committed the Quran to memory. The loss of so many of Muhammad's companions appalled Abu Bakr, for no final edition of the Quran had been prepared and many of the suras were not yet written down. He gave orders to Muhammad's secretary Zayd ibn Thabit to collect as many suras as possible, and the work of compiling the Quran continued slowly during the following years. To Zayd's carelessness and incompetence must be attributed the curious state of the Quran, with revelations clearly received in Mecca inserted haphazardly among revelations received in Madinah.

Meanwhile the work of pacification was continuing. All through the first year of Abu Bakr's reign the flying columns reached out across Arabia. Bahrayn, Uman and Yaman submitted to Madinah, and their troops were incorporated in the Muhammadan army. Inevitably the character of the revolution was changing. The oldest companions of Muhammad were dying out, to be replaced by converts, with the result that the army and many of the Caliph's chief advisers were being recruited from the ranks of recent enemies. Christians, Jews and Bedouins flocked to the standards, inspired by hopes of booty, announcing their conversion only because they felt the need to identify themselves with the winning side. Such an army, closely disciplined, lacking any common morality or a common faith, soon became the instrument of self-seeking generals. Within a year of Muhammad's death the Quraysh, who had fought so bitterly against Muhammad, were in the ascendancy.

Ironically Abu Bakr seems to have been unaware of the change coming over the movement which Muhammad had brought into being. Gentle and trusting, his deep-set eyes lighted with the fires of contemplation, careless of his appearance—he usually wore two sheets of reddish-brown cloth, one folded round his shoulders, the other round his waist and legs, and because he was bent a little this one was always slipping down—he behaved as Caliph exactly as he had behaved when he was the trusted adviser of Muhammad. For the first six months of his reign he continued to sell cloth in the market-place of Madinah, saying he saw no reason why he should not earn his living. He kept the treasury of the empire in an unlocked box in his house. Half the night he prayed to God, and half the days of the week he fasted. He had fought beside Muhammad during the battles of Badr, Uhud and Hunayn, but as old age came on he seems to have allowed his lieutenants full control of the army. Stern only when the power and majesty of Islam were directly involved, he was especially gentle to widows and orphans, and it is unlikely that he knew or cared what the army, moving with its own momentum, was doing.

He did, of course, make some appointments and he allowed commands to be issued over his name. He appointed Abu Sufyan, once Muhammad's most relentless enemy, governor of Nadj and Hijaz. Abu Sufyan's sons, Yazid and Muawiya, were given leading posts in the army. Amr ibn al-'As, who had defected from Mecca at the same time as Khalid, was also put in command of a column. And when Abu Bakr summoned the faithful to take part in a *jihad*, or holy war, against Syria, most of the commands were in the hands of men who had only recently fought against Muhammad, thus arousing the suspicion that the holy war was brought about by men who were less interested in propagating the faith than in acquiring booty. Abu Sufyan and his sons belonged to the Umayyad tribe, the aristocracy of the Quraysh; and soon the vast treasure of the empire was to fall into their hands.[1]

---

[1] The historian al-Baladhuri says that in the late summer of A.D. 633 Abu Bakr 'wrote to the people of Mecca, Taif, Yaman and all the Arabs in Nadj and Hijaz summoning them to a *jihad* and reminding them of the booty to be got from the Greeks'. But it is unlikely that Abu Bakr would ever have written these words.

At first, when the expedition set out for the north, there was no indica-
tion that the Umayyads were preparing for their triumph. Overall command was placed in the hands of Abu Ubaydah, the *éminence grise* of whom
little is known except that he was the treasurer of the kingdom and a close
companion of Muhammad, a man who kept severely to the background,
for few stories were ever told of him. In the autumn of A.D. 633, the three
columns, each consisting of about 3,000 men, made their way towards
the Dead Sea. Yazid commanded one column, his brother Muawiya
acting as standard-bearer. Another column was commanded by Amr ibn
al-'As, and the third was commanded by Shurahbil ibn-Hasanah, who
had assisted Khalid in the bloody battle of Yamanah. These columns met
the weak levies of Sergius, the patrician of Palestine, at Wadi Arabah
south of the Dead Sea, and overwhelmed them by surprise. A series of
raids and *razzias* followed, with the remnants of the Byzantine frontier
forces in orderly retreat. The Emperor Heraclius, a man of simple dignity
and quiet courage who had fought the Persians through Syria and Egypt,
had for some time been expecting the Muhammadan forces, but his troops
were weakened by six years of continuous campaigning and he was in no
mood for joining battle except on his own terms. Hurrying from Edessa
he recruited a fresh army and placed it under the command of his brother
Theodore. Then he prepared a defence in depth, and, realizing that he
would eventually be forced into a major battle, he hoped to select his own
battleground. He was already threatening the Muhammadans and preparing to drive them out of Palestine when news was brought to him that
an Arab army, which seemed to have arisen out of the earth, was gathered
around the walls of Damascus in his rear. This army was under the command of Khalid, 'the Sword of God'.

After the battle of Yamanah, Khalid had been sent on a marauding expedition against the frontier posts of Persia on the Euphrates. He conquered al-Hirah in June, A.D. 633, and went on to conquer a host of small
towns and villages, his raids taking him almost to the Tigris. Abu Bakr
had proclaimed him governor of Iraq. Suddenly, when news that Muhammadan troops in Palestine were being hard pressed reached Madinah, Abu
Bakr or one of his lieutenants issued the order that Khalid was to race immediately to their rescue. Khalid was a close friend of Ali and an enemy
of Umar ibn-Khattab, who perhaps was Abu Bakr's chief adviser. He
seems to have believed the order was a punishment for a recent swift and
unauthorized pilgrimage to Mecca, but he made haste to obey. With six
or seven hundred troops he led a forced march across the desert from the
Euphrates to Damascus in eighteen days, a feat of unparalleled daring.
Then he marched southwards through Transjordan to join forces with the
harassed columns under Abu Ubaydah. His coming was so swift that
Heraclius had no time to prepare for a war on two fronts; and on July
30, A.D. 634, on the plain of Ajnadayn west of Jerusalem, the combined
Muhammadan armies routed the army of Heraclius, who fled with the
survivors to Antioch. The whole of Palestine was now open to the Arab
raiders.

No one knows whether Abu Bakr ever heard that a new province had been added to his empire. That summer he was already ailing. He was suffering from fever, and like Muhammad he liked to take cold baths, but the baths only made the fever worse. For fifteen days he lay in bed, while the strength slowly drained from him. It is possible that he made arrangements for the succession, but many competent historians maintain that the carefully written testament in which he named Umar ibn-Khattab as the second Caliph is a forgery. Tabari, in *The Book of Religion and Empire*, tells the story of how, as he lay dying, Abu Bakr was asked how much had been added to his private fortune during the Caliphate, and answered: 'I have acquired nothing but a young camel, an Abyssinian slave to look after my children and polish swords, and a mantle.' Then he spurned the mantle with his foot and said: 'I have given back all that, and I am well and happy.' He asked what day Muhammad had died. Told it was on Monday, he said: 'I hope I shall die on that day.' He died on August 23, A.D. 634, in the modest house where he had long lived, and was buried beside Muhammad. He was sixty-three, and his Caliphate had lasted for no more than two years and three months.

He was the greatest of the Caliphs, the most generous, the most devout, the most learned. Of his manner and appearance we know more than we know of most of his successors. He was tall and slender, with a fair complexion, with a narrow face, deep-sunken eyes and a bulging forehead. He walked with a kind of shuffling gait, and was stooped, and his clothes hung loosely on him. He had long thin hands 'with almost no skin on his fingertips', but there were knotted swollen veins on them. He dyed his hair with henna and wore a ring inscribed with the words: 'How good is Almighty God!' None of his successors believed so firmly in the goodness of God, and none was so saintly.

Umar, the second Caliph, was made of sterner stuff. There was no aristocratic blood in him, but he behaved like an aristocrat. Calm, unyielding, demanding and receiving instant obedience, he sometimes gave way to ferocious bursts of temper. No one loved him, but everyone respected him. The story is told that Umar once visited Muhammad and found the womenfolk chattering excitedly, but the moment Umar appeared they ran behind the curtains and fell into a strange silence. Umar asked angrily why the women were showing less respect to Muhammad than to himself. Muhammad laughed and answered: 'Umar, if the devil himself were to meet you in the street, he would dodge into a side alley!'

Umar was hard, but he had need to be. He lived strictly, almost ascetically. They said he lived only on bread and olive oil, and his clothes were always patched in a dozen places—he patched them himself with strips of leather. His role—the role which he assigned to himself—was that of the strict teacher and legislator, the organizer of victory. He alone possessed the authority to marshal the many Muhammadan armies surging across North Africa, Syria and Persia, and to complete the transformation of Arabia and the conquered lands into a theocratic state. The tangled threads of conquest passed through his hands, and no one else could straighten them out.

When Umar entered upon his Caliphate, there was only one Muhammadan army outside Arabia, and it was still in difficulties. The victory of Ajnadayn was followed by a long series of indecisive raids. Theodore remained in Galilee, Heraclius was massing his troops in the Orontes valley, preparing to deal with the Arabs as he had dealt with the Persians. He had lost battles before. Even when Damascus fell the following year, betrayed to Khalid by malcontent Christians—among them the grandfather of St. John Damascene—he had hopes of eventual victory. Umar sent up reinforcements to aid the hard-pressed Muhammadans, and then at last, after two years of skirmishes, the two armies met in force in the hottest month of the year in one of the hottest places on earth: the mouth of the Yarmuk in the Jordan valley. It was August 20, A.D. 636, and the battle had hardly begun before a thick dust storm darkened the sky. The imperial infantry stood firm, but the Arabs scouted round them, protected from the dust and sand by their burnooses, making continual sallies against the massed ranks of the regulars, challenging them to individual combat. Tabari tells the not improbable story of Khalid challenging George, the sone of Theodore. As usual, the challenge began with taunts. 'I hear,' said George, 'that you are known as the Sword of God, and therefore always win victories.' The irony was lost on Khalid, who answered in the accepted manner of an Arabian moralist: 'God sent Muhammad (peace be upon him) among us to preach the faith, but at first no one paid any attention to him, and I was one of those who fought against him; and when at last I bowed before him and accepted the faith, Muhammad said to me: "O Khalid, you are a sword from the swords of God, which have been drawn from their scabbards to fight the infidel!"' Tabari adds that George (Jarja) was so impressed with Khalid's words that he instantly accepted Islam and fought with the Muhammadans.

While Arab historians are inclined to see the hand of God hovering benignly over the standards of Khalid, others are more inclined to blame the Byzantine defeat on the storm. Blinded by the sand and maddened by the thrusts of the Muhammadans, the imperial infantry panicked, some to be slaughtered on the spot, others to be driven relentlessly into the river, while those who deserted were summarily executed. Theodore was killed, and the Emperor Heraclius abandoned the field. He made no further effort to prevent Syria from being overrun, but withdrew across the mountains. As he departed for Constantinople, he is supposed to have said: 'Farewell, Syria! Oh, that so fair a country should belong to my enemies?'

The swift conquest of Syria has puzzled historians and military strategists, for the same reasons. No one knows the exact details of these campaigns: we do not even know the exact sites of the battles, or when they took place, and we can only guess at how they were fought, for there are wide differences even in the accounts of the Arab historians, who tend to describe the adventures of their heroes as though they were describing legendary warriors, drawing them ten times larger than life, so that their behaviour becomes increasingly unreal, and their motives improbable. What is certain is that Syria, then as now, belonged to the uncommitted frontier, where a hundred sects were at war with one another. For centuries there had been no peace, as the Persians and the Greeks fought for mastery over their common border. Heraclius wrested Syria from the Persians only ten years before the Arab conquest, but he had neither the time nor the energy to drive deep stakes in the country. An air of improvisation hangs over his attempts to keep the Arabs at bay.

The Arabs, too, were showing a talent for improvisation. More congenial than the Greeks, less tyrannical than the Persians, their victory had overwhelmed them with its speed; and since they had no experience with foreign conquests, they were compelled to rely on the existing bureaucracy in order to keep control over the people. Murderous in battle, the Arabs could be, and often were, surprisingly gentle to the inhabitants of the conquered cities. The terms for the capitulation of Damascus, which served as a model for future capitulations, suggest that the Arabs were chiefly interested in acquiring a proper share of the tax money:

> In the name of God, the Compassionate, the Merciful! I, Khalid ibn-Walid, grant to the people of Damascus the following terms. I promise them security for their lives, property and churches. The city wall shall not be laid low, nor shall any Muhammadan be quartered in their houses. So we give them the peace of God and the protection of His Messenger, and of the Caliph, and of the believers. So long as they pay the poll tax, nothing but good shall come to them.[1]

That the Muhammadans could on occasion behave with an almost forbidding gentleness was demonstrated when at last Jerusalem, which had fought stubbornly against the invaders long after Heraclius had left the country, offered to capitulate only on condition that the Caliph in person came to sign the treaty. Since Jerusalem possessed a special importance in the eyes of believers, Umar permitted himself the luxury of a private triumph. He entered Jerusalem on a camel, accompanied by only a few attendants, his clothes dust-stained, giving an impression of ostentatious simplicity. Sophronius, Patriarch of Jerusalem, was dressed in his glittering robes, and he seems to have been a little surprised by the strangeness of the occasion, for he remarked in a whisper to one of the priests by his side: 'So this is the abomination of desolation spoken by Daniel the Prophet as standing in the Holy Place!' There was an amicable exchange of gifts, and the treaty was drawn up by the Caliph and his advisers, and signed by Khalid, Muawiya, Amr ibn al-'As, and Abdal Rhaman ibn 'Auf, who had been one of Muhammad's closest companions, an old man who had lost all his teeth in the wars. The treaty resembles the earlier treaty with Damascus, but with important differences:

> In the name of God, the Compassionate, the Merciful! This is the covenant of peace which Umar, the servant of God and commander of the faithful, has made with the people of Jerusalem.

[1] Philip K. Hitti, *History of Syria* (New York: The Macmillan Company, 1951), p. 415.

This peace which is vouchsafed to them guarantees them security for their lives, property, churches, and the crucifixes belonging to those who display and honour them. Their churches shall not be used as dwelling houses, nor shall their walls be laid low, nor shall they be damaged in any way: likewise the houses attached to the churches, the crucifixes and any other belongings whatsoever. There shall be no compulsion in matters of faith, nor shall they be in any way molested. Nor shall Jews reside with them in Jerusalem.

It is incumbent on the people of Jerusalem that they pay the poll-tax, as other towns do. They must also rid themselves of Greeks and other robbers. Whoever of the Greeks leaves the city, his life and property shall be protected till he reach a place of safety; and whoever shall stay in Jerusalem, he shall be protected, but he must pay the poll-tax like the rest of the inhabitants. And whoever wishes to depart with the Greeks, leaving their churches and crucifixes behind, there is protection for them as well. Their lives, property, churches and crucifixes shall be protected till they reach a place of safety.

All that is contained in this treaty is under the covenant of God and His Messenger, and under the protection of the Caliph, and of the believers, so long as the people pay the poll-tax.[1]

This document, with its precise accounting of the rights of Christians, its legalisms, its peculiar references to crucifixes, so often repeated, its threats uttered in the formal language of conquerors and the menaces concealed in circumlocutions, suggests like nothing else the temper of the Arab mind during the early months of conquest. Almost we can hear the grave voice of the Caliph as he announces himself as the Protector of the Christians. It was a role which he played with considerable unction, for Eutychius records that he visited the Basilica of Constantine and prayed at the top of the stairs leading to the entrance, remarking that if he entered the Basilica the Christians would believe he intended to convert it into a mosque, but afterwards he made the journey to Bethlehem and prayed in the Church of the Nativity. It is possible that he ordered the construction of a mosque in Jerusalem, but Arab historians are silent on the matter and Christian historians describe the mosque with so many legendary details that they remain unconvincing. It is likely that in their first brush with Christianity the Arabs were content to leave well enough alone.

For the first time in his life Umar had left Arabia and entered a foreign country. The experience, however, did not broaden him. He had been stern before; he became sterner. The gentle Abu Bakr was followed by the revolutionary dictator, a man of inflexible will, who in the course of time rode roughshod over the wishes of his people, introduced harsh punishments, placed the whole nation on a war footing, regimented whatever could be regimented, and dealt remorselessly with any generals suspected

[1] Malauna Muhammad Ali, *Early Caliphate* (Lahore: Ahmadiyyah Anjuman Ishaat Islam, 1951), pp. 135–6.

G

of undermining his position. In so doing he followed one by one the tenets which have been proclaimed by revolutionary dictators throughout history; and he met the fate which is usually reserved for revolutionary dictators.

Khalid had been the first to sign the Treaty of Jerusalem, and he was the man most responsible for the victories in Syria and Palestine. Thin and eager, with a beaked nose and a gay manner, he was worshipped by his troops and envied by his fellow generals. He was inclined to flaunt his power, wear fine clothes and grant generous gifts out of the treasuries of conquered cities to his companions-at-arms without reference to the treasury in Madinah. Umar was incensed by the rich costume worn by Khalid when the young general came to meet him at al-Jabiyah on the way to Jerusalem; and when Khalid remarked that it was unworthy of the Caliph to appear in such sombre and simple garments, there was a moment of terrible tension before the Caliph replied that he was the best judge of the clothes he would wear. Close-fisted, the Caliph disliked Khalid's extravagance almost as much as he disliked his popularity. Soon after the capture of Jerusalem, Khalid was ordered to resign all his posts and return to Madinah. One day, when it became known that Khalid had tossed a thousand dinars to a poet who had celebrated his prowess, Umar called for an explanation. At first Khalid refused, suspecting there were other reasons for the summons. Umar was incensed. He ordered Bilal to remove Khalid's turban and then tie it round his hands—the sign that he was found guilty. Khalid exploded, and asked what harm he had done in rewarding a poet from his own private purse. Umar, who had heard that Khalid was using money from the treasury, relented and gave him his freedom, though he was never again allowed to command an army. There were murmurings among the soldiers. Umar wrote an order of the day, explaining that Khalid had been removed for reasons of state which in no way reflected on his honour: he had been removed simply because the Caliph was afraid the people would attribute the conquests of Islam to Khalid's prowess on the battlefield. Not Khalid, but God, had won the war.

Some years later, visitors to the town of Hims in northern Syria were accustomed to see a gaunt and wizened beggar in the streets, who sometimes spoke of the days when he was known all over the empire as 'the Sword of God'. There, or perhaps in Madinah, he died in A.D. 641, forgotten by everyone.

Other generals were luckier, or more cautious, in their dealings with the Caliph. When Umar was in Jerusalem, Amr ibn al-'As, one of the signatories to the treaty, asked permission to invade Egypt. Characteristically Umar neither consented nor refused, thus suggesting by his silence that if the venture was successful, he would be rewarded; if unsuccessful, discredited. Amr was at the height of his powers: he was forty-five, as hard as steel, as resourceful as a fox. With 5,000 men he rode out of Caesarea in December, 639, and made his way towards the Egyptian frontier, following the route which Alexander had taken before him. At the frontier a letter from the Caliph awaited him. A small gulley traditionally divided Palestine from Egypt, and Amr decided to walk across it before opening the letter, which read: 'If my letter ordering thee to turn back from Egypt overtakes thee before thou hast entered any part of the country, then turn back; but if thou hast invaded the land before receiving my letter, then proceed, and may God help thee!' Amr had already crossed the frontier, and felt that the auspices were in his favour. He struck at Pelusium, captured it, and marched on to Babylon on the Nile, which was so strongly defended by Cyrus that he was forced to pitch camp at Heliopolis and await reinforcements from Umar, who sent al-Zubayr, the cousin of Muhammad, with 5,000 troops to his rescue. Babylon was taken at the end of a seven months' siege, and the road was open for the attack on Alexandria, after Constantinople the most splendid city in the world.

Alexandria was a prize worth dying for. As seaport and naval base, centre of learning and the arts, with its racetrack and theatres and well-equipped library, with the noble Cathedral of St. Mark overlooking the two harbours, it had remained Greek through all the nine hundred years of its existence. There followed a long siege, which did not unduly alarm the Alexandrians, who continued to receive supplies by sea; and the city fell only through the treachery of Cyrus, who hoped to administer the city as an independent enclave within the Arab empire.

While the siege was in progress Umar asked Amr to describe the sea for him, and Amr answered with that typical sobriety which characterizes the Arab when he confronts something he cannot understand: 'The sea is a great creature upon which weak creatures ride—like worms upon a piece of wood.'[1] For Amr, all Western civilization took on the aspect of 'worms upon a piece of wood'. When Alexandria fell at last, he rode in triumph through the Gate of the Sun and along the Canopic Way, past the great Pharos and the glittering tomb of Alexander, which has since disappeared as completely as though it had never been. And with his coming, Alexandria fell into a long decline. In the words of E. M. Forster: 'Though they had no intention of destroying her, they destroyed her, as a child might a watch. She never functioned again for over a thousand years.'

When the treaty was signed, Amr wrote jubilantly to Madinah: 'I have captured the city, but I shall forebear describing it. Suffice to say that I have taken therein four thousand villas, four thousand baths, forty thousand Jews liable to poll-tax, and four hundred pleasure palaces fit for kings.' The Caliph rewarded the bearer of the letter with a meal of bread and dates, and held a brief service in the mosque to celebrate the addition of imperial Egypt to his empire.

Egypt was not the only empire to fall into his hands. When Khalid left the Euphrates front, command of the Arab guerrillas was placed in the hands of the Bedouin tribesman Muthana, who fought a series of brilliant campaigns from his headquarters at al-Hirah. Umar distrusted the

---

[1] Nearly all Amr's recorded words have a wonderful pithiness. As he lay dying, someone asked him how he felt. He answered: 'I feel as if heaven lay close upon the earth and I between the two, breathing through the eye of a needle.'

Bedouins, and sent Sa'd ibn-abi-Waqqas, one of the oldest companions of Muhammad, perhaps the fourth to accept the faith, to take the command. Al-Hirah was occupied by the Sasanian general Rustam, and the Arabs camped in the nearby village of Qadisiyah; there the two armies remained, facing each other and waiting for reinforcements. Months passed. Neither side was prepared to begin the inevitable battle, and both sought for advantages. Tabari, who is generally accurate in essentials, tells how fourteen Arabs made their way to the palace at Ctesiphon and demanded of the young Persian Emperor, Yazdagird III, that he accept Islam and pay tribute to Madinah. The Emperor, surprised by their effrontery, exclaimed that he had never in his life seen such pitiable creatures as these ambassadors, whose food was mice and lizards and whose clothing consisted of camel's hair and wool. He ordered them to return to their lands, and out of pity promised them provisions for the journey. He also promised to name a governor over Arabia. At this the leader of the Muhammadan ambassadors leaped up and exclaimed: 'By God, he is right! Hunger and nakedness were our lot in the past, but God gave us a Messenger and through him we have grown strong. The Caliph has sent us to demand that you pay tribute and accept our faith or fight.' The Emperor said: 'I will give you some earth to carry on your heads, and you will return with this earth to your own country.' The fourteen ambassadors thereupon left the city, each carrying a sackful of earth on his head, and promising revenge.

Revenge came in the hot summer of A.D. 637, when the imperial field marshal Rustam finally decided that the time had come to stamp out the small Muhammadan army camped at Qadisiyah, and ordered that the canal separating the two armies be filled up to allow the progress of the Persian elephants. Sa'd was ill, and directed operations from his bed. The battle lasted three days, and most of it was fought during a blinding sandstorm. Arab chroniclers have divided the battle into three periods: the day of confusion, the day of succour and the day of distress. On the first day a Syrian division stationed in Mesopotamia came to the relief of the hard-pressed Muhammadans, but did little to effect a decision. The fighting continued through the night, and through the night of the next day, with the Persian elephants standing like a wall against the Muhammadan cavalry, and Rustam in complete command of the situation, superintending the attack from his high thronelike command post.

On the morning of the third day, about noon, when the air was dark with driven sand, a small band of dedicated Muhammadans fought their way to Rustam's command post and toppled him from the throne. Wounded, he was able to reach the baggage train and was about to drive away with the treasure when he was discovered and killed. The holy standards of Persia were seized; and the Persian army dissolved in panic, while all the fertile lowlands of Iraq lay open to the Muhammadans.

Sa'd recovered from his illness and pushed on towards Ctesiphon, the fortified capital of the Sassanian empire, where Yazdagird III lived in a more splendid state than any emperor or king before him. In his White

Palace there lay a great carpet made to represent a garden, with a border of emeralds and a centrepiece of pearls. A crown of solid gold set with jewels hung on chains from the roof above the Emperor's head. Beside the throne stood a golden horse with teeth of emeralds and a ruby mane. Protected by the Tigris, the city might have held out indefinitely, but Yazdagird, fearing assassination, withdrew to Hulwan at the foot of the Zagros Pass with the imperial treasury; and while he was escaping, six hundred Arabs hurled their horses across the raging river and surprised the garrison. Ctesiphon fell into their hands. The next day Sa'd marched through the city in triumph, so elated that he could not prevent himself from shouting the prophetic verses of the Quran: 'How many the gardens they abandoned, and springs and rich fields and magnificent mansions where they lived! Even so, we gave them as a heritage to another people!'

Even in Alexandria there had not been such a heritage of treasure to be packed off to Madinah. The spoils included the sold golid breastplate and helmet of the Emperor, innumerable jewelled diadems and necklaces, and the great banner of the empire. For days the great *maidan* outside the White Palace became a market-place where the conquerors rivalled one another in bargaining over their treasure. The story is told of an Arab warrior from al-Hirah who sold a nobleman's daughter for a thousand dirhams, and when he was blamed for selling her so cheaply, he replied: 'I never thought there was a number above a thousand!' It was remembered that when Muhammad was escaping from Mecca, he was overtaken by a certain Suraqa, whose horse stumbled; and believing the stumbling of his horse was a sign that Heaven protected the fugitive, Suraqa had simply begged Muhammad's pardon and allowed him to go free. Pleased, Muhammad replied: 'I see the gold bracelets of Chrosoes on thy wrists.' When the spoils reached Madinah, Suraqa was summoned by the Caliph and the golden bracelets of Chosroes were placed on his wrists, that the prophecy might be fulfilled. Other prophecies were remembered. At the time when the people of Madinah were digging a ditch to defend themselves against the Quraysh, Muhammad had dropped down into the ditch, and when he struck at the rocks with a pick, three times the lightning flashed from the tip of the pick. Salman al-Farisi had asked the meaning of the lightning, and Muhammad answered: 'Did you really see that, Salman? The first means that God has opened up to me the Yaman; the second Syria and the west; and the third the east.' Now the east had fallen into the hands of the successor of Muhammad, and no one knew how many hostages to fortune were being prepared.

Umar never knew, but he may have guessed. When the spoils of Persia were laid at his feet, he wept and said: 'I fear all this wealth and luxury will in the end ruin my people.' And when Ziyad, who had escorted the treasure to the capital, asked the Caliph's permission to march against Khurasan, he answered: 'I would prefer to see insurmountable mountains between Iraq and those other lands, so that they could neither attack us, nor could we attack them.' But as the army gathered strength and speed, the momentum of victory carried it beyond the mountains into regions where the Caliph had little control, and the governors of the new provinces often acted as independent satraps, paying only lip service to Madinah.

Umar was not always able to control his governors, but at least he could impose his views on social order and establish a constitution for the Islamic Empire. Tax moneys poured into Madinah, and from a hundred cities came gifts and tribute; the wealth so gathered could be employed in supporting a vast bureaucracy to supervise the actions of the conquerors, and report on them. The Caliph was assiduous in sending teachers of the Quran to all the provinces, and these teachers sometimes performed the function of political commissars. He built jails, organized a police force, established a census for the purpose of acquiring accurate muster rolls, and saw that the conquered lands were accurately surveyed so that the proper taxes could be assessed. He introduced a new code of laws based upon the legislative precepts in the Quran, but harsher—adultery was punished by stoning, and drunkenness by eighty lashes of the whip. When his own son Was found guilty of drunkenness, the Caliph scourged him to death.

Proud and imperious, remote from the people while at the same time capable of acts of astonishing humility and selflessness towards the very poor and the sick, he laid down the law with a heavy hand. Muhammad had ordered that the Jews in Khaybar and the Christians in Najran should be allowed full protection. Umar simply disregarded the treaties signed by Muhammad and expelled them to Syria, having come to the conclusion that only Muhammadans should be permitted to live in Arabia. As for the Muhammadans beyond the frontiers of Arabia, they were to form an embattled aristocracy whose sole purpose was to keep the conquered peoples in a state of permanent subjection. No Muhammadan was allowed to cultivate land outside the peninsula, own property, or marry an infidel. Muhammadans were to be armed at all times, while infidels were never permitted to bear arms. An infidel must never wear the clothes of a Muhammadan, and must dismount whenever a Muhammadan passed him by. He must not pray aloud, or ring bells in church, and he must not expect his word to be believed against the word of a Muhammadan. In general the fate of the infidel was to be the silent and undemonstrative slave of the warrior caste, forever at the mercy of the conqueror. It was a simple division of the world, not unlike that envisaged by Hitler; and it failed because such simplicities bear in them the seeds of their own corruption.

Umar himself seems to have been aware of the corruptions of power. Once he asked Salman al-Farisi whether he was Caliph or Emperor. Salman replied diplomatically that he could be called Emperor only if he misappropriated money from the state treasury for his own use. 'By God!' said Umar. 'I know not whether I am Caliph or Emperor. And if I am Emperor, it is a fearful thing!' It was a strange and revealing remark from a man who lived in ostentatious poverty, possessing at his death when he was Emperor of half the known world even less than Abu Bakr possessed— his total possessions amounted to one patched shirt and a mantle.

He died as the result of an obscure quarrel over a few pennies. A Persian slave, a convert to Christianity, stabbed him one morning when he was entering the mosque, believing he had received an unjust verdict from the Caliph. The weapon was a double-bladed dagger, which the Persian afterwards turned upon himself. The Caliph knew he was dying: the wounds were deep and the bowels were cut. He asked who had struck him, learned that it was a certain Abu Lu'lu'ah Firoz, a Persian, and gave thanks that he had not been killed by a believer. Then he summoned Ayesha and asked to be buried beside Muhammad, a request which Ayesha granted immediately. A man of towering height and imposing physique, he survived for four more days, dying on November 23, A.D. 644. He had reigned for ten years, and in his reign the boundaries of Islam reached across North Africa and far into Asia.

No one ever accused Umar of being niggardly or given to nepotism, but Uthman, his successor, suffered from all the minor vices, and was consumed with pride. He had no flair for government, and almost no understanding of the forces which Muhammad had brought into being. He was seventy when he came to power: old and feeble, with a reputation for running away from battle, rich and sanctimonious, acutely conscious of his Umayyad ancestry, generous only to his innumerable relatives.

With all his faults Umar had shown a steady hand at the helm, but Uthman was one of those men whose opinions were based on the latest voice to reach his ear; and only the voices of the Umayyad clan were permitted to reach him. There was something awe-inspiring in the extent of his nepotism. Within a decade nearly all the governorships and all the high offices of state were in the hands of his close relatives. The once detested Umayyads were in the seat of power.

Perhaps it was not entirely his fault. Quite early he became the captive of the Umayyad conspiracy, which seems to have been organized immediately after the fall of Mecca, with Abu Sufyan playing the role of chief conspirator while successfully ingratiating himself with Muhammad. Uthman began by deposing Sa'd ibn-abi-Waqqas, the conqueror of Persia, in favour of a near kinsman on his mother's side, who proved to be a drunkard and a profligate and was therefore flogged within an inch of his life in the public square of his own capital at al-Kufah, only to be succeeded by another relative, an inexperienced youth, who was so incompetent that he allowed the street rowdies to take control, and so he too had to be dimissed. Amr ibn-al-'As, the conqueror of Egypt, was deposed and replaced by Abdallah ibn-Sa'd, Uthman's foster brother. Sa'd ibn-abi-Waqqas disappeared into private life, tending his vast estates until the day he died and refusing all offers to take part in government, while Amr ibn-al-'As made his way to Syria, becoming the chief lieutenant of Muawiya, another Umayyad nobleman, who regarded Syria as his own private fief.

But this was only the beginning. Umayyads were in control of the imperial treasury, of the police, of the annual pilgrimage, of the inspectorate, of the armed forces all over Arabia and beyond. Umayyad influence pervaded all branches of government: nearly all the wealth of the empire was concentrated in their hands. Moreover, some of Uthman's appointments gave the impression of being deliberate affronts to the memory of Muhammad. Abdallah ibn-Sa'd, the new governor of Egypt, was one of the ten men proscribed by Muhammad at the time of the conquest of Egypt, and he had been saved from death only by the intervention of Uthman. For a long time Muhammad had deliberated whether to allow the man to go free. Afterwards one of the Companions asked him why he had deliberated so long, and he answered: 'I was hoping one of you would strike off his head!' All the wealth of Egypt belonged to this man who escaped death by a miracle. One of Uthman's half brothers, who became governor of Persia, had spat on Muhammad's face.

Though Uthman was incompetent, the Muhammadan armies, surging forward with the momentum acquired in the last years of Muhammad's life, continued to gain victories. From Syria, Muawiya had long hoped to launch an expedition against Cyprus, saying that the island was so close that he was being kept awake at night by the barking of Cypriote dogs. Umar, who feared the sea, had refused his permission, but Uthman was more tolerant of naval adventures; and then for the first time a Muhammadan navy sailed out against a Byzantine naval base. Cyprus fell, and then it was the turn of Rhodes, which fought off the invaders, but not before losing to the Muhammadans the remnants of the great statue of the Sungod designed by Chares of Lindos, one of the seven wonders of the world. The statue, which had fallen in an earthquake hundreds of years before, was cut up and shipped to Syria, and nothing more was ever heard of it except that a junk dealer was reported to have employed 900 camels to carry the immense bronze fragments away.

Meanwhile the relentless expansion of Muhammadan power continued in the east and west. Abdallah ibn-Sa'd advanced along the Mediterranean coast almost to Carthage, which was forced to pay tribute. He brought the Berbers into the Islamic fold, and fought the Christian Nubians in the south. In the east, Afghanistan, Turkestan and Khurasan were added to the empire; and the flag of Islam fluttered on the coast of the Black Sea.

But while these conquests increased the power and prestige of the Caliph and the far-flung family of Umayyads, they were a source of constant quarrels in the army, where it was felt that too great a share of the wealth was pouring into the state treasury. Baggage trains filled with treasure sometimes disappeared on their way to Madinah. The army was disturbed too, by the inflexible nature of the theocratic state: the revolution had stopped in mid-flight, with no attempt on the part of Uthman or his lieutenants to understand the new social forces at work. Uthman seems to have been conscious of the ever-present danger of a military *coup d'état*, but he was too old and feeble to take proper precautions. A vast new empire had come into being, and a shadow governed it.

A vigorous and gifted man might have saved the day, but Uthman was no Augustus Caesar throwing the mantle of his imagination over an entire empire. The military were in the saddle, and the best of them were disheartened by the evidence of constant nepotism. Uthman added nothing new. The military organization of the conquered territories in his reign followed exactly the principles laid down by Abu Bakr and Umar. Taxes, pensions, public works, chains of command, methods of communication, all these remained unchanged. Even Uthman's revision of the Quran, his chief claim to fame, was derived from a decision made by Umar, with the important difference that Uthman took care that Muhammad's violent attacks against the Umayyads were expunged, and there was tampering of the text. Abdallah ibn-Masud, Muhammad's secretary, announced publicly that the canonical version of the Quran as revised by Uthman was a monstrous falsification. Unfortunately, since Uthman gave orders that all the copies of the Quran in the provincial libraries should be publicly burned, and since he took possession of the copies belonging to Muhammad's family and destroyed them, his version is the only one that has survived.

Inevitably there were murmurings of discontent. Some, like Abu Dharr, raised their voices against the vast wealth of the Umayyads, quoting the Quran: 'Ye who hoard up gold and silver and spend it not in the way of God, know that ye shall receive a fearful punishment.' Abu Dharr was one of Muhammad's closest companions, and his bitter complaints were regarded so seriously that Muawiya sent him for trial to Madinah, where he continued to proclaim his own views until he was banished to an obscure town in the provinces. Ali remained quiet, but all over the empire, and especially in Iraq, small groups of his followers were proclaiming that Uthman was a usurper and Ali was the rightful emperor. According to them, Ali alone was in the direct line of apostolic succession, and he alone was worthy of the high position.

The revolt, when it came, bore all the hallmarks of being hastily prepared by plotters who were uncertain of their aims and appalled by the responsibility they had assumed. The conspiracy, which seems to have begun in Iraq, had at first no particular aim except the removal of the Caliph and the Umayyad governors. Ali, who held himself remote from the conspirators, seems to have warned the conspirators in Iraq against immediate action, but his warnings failed to reach Muhammad ibn Abu Bakr, the son of the first Caliph, who was in Egypt. At the head of 500 men, Muhammad ibn Abu Bakr marched on Madinah, pretending to be taking part in the pilgrimage. Once in Madinah, they entered the mosque and demanded the resignation of the Caliph, who stoutly maintained that he had no power to resign, but would listen to their grievances. 'I will not abdicate,' Uthman said. 'How can I throw off the mantle which God has placed about my shoulders?' The conspirators decided upon sterner measures. They would prevent the Caliph from exerting his authority; they would prevent him from speaking; they would reduce him to insignificance by making him the laughing-stock of the people of Madinah. They heckled him in the mosque and threw dust in his face. When these tactics failed, they threw stones at him. Covered with blood, the Caliph was borne unconscious out of the mosque, which he never entered again.

The conspirators were divided among themselves. Some hoped the Caliph would resign, others that he would accept their demands and while retaining his title surrender his power to someone outside the Umayyad aristocracy. Ali, who cared nothing for the Caliph and little for the rebel leaders, maintained a malevolent neutrality. Ayesha, who detested Ali and the Caliph equally, set off for Mecca on pilgrimage. Her role in the conspiracy was never made clear, but her sudden departure at this time suggests that she was deeply implicated. As the days passed, and the Caliph remained in his house recovering from his wounds, the conspirators determined upon extreme measures: they would take the house by assault, kill the Caliph and leave the election of a new Caliph to the future. If Ali refused to become Caliph—he showed every sign of refusing to come to power as the result of a *coup d'état*—they proposed to choose between Zubayr and Talhah, two veteran companions of Muhammad. They had already decided to attack the house when they observed that Ali, Zubayr and Talhah had all sent their sons to guard it. The sons were armed, and prepared to fight. Undaunted, the conspirators determined upon a ruse. They sent some men against the youthful guards to distract their attention, while the armed ringleaders went to the house next door, climbed on to the roof, jumped across the gap between the two houses and let themselves down into the inner courtyard of the Caliph's house. Uthman was reading the Quran surrounded by his family. Watching him there, his assailants hesitated for a moment, until Muhammad ibn Abu Bakr sprang forward and held him by the beard, preparing to strike at his throat. Uthman was not alarmed. He was nearly eighty-three, and he had been expecting death for some time. He said quietly: 'Son of my brother, if thy father were alive, he would know better how to treat these white hairs.' Someone else stabbed him in the throat, and soon all the conspirators were stabbing wildly. Nailah, the Caliph's wife, threw herself on the body, and three of her fingers were cut off by a sword. The blood of the Caliph flowed over the page of the Quran he was reading. The house was pillaged. Some time later Ali entered the house, found Uthman dead, summoned Hasan and Husayn, asked them what they had done to defend the Caliph, and when their replies proved unsatisfactory Ali struck them. From Nailah he learned that the murderer was Muhammad ibn Abu Bakr, but he seems not to have believed her. That night the body of the Caliph was buried secretly by his wife and a few friends, while the rebels celebrated their triumph. It was June 17, A.D. 656. The Caliph had ruled for twelve years over an empire he had never seen.

For the first time a Caliph had been murdered by members of his own faith, and all Madinah trembled. For five days Ali deliberated whether he would allow himself to become Caliph, at last accepting the high office only because he felt the empire would disintegrate if he refused. He had held aloof from the conspiracy; he knew he had little gift for ruling an empire; he was ageing rapidly. He entered upon his Caliphate with foreboding, and from the very beginning he seems to have guessed it would end in tragedy for himself and for all those who were close to him.

The election passed without incident. Leaning on his long bow, he received the oath of allegiance from the people of Madinah. Talhah and Zubayr swore to be loyal to him, and soon left for Mecca, where Ayesha was already secretly urging revolt. Three months later the town criers of Mecca were proclaiming that 'the Mother of the Faithful and Talhah and Zubayr are riding to Basrah—whoever therefore desires to strengthen the faith and fight to avenge the death of Uthman, if he has any conveyance for riding let him come!' Talhah and Zubayr had fallen under Ayesha's spell, and with 3,000 Meccans, always hostile to Madinah, they marched towards Basrah and took the town by storm.

Ali was walking through quicksands; wherever he looked, there was treachery and conspiracy. He appointed new governors to the provinces, only to discover that his appointees were enemies, and the old governors refused to obey his orders. He demanded the allegiance of Muawiya, the governor of Syria, and received in reply a letter which bore only the words: 'In the name of God, the Merciful, the Compassionate——' Startled, Ali asked the messenger what the words meant. The messenger replied: 'I have seen sixty thousand men at the mosque at Damascus, weeping at the sight of Uthman's bloody shirt and cursing the murderers!' Ali was innocent, but he must have known that his silence at the time of the murder was regarded by many of the believers, especially among the still-powerful Umayyads, as complicity in the crime. Puzzled and angry, he decided to fight. When his son Hasan attempted to dissuade him from leaving Madinah he answered: 'Would you have me lurk in a hole like a wild beast till she is dug out?' With 900 men he marched north to save the empire. His evil genius, Muhammad ibn Abu Bakr, the murderer of Uthman, rode by his side.

When Ali set out in the hope of establishing a new capital at al-Kufah on the banks of the Euphrates, he was no longer the well-knit, muscular and clear-sighted warrior who had fought through all the battles which brought his father-in-law to power. At fifty-six he was enormously fat, completely bald, with a thick white beard reaching to his waist, and he walked slowly and ponderously. All his life he had been a contemplative who would arouse himself from contemplation to perform fantastic feats of valour; but as he grew older he seems to have lost his genius for war. He was still a living legend, but he was a legend fighting against a ghost—the ghost of Uthman, whose bloody shirt hung in the mosque at Damascus with the three severed fingers of his wife pinned to it and the bloody page of the Quran below it. Because he refused to punish the murderers, or was unable to punish them, the ghost of Uthman haunted him to the end of his life.

Ayesha, too, was haunted by a ghost—the ghost of her husband Muhammad. On her way to Basrah, she came to a place called the Valley of Hawab, and suddenly she heard dogs howling. There were some Bedouins in an encampment nearby, and the dogs belonged to them. She screamed: 'Take me away! I remember Muhammad saying once when he was among his wives: I wonder which one of you the dogs of Hawab will bark at.' 'Hawab' means 'crime'. Guilt plagued her, as it plagued Ali, and she remembered the barking of the dogs to the end of her life.

Ali caught up with Ayesha at Basrah, and after an abortive attempt to make peace, he joined battle with her. By this time both their armies had swollen, and there were about 30,000 on each side. At dawn on December 9, A.D. 656, Ayesha took her place in the howdah of her camel after removing the curtains so that her soldiers could see her and derive what courage they could from seeing the wife of Muhammad leading them into battle. She fought like a tiger; Ali fought like a lion. Neither side gave any quarter. At the sight of the slaughter, Zubayr had qualms of conscience and rode off in the direction of Mecca, only to be discovered by one of Ali's followers, who cut off his head. Talhah, wounded in the leg, was thrown from his horse as he was trying to escape from the battlefield, and died of his wound. As the day progressed, the fiercest fighting was waged around Ayesha's camel, the basketwork litter, which was painted scarlet, bristling with arrows like the back of a porcupine. Seventy men were killed one after another while trying to defend her, and the camel was hamstrung. Then the battle came to an end, with 13,000 lying dead on the field. Taken prisoner, Ayesha offered her support to Ali, but the offer was refused. He sent her back to Madinah in the guard of his two sons, Hasan and Husayn, ordering her to meddle no more in affairs of state. So she passes out of history, a strange querulous woman with a passion for intrigue, dying twelve years later. Ali was recognized as Caliph throughout Iraq.

There remained Muawiya, whose genius for intrigue rivalled that of his father. He had a brain which moved like lightning, and he could wither people with a glance. Fleshy and handsome, with remarkably large buttocks, he was one of those who had embraced the faith only to increase the Umayyad name. On him there devolved the duty of avenging Uthman's death.

Ali's duties were more complex, for his task was to preserve the empire and to ensure the continuity of the faith. Of all the surviving companions he alone possessed the authority to speak in the name of Muhammad. As he grew older his fault was that he despised the world and wished himself rid of all the tormenting problems which went with the Caliphate. 'The world is carrion,' he said once. 'Whoever wants a part of it must be satisfied to live with dogs.' The most dangerous of the dogs he ever encountered was Muawiya, whose strange name means 'a barking bitch'.

Months passed in futile negotiations, while Ali and Muawiya confronted one another across the Syrian desert. At last, in the spring of A.D. 657, Ali marched northwest to meet Muawiya's army on the plain of Siffin on the west bank of the Euphrates. The armies were well-matched, with Ali's 50,000 Iraqis confronting an equal number of Syrians. Neither side was anxious to begin fighting, and for some days the negotiations were renewed. Ambassadors were exchanged. There was an almost festive air about the two great encampments facing one another. But whenever Ali insisted on the unity of the empire under one Caliph, Muawiya answered: 'There can be no unity until Uthman's murderers are punished. The sword divides us.' The fighting when it started was halfhearted, with Ali dividing his army into eight divisions and making a show of fighting with only one of these divisions each day. They had been fighting in this indecisive manner for about a week when the sacred month of Muharram came along, and then there were more negotiations, more attempts to bridge the unbridgeable gap between them. The sacred month came to an end. There were skirmishes for a few days; then outright war, with the battle raging for three days and nights, and no quarter shown. Ali's forces were on the point of victory when the wily Amr ibn-al-'As, the conqueror of Egypt, decided upon a ruse. He ordered his spearmen to tie pages of the Quran to their spears and hold them aloft. This gesture was interpreted as an appeal for arbitration by holy men: God must be the arbiter. From the soldiers there came a great cry of relief, but Ali remarked bitterly that victory had been dashed from his hands.

Once more there was an exchange of ambassadors, as Ali sought to discover exactly what was meant by this strange appeal to the Quran. Muawiya explained that the time had come for arbitration 'according to the book of God': each side would choose a representative; they would meet in some distant place; and meanwhile the armies would return to their bases, Muawiya's to Damascus and Ali's to al-Kufah.

Within the armies weariness had set in, and both Ali and Muawiya seem to have been glad of the respite. Yet Ali had most to lose, for time had been fighting on his side. He returned to al-Kufah in a mood of baffled indecision, leaving to his lieutenants the work of arranging the arbitration conference.

Months passed, and it was not until January, 659, that the arbiters met at Adhruh, halfway between Madinah and Damascus. Against his will Ali had been persuaded to select as representative Abu Musa, a man of extreme piety, but no political experience. Muawiya selected Amr ibn-al-'As, who had spent the intervening months in Egypt fighting against Muhammad ibn Abu Bakr, whom Ali had appointed to the governorship. Muhammad ibn Abu Bakr was killed,[1] and all of Egypt had fallen once again under the control of Muawiya. Striding into the tent at Adhruh, Amr ibn-al-'As came as a conqueror with no intention of abiding by the book of God. He tricked Abu Musa into proclaiming that both Ali and Muawiya should be deposed from the Caliphate; but since Muawiya was only the governor of a province and had never been Caliph, and by Abu Musa's declaration was now placed on an equal footing with Ali, the advantages all turned on Muawiya. The strange conference ended with a brawl, neither arbiter accepting the judgment of the other. But the

---

[1] Muawiya's vengeance against the murderer of the Caliph Uthman was complete. When Muhammad ibn Abu Bakr was captured, Muawiya vowed he would dress him in an ass's skin and burn him alive, but he was so overcome by hatred and horror that he stabbed his prisoner. Aghast as what he had done, he then had the dead Muhammad dressed in an ass's skin and burned.

damage was done. Muawiya was master of Syria and Egypt, and time
was fighting on his side.

From his headquarters in al-Kufah, Ali was preparing to invade Syria
when he learned of Amr ibn-al-'As's victory at the conference. Others
heard of it, including some disaffected elements in the army, fanatics who
proclaimed that Muhammadanism should return to its primitive roots,
with the Caliph elected by the votes of the faithful. They hated Ali as
much as they hated Muawiya, for the same reasons. They wanted no
government that was not elective; they rejected the doctrine of justifica-
tion by faith without works; and they placed the seal of their approval on
religious murder. Democratic, puritanical, hostile to nearly all forms of
authority, they represented a force which all succeeding Caliphs had to
reckon with. When 4,000 of these dissenters pitched camp outside al-
Kufah, and then marched on Ctesiphon, which they sacked until the
streets ran with blood, Ali knew that the invasion of Syria would have to
be postponed. At the obscure village of Baghdad, later to become the
capital of the Abbasid empire, Ali caught up with them. The dissenters'
camp lay along the Nahrawan Canal, and there the battle was fought
which put an end for a while to armed resistance by the dissenters. Ali
returned in triumph to al-Kufah only to discover that his whole army was
disaffected, and the invasion of Syria had to be indefinitely postponed.

He had only a few more months to live. Almost he was a prisoner in a
town given over to treachery and conspiracy. At the end of May, 660,
Muawiya proclaimed himself Caliph in Jerusalem, and Ali could only
watch the emergence of his rival from a distance. At dawn on January
24, 661, Ali was leaving his house when he heard the sudden honking of
geese belonging to some children. One of his servants wanted to chase the
geese away. 'Let them cry,' Ali said. 'They are weeping for my funeral.'
He was making his way down a narrow passageway leading to the mosque
when he was attacked with a poisoned sword by a certain Abdal Rahman
ibn-Muljam, who had sworn to pay a bride-price for his wife of 3,000
drachmas of silver, a slave, a maid and Ali's head. The sword penetrated
Ali's brain, but he lingered for three more days in great pain. Carried to
his own house, he summoned his assassin and ordered Hasan to keep guard
over him. Almost his last request was to instruct his followers to treat the
assassin mercifully; there must be no torture; he must be well-fed and comfortably accommodated; and if the Caliph died, then Abdul Rahman must
be executed with a single clean stroke of the sword.[1]

So died Ali after a troubled reign of a little more than five years. He
was the last Arabian Caliph, the last of the companions of Muhammad to
rule over the empire. Many titles and many great offices of state had
fallen to him, but the title he preferred most was 'Abu Turab', meaning
'Father of the dust', which Muhammad had given him after seeing him
stretched out at full length on the dusty floor of the mosque, and the greatest of his offices of state was to act as Muhammad's perpetual champion.

[1] Masudi says the clean death was not given to him. His hands and feet were cut off,
then red-hot nails were thrust into his eyes, and he was finally roasted to death.

Like Abu Bakr and Umar he died in poverty, his personal estate amounting to only 600 dirhems. On the night of his death Hasan went to the mosque and addressed the people of al-Kufah. He said: 'You have killed a man on the same night as the Quran descended from Heaven, and Jesus (upon whom be peace) was lifted up to Heaven, and Joshua the son of Nun was laid low. By God, none of his predecessors exceeded him, and none of his successors will ever equal him!' It was no more than the truth.

Dead, Ali was more alive than ever, recovering in a day everything he had lost. He became a canonized martyr and saint, the mediator between God and man, the divine exemplar and the perfect knight of the faith. Among the Shi'a Muhammadans he assumed a place even higher than Muhammad as the guardian of the gates of Heaven and the closest of God's companions. Some saw divinity incarnate in his person, and said that blessings flowed from him. His defects of indolence and political immaturity, his stubbornness and senseless devotion to treacherous friends, were forgotten, or regarded as virtues. They remembered him as a man whose supreme achievements on earth were only equalled by his supreme achievements in Heaven. The Persians especially demanded in their religious heroes the blaze of glory, a divine radiance; and in the etherealized figure of the maryred Ali they found their saviour.

At the time of his death none of his followers had any conception of the heights he would attain. He was buried obscurely outside the town, close by the dyke which protected the town walls from the inundations of the Euphrates; and for many decades the site of his tomb was unmarked. In A.D. 977 the Perians erected a sumptuous mosque above the place where they believed he was buried. For millions of Shi'a Muhammadans this place is more sacred than the tomb of Muhammad in Madinah or the Kaaba in Mecca.

THE CALIPHS OF DAMASCUS

IN THOSE days Damascus was still a Hellenistic city filled with Greek statues and Christian churches and wide avenues divided by rows of Corinthian columns. From their marble arcades shopkeepers sold damask cloth and damascene blades, and along the roads paved with amber-coloured limestone passed all the caravans of the East. No city in Syria was wealthier, or more licentious, or so given to trade; and no other city in the world was so well-favoured with running streams and canals. The gardens were a riot of colour with so many flowers that the Arab chroniclers grew weary of listing them, and the air tasted like wine. From the south-west the snow-capped heights of Mount Hermon looked down upon a city so unbelievably beautiful that many, including Muhammad, are reported to have hesitated before entering it, afraid of entering Paradise too soon.

As he sat in his palace a stone's throw from the great Church of St. John the Baptist, Muawiya may have reflected on the strange turn of events which had brought him, the son of Abu Sufyan, to power. The Umayyads had hoped to kill Muhammad and strangle the faith at birth; instead, without exerting themselves, employing patience and cunning as their weapons, they had acquired the title-deeds of the faith and the worship of the faithful. Those who had fought Muhammad had inherited the empire which Muhammad had built. It had all happened so effortlessly, in so brief a time, that he might have been excused if he had trembled at the thought of the appalling responsibilities he had assumed. But there was no reason to tremble. The empire was at peace. There were no rivals in sight. Ali was dead; his sons Hasan and Husayn possessed only a handful of followers; and most of the surviving companions of Muhammad were hurrying to Damascus to pay tribute in the name of the Messenger of God to a prince who believed only in his own magnificence.

Muawiya was the perfect type of the Machiavellian *condottiere*. Handsome, elegant and suave, delighting in luxury and power, amused by his own behaviour and capable of surprising acts of toleration, outwardly warm but possessed of an inner core of cold steel, he was in every way the opposite of Muhammad, whose secretary for a short time he had once been. There was no fanaticism in him. He was cruel with the casual cruelty of a snake which strikes at everything in its path, but on occasion he could be gentle as a woman. There was a streak of femininity in him. He was the same age as Ali, and therefore about sixty when he became Caliph, but he looked younger. From the beginning of his Caliphate he decided that the empire was to be enjoyed.

Surprisingly, he was a good ruler, quick to reward the deserving, always listening carefully to his advisers before making up his own mind, his brilliance never at war with his judgment. Sitting cross-legged on a throne covered with richly embroidered cushions, he sometimes gave the impression of being asleep when he was wide awake. He had few vices. He liked women, wine and song, but in moderation. Of all the Caliphs of the dynasty he founded, he was the one who suffered least from his conscience, though he committed the most crimes. His forbearance was famous, and he was the first Caliph known to crack jokes with his subjects. When a certain Khuraym came to audience with his lower garments tucked up, showing well-turned legs, Muawiya said: 'By God, if only those legs were on a woman!' 'The same for your buttocks, Prince of the True Believers,' replied Khuraym, and went unpunished.

Though Muawiya shows an astonishing modern temper in his mingling of indolent ease and efficient ruthlessness, he remained a man of his own time. Beneath the silks and damasks he remained essentially an Arab at war with the incomprehensible civilized world, hating Byzantium with an inextinguishable passion, employing Christians in his service only because he needed them as scribes and teachers and government officials, and because he could himself learn from them. His aim, like Muhammad's, was to conquer the whole world.

During the twenty years of his reign he waged war, often simultaneously, on three immense battlefronts—against the East, against Byzantium and against Africa. His first task when he came to the throne was to destroy Ali's son Hasan, who had assumed the Caliphate at al-Kufah in the place of his martyred father. Hasan, a man without convictions who had spent his life making and unmaking innumerable marriages—a hundred are recorded, and some two hundred others are suspected—was an easy prey, especially after being wounded by malcontents in his own capital. Muawiya disposed of him by bribery, sending him a letter acknowledging that the grandson of Muhammad had claims to the Caliphate, but pointing out that he, Muawiya, possessed greater skill in managing men. Enclosed with the letter was a blank sheet bearing Muawiya's signature, on which Hasan was invited to write out the details of the bribe. Hasan asked for himself a pension of five million dirhems and the revenues of a district in Persia, and for his brother Husayn, whom he detested, a pension of two million dirhems. In the agreement finally drawn up between Muawiya and Hasan, it was explicitly stated that the Caliphate, should revert to the family of Muhammad on Hasan's death. And when Hasan died ten years later of consumption in the obscurity of his small palace in Madinah, Muawiya, who had never intended to abide by the agreement, simply disregarded it. He had already decided to found a dynasty, with his son Yazid as his successor.

Hasan dead was more dangerous to Muawiya than he had ever been alive. There grew up the legend that he had been killed by one of his wives, who washed his body one night with a poisoned napkin. The woman was said to be in the pay of Muawiya. In time the easy-living Hasan, who was said to bear an extraordinary resemblance to his grandfather, came to be known as 'the *saiyid* [prince] of all martyrs'.

H

With Hasan no longer a contender for power, Muawiya was free to
launch the series of great campaigns which brought his armies to the frontiers of China, along the whole coast of northern Africa and to the walls of
Constantinople. Only four years after he came to the throne his ships,
sailing from Tyre, raided Sicily. He established a naval base at Cyzicus
on the Sea of Marmora. In 669, and again in 674, Muhammadan armies
fought against the Byzantines in sight of Constantinople, only to be thrown
back by the mysterious weapon known as 'Greek fire', of which the secret
is still unknown. From Basrah his armies advanced through Khurasan
and deep into Transoxiana, where the ancient cities of Balkh and Herat,
later to become brilliant centres of Islamic culture, were first introduced
to the faith. The most resourceful of these campaigns led his armies to the
Atlantic.

Under Uthman the Arabs had already advanced as far as Carthage,
but when Amr ibn-al-'As was forced to withdraw as a result of the civil
wars the small Arab garrisons were soon overwhelmed by the Byzantines,
who retained command of the sea and could bring up forces along the
African coast without warning. Muawiya was determined to secure if
possible the whole of north Africa. Uqbah ibn-Nafi, the nephew of Amr,
the conqueror of Egypt, was given the task of consolidating the African
empire. By 670 he controlled most of modern Tunisia, and in that year
he founded the fortified military colony at Qayrawan, later to become a
great and important city. He levelled the surrounding forests and set up a
chain of military posts, to prevent the marauding Berbers from infiltrating
into northern Tunisia and to keep the Byzantines at bay. He was recalled,
but twelve years later, when Berbers and Byzantines were again attempting to overrun his military posts, he was sent out once more as governor
of Africa. This time he decided to make a show of force, and advanced
into Morocco. It was a dangerous journey, for the Greeks hung about his
flanks and cut off stragglers, and the Berbers threatened to cut off his
retreat. When he reached the Atlantic, Uqbah was disturbed by the
thought that he could go no farther. He spurred his horse into the sea,
raised his hands to heaven and exclaimed: 'Almighty God, but for this
sea I would have gone into still remoter regions, spreading the glory of
Thy name and smiting Thine enemies!'

The brilliant march of Uqbah and the crushing blows he inflicted on
the Byzantines and the Berbers had the effect of keeping the country
quiet for no more than a few months. In the following year, when he was
encamped at Tahudah on the edge of the Sahara, a horde of Berbers, issuing from the mountains and valleys of the Atlas, poured upon the camp
and massacred nearly everyone in it. Uqbah fought to the end. He broke
the scabbard of his sword as a sign that he expected no quarter, and
charged into his enemies. A handful of survivors made their way to Egypt.

In all his campaigns Muawiya and his lieutenants showed an astonishing resilience. They dared what no one had dared before, fighting offen-
sive campaigns on three widely separated fronts. The old forms of Arab
warfare were abandoned in favour of formations which followed the

Byzantine model; the solid square gave way to the phalanx, protected by cavalry on the wings. Arab and Byzantine armour were so alike that it was hard to distinguish between them in battle, and they employed the same weapons. The armies of Muawiya had little in common with the armies that moved across Arabia in the time of Muhammad. So, too, with the naval forces. In shipyards abandoned by the Byzantines, Muawiya found the models for the ships which he sent against Constantinople. He adapted and transformed whatever he found at hand in a ceaseless experiment with novelty. Unlike Uthman, he did not view society in terms of an unchangeable division between believers and infidels, but permitted and encouraged infidels to hold high posts in the government. The family of the Sarjunids, from which St. John of Damascus was descended, was placed in charge of the treasury, and all its members were Christians. The court poet Alkhtal was a Christian; and in this tolerant age it was not thought remarkable that he should be led in a robe of honour through the streets of Damascus while a herald proclaimed: 'Behold the poet of the Commander of the Faithful! Behold the greatest of all Arabian poets!' Akhtal would appear at court dressed in sumptuous silks with a gold cross hanging round his neck from a gold chain, wine drops trickling down his beard. Muawiya delighted in the poet who proclaimed in magnificent verse that everlasting glory attended the Umayyad dynasty. 'I am the first of the kings,' Muawiya said once. He was also the first of the innovators.

As a king he felt it his duty to live in a state rivalling the Emperors of Byzantium, and his glittering court followed the Byzantine model, with one important difference. Where the Byzantine Emperor remained remote from the people behind an impregnable barrier of officials, Muawiya threw the doors wide open. He held his first audience, attended by his ministers, at breakfast. Then he proceeded to the mosque, where anyone who wanted to see him could approach him with petitions—the poor, the destitute, women, children, wandering Arabs from the desert. He would inquire into their needs, order gifts of money to be given to the deserving and send officials to make inquiries in cases where summary justice was not desirable. Then he returned to the palace and held court, with more petitioners entering while lunch was being served. The historian Masudi says as many as forty petitioners came to the throne during lunch and they shared the Caliph's meal. Lunch was followed by noonday prayers at the mosque. Afterwards the Caliph returned to the palace for another audience with his ministers, serving them with pastries and sugared curd tarts. This audience went on to the middle of the afternoon, when the Caliph recited the afternoon prayer and retired. No petitioners were admitted at the evening audience, when supper was served. These evening audiences sometimes continued long into the night; and when at last the Caliph went to bed, he was often sleepless and spent the night listening to poets and secretaries who had memorized whole chapters of historical books. He especially liked the chapters which dealt with the secret stratagems of kings.

It is a pity that no portraits of Muawiya have survived. This amused, tolerant, infinitely gentle and infinitely treacherous king seems to gaze at us across the pages of history with an air of mockery. He was the supreme realist. He said once: 'I do not use my sword when my whip will do; nor my whip when my tongue will do. Let a single hair still bind me to my people, I will not let it break. When they pull, I loosen; and if they loosen, I pull.' When he lay dying at the age of eighty, he asked that he should be buried with some hairs of Muhammad and a paring of his nail. 'And when you have done that,' he said, 'leave me alone with the Most Merciful of the merciful.' It was perhaps no more than an amused tribute to the God who had given him so much unexpected magnificence.

His successor was Yazid, his son by his Christian wife Maysun, who was a gifted poetess. Yazid was an amiable prince with a talent for music and poetry which he inherited from his mother, and a strange awkward ruthlessness, unlike the cultivated ruthlessness of his father. A contemporary Christian chronicler, Isidore of Hispalis, said that he had an extremely happy nature—*jucundissimus*—and wished to live peacefully with all men. Except for a brief appearance at the siege of Constantinople, where he distinguished himself by his reckless bravery, he spent most of his life among the royal hunting lodges. He was the first Caliph to employ cheetahs at the hunt, and the only Caliph of whom it was related that he was drunk every day. The three-year reign of the jocund prince was an unrelieved tragedy.

The deft hand of Muawiya had kept the empire at peace, but with his death there was hardly anyone in Damascus who could not foresee the coming storm. On his deathbed Muawiya had foreseen the danger that would come from Arabia. He summoned Yazid to his bedside and said: 'The restless people of Iraq will encourage Husayn to attempt the empire. Defeat him, but afterwards deal gently with him, for truly the blood of the Messenger of God runs through his veins. It is Abdallah ibn-Zubayr I fear most. He is fierce as a lion and crafty as a fox, and must be destroyed root and branch!' Muawiya's fear of Abdallah ibn-Zubayr was justified. Son of Zubayr and grandson of Abu Bakr, he was a determined warrior, an undying enemy of the Umayyads and the one man after Husayn whom the people of Madinah wanted to elevate to the Caliphate.

When Yazid came to the throne, he sent ambassadors to Madinah to demand the allegiance of Husayn and Abdallah. Allegiance was refused. In al-Kufah, where Ali and Hasan had proclaimed themselves Caliphs, there arose a movement to install Husayn as the legitimate Caliph in opposition to Yazid. For weeks Husayn debated with himself and with his family whether to accept the offer of the Kufans, who promised to place an army at his disposal. He sent a messenger to al-Kufah to sound out the people, and learned too late that the messenger had been murdered. By September he was already on his way, riding at the head of a pathetic group of relatives and family retainers across the desert. Some soldiers joined him on the road, until his small force numbered perhaps two hundred men and boys, and another hundred women and girls. He seems to have known he was doomed, but he marched straight to the walls of al-Kufah, and there outside the walls he received news for the first time that his messenger had been decapitated, and the headless body had been thrown from the roof of the palace. The head was sent to Yazid.

Ubaydallah ibn-Ziyad, a nephew of Muawiya, was governor of Iraq with orders to take Husayn dead or alive. He had established outposts on the roads leading to the city; there was a reward for the head of Husayn, and the cavalry patrolled the roads ceaselessly. Thinking to avoid the patrols, and to put them off the scent, Husayn skirted al-Kufah and marched northwest. One night a ghostly horseman rode up to him and said: 'Men travel by night, and their destinies travel by night towards them.' It was a dream, but a strangely convincing one. And when destiny finally caught up with him, it was not at night but in broad daylight, the fires burning, a river flowing nearby, and his men dying of thirst.

On October 1, Husayn's small column reached the plain of Karbala, on the western bank of the Euphrates about twenty-fives miles northwest of al-Kufah, on the edge of the desert. Here he pitched his tents beside the reeds and tamarisks, to await the arrival of the cavalry patrol he had seen in the distance. It was led by a man who had sworn to kill Husayn with his own hands. He rode up to the camp and, speaking in the name of Yazid, demanded Husayn's immediate surrender and promised the protection of the Caliph. If Husayn did not surrender, the army had orders to destroy him and everyone in his camp. Husayn asked permission to give his decision the next day. This was granted to him. Most of the patrol kept watch on the camp during the night, while a messenger was sent to Ubaydallah.

That night Husayn gave orders to cord the tents close together so that the enemy would not be able to pass between them. The next morning Ubaydallah rode up to accept Husayn's surrender; but Husayn still retained some of his old authority. He made a speech and suggested that there were alternatives to surrender. There were three alternatives: he could return quietly to Madinah, or he could be sent to Damascus under safe-conduct, or—since these two alternatives might be regarded as favouring his own interests—he could go into exile in some obscure frontier post on the Turkish border. He refused to surrender without a guarantee of safety for his women, and while the negotiations went on during the day, he spent the nights debating with his followers how they could escape from the trap. By the tenth day Ubaydallah had sent up his entire army of 4,000 men under the command of Umar, the son of Sa'd ibn-abi-Waqqas. Husayn was surrounded on all sides. He had made the mistake of pitching his tents some distance from the river, and now Ubaydallah's archers stood between the river and the tents.

There had been skirmishes, sudden flares of anger which resulted in brief engagements, but there was no battle until the tenth day, when Husayn rejected Ubaydallah's final ultimatum. As usual the battle began with single combats: in these Husayn's men were victorious. Emboldened by the success of his champions, dazed by the heat and suffering from thirst, Husayn ordered a charge after first putting fire to a barricade of tamarisk branches and so safeguarding his rear. For about an hour there was confused fighting, with Husayn's men fighting with the courage of despair; and when Umar ibn-Sa'd ordered his men to pull down the tents, Husayn wheeled on these foot soldiers who dared to come near his women and slaughtered them to a man. But if Husayn could use fire, so could the enemy. Flaming brands were tossed at the tents, and javelins were hurled into them. The women ran out screaming. Above the roar of the conflagration, Husayn was heard shouting: 'You shall burn in hotter flames than these—you shall burn in hell fire!'

Then it was noon and the time of prayer, while everyone knelt and proclaimed the greatness of God, whose only Messenger was the grandfather of Husayn. The remnants of Husayn's shattered column were gathered together, to implore the aid of Heaven. Husayn recited 'the prayer of fear', which is never used except in cases of extreme danger. A moment later the fighting was renewed, with all the advantages of number and position belonging to the enemy. From a safe distance Umar ibn-Sa'd's archers picked off the few survivors one by one. Husayn was covered with wounds, but still fighting. When a sword-thrust split his helmet, he threw the helmet away, bound his head in a turban and continued fighting. During a lull he sat at the door of his tent, taking his son Abdallah on his knees. He was fondling the boy, who was only one year old, when an arrow from one of the distant archers pierced the boy's ear and penetrated the brain, killing him instantly. Husayn was half mad with grief. He filled his hands with blood from the boy's wound and flung it to the heavens, praying for aid. He was suffering from thirst, and called out to his women for water. A little water was brought to him. He was drinking when an arrow buried itself in his mouth. He fell to the ground, and while he was groaning one of his nephews ran out of the tent to console him. The boy was very handsome, with jewels in his ears, and the favourite among all his nephews. A horseman rode up, cut off the boy's arm with a swinging sabre, and then rode away to safety.

Husayn was now alone on the field, for all the men and boys who had fought with him were by now dead or wounded. The enemy was making sport with him. For them it was a sweet victory, to be savoured as long as possible He was entirely at their mercy as he stood there at the door of his tent, while the women sobbed and the tamarisks burned.

Suddenly, as though hurled forward by the impetus of despair, Husayn rushed at the enemy, determined to kill as many as possible before he was himself killed. He broke through their lines as though they were chaff. He was bleeding from a deep head wound and from the mouth and from many other wounds, but no one could stop him. At last one of the enemy soldiers thrust at his shoulder, almost severing an arm. Husayn continued fighting for a little while longer. A sword-blow at the neck knocked him to the ground. He fell on his face, and as he lay there a spear was driven into his back, and a moment later his head was cut off. From the time when he dashed from the tent to the time when his head was cut off, only a few minutes passed. 'It was very short,' one of the enemy soldiers said later. 'Just time to slay and dress a camel, or take a short nap.'

Guilty men attempt to obliterate the evidence of their crimes. So Ubaydallah gave orders that the headless trunk should be stripped, and the dead Caliph's shirt and underclothes, his corselet, turban and sword, were divided among the soldiers who had helped to kill him. Then Ubaydallah ordered his horsemen to ride over the naked body, trampling it underfoot until it was unrecognizable. But before this was done one of his men took careful note of the wounds. According to Masudi, there were twenty-three wounds from spears and thirty-four from swords. The body was left on the field for the daws to peck at.

The head, however, was carefully preserved according to Arab custom, to be shown to Yazid. There is a story, perhaps apocryphal, that when Yazid saw it, he brought his fist against the dead mouth, bruising it with his heavy rings. A certain Abu Barzah standing nearby was heard to say: 'Gently, O Caliph! Have I not seen those very lips kissed by the Messenger of God?'

The subsequent history of the head has puzzled historians. According to one report it was given to Husayn's sister, who carried it with her to Madinah and buried it in the grave of her mother Fatima, the daughter of Muhammad. Others say that it was placed in the tomb at Karbala which later became his shrine, and has remained there to the present day. In the most sacred mosque in Cairo, known as the Mosque of Hasan and Husayn, a head deep below the pavement under the dome is said to be Husayn's. It is said that the head was brought to Cairo in A.D. 1153 from Ascalon, and for some years was kept in the Caliph's palace. Contemporary travellers speak of the great treasures of gold and silver squandered on embellishing the mosque. Damascus also claims the head, for in the eastern end of the great Umayyad Mosque there is a small chamber where the head is supposed to lie, concealed by a black silk curtain and enclosed in a silver niche. Not far away lies the Shrine of St. John Baptist, which perhaps contains the head of the Baptist.

Yazid had defeated Husayn, but he had still to defeat Abdallah ibn-Zubayr, who defied the Caliph from his sacred asylum at Mecca. Abdallah ibn-Zubayr had encouraged Husayn to take the dangerous journey to al-Kufah. He was a man of violent temper and great determination, and he saw that the time was ripe for destroying the Caliphate at Damascus. By stirring up the people of Mecca and Madinah against the local governor appointed by Muawiya, he was able to bring about the recall of the governor and the appointment of another more sympathetic to his claims. Yazid, however, recognized the signs of the coming rebellion and to forestall it sent an army of 12,000 Syrians under the command of the one-eyed general Muslim ibn-Uqbah, the son of the conqueror of Africa. In August, 683, Muslim, an old man and close to death, camped on the Harrah, the lava fields north of the city, and a few days later met the Madinese army and defeated it. He showed no mercy. For three days his soldiers were permitted to rape and pillage and destroy. The mosque of

Muhammad was turned into a stable; colleges, hospitals and public buildings were destroyed. Abdallah ibn-Zubayr escaped to Mecca, but those
who fought with him and failed to escape in time were either executed
or branded on the neck. Madinah, which had been the capital of the
empire until A.D. 660, in less than twenty-five years became a wilderness.

Madinah destroyed, the Syrians marched on to Mecca, where Abdallah
ibn-Zubayr had already proclaimed himself Caliph and Commander of
the Faithful. The Syrians took the heights overlooking Mecca, set up
ballistas and mangonels, and hurled stones and pots filled with flaming
pitch into the city. During the bombardment the Kaaba was burned to
the ground, and the Black Stone split into three pieces. The Kaaba resembled 'the torn bosoms of mourning women', says Tabari, meaning
perhaps that the ruins were thick with the blood of the Meccans who had
pitched their tents around it in the hope of being able to defend it.
Abdallah wrapped the three pieces of the Black Stone in brocade and kept
it in his house. The siege was raised when runners brought the news that
Yazid had died, apparently of consumption, on November 10. He was
succeeded by his young son, Muawiya II, who died of the plague less than
two months later.

In its plight Damascus turned to another branch of the Umayyad
family for a Caliph to set against the anti-Caliph Abdallah ibn-Zubayr.
They chose the venerable Marwan ibn-Hakam, who had been Uthman's
secretary and who had been severely wounded during the attack on
Uthman's house, but whose principal claim to the affections of Damascus
was that he was the head of the Umayyad house. He was a short and pon-
derous man with a high colour, and he had modelled himself on Uthman;
and no one knows whether he would have made a good Caliph, for he
died nine months later. In a single year three Caliphs had died, and all of
them brought ruin on their empire.

Abd-al-Malik, the son of Marwan, was made of sterner stuff. News of
his elevation to the Caliphate came to him when he was reading the
Quran. He immediately closed the book, whispered, 'This is our last time
together,' and went to the palace for his inauguration. For the next
twenty-one years he fought tenaciously to preserve the empire.

He was a man without affability, precise, murderous, dedicated only to
the preservation of the empire. They called him 'the sweat of a stone',
because he was avaricious, and 'the father of flies', because his bad breath
was reputed to kill the flies that settled on his lips. One day he announced
from the throne: 'I am weary of being told to fear God. I shall smite the
neck of the next person who warns me against God's punishments on
Caliphs.' He was the first of the Caliphs to rule with absolute power, the
first to prohibit talking in his presence, the first who was never known to
smile.

When he came to the throne, half the empire acknowledged the anti-
Caliph Abdallah ibn-Zubayr, the Byzantines were attacking from the
west, Africa was in revolt, Damascus was seething with unrest, and even

in Syria there were armies moving against him. Ruthlessly Abd-al-Malik set about restoring order. He threw back the Byzantines; crushed the uprising in Syria; stormed Iraq; sent a punitive expedition to Mecca; destroyed the power of Abdallah ibn-Zubayr, who was killed while defending the Kaaba for the second time after thirteen years of independence; and by a series of brilliant campaigns in North Africa fought against a mysterious sorceress known to Arab chroniclers only as 'the woman who makes spells', he recaptured Africa. His armies penetrated into Afghanistan and deep into the Sahara. He was a conqueror who possessed no other virtue than his truthfulness. Asked why he waged war so mercilessly, he replied: 'I enjoy it!'

His chief lieutenant in the wars against Arabia and Iraq was a former schoolmaster from Taif called Hajjaj ibn-Yusuf, who also enjoyed making war. He was only thirty-one when he quelled a rebellion in al-Kufah with no more assistance than that provided by the twelve cameleers who accompanied him on a secret journey to the city. Hajjaj rode straight to the mosque, disguising himself by allowing his turban to fall over his face. No one knew he was coming. He was the most feared man in the empire. He rode straight to the mosque, tore the turban from his face and made a speech which terrified the people standing in the mosque and which even in translation can send shivers down the spine. He began by quoting two verses by the poet Suhaym ibn Wathil, and then launched into a ferocious judgment on his enemies:

'I am he that scattereth the darkness and climbeth the heights: As I lift the turban from my face, ye shall know me!'

O people of al-Kufah! I see before me heads ripe for the harvest and the reaper; and verily I am the man to do it. Already I see the blood between the turbans and the beards.

The Prince of the True Believers has spread before him the arrows of his quiver and found in me the cruellest of all arrows, of sharpest steel and strongest wood. I warn you, if you depart from the paths of righteousness, I shall not brook your carelessness, nor listen to your excuses. You Iraquis are rebels and traitors, the dregs of dregs! I am not a man to be frightened by an inflated bag of skin, nor need anyone think to squeeze me like dry figs! I have been chosen because I know how to act. Therefore beware, for it is in my power to strip you like bark from the tree, to pull off your branches as easily as one pulls off the branches of the *selamah* tree, to beat you as we beat the camels which wander away from the caravans, and grind you to powder as one grinds wheat between mill-stones! For too long you have marched along the road of error. I am Hajjaj ibn-Yusuf, a man who keeps his promises, and when I shave I cut the skin! So let there be no more meetings, no more useless talk, no more asking: 'What is happening? What shall we do?'

Sons of prostitutes, learn to look after your own affairs. . . . Learn that when my sword once issues from its scabbard, it will not be sheathed, come winter, come summer, till the Prince of the True Believers with God's help has straightened every man of you that walks in error, and felled every man of you that lifts his head![1]

In such terms had Muhammad spoken in the days of his rage, but never with such concentrated venom, such glory in destruction, such power to kill by words alone. Hajjaj belongs to the small band of destructive conquerors, glorying in bloodshed, who have descended at intervals to haunt the world. That he was the pure nihilist, a man who believed in nothing, is suggested by his famous phrase: 'God wrote upon this world the word *annihilation*, and on the world to come He wrote *eternity*.' Once, when someone accused him of being an infidel, he laughed, and for a long time debated with himself whether it was worth while executing a man who had spoken so truthfully. Masudi says his whole life was like a trail of blood, and among his victims, not counting the innumerable soldiers who died in his wars, were 120,000 innocent men and women. At his death his prisons were choked with 80,000 prisoners, and Masudi notes as a sign of his especial inhumanity that 'six thousand of these prisoners were completely naked and made to shift for themselves'. As he lay dying at the age of fifty-four of cancer of the stomach, having been virtual ruler of the empire for nearly twenty years, the former schoolmaster from Taif is supposed to have said: 'Pardon my sins, O God, and grant me a kingdom such as none will enjoy after me.'

Reading the chroniclers of the Umayyad empire, one is continually being reminded of Elizabethan England or the age of the Italian despots. Horsemen robed in splendid silk ride out to massacre defenceless villagers. Luxury, almost too great to be borne, sits cheek by jowl with intolerable poverty. Blood flows; heads are impaled on gibbets; there is treachery everywhere. While murderous intrigues occupy the attention of the court and empires rise and fall, the Emperor himself is writing the most exquisite poetry and ordering the construction of buildings of unearthly beauty.

The Caliph Abd-al-Malik himself may have been responsible for the design of the greatest building erected during his reign—the exquisitely beautiful Dome of the Rock (*Qubbat al-Sakhrah*), built on the site of the Temple of Solomon in Jerusalem. According to contemporary chroniclers, Abd-al-Malik himself designed the small treasure-house known as the Dome of the Chain (*Qubbat al-Silsilah*), which lies close to the Dome of the Rock, and this design, immensely magnified, was employed by the architects in building the great shrine-temple which rises high above Jerusalem.

Here on the summit of Mount Moriah, where the Jews built the Altar of Burnt Offering, destroyed by the Romans during the sack of A.D. 70,

---

[1] There are minor variants in the speech, and I have here followed Masudi. It is possible that none of the recorded versions represent exactly what Hajjaj said. The speech, for all its violence, has the air of a set piece carefully revised by a scholar who may have heard the speech and recast it in literary form. Whoever wrote it shared Hajjaj's peculiar nihilism, his contempt for the world and all who live in it. The speech has become an Arabic classic and is eagerly studied by schoolboys.

and where Justinian later built a church dedicated to Mary, Abd-al-Malik built a monument to himself bearing a famous Kufic inscription in yellow and blue mosaic around the base of the dome: *The Servant of God, Abd-al-Malik, Commander of the Faithful, built this dome in the year Seventy-two. May God find favour in him and bless him. Amen.* He had reason to be proud of his handiwork. It is one of the four or five truly noble buildings in the world, to be compared with the Parthenon, the Masjid-i-Shah in Isfahan and the Taj Mahal.

In its origins, however, the Dome on the Rock was a political device. Mecca was in the hands of the anti-Caliph Abdallah ibn-Zubayr, and Abd-al-Malik was concerned that the faithful should possess in the territory he ruled an object of veneration as important as the Kaaba. Such an object lay ready at hand in the huge mass of black rock, its surface scored like a breaking wave, which for untold centuries had reposed on top of the highest hill in Jerusalem. Legends had accumulated around this rock. Here Abraham, the father of the Arabs, had almost sacrificed Isaac. Here Muhammad ascended to Heaven, and here too all the prophets of God up to the time of Muhammad came to pray. Beneath the rock, invisible to human eyes, lay the fountain from which there came all the sweet water which ever poured over the earth. Abd-al-Malik sent out feelers to his people, and came to the conclusion that a shrine-temple over the rock would answer his purposes. In every possible way he would follow the existing example of the Kaaba. There would be ambulatories around the rock, so that the pilgrims could perform the *tawaf*. Here, too, he would exhibit his most costly and most ancient treasures. When the Dome of the Rock was built, the rock itself was surrounded by a lattice of ebony and curtains of brocade. Suspended over the rock, hanging on a chain, were the very horns of the ram which Abraham had sacrificed, together with a pearl of immense size and the jewelled crown of the Persian Emperor Chosroes. In A.D. 680, Bishop Arculf visited Jerusalem and saw on this spot an old mosque, perhaps the same which was built by the Caliph Umar when he came to accept the surrender of the city. Arculf says the mosque was 'built very roughly of beams and planks raised over some ancient ruins'. Eleven years later, Abd-al-Malik had built a shrine so brilliant and colourful it took men's breath away.

The Dome of the Rock, as we see it today, has not changed very much since the time when Abd-al-Malik built it. The roofing of copper gilt has gone, and so have some of the mosaics of angels and earthly palaces which decorated the interior, and the palisade around the rock itself was added in the twelfth century. In his time the whole of the exterior wall, including the drum, was covered with gold and polychrome mosaic, which survived until the middle of the sixteenth century, to be replaced by the most delicate blue and green and yellow tiles. Today the pilgrim gazing at the mosque at sunset, when the dome turns to gold, can recapture almost without effort the splendour and the freshness which merged for the first time when Abd-al-Malik attempted to build a shrine as superb as the Church of the Holy Sepulchre; and perhaps it was inevitable that the

Dome of the Rock should resemble a pleasure palace, but of such noble proportions that it becomes worthy of its object.

There are mysteries here. Nothing we know about Abd-al-Malik suggests that he was a man of taste in architecture, capable of sketching the wonderful Dome of the Chain on the drawing-board. Stern and pitiless, capable of murdering men with his bare hands, he gloried in his conquests and allowed the insufferable Hajjaj free rein in all his sanguinary exploits. He placed his own relatives in command of all the provinces except Iraq, where Hajjaj assumed complete control, acting more like a viceroy than like a governor. He was the first to mint an Arabic coinage, and the first to insist that treasury accounts should be kept in Arabic, with the result that the coinage was soon debased and the treasury, formerly placed in the hands of the Christian Sarjunids, who behaved with the admirable discretion of civil servants, became a hotbed of intrigue. Taxes were farmed out to the provincial governors, with the result that the peasants despaired and throughout the whole course of his reign there were uprisings. The civil wars were complicated by outbreaks of war between sects. There were families split between loyalty to the Caliph, the anti-Caliph, and obscure revolutionaries who called themselves Messengers of God.

The followers of the martyred Husayn cried out for vengeance. They found their leader in the resourceful guerrilla chieftain Mukhtar ibn-abi-Ubayd, who had known Ali as a youth and whose uncle when governor of Ctesiphon had introduced him to the world of conspiracy. Mukhtar raged through Iraq like an avenging flame. He possessed prophetic gifts, hinted that he had been sent by direct command of the Archangel Gabriel to punish the Umayyads, preached in an obscure rhymed prose modelled on the Quran, and spoke of the coming of the *mahdi*, the divine deliverer and restorer, who would bring peace and justice to earth. Armed bands of Iranians and Iraqis under Mukhtar's leadership found themselves fighting an Umayyad army commanded by the hated Ubaydallah ibn-Ziyad, the man most responsible for killing Husayn. Mukhtar won the battle, and in a solemn ceremony in the palace at al-Kufah the head of Ubaydallah was presented to him. The followers of Husayn rejoiced, but not for long. Mukhtar incurred the enmity of the anti-Caliph, who sent his brother Musab ibn-Zubayr against the heretic. Mukhtar shut himself up in the fortress at al-Kufah, and was killed when making a sortie in the hope of breaking the four months' siege. The head of Mukhtar was solemnly presented to Musab. Abd-al-Malik, incensed by the growing power of the anti-Caliph, led an expedition against al-Kufah, and for the fourth time in living memory the head of a saint or a general was solemnly laid at the foot of the throne. An old Arab who was present when the Caliph received the head of Musab complained: 'There is no end to it! First I see the head of Husayn lying there, and Ubaydallah ibn-Ziyad takes it in his hands. Then I see the head of Ubaydallah ibn-Ziyad, and Mukhtar takes it in his hands. Then I see the head of Mukhtar, and Musab takes it in his hands. And now I see the head of Musab, and the Caliph takes it in his hands.'

It was like a dream drenched in blood, with no end to the wars, no end to tears. Abd-al-Malik, who loved war, died peacefully in bed. On his deathbed he is supposed to have summoned his son Walid and said: 'Why are you mourning? When I am dead, put on your leopard-skin, gird yourself with your sword, and cut off the head of everyone who gets in your way!' Abd-al-Malik seems to have had little hope for his son, but in this he was wrong. In the reign of Walid I, the Islamic empire reached its greatest extent, stretching from Spain to the borders of China.

Walid was Muawiya all over again, ruthless and gentle by turns, a terror to his enemies, a great benefactor to the Syrians, who never tired of singing his praises. He established orphanages for poor children, founded schools and hospitals, granted pensions to the old and impoverished, built roads and canals and frontier posts, and took careful note of the cost of living by visiting the market-places. Abd-al-Malik was unapproachable; Walid could be approached by anyone. He built the first lunatic asylums and the first hospices for the blind. He was especially gentle to women and never known to lose his temper, yet he kept Hajjaj in his employment against the advice of his wife, who was permitted to berate the bloodthirsty general and call him a murderer to his face. His armies overran Transoxiana, penetrated deep into India, and in three short years conquered all of Spain.

Almost his first act when he came to the throne was to order the rebuilding of the mosque at Madinah where Muhammad lay buried. Hundreds of Greeks and Egyptians were employed in the work. Muhammad's mosque was changed beyond recognition; the huts where he had lived with his wives were swept away; mosaics glittered on the walls. Having saluted the Messenger of God, Walid turned his attention to a memorial worthy of himself and ordered the construction of a great mosque at Damascus, choosing as his site the Church of St. John Baptist, which itself had been raised on the site of a temple to Jupiter Damascenus. Known as the Great Umayyad Mosque, it survives to this day, altered by time and fire, but still recognizably the mosque he built with its wide-sweeping court, its pavilions and sanctuaries, and walls thick with mosaics. If the Dome of the Rock was an act of pure mercy, a sudden spring of beauty issuing above a rock which had seen too many sacrifices, the Great Umayyad Mosque was an act of the purest beneficence. We learn nothing about Abd-al-Malik by gazing at the Dome of the Rock, but we can learn all we want to know about Walid by gazing at the Great Mosque, where the courtyard resembles a great barrack square and the interior with its marble floor and wooden roof and delicate traceries resembles nothing so much as a queen's palace. *Luxe, calme et volupté* are its guardian angels, and there is more than a hint of Byzantine magnificence, yet without stiffness.

Byzantium, indeed, contributed greatly to the mosque. According to Arabic chroniclers, Walid summoned a fabulous army of Byzantine craftsmen (one writer says 1,200, another says 12,000) to decorate it with mosaics. Six hundred lamps hung on golden chains from the roof. The whole of the floor was glittering white marble, all the capitals were gilt, and the dome was covered with a sheeting of gold. For seven years the entire revenue of Syria was spent on building the mosque, not counting eighteen shiploads of gold and silver from Cyprus. From the Church of St. Mary at Antioch and from a hundred other churches columns were looted to decorate the interior and the colonnades. Precise figures and details of the construction have been handed down. We know, for example, that the cost of the cabbages eaten by the workmen amounted to 6,000 dinars. When the building was completed, Walid refused to look at the account books which were brought to him on eighteen laden mules, but ordered that they should be burned. And at the ceremonial opening of the mosque he made it clear that the mosque was a present to Damascus. To the crowd gathered in the mosque he said: 'O people of Damascus, five great gifts have been given to you! The first is the sweetness of your water, the second the sweetness of your air, the third the succulence of your fruits, the fourth the number of your bath-houses, the fifth is this mosque!'

Three times the mosque has been destroyed by fire almost to the foundation walls—in 1069, when it was set on fire during riots between the Fatimids and the Shi'as; in 1400, when Damascus was sacked by Timurlane; and most recently in 1893—but each time it has arisen phoenix-like from the flames. According to the Syrian geographer Muqaddasi, who wrote at the end of the tenth century, the whole mosque inside and outside gleamed with mosaics depicting all the cities of the known world, and all these mosaics were a present from the Byzantine Emperor. Muqaddasi added that all these cities were uninhabited, in deference to Muhammadan distaste for making portraits of people. We may doubt whether the Byzantine Emperor was so generous, and until recently it was permissible to doubt whether the Great Mosque once contained an immense mosaic picture gallery of cities. In 1928, when whitewash was cleared from the walls, remnants of Walid's mosaics were found in a perfect state of preservation. They glittered brilliantly. They depicted cities. They showed clearly the influence of Byzantine craftsmen. The French archaeologist De Lorey, who uncovered the mosaics, found an immense strip of mosaic 115 feet long and nearly 24 feet high depicting Damascus itself as it was 1,300 years ago, with the details of summer palaces and kiosks and highways readily identifiable from the descriptions left by the geographer Istakhri. We recognize the bridge, surprisingly like the Rialto at Venice, soaring over the golden flood of the Barada River, the palaces amid the cypresses, the minarets of the innumerable mosques. Houses pile on houses, as they always do in Byzantine mosaics, and there is nothing in the least singular in the absence of people wandering in that landscape at the first touch of dawn, when the air is fresher and the eye sees farthest. It is almost a relief to see mosaics which are not filled with saints in postures of hieratic prowess. Byzantine churches are filled with so many blazing and accusing eyes, so many muscular folds of draperies, that we turn with relief to these mosaics where nothing is being proved and where the aim of the artist is to demonstrate only the greatness of man's creations under the sun. Here there are no Pantocrators summoning men to judgment, only quiet cities gleaming in a summer light.

Accustomed to tracing Biblical legends in mosaics, we forget that mosaics have a life of their own, continually quivering; and to set people wandering in them is to invite a reduplication of life. There is a perfection in these mosaics equalled nowhere else except perhaps in those rare architectural details which appear in the mosaics of Monreale and in the great tumbling fountain of the Prayer of St. Anne at Daphni, where the waters of life are held in continual motion by the refraction of the ever-changing light on them; but these mosaics belong to another age. They lack the essential gentleness, as they lack the formal abstract quality, of the mosaics in Damascus. Here and there among the scraps of mosaic preserved in the Great Umayyad Mosque, other cities can be recognized—Jerusalem, Mecca, perhaps Antioch, all of them represented with an exquisite refinement in subtly shaded green, blue and gold. In these mosaics we are made aware of Byzantine technique operating within the formal limits of the Muhammadan imagination. The Christian, pausing in the galleries of the Great Umayyad Mosque or standing on the terrace which surrounds the Dome of the Rock, cannot but observe a quality conspicuously lacking in most of Christian art—the quality of an extreme serenity. Within three generations of Muhammad we are already far removed from the preoccupations of the desert dwellers and from Muhammad's fiery and reckless imagination as he contemplated the flames of the Last Day. This extreme serenity, if it comes from anywhere, must come from *islam*, the complete submission to the will of God.

The Umayyads settled the course of Muhammadan art for centuries to come. Nothing greater than the Dome of the Rock or the Great Umayyad Mosque was ever conceived. The marriage of Byzantine and Hellenistic techniques to the driving force of the Muhammadan imagination was long enduring. There were to be subtle changes later. The Damescene spring was to ripen into a Persian summer: in time the colours and shapes of Persia were to overlay the simpler contours of Damascus and Jerusalem, adding always an element of restlessness. But in remote provinces of central Asia, in Spain and Africa, wherever the Muhammadan artists were at work, we shall be continually reminded of the early beauty.

Serenity was the aim, but there were many restless paths to it. Surviving Umayyad art reflects the path of contemplation, but every religious movement involves a variety of different approaches to God. There is the way of faith, the way of illumination, the way of ritual, the way of the sword. Muhammad envisaged a time when the whole world would be conquered by the sword for Islam, and Walid very nearly did conquer the world.

In the east the Arab armies under Qutaybah ibn-Muslim captured Ferghana and reached the frontiers of China. In Africa Musa ibn-Nusayr, the son of Muawiya's chief of police, dominated the lands from Egypt to the Atlantic. Muhammad ibn-Qasim, the son-in-law of Hajjaj, drove out of southern Persia and Baluchistan until he reached the sea near the modern Karachi, conquering most of the area represented by present-day Pakistan and so drawing northwestern India forever into the Muhammadan fold. Preparations for the conquest of China had advanced to the stage where a governor and administrators were being appointed. The most dramatic of these conquests was provided by an obscure Berber freedman called Tariq ibn-Ziyad who crossed the narrow straits between Africa and Spain, took possession of the Rock of Gibraltar, which has ever since borne his name (*Jabal Tariq*), and then with 7,000 men, mostly Berbers, descended upon the province of Algeciras and routed an army of 25,000 under Roderick, the last of the Visigothic kings. With the remnants of Roderick's army in full flight, the gates of Spain were thrown wide open. In three years there were Arab armies on the Pyrenees.

When the first reports of Tariq's victory were received, Musa ibn-Nusayr wrote to the Caliph in Damascus: 'O Commander of the Faithful, these are not common conquests: they are like the meeting of nations on the Day of Judgment.' Similar reports could have been sent from all the embattled frontiers of the empire. The earth trembled. Panic seized the enemies of Islam as they watched the approach of small and relentless columns which marched by night and fought during the day, and carried everything before them. Cordova fell by a ruse; Malaga surrendered; Elvira was taken by storm; so it was throughout the peninsula as the Visigoths, divided among themselves, fell back towards the mountains of the Asturias. The Visigothic capital Toledo was found to be undefended, and when Tariq entered it in triumph most of its treasure, including a jewelled table said to have belonged to King Solomon, was intact.

The speed of Tariq's march brought Musa ibn-Nusayr, Viceroy of Africa, out of his fortress city of Qayrawan to inspect this new addition to the empire. In the summer of 712, a year after Tariq's columns began their march across Spain, he sailed with 10,000 Arabians and Syrians across the straits and amused himself by attacking the cities which Tariq had by-passed. He caught up with Tariq in Toledo, and there is a story that he ordered the conqueror of Spain to be whipped and held in chains. But some months later we hear of further conquests by Tariq, and though there seem to have been disagreements between them, it is unlikely that they were serious. In the autumn of 713, both generals were recalled to Damascus. The Caliph appears to have been mildly disapproving, but permitted them to return in triumph at the head of an army of prisoners, which included 400 of the Visigothic nobility wearing their coronets and massive gold belts of office, with the treasure of the captured cities. A thousand Spanish virgins took part in the triumphal march of Musa ibn-Nusayr across North Africa, and the Arab poets delighted to dilate on the beauty of these fair-haired prisoners, the number of the slaves, the wealth of gold plate and jewels in the baggage trains. Nothing quite like this brilliant cavalcade had ever taken place before since the Roman triumphators marched through the streets of Rome to the Temple of Jupiter Capitolinus. At last in February, 715, after more than a year of

The leaning minaret of the Great Mosque, Mosul, built in A.D. 1172. The brickwork is typical of Atabeg decoration, at one time prevalent in this part of Iraq

(*Above*) The Friday Mosque, Samarra. The spiralled tower and massive buttressed walls were erected by Caliph Ja'far-al-Mutawakkil after Samarra had become the capital of the Abbasid caliphate. Later the city was abandoned when the caliph moved his capital back to Baghdad

(*Left*) An arabesque from the Abbasid Palace, Baghdad, characteristic of the decorative style evolved by the early Islamic masons

marching, the prisoners were assembled in the vast courtyard of the Great Umayyad Mosque, recently completed, and presented to the Caliph. All the treasure of Spain lay at the Caliph's feet, and never in the history of Damascus had there been so great a triumph.

Walid was already ailing when the Spanish captives were brought to him. He died a few weeks later at the age of forty, having reigned for nearly ten years. The Syrians still remember him as the most beloved of their kings.

The Umayyads never reached these heights again. For thirty-five more years they ruled over their empire, fought battles, vigorously pursued their aim of conquering the whole world, and watched the tide rolling back. A succession of brilliant Caliphs attempted to organize a seemingly perpetual victory which God had granted to the Umayyads. They were cultivated men, scholars and poets, and most of them inherited the great gifts of Abd-al-Malik, who gave four sons, two nephews and three grandchildren to the Caliphate.

Arab chroniclers delight in describing the private lives of rulers: so it happens that we know the numbers of their mistresses, their behaviour during drinking parties and in the boudoir, and what animals they pursued as they rode out of their hunting lodges in Syria and Palestine. We know, for example, that Walid's successor, his brother Sulayman, was a fat voluptuary with a passion for the soft Yamanite silks known as *wachi*, which he wore on all occasions, even demanding that he should be buried in them, and we are told that he kept plump cooked chickens in his sleeves and would suddenly gnaw at them in the middle of an audience. No doubt these stories are true, but it is also true that during his brief reign he organized the greatest of the Umayyad expeditions against Constantinople. He conquered Pergamum and Sardis, crossed the Dardanelles at Abydos and blockaded Constantinople by land and sea, throwing a chain across the Golden Horn, so preventing the Byzantine fleet from sailing out of the harbour. Of all the Arab assaults on Constantinople this was the most threatening, the closest to success. It failed only because the pestilence broke out on his ships.

Sulayman possessed the resilience of Muawiya, and much of Muawiya's ruthlessness. He had always detested the excesses of Hajjaj, who had died during the reign of Walid, and his first act on coming to the throne was to open the prison doors and set free the prisoners thrown by Hajjaj into the countless prisons of the East. For this he was granted among the people the title of 'the Key of Blessing'; and for long afterwards it was remembered that he not only freed the prisoners, but gave them gifts and asked for their pardon. His rages were as sudden as his acts of generosity. For some unexplained reason the weight of his hatred fell on Musa ibn-Nusayr, the conqueror of Spain. Hot words were exchanged, and suddenly the Viceroy of Africa was deprived of his rank and titles, and reduced to penury. He shared the fate of Khalid, 'the Sword of God', and when last heard of he was a wandering beggar in a remote village of the Hijaz.

Sulayman, the fat voluptuary, belongs to the great tradition of Umayyad

I

monarchs: he possessed, like many enormously fat people, a steady, driving intelligence. He died of the plague in 717, and was succeeded by his saintly brother Umar, a gentle ascetic, of whom it was said that he was always praying and most of the things he prayed for came true. Umar had been kicked by a mule when a child, and bore the marks of the mule's hoof on his face for the rest of his life, but no one thought the worse of him for his strange appearance. Brilliant, gentle and unassuming, he liked to wander among his subjects wearing such old patched clothes that it was difficult to recognize him, and petitioners complained of how they had spent days in search of him even when he was known to be in the streets of Damascus. He had a fondness for discussing theology, but he was no unworldly theologian, and allowed the Arab troops on the borders of France to penetrate deep into the interior, conquering Septimania and setting up their headquarters at Narbonne, apparently with the intention of colonizing all southern France and pushing on to Italy. He restored to the Christians and Jews the churches which had been taken from them, and attempted to conciliate the followers of Ali by restoring to them the oasis at Fardak, which Muhammad had claimed as his private property. When he came to the throne he ordered the horses of the royal stables to be sold in public auction and deposited the proceeds in the state treasury; and wherever possible, he remitted and reduced taxes.

Such evident goodness had its penalties. He was sometimes greeted in the streets with the reverence reserved for divinities. During his life a cult arose around his name, and he was believed by some to be the *mahdi*, 'the guided one', the one who will lead the world into the paths of peace. On his mother's side he was descended from the first Caliph Umar, whom he resembled. He was completely bald, wore a heavy black beard and was so thin that his ribs could be counted by the naked eye.

Innumerable stories were told concerning his piety, his fastings, his night-long prayers, his terror of death, the sweetness of his smile. One day his seventeen-year-old son spoke to him half-reproachfully about the evils in the society of his time. According to the son, these evils should be rooted out by a stern Caliph. 'Stern measures?' the Caliph exclaimed. 'That means the sword, and there are no good reforms which can be accomplished by the sword.' He died after a reign of two years, perhaps as a result of his austerities, and his grave became a place of pilgrimage. Arab historians rank him among the small group of 'righteous' Caliphs, which includes Abu Bakr, Umar and Ali. The Umayyad Caliph Umar was the gentlest of them all, and no more gentle Caliphs came after him.

Umar was a nephew of Abd-al-Malik, and was succeeded on the throne by two more of Abd-al-Malik's sons. Of Yazid II, who was married to the niece of Hajjaj, little is known for certainty, though legends have proliferated around him. He is described as the perfect type of the aesthete, in love with music and poetry, content to waste his days among his singing girls instead of ruling his empire. It is related that when he playfully threw a grape into the mouth of his favourite singing girl Hababah, she choked to death and the Caliph died a few days later of a broken heart.

It may have happened, but it is unlikely. A more pleasant story related about him concerns Fatima, the daughter of the martyred Husayn, who was living in retirement in Madinah. The governor of Madinah was pestering her with his attentions, threatening her with ill treatment. Fatima appealed to the Caliph, who deposed the governor and severely punished him.

With Hisham (724–43) the Umayyad dynasty comes virtually to an end. Strong, proud, relentless in his determination to wield power over the empire, Hisham lacked the quality of resilience which had maintained so many of his predecessors in office. He had all the virtues; he was thrifty, generous, devoted to handicrafts. He encouraged weaving, improved the art of the armourer, and was especially interested in drainage works, but his virtues were equalled only by his vices. He was suspicious, bigoted and utterly unforgiving. When Zayd ibn-Ali, the grandson of Husayn, and still only a boy, raised the standard of revolt in al-Kufah, Hisham gave orders that the revolt should be put down mercilessly. Zayd was wounded by an arrow lodged in his forehead, and taken to a doctor who removed the arrow so carelessly that he bled to death. The doctor feared the consequences of having treated an enemy and secretly buried the body near a canal and then diverted the canal to flow over the body. He left a marker near the place, and vowed everyone who knew about the burial of the boy to secrecy, but Hisham heard of it—his spy system was accounted the best among the Umayyad Caliphs. In a rage Hisham ordered the body dug up and demanded that the head be sent to Damascus. 'As for the rest of his accursed body,' he wrote, 'let it be hung on a gibbet until nothing is left of it.' For weeks the people of Damascus were forced to look on the head of a descendant of Muhammad fixed to a palm tree.

A bitter man, who had lost one eye in his youth, Hisham raged remorselessly against his enemies. He had enemies everywhere. There were uprisings in Africa and Iraq; corruption was rampant in the government of the provinces; the Byzantine armies were surging across Asia Minor. He was always building castles on the frontiers, but the tide was already turning, threatening to engulf him and his house.

It is possible that he paid very little attention to an event that occurred on the borders of his empire in the west, near an old Roman paved road, among the forests overlooking the Loire. No doubt some reports of this obscure skirmish with the Austrasian Franks must have reached him, but it is unlikely that he did more than glance at them—there were more important battles being fought in other parts of the empire.

In October, 732—it was a hundred years after Muhammad's death—a scouting party belonging to the army of Abd ar-Rahman ibn-Abdallah, the governor of Spain, made contact with the Frankish army of Charles of Heristal, the mayor of the palace of the Merovingian court, along the road between Poitiers and Tours. The Arab commander did not know that a trap had been set for him. Eudo, Duke of Aquitaine, had been besieged between the Garonne and the Dordogne and fled in the direction of the Loire with the Arabs in hot pursuit. Unexpectedly the Frankish commander, thought to be in some other part of France altogether, stood across the Arab line of march. Abd ar-Rahman called a halt. He wanted to discover the strength of the enemy, and he hoped the Franks, if not too numerous, would attack. What frightened him most of all was the possibility of losing his army among the forests and the streams.

For seven days Charles of Heristal remained on the edge of the forest, waiting for the attack. It was bitterly cold weather, with the Arabs still dressed for their summer campaigns. The wolf pelts of the Franks helped them in the icy cold. At last on the morning of the seventh day Abd ar-Rahman decided to attack. Charles held firm, forming his men in a hollow square to take the main charge of the Arabs while dispatching raiders along unfrequented forest pathways to attack the Arabs in the rear. The Arabs, once guerrillas, had reverted to a classical mode of warfare, and were no match for the Franks, who numbered many more well-equipped soldiers than the Arab spies had indicated. Also, the Franks were fighting with the river at their back, and could not retreat even if they had wanted to. The Arabs marching through France had acquired immense booty, and this too worked in the favour of the Franks, who were not weighed down with the task of guarding their treasure, nor did they possess baggage trains of any kind. Most of them were foot soldiers, but there were some companies of cavalry.

As the battle progressed, the Franks began to waver. Not in vain had Hisham ordered his best metalsmiths to study the problems of armour. Behind their coats of mail, their pointed helmets, their horses clothed in chain mail, the Arabs were almost impregnable. They were on the verge of victory when the Franks fought their way towards the treasure carts. Instead of fighting in column, the Arabs flew to the defence of the treasure, and panicked when they saw the carts being driven away by enemies. Abd ar-Rahman ordered his troops back into line, but he was too late. A lance killed him. Then, while the armies were still fighting confusedly, night fell. Both armies retired to lick their wounds.

All through the night the spies of Charles heard the clash of arms as the lieutenants of Abd ar-Rahman quarrelled bitterly over the election of a new leader. A small-scale civil war was being fought by the Arabs over the treasure carts. Towards dawn the sounds of fighting ceased, and when the sun came through the clouds on that cold October Sunday, Charles saw that the enemy had vanished. They were hurrying south, away from the northern winter and smell of defeat in the marshes of the Loire.

To the Arabs the battle is known as *balat al-shuhada*, meaning 'the pavement of martyrs', after the paved Roman road which ran along the edge of the forest. It was the turning point of the undeclared war against western Europe which had become inevitable once Tariq had captured Gibraltar. At the time, however, neither the Arabs nor the Franks were aware there had been a turning point. Checked near Tours, the Arabs continued to send expeditions across France. They crossed the Rhône, captured St.-Rémi, and marched against Avignon, which surrendered after a short siege. They advanced on Valence and Lyons, spread into Burgundy and threatened Paris. Charles, who assumed the title of Martel, or 'the Hammer', meaning that he regarded himself as the hammer appointed by God to punish the Arabs, summoned the assistance of the Lombards, instigated a revolt by the Basques and Gascons in the south, and harried the enemy unmercifully. Avignon was recaptured for the Franks, and Nîmes, long occupied by the Arabs, was put to flames. Terror in France led to terror in Spain, where the governor was taken prisoner and killed by rebels. Narbonne was abandoned by its commander, and one by one the captured cities of France were reconquered by the Franks.

In another age, under happier auspices, Hisham might have been able to hold back the tide. He held off the threatened collapse of his empire, but he was unable to pour into it any revivifying strength. The Berbers in Africa, the Persians and the Turks in Transoxiana, were in a state of constant revolt; and everywhere he looked he could see the disintegrating frontiers. Much sooner than he expected a small band of determined men would attack the empire at its heart and destroy it utterly.

During the last years of his long reign—he ruled for nearly twenty years—Hisham gives the appearance of a sleepwalker. He seems not to have known or cared what was happening, as he amused himself with his horses on his estate at Rusafah on the Euphrates. He liked horses more than he liked men, and no other king ever had such a vast stable: he was reputed to have 4,000 horses. Arab chroniclers credit him with being the inventor of horse racing. He died at the age of fifty-three at his beloved Rusafah, far from the capital, having in one of his rare moments of imprudence assigned the succession to his nephew Walid, the son of Yazid II. Under Hisham the fruit had ripened; under Walid it rotted.

At first Damascus greeted the arrival of the new Caliph with jubilation. Of all the Umayyad princes he was the most handsome, the keenest-witted, the most generous. He was a reckless horseman, an exceptional poet, a gifted musician. He came to the throne with all the talents, and was immediately corrupted by power. We know of countless rulers who suffered on themselves the processes of corruption, but few were corrupted so easily or rejoiced in it with so much grace and ease. There was something almost heroic in his acceptance of the role of a corrupt emperor at a time when the empire was shuddering at the foundations. From his uncle he had inherited an empire which stretched from the steppes of Mongolia to Morocco, included Arabia, Egypt, Spain and North Africa, and most of the islands of the Mediterranean—Majorca, Minorca, Corsica, Sardinia, Crete, Rhodes, Cyprus, a part of Sicily and nearly all the islands of the Aegean. There was hardly another man in the empire less fitted to rule than this Caliph who possessed to such an exaggerated degree the typical virtues and vices of the Umayyads—ruthlessness, artistic sensibility, physical beauty, charm, gentleness, furious impatience.

None of the histories written by the Umayyads have survived, and we see them now through the eyes of the historians who came later and who owed allegiance to another dynasty. We do not have to believe everything they say about his profligacy, his wine-bibbing, his atheism. He said once:

'I wish all women were lionesses so that only the strong and courageous would dare to approach them,' and the phrase, which would have pleased the poet William Butler Yeats, rings true. He thought more of poets than of politicians, and that is no crime except in emperors. He summoned to his court all the best singers and dancers of the empire, and rewarded them with an open hand. He raised the pay of the soldiers, and increased the allowances of the poor, the blind and the insane, following the example of Walid I. He followed the Umayyad custom of hounding the descendants of Ali. Yahya, the son of the murdered Zayd, raised the flag of revolt, and Walid gave orders that he should be hunted down. Yahya was determined to die fighting, rather than to be killed like vermin. He died in the way he had sought, and his head was sent to Walid and his body impaled on a cross. Such ruthlessness was commonplace; and in this, as in so many other things, Walid was only obeying the traditions of his house. But to these typical virtues and vices there was added after he came to power a ferocious and untamable pride, a sense of magnificence which went far beyond the self-regarding splendours of Muawiya. Masudi tells the story of how he was one day reading the Quran when he came upon the verses demanding of all men their complete submission to the will of God. Walid was enraged. He set up the Quran on the other side of the room and shot arrow after arrow at it, until the pages were reduced to tatters, and then this accomplished poet, who must be accounted among the best of his time, wrote the terrible verses:

> Dare you threaten me in my proud rebellion?
> I am Walid—the most rebellious of men!
> O Quran, when you appear at the Judgment Seat,
> Tell God who it was who tore you to shreds!

We do not have to believe Masudi's story entirely to know that Walid was corrupted by power and pride, and was tempted to wrestle with God. He comes to us like one of those emperors in the plays of Christopher Marlowe who are not content with making war against earthly princes, but must measure themselves with angels, and like those tragic heroes he must suffer for his sins. He had been ruling for only a year when Yazid, the son of Walid I by a Soghdian princess, entered Damascus in disguise and, after discovering a store of weapons hidden in a mosque, announced publicly that he was preparing to destroy the most profligate of Caliphs. The Damascenes flocked to his standards and marched towards Bakhra, south of Palmyra, where Walid was at that time living in a fortress castle. Walid tried to parlay with the insurgents, and then with his small company of guards fought them. At last, knowing he was outnumbered, he retired to an inner room of the castle, opened the Quran, and waited for the death blow. His head was cut off and paraded through the streets of Damascus on a spear, and the son of the Soghdian princess, under the title of Yazid III, came to the throne.

Yazid was known as 'the retrencher' because he reduced the pay of his soldiers. He was the first Caliph to be born of a slave mother, and gave promise of strong leadership. In his inaugural speech from the throne he explained why he was compelled to revolt against his cousin, promised to fortify the frontiers, to place the cities in a proper state of defence, to remove the heavy burdens of taxation on the common people, and to rid the empire of dishonest officials. These plans were admirable, but time was running out; and when he died mysteriously in 744 after a reign of five months and two days, to be succeeded by his brother Ibrahim, who reigned for only two months and is therefore not included among the list of Umayyad Caliphs, everyone knew the empire was disintegrating for lack of a central authority. A slight blow, coming from some unexpected direction, might reduce the whole empire to fragments, unless a dictator could be found.

A dictator was found in the person of Marwan ibn-Muhammad, a grandson of the Caliph Marwan ibn-al-Hakam, a professional soldier with a stern sense of duty and an undying distaste for amateur Caliphs. He was known as Marwan al-Himar, meaning Marwan the Ass, not in derision, but in acknowledgment of his noble appearance and his powers of endurance. He lived with his soldiers, and ate their fare: the army was passionately loyal to him. If the problems of a failing empire could be solved by a sixty-year-old soldier who was genuinely worshipped by the people, the Umayyad dynasty might have been preserved. But around the real and imagined descendants of Ali explosive forces congregated. Sanctity was theirs; they could do no evil; to them had been entrusted spiritual powers which outweighed the temporal powers of the Caliphs of Damascus. In the Persian province of Khurasan especially there existed a deep-lying bitterness against the Umayyads for having murdered so many of Ali's descendants. A saddler called Abd ar-Zahman, who assumed the name of Abu Muslim, raised the black flag of rebellion in 747. Then within a few months the whole patiently acquired empire which had endured for ninety years toppled over and went to its death.

Like so many of those strange revolutionaries who emerged out of Khurasan at regular intervals in the history of Persia, Abu Muslim was a figure of mystery. Part of the mystery was of his own making. He was originally a Persian slave sold in the markets of Mecca to the head of the branch of the Quraysh clan which was descended from the Prophet's uncle al-Abbas. The slave soon identified himself with the claims of the Abbasids, who believed that the sacred blood of Muhammad in some mysterious fashion flowed through their veins. They were unlikely claimants to the Caliph's throne, but they could truthfully call themselves Ahl al-bait, or 'People of the House', and these words became the watchword of the people of Khurasan as they sought for some way to put an end to the accursed Umayyads.

On June 17, 747, Abu Muslim summoned the people by lighting large bonfires on the hilltops, and explained the purpose of the revolt. It was a very simple purpose—the destruction of the Umayyads to the last man by bands of dedicated and remorseless men. They flew the black banners of the Abbasids and wore black clothes, and saluted the banners known as 'the Cloud' and 'the Shadow'. The symbolism was deliberate: like clouds and shadows the armies of the Abbasids would pour out of Persia on to the plains of Iraq, and so to the coasts of Syria. Soon the Arab garrisons in Khurasan were disaffected, and the provincial governor Nasr ibn-Sayyar wrote a desperate appeal to Marwan for assistance. In the fashion of the day he wrote in verse:

> I see the red coals glowing among the embers, about to blaze:
> Fire springs from the rubbing of sticks, and out of words comes war.
> I cry in dismay: Are the Umayyads asleep, or will they ever awake?

The message reached the Caliph when he was busy with rebels in Jordan and Syria; no help reached Khurasan. Merv fell, then Nihawand, and the road was open to Iraq. Abu-l-Abbas Abdallah was at that time the head of the Abbasid house, and when the army under Abu Muslim reached al-Kufah he emerged from hiding, marched to the cathedral mosque, pronounced a sermon on the virtues of his family and was elected Caliph by acclamation. War between the Umayyads and the Abbasids had become inevitable.

With an army 120,000 strong, Abu Muslim and Abu-l-Abbas Abdallah forded the Tigris and pitched camp between Mosul and Arbela on the river Zab. The two armies met in January, 750, and the battle raged for nine days. The legions of the Abbasids were clothed from head to foot in black, in mourning for the martyrs, with camels, horses and standards all draped in black, and in their solemn appearance they looked, said one Arab chronicler, like deaf-mutes. They moved silently. They behaved like automatons. Like Abu Muslim, who was famous for his impassivity, they deliberately assumed the air of people who did not belong to this earth; they resembled avenging angels. Marwan was a professional soldier and not unduly impressed. He led the charge, and the Abbasids gave way. The turning point came, as it came so often, when the commanding general was thrown from his horse; at the sight of Marwan's riderless horse plunging through the battlelines, the Umayyads panicked. Marwan fled to Mosul and then to Harran, and so to Damascus, with the Abbasids in hot pursuit. For a few weeks Marwan held off the Abbasids, but in April they stormed the city and stabled their horses in the courtyard of the Great Umayyad Mosque; and Marwan was in flight again. The black flag of the Abbasids waved over Damascus while Marwan hurried south, hoping to gather enough troops to make a stand, running like a frightened hare through Palestine and across the desert until he came to Egypt. One night in August he was resting in a Christian church at Busir in Lower Egypt when he heard a voice shouting in Persian. He had thought he was safe, but the Persian voice told him that the Abbasids were gathered round his hiding place. Suddenly there was a roll of kettledrums, and the air was full of black flags waving in the wind. Marwan put on his cuirass and rushed out of the church sword in hand. There was a brief battle, and then Marwan fell with a javelin in his stomach. Some time later one of Marwan's followers revealed where the sacred emblems were hidden. They had been buried a little way from the church. So it happened that the mantle of Muhammad, his finger ring and staff, fell into the possession of Abu-l-Abbas Abdallah, who called himself *as-Saffah*, or 'the Shedder of Blood', and a new dynasty which was to last for five hundred years was founded.

The Umayyads had attempted to destroy all the descendants of Ali. The Abbasids even more ruthlessly attempted to destroy the last vestiges of Umayyad rule. They exterminated all but one of the entire caliphal family. Eighty Umayyad princes were invited to a banquet near Jaffa on the promise of an amnesty; the banquet had hardly started when the executioners entered, strangled the princes one by one, and covered the bodies with leather cushions while the banqueters went on feasting. With unheard-of ferocity they hounded down their enemies. Princess Abdah, the daughter of Caliph Hisham, refused to divulge the place where she had hidden her jewels, and was cut down with a sword. Sometimes they murdered by mockery. Prince Aban, a grandson of the same Caliph, with one hand and one foot cut off, was led on an ass through the villages of Syria while a herald cried: 'Behold Aban, son of Muawiya, the most renowed cavalier of the Umayyad house!' The Abbasids were not content to kill the living, but wreaked vengeance on the dead. They dug up the graves of the Caliphs and amused themselves by whipping the poor remnants of their bodies, and then throwing them to the flames. They found the long-dead Caliph Hisham in his robes of state, well-preserved except for his nose, which had gone—he received eighty strokes of the whip as a posthumous punishment. Fat Sulayman had become a skeleton, but they burned it. The tomb of Walid I was empty, and in the tomb of Abd-al-Malik there was only a skull, and in the tomb of Yazid I only a single bone and a little black dust. Thus in the first days of the new dynasty the ceremonies of purification were performed by men weighed down by a sense of outrage: the past must be purified by being put to the flames. Significantly, the rebellion had its origins in Khurasan, where until the Arab conquest men worshipped, not the One God, but the living flame of the sun.

Henceforward the influence of Persia was to be felt increasingly in the Muhammadan world. The Umayyad Caliphs, emerging from Arabia, descendants of the obscure nobility of Mecca, had gradually assumed the temper and the panoply of Byzantine emperors. Inevitably the Caliphs of the House of Abbas, emerging from Khurasan, assumed many of the habits, the rituals and the brilliant colouring of the great Sassanian emperors, whose dynasty was destroyed by the Arab conquerors. The Arabs began to lose their influence, not only in the army and at court, but in society. The highest positions were given to Persians, who were never able to divorce themselves completely from the tenets of Zoroaster, with the result that Muhammadanism began to lose its rough-hewn character, and survived as a delicate balance of forces, a compromise between incompatible passions. In every Persian breast Zoroaster and Muhammad were at war with one another; and only the Persian genius for mysticism and his unrivalled sense of the delicate and often contrary patterns running through the universe permitted this war to be fought without too much bloodshed. Muhammad, seen through Persian eyes, resembled one of the great kings of the Achaemenian dynasty, another Cyrus. They made Muhammad over in their own image; and, possessing an instinct for martyrdom, they gave to Ali, Hasan and Husayn an especial place of honour equal to that of the Messenger of God. It is one of the greater ironies of history that within a little more than a hundred years of Muhammad's death, Islam was conquered by the Persians whom Muhammad regarded as the most effete nation on earth.

In their efforts to stamp out the influence of the Umayyads the Persians were not completely successful. One of the few who escaped was Abd-ar-Rahman ibn-Muawiya, the brother of the mutilated Prince Aban, grandson of the tenth Umayyad Caliph Hisham. Red-haired, handsome and superbly well-equipped to be a soldier, he was nineteen years old when the Abbasid Caliph Abu-l-Abbas ordered the proscription of the entire Umayyad family. One night he fled to the safety of a Bedouin camp on the left bank of the Euphrates River. He was not alone: with him went his thirteen-year-old brother Yahya, two sisters and his four-year-old son Sulayman. Abd ar-Rahman was ill in bed, suffering from inflammation of the eyes, when he was startled by the sudden cries of Sulayman, who shouted that horsemen with black banners were approaching. There was little he could do for his sisters except to provide them with money and commend them to the mercy of the enemy. With Yahya and his son he fled along the riverbank, hotly pursued by the cavalry patrol; and when the cavalry had almost caught up with him he jumped into the river with his son in his arms, while Yahya, terror-stricken, followed him, only to turn back when the captain of the patrol shouted: 'Return! We mean no harm!' Yahya swam back to the shore, and was immediately seized and beheaded, while Abd ar-Rahman continued his flight, making his way slowly towards Morocco, perhaps because his mother was a Berber princess and he knew he would find relatives there. After five years of wandering in disguise, he landed in Spain at Almuñecar on the coast between Málaga and Almería. Within eight months he had gathered a small army and was ready to attack the governor of Spain; and at the battle of Musarah, west of Cordova, on the banks of the Guadalquivir, on May 14, 756, he defeated Yusuf al-Fihri, a descendent of Uqbah, the conqueror of Africa, and immediately afterwards established his capital at Cordova. The Umayyads had lost the world and acquired Spain.

Abd ar-Rahman was the exception. Tall and lean, hawk-faced, with enormous eyes and a winning smile, he possessed the characteristic virtues of the Umayyads and none of their vices. He ruled like a benevolent despot, built canals, introduced peaches and palm trees to Spain, wrote excellent poetry, and delighted in embellishing the cities he had conquered. He did not assume the title of Caliph 'out of respect for the seat of the Caliphate, which is still the abode of Islam and the meeting-place of the Arabian tribes'. Instead he called himself 'emir of Spain'. He founded a dynasty which ruled for nearly three hundred years.

One day shortly after the conquest of Damascus, the new Caliph's brother Abu Ja'far, known to history as al-Mansur, was discussing with a group of friends the reasons for the fall of the Umayyads. They were, after all, very simple reasons. None of the Caliphs—there were a few exceptions—were men who possessed the gift of rulership. There was Abd al-Malik, a man of such violent temper that he scarcely knew what he was doing at any given moment; there was Sulayman, who thought only of his stomach; there was the pious Umar, 'a blind man among blind men'; the only real ruler among them had been Hisham. These verdicts were caustic, and modern historians would have difficulty in substantiating them, yet they pointed to the defects in the Umayyad character—violence, ruthlessness, insensitivity, too great a love of luxury. At that time Abu Ja'far was in Nubia, taking part in the mopping-up campaign which was the inevitable consequence of the conquest of Egypt after the death of Marwan. It happened that Abdullah, the son of Marwan, had been taken prisoner a few days earlier. The friends decided to ask Abdullah, a man who had occupied high positions of state, for his own verdict on his family. He answered:

These were our faults—we gave to pleasure the time we should have devoted to government. We laid heavy burdens on our people, and so alienated them from our rule. We taxed them so heavily, and gave them so little opportunity for redress, that they prayed for deliverance from us. We left our fields uncultivated, and our treasury was empty. We trusted our ministers, but they pursued their own selfish interests and governed the country in their own right and left us in ignorance. The pay of the army was always in arrears, and so in the hour of danger they sided with the enemy; and our allies failed us when we needed them most. But the chief causes of the fall of our empire lay in our ignorance in government and our innocence, for we never knew what was happening.

We never knew what was happening. . . . There is a sense in which none of the Umayyads had ever known. They had stolen the sword of Islam and the thunder of Muhammad without ever knowing how they could be put to use in the service of mankind. Muhammad had spoken of 'the brotherhood of the faithful', but the Caliphs of Damascus had destroyed that brotherhood by elevating themselves to the ranks of earthly emperors. In time the House of Abbas, ruling from Baghdad, was to fall by the same defects, the same presumptuous innocence.

THE CALIPHS OF BAGHDAD

THERE IS a glow in the Persian imagination, as of softly burning coals: and sometimes the flames leap with startling brilliance only to die down again into a troubled darkness, but at the moment when all hope is lost, when there are no more flames and the embers are cold, there will emerge a great flare of flame, dazzling like the dawn. Again and again in the history of Persia there have been these sudden explosions of flame, and when the Persians captured Muhammadanism they drenched it in their own colours and gave it their own vivid intensity.

In nearly everything the Persian temperament differed from the Arab temperament, and had little enough in common with the strange mixture of oriental craft and western formality which characterized the Syrians. The Persians were of the east, eastern, not rootless like the Syrians, who were at the mercy of every wind that blew across the deserts of Judaea and the mountains of Lebanon. They were a settled people, who liked bright colours, luxury after hard riding and hunting, the majesty of kings. Muhammad said all men were brothers, Muhammad himself being brother to the meanest Negro slave, while the Persians wondered how a slave could be the brother of a nobleman. They were feudal and caste-ridden and believed deeply in the portentous God-given power of kings, visible or invisible. They were both gay and disputatious by instinct, and did not take easily to dogma. For more than a thousand years they had worshipped fire and regarded the summer and winter palaces of their Kings as the centres from which the beneficent influences of Ahura-mazda spread out like the rings on the surface of a pool when a stone is flung. They were passionately fond of women, flowers and animals; they saw no reason to dissemble their passions. The stern morality of Muhammad met the fierce Persian delight in luxury, their love of the splendour in all created things. It was inevitable that Muhammadanism under the influence of the Persians would become in time profoundly different from the Muhammadanism practised by the Arabs in Madinah and Damascus.

Yet in the early years of the Abbasid Caliphate there was little to suggest the splendour to come. The Caliph as-Saffah, 'the Shedder of Blood', the undisputed master of Asia and Egypt, was feared as much by his subjects as by those he had conquered. A morose, heavily built man, whose face sometimes lighted up with a fleeting smile, he surrounded himself with theologians and jurists, and, like Muawiya before him, amused himself by collecting *hadiths*. Harshly puritanical, he introduced many of the worst features of Sassanian rule. Beside the throne stood the executioner with the leather mat ready for the head of the victim. The Caliph regarded himself as the incarnation of the vengeance of God, a man more

than half divine, and brother to Muhammad, whose striped mantle he
sometimes wore at audiences. He wrote poetry filled with his lust for
blood:

> Our swords are dripping with blood, and they have brought vengeance:
> The great princes of the past brandished them on the battlefield:
> And the heads of our enemies are broken to fragments, like smashed ostrich eggs.

Such men found dynasties, but leave little trace of themselves. As-
Saffah built his capital at Hashimiyah in northern Iraq, and embellished
it with the treasure of Damascus, but the capital was soon abandoned. He
left no monuments to himself, and when he died of smallpox in his early
thirties he gave orders that his body should be buried in a secret place, because he feared the same treatment he had meted out to his fallen rivals.

His successor, his brother Abu Ja'far, called al-Mansur, 'the Victorious', was a man of a wholly different stamp. There was a fierce rage
in him, but he liked to keep it under control. He was harsh, gloomy and
austere, and they called him 'the Father of Farthings' because he was
avaricious, but he was not obsessed with the need for bloodshed and possessed a brilliant knowledge of the social and political forces at work.
As-Saffah was a tribal chieftain suffering from blood lust; al-Mansur was
an emperor.

The proud boast of the Abbasids was that they introduced a *dawlah*, or
new era. Al-Mansur brought peace and security to wide areas of his empire, and set out the laws which were to be followed in varying degrees by
his successors—those thirty-five Caliphs who were descended from him.
Tall and lean and very graceful, with a rosy complexion, he concealed his
passions under a mask of austerity, and relied heavily upon his Persian
advisers, his bodyguard from Khurasan and his astrologers, who were often
the descendants of Zoroastrian priests. His chief adviser was Khalid ibn-
Barmak, who had been as-Saffah's secretary and companion-at-arms, a
man of prodigious talent. His father was the chief priest of the fire temple
at Balkh, or perhaps—for accounts differ—the abbot of a Buddhist
monastery at the same place. Whether Buddhist or Zoroastrian, he was a
Persian and the man most responsible for bringing Persian customs and
attitudes to the court. He was so close to as-Saffah that his daughter was
nursed by the Caliph's wife, whose daughter in turn was nursed by
Khalid's wife. Men said there was never any difference of opinion between
the Caliph and his secretary: they could read each other's thoughts and
behaved like one man.

When al-Mansur came to the throne, he inherited Khalid and depended
upon him as his brother had done. Together they fought their wars and
worked out the principles of government, and it is almost certainly due to
Khalid that al-Mansur continued to rule like his brother with all the
trappings of a Sassanian king, wrapped in the inaccessible mantle of
kingship. The weapons of the new Caliph were tyranny and terror, more
violent and in their effects more sudden than the sporadic ruthlessness of
'the Shedder of Blood'. He hit hard, and then relaxed, to enjoy the peace
he acquired at the price of violence.

In the early years of his reign there was no end to violence. The mysterious and capable Abu Muslim had almost singlehandedly brought the Abbasids to power, and now demanded a position equal to his talents. In Khurasan a secret army waited to do his bidding. Offered the governorship of Egypt, he rejected it, preferring to remain among his own soldiers. In February, 755, when al-Mansur had been on the throne only a little more than six months, he lured Abu Muslim to his camp outside the walls of Ctesiphon on the plea that he needed advice and would not detain the great general for more than a little while. Abu Muslim came with his Khurasanian guards, and all the pomp at his command. Honours were heaped on him; he was permitted to ride on horseback right up to the Caliph's tent; the greatest friendliness was shown to him. Suddenly al-Mansur showed his true hand. He began to upbraid the general. He recalled one by one the crimes committed by Abu Muslim, who had once placed his own name before the Caliph's, and at another time demanded the Caliph's aunt in marriage, and even claimed to be a descendant of Abbas. The Caliph clapped his hands. The guards rushed in. Abu Muslim was armed, and fought off the guards for a few moments, but when his foot was sliced off, he knew the end had come, and fought no more. His body was wrapped in a mat and tossed into a corner of the tent. The Caliph called in one of his generals, Ja'far ibn-Hanzala, and asked him what he thought of Abu Muslim. The general, who knew or suspected that Abu Muslim was in disfavour, answered: 'If you have plucked as much as a single hair from his head, then you must kill, and kill again, and kill again.' 'Look under the mat,' the Caliph said, and when Ja'far had looked, he turned to the Caliph with a pleased smile and said: 'This day must be counted the first of your Caliphate.' 'Yes,' said al-Mansur, and he quoted the verses:

> The traveller threw away his staff at last:
> At the end of the journey he lay down to rest.

Some time later that day the body of Abu Muslim was thrown into the Tigris, and for the rest of his reign al-Mansur went without fear of a rival.

Abu Muslim represented the dissidents connected with the House of Abbas; there were others who were followers of the descendants of Ali. Against these al-Mansur fought remorselessly. Among them was Muhammad, a great-grandson of Hasan living in Madinah. He dug a ditch on the model of the famous ditch which had been dug by his great ancestor, and invited the Caliph to attack him. An army was sent to Arabia, the ditch was crossed, and Muhammad was killed. Within a year al-Mansur had killed so many of the followers and descendants of Ali that popular imagination pictured the Caliph as a nightly visitor to an immense chamber filled with their bodies: in the ear of each there was a label with his name and genealogy neatly written. Afterwards, when the Caliph's son Muhammad came to the throne, it was whispered that he was so horrified by the bodies he found in the chamber that he caused them to be buried.

It was a time of feverish excitement, of intense planning, of strange forms of worship. The Rawandiyah, a sect of Persian extremists, flocked to the court and paid the same tribute to the Caliph they would have paid to God. They worshipped him openly, hurled themselves before him when he was out riding, and became such a nuisance that the Caliph ordered them exterminated. It was counted in the Caliph's favour that he ruthlessly destroyed those who paid him divine honours.

Al-Mansur's aim, above all others, was to secure his dynasty, and as soon as the domestic situation was well in hand, he set about building a great capital from which he could rule his vast empire and where his safety could be assured. He chose the district called Baghdad, which may be a Persian name meaning 'the gift of God', on the lower west bank of the Tigris, as the site. In this district, once the summer camp of Sassanian emperors, sixty small villages largely inhabited by Christians had grown up. The villagers were indemnified, the ground was levelled, and in the spring of 762, with Sagittarius rising, the Caliph attended the solemn ceremony of marking the bounds of the new city. An immense circle 3,000 yards in diameter was cut into the sand, and along the cut cotton soaked in naphtha was set alight. At the beginning the city was a circle of fire; and so it was again five hundred years later, when a Mongolian emperor put it to the flames.

No great city has ever been built as quickly as Baghdad. In four years the city was virtually completed. A hundred thousand labourers in forced levies were employed to bring immense blocks of stone from Jabal Hamrin, eighty miles distant. About a third of the fortress city of Ctesiphon was demolished and brought to Baghdad. There was a double surrounding wall of brick, a deep moat, and a third inner wall ninety feet high surrounding the royal palace. The top of the main wall was provided with a roadway forty-two feet wide. There were four main gates named after Khurasan, Damascus, al-Kufah and Basrah, with an audience chamber above the archways. In the palace, known as the Palace of the Golden Gate, was the famous Green Dome surmounted by a gilded horseman whose lance was said to point in the direction of the Caliph's enemies. The Round City took its water supply not from the Tigris, which it overlooked, but from the far more dependable Euphrates, which was only thirty-five miles away. When the city was completed it was given the name of Madinat al-Salam, 'the City of Peace', but the people continued to use the old name, which had fewer ironical overtones.

To this city, built so close to the ancient cities of Akkad, Babylon, Seleucia and Ctesiphon, there flocked all the talents of the empire: no court on earth excelled the splendour of the Abbasid court in Baghdad. For seventy years it remained the glory of Islam, and for four hundred more it continued to be, in name if not in fact, the capital of the empire. Artists, poets, philosophers, philanderers and soldiers flocked to the city in increasing numbers, until Baghdad could no longer hold them and spilled out beyond its own walls.

Al-Mansur had little taste for the arts, but did nothing to prevent others from enjoying them. Soon Baghdad was famous for its musicians and dancing girls, its taverns and market-places, its water carnivals and gaudy processions through the streets, its colleges and hospitals and hotels. For the first time translations from Persian, Syriac and Greek were made into Arabic, and the Caliph handsomely rewarded the translators. The tall, dark, slender man with the thin beard and the look of a hungry hawk had a penchant for hard work, read voluminously, spent whole days supervising the accounts, took little interest in his harem and drank no wine. Occasionally he permitted himself to be amused by the antics of the court poet Abu Dulama, who was nearly always drunk, but such occasions became increasingly rare as the Caliph grew older. More and more the Caliph devoted himself to the raising of money—'the Father of Farthings' was also 'the Father of Millions'. He took from his friends and especially from the governors of provinces, who were in positions to raise vast sums of money, whatever he needed. One day he called upon the aged Khalid to disgorge 3,000,000 dirhems, and when Khalid complained the amount was reduced to 2,700,000. The Caliph's brother Abbas was compelled to surrender all the money he had squeezed out of the people when governor of Mesopotamia. At Basrah there lived a small colony of descendants of Abu Bakr who had made fortunes; the Caliph ordered nine-tenths of these fortunes to be handed over to the treasury of the empire. 'Never sleep,' he told his son, 'for your father has never slept since he came to the Caliphate; and even when sleep overcame him, his spirit was wide awake.'

The unsleeping Caliph prepared the way for that great explosion of intellectual energy which followed upon his death. He inaugurated a postal service which brought news from the most distant provinces in a matter of days; he built roads, constructed canals, designed cities and superintended the making of maps. None of the Umayyad Caliphs possessed his complete devotion to the art of government. In the forenoon and evening and late into the night he gave orders and listened to reports; only a few hours in the afternoon were spent with his family.

He enjoyed his family, but could be relentless with his relatives. As-Saffah had nominated Isa ibn-Musa, al-Mansur's cousin, as the successor to the throne. Isa ibn-Musa, a saintly man, deeply religious and much loved, had distinguished himself on the battlefield and also as a canal builder, and he seems to have accepted al-Mansur's Caliphate with good grace, demanding only that he should become the next Caliph. Accordingly there was a solemn ceremony at which al-Mansur promised on the Quran that the succession should go to his cousin. A few weeks later al-Mansur was plotting to get rid of his cousin, who was given poison, but though he fell ill and lost his hair and beard, he recovered and appeared at court to warn the Caliph against breaking agreements signed on the Quran. In this extremity the Caliph called upon the services of his vizier, who suggested that witnesses be brought to swear that there had been no solemn agreement between the Caliph and his cousin. This was done, but Isa ibn-Musa brought more witnesses to prove the contrary. In despair the Caliph decided upon a ruse of his own. He summoned Isa ibn-Musa

The courtyard of the Abbasid Palace, Baghdad, the residence of the caliphate from the abandonment of Samarra to the Mongol invasion of the thirteenth century. The palace is richly decorated with ornamented bricks

The Hall of the Ambassadors, the Alcazar, Seville. The caliphs of Cordova were responsible for much of the wonderful Moorish architecture in Spain, of which the horseshoe arch was a peculiarity

The fifteenth-century Mosque of Kait Bey Outside the Walls, Cairo. The building, which dates from the last decades of Mamluk rule, is a fine example of the elaborate elegance frequently seen in late Arab architecture

to appear at court with his young son. From the throne the Caliph ordered the boy to be executed. The executioner stepped forward. The leather thong was drawn tight round the boy's neck and he was half-strangled. Isa ibn-Musa protested no more. Taking his son with him, he lived out the rest of his life on his country estate near al-Kufah as a millionaire recluse, for during the last act of this atrocious drama the Caliph gave his cousin a vast fortune. The succession was reserved for his own son Muhammad.

Al-Mansur's greatest claim to the affections of Muhammadans derives from the peace he brought to the empire. There were, of course, the usual border incidents. The tribes on the southern borders of the Caspian Sea remained unsubdued, but Tabaristan (Mazanderan), where descendants of Sassanian rulers maintained an independent dynasty and kept up the Zoroastrian religion, was conquered, and added to the empire. There was the usual trouble in Merv, the capital of Khurasan, when al-Muqanna, 'the veiled one'—he wore a gold-embroidered veil supposed to obscure the radiance of his divinity from profane eyes—revolted and for a while held the whole province at his mercy. There were brief rebellions in Egypt; and when in 767 al-Mansur received reports that the rebels were threatening to use the ancient Pharaonic Canal, he immediately ordered the canal to be filled in, and so it remained, a barren and waterless waste, until De Lesseps carved it out again.

His greatest failure was in Spain, where Abd ar-Rahman, the last survivor of the Umayyad princes, had entrenched himself. Al-Mansur, underestimating Abd ar-Rahman's power, ordered al-Ala ibn-Mughith, the governor of North Africa, to attack Spain and bring it back to the Abbasid fold. In a series of sharply fought campaigns Abd ar-Rahman succeeded in destroying the enemy at Badajoz; and the heads of al-Mansur's governor and his lieutenants were embalmed in salt and camphor and wrapped in a black Abbasid flag, and entrusted to a merchant of Cordova making a pilgrimage to Mecca. One day when al-Mansur was on pilgrimage to Mecca, the head came rolling over the carpet while he was holding court. Attached to the ears were tags written by Abd ar-Rahman giving the full name, titles and honours of the dead governor. 'This man is the devil himself!' al-Mansur exclaimed. 'Thanks to God for putting the sea between me and such a foe!' At that time Abd ar-Rahman was busy building a fleet and contemplating the capture of the Islamic empire from the ports of Spain.

Al-Mansur made many pilgrimages to Mecca, his last taking place in 775. On the journey he complained of illness and a sickness of the bowels. It had been a very hot summer, and he was exhausted and close to death when he reached Bir Maimun, an hour's journey from Mecca. Only his freedman Rabi and a few servants were present when he died. At his orders a hundred graves were dug for him, and he was buried surreptitiously in one of them, so that no one should ever know where he was buried. He was seventy years old, and he had ruled the empire for twenty years. He was the real founder of his dynasty, and those who came after him were lesser men.

K

Shortly before he died, al-Mansur summoned his son Muhammad to the presence. As so often before, the Caliph spoke about Baghdad. 'The city is a treasure,' he said. 'Beware of exchanging it for another, for it is your home and your strength. In it I have gathered so much wealth that even if the land revenues were cut off for fifteen years you will have sufficient for the supplies of your army and for every kind of expenditure.' Muhammad, who came to the throne with the title of al-Mahdi, 'the guided one', showed himself to be as solidly rooted as his father, without his father's vices of acquisitiveness and cruelty. He was thirty-three, tall and well built, with an amiable expression. He opened the prisons of all except the worst offenders and returned to the few living descendents of Ali the properties confiscated from them. He gave pensions to lepers and to the poor, and built resthouses along the road to Mecca. When one of Marwan's sons rose in rebellion in Syria, al-Mahdi defeated him in battle, took him prisoner, and later gave him a substantial pension; and his wife Khayzuran, a princess from Tabaristan, protected and favoured the widow of Marwan. It was a time of consolidation, and the gathering of the harvest.

With the vast wealth inherited from al-Mansur, al-Mahdi was able to renew the 'holy war' against Byzantium. In 782, he marched by way of Mosul and Aleppo almost to the gates of Constantinople, leaving his elder son Musa (Moses) as regent of Baghdad. His younger son Harun, who had already distinguished himself in war in Asia Minor—he had led expeditions to Ephesus and Ankara fifteen years earlier—advanced as far as the ancient Chrysopolis (Scutari), thus forcing the Empress Irene to sue for peace under a humiliating treaty involving the payment of an annual tribute of 90,000 dinars. Harun so distinguished himself that he was granted by his father the title al-Rashid, 'the Upright', and designated his elder brother's successor to the throne.

Al-Mahdi died while out hunting. He was pursuing a stag, with the hunting dogs barking at its heels, when he lost control of his horse and was thrown against the gate of a ruined palace; the concussion broke his spine. He died later that day in the presence of his son Harun. He was forty-three and had ruled for ten years, and some said afterwards that those were the best years enjoyed by the Abbasid Caliphs and the people they ruled over.

Harun might have seized the Caliphate, but refused, even though he had little liking for his elder brother Musa. Accordingly he took the ring from his father's finger and sent it with the Prophet's staff and mantle to his brother, together with his oath of fealty. Musa became Caliph under the title al-Hadi, meaning 'the guide'. He was twenty-four, a headstrong and thickset man, obstinate and generous, with a passion for poetry and no particular talent for ruling. In his reign Idris ibn-Abdallah, a grandson of Hasan, made his way to Morocco and founded the Idrisid dynasty; Morocco was henceforth lost to the empire.

The loss of Morocco passed almost unnoticed in Baghdad, the capital of an unwieldy empire. Revolts on the frontiers were commonplaces of the time: there were continual wars in Transoxiana, continual uprisings in Khurasan and Arabia, and these were put down with a heavy hand. Most of al-Hadi's reign was spent in attempting to secure the succession for his young son Ja'far, against the advice of Yahya ibn-Khalid, who became vizier on the death of his father. For demanding that the succession pass into the hands of Harun al-Rashid, Yahya was thrown into prison; and Harun, suspecting that he would be poisoned if he remained at court, hurried out of the capital and spent the remaining months of his brother's reign in a prolonged tour of the distant provinces. In September, 786, al-Hadi died of a lingering disease at Isabad, a day's journey from Baghdad; there were rumours that the disease took the form of slow suffocation. Two slaves in the pay of his mother are said to have smothered him with pillows when he was lying in bed in his harem.

Young, elegant, superbly handsome, with his father's ruddy complexion and his mother's dark and deep-set eyes, Harun possessed the virtues of his grandfather and the graces of a woman. There was something feverish and feminine in him from the beginning. He looked upon the world as though it were there for his enjoyment, to be continually caressed. He adored his own majestic presence, and he adored Baghdad; and since the man and the city were conceived in the same year, he came to represent its failings and its splendours like no other Caliph before or after him. We think of him as the hero of the *Arabian Nights*, wandering in disguise through the taverns of Baghdad, forgetting that he was deeply religious, a brilliant soldier, an exceptional administrator. 'He used to weep over his own extravagance,' wrote an Arab chronicler, 'and he wept for his sins.' Indeed, he was counted among the weepers, of whom Abu Bakr was the most renowned. It is related of him that when he heard for the first time the *hadith*: 'I would I might do battle for God's sake and be slain, and then be quickened again, and so slain again,' he sobbed as though his heart would break.

Harun's abundant virtues even startled his contemporaries. To a precocious intelligence he added an exquisite sensibility and an almost morbid refinement. He saw himself in the endless mirrors of his own magnificence; and if sometimes he gave the impression of a man too much in love with his own image, he also possessed a becoming humility and a gift, rare among the Abbasid Caliphs, of putting people at their ease. Proud and imperious, he was the most human of Caliphs, and at times the gentlest.

In Harun's time Baghdad reached the height of its glory. Along the wharves, to a length of nearly twenty miles, were moored hundreds of vessels ranging from warships to pleasure boats, from immense high-prowed Chinese junks to rafts floating on inflated sheepskins and the little gondolas called *zourak*, decked with flags, which carried the Baghdadis from one part of the city to another. Baghdad was more than the Round City; it had spilled over on to the opposite shore of the Tigris until it reached Karkh, the military camp built by al-Mahdi, which had become a full-fledged town. Into the *suks* came rice from Egypt, glass from Syria, silks, perfumes and fruits from Persia, lapis lazuli from Khurasan, gold and rubies from Transoxania, dyes and spices from India, porcelain and silks from China, furs and slaves from Russia, ebony and more slaves from Africa. All the provinces of the empire sent their products by sea or river, or along the highways to Baghdad, which had become the centre of the world and the greatest trading port in history. Of this period people said: 'It was one long wedding-day and an everlasting feast.' It was so glorious a time that people doubted their good fortune and wondered whether they were dreaming.

Harun was perfectly aware of his good fortune, and of the brilliance of his city, which seemed to be no more than the reflection of his own brilliance. At dusk, when a grateful coolness rose from the river, the Caliph's palace was lighted up. This was the hour when he received guests, sitting in state on his divan, sometimes beckoning to a distinguished visitor to sit beside him. Usually, not far from the presence, there would be the sons of his tutor, Yahya ibn-Barmak. There were four sons, Ja'far, Fadhl, Musa and Muhammad, all of whom received high administrative posts. Ja'far was the handsomest, remembered for his long and graceful neck and his dark glowing eyes. Sometimes at these evening audiences the Caliph's wife Zubayda—the name means 'little creamy one' and was given to her by her grandfather al-Mansur—was present in all her finery, wearing her rich brocades which sometimes cost 50,000 dinars, with jewel-studded slippers on her feet, and with ropes of heavy pearls around her neck. Zubayda set the fashions. She dressed her handmaidens as page boys, and organized a body of mounted palace servants to run her errands, and rode about Baghdad in a palanquin of silver, ebony and sandalwood. She revelled in luxury. Harun enjoyed luxury, but sometimes regarded it as a necessary evil, to be viewed with an air of cultivated distaste.

At these evening audiences Harun was in his element, surrounding himself with theologians and alchemists, astronomers and jugglers, judges and poets, soldiers and administrators. Poets were especially rewarded, and he was appreciative of dancing girls. So the evenings passed with drinking and songs and long arguments, while the incense burned and sometimes the Caliph would hold his robe up to his eyes to prevent them from smarting from the fumes of the incense which clouded the air, making everything appear strangely blue or purple. Just before dawn there were morning prayers with the guests standing rigid as statues, and afterwards the Caliph would wander away to his harem or with Ja'far, his favourite, he would wander out in disguise through his city.

For Ja'far the Caliph possessed an affection which he showed to no one else. When Yahya ibn-Khalid grew too old for the task, his eldest son Fadhl was made Vizier of the empire, but the appointment lasted only a few months. Fadhl was abrupt in his manner, and strangely reserved. Ja'far was gay, affectionate, brilliant, impulsive, quick to share the Caliph's moods. For nearly seventeen years they were inseparable, and it was rumoured that the Caliph loved Ja'far so dearly that he ordered a robe with two collar openings, so that they could wear it together. There were rumours, too, of a homosexual affection between the light-skinned Caliph and the darker-skinned Vizier whose mother was a mulatto from Madinah with Abyssinian or Negro blood in her.

Inevitably there were complaints. Ja'far, loaded with honours, the wealthiest man in the empire after the Caliph, became the target of influential scandalmongers. Perhaps the Caliph wearied of his long friendship, but it is more likely that he gave way to a sudden uncontrollable rage, like those bloodthirsty rages which accompanied as-Saffah through all his campaigns. On January 29, 803, shortly after returning from a pilgrimage to Mecca, the Caliph gave orders for Ja'far's execution. The head was placed on the central bridge of Baghdad and the two halves of his body on the other two bridges. Immediately afterwards the Caliph abandoned Baghdad for his summer palace at al-Raqqa, and rarely returned to his capital. It was as though he was haunted by the presence of his dead friend.

Arab chroniclers have delighted in telling the story of Ja'far's fall from grace. For them the story has some of the elements which appear in the story of the martyred Husayn—the murder so purposeless, and yet inevitable, the bloodshed somehow redeeming the time. They have embroidered upon it until there is hardly a single detail which remains entirely credible, but the whole remains vivid and true.

According to the chroniclers Ja'far was murdered for having fathered two sons on his own wife. His wife was Harun's favourite sister Abbasa, and the marriage was arranged because Harun loved Ja'far and his sister equally, and wanted to be with them at all hours of the day and night. It was agreed, however, that Ja'far would never be alone with his wife, and he would never be in the same house with her unless the Caliph was present. Ja'far, who felt highly honoured by this marriage into the caliphal family, was prepared to abide by the strange agreement, but had not counted on the princess's capacity for intrigue. One night, returning drunk from an audience in the palace, he went to his mother's house. Too befuddled to know what he was doing, and mistaking the princess for a pretty serving maid, he slept with her: the child she bore was called Husayn and spirited secretly to Mecca. Some time later another child called Hasan was born to them, and this too was sent secretly to Mecca. The Caliph was kept in ignorance of the affair until the end of 802, when he was on pilgrimage in Mecca. Vague rumours had reached him during the journey, and as soon as he reached Mecca he set about discovering the children. They were brought to him. They were very handsome, and he gazed at them for a long time, speaking to them very gently, inquiring about their health and their schooling, as though he wanted to delay the inevitable moment of decision. They were strangled shortly after he had dismissed them with presents. Returning to Baghdad, the Caliph was overwhelmed by the knowledge of treachery in his own family. He had changed remarkably. There were heavy lines on his face. He had killed the children to prevent them from obtaining the succession, and now he determined to kill both his favourite and his sister.

The princess was killed first. To Masrur, his bodyguard and executioner, he said: 'When it is dark, bring me ten masons and two servants.' In the dark they went to the princess's palace. She was standing in the middle of the room, welcoming them, when the Caliph gave the order for her death. Masrur was a black eunuch, very strong, and she was soon killed. When Masrur asked where she should be buried, the Caliph answered: 'Bury her where she is,' and the masons went to work, digging through the floors of the palace until they reached water level, while the Caliph looked on, sitting in a chair. At last he gave orders for the body to be thrown into the water and the grave filled in. When the work was finished, he turned to Masrur and said: 'Give the workmen their due.' The ten masons were sewn into sacks and thrown into the Tigris.

The next day was Thursday, the day on which Ja'far was accustomed to lead the parade in front of the palace. At the audience following the parade, Ja'far was allowed to sit close to the Caliph. It is possible that he knew his life was in danger, for he asked permission to leave for his estates in Khurasan. Harun answered: 'We must ask the astrologers,' and set about consulting the astronomical tables. Finally he said: 'No, Ja'far, I believe it is an evil day for you. Better stay for the Friday prayers, when the stars will be more propitious.' Ja'far was puzzled. He had taken the precaution of consulting the stars and the almanacs, and he had been assured he had chosen a propitious day for the journey. When he left, the Caliph accompanied him to his horse and helped him to mount—a sure sign that he was still in favour.

That night he was summoned to return to the palace by a messenger who said that letters had come from Khurasan, and the Caliph wanted him to open them. Terrified, and suspecting the worst, he rode to the palace with Masrur and his own escort. Soldiers at the palace headed off his escort, and he went into the inner apartments alone with Masrur. Harun had put up a Turkish tent within his own apartments. He was waiting there with his stick in his hand and the sweat streaming down his face, and from time to time he would bite at the handle of the stick.

When Ja'far knew that his end had come, he was so paralysed with fear that he threw himself on the ground and implored Masrur for mercy, reminding him of the many gifts he had given him, and the many more that would be his if he would spare the Vizier's life. Masrur may have been half tempted by the great wealth that would come to him, but he feared Harun's vengeance if he let Ja'far free.

'Then do not kill me here,' Ja'far cried. 'Let me into the presence. He will not kill me if he sees me.'

'I dare not face the Caliph without your head,' Masrur said. 'I know there is no chance for thee!'

'Then give me a little time,' Ja'far replied. 'Go to the presence and say: I have done your bidding. See what he says, and after that do whatever has to be done. If you do that, then God and the angels are my witness I will give you half of what I have.'

Masrur was tempted, and after removing Ja'far's sword and putting him in charge of forty black slaves, he went to where the Caliph was sitting in his Turkish tent.

'I have done your bidding,' Masrur told the Caliph.

'Then where is the head?'

'It is outside.'

'Bring it to me.'

There was nothing left for Masrur to do but obey the order. He returned, cut off Ja'far's head, and, taking it by the beard, he threw it at the Caliph's feet. There was a moment of silence, as the Caliph gazed at the familiar head, and then there burst from him a strange animal-like sob, and he began to scream and shout at the head as though he expected it to answer him, and all the time he was digging the stick deeper into the ground. A little later he gave orders to have Ja'far's brother Fadhl, and his venerable old father Yahya, imprisoned.

That night one of the officers of the guard, al-Sindi ibn Shakik, was awakened from a bad dream:

> I was sleeping in the upper room of the guard-house which is on the west side of Baghdad when I saw Ja'far in a dream. He stood before me in a robe dyed with saffron and inscribed with strange terrifying verses. I awoke in horror, and told what I had seen to one of my friends, who said: 'Not all that a man sees in sleep can be interpreted.' I then returned to my couch, but I had scarcely closed my eyes when I heard the challenge of the sentries, the ringing of the bridles of the post-horses and a loud knocking at the door of my chamber. I ordered it to be opened, and the eunuch Salam al-Abrash (whom Harun never sent out except on important business) came upstairs. I shuddered at the sight of him, and my joints trembled, for I imagined he had some orders for me. The eunuch handed me a letter telling me to seize and imprison Yahya and all his relatives.[1]

So Ibn Khallikan tells the story in his *Book of Names*, that enormous biographical dictionary which corresponds to an Arabic *Who's Who*; and of all the accounts written about that night, this is the one with the most authentic *frisson*, perhaps because it only hints at the atrocities to come.

When Yahya and his three remaining sons, and their families, were thrown into prison, an inventory was made of their estates, which amounted to 36,676,000 dinars (£50,000,000). Harun was still not satisfied and ordered Fadhl tortured, to reveal where he had hidden the treasures not included in the inventories. One evening Masrur arrived at the prison accompanied by several slaves, each holding folded napkins in their hands. Such napkins usually concealed presents, but this time they concealed whips with knotted lashes. Fadhl proclaimed his innocence: he had revealed everything, and hoped only to spend his last days in peace. Masrur told the slaves to give Fadhl two hundred lashes. He was whipped within an inch of his life and afterwards his body was drawn

[1] Ibn Khallikan, *Biographical Dictionary*, tr. Baron MacGuckin de Slane (Paris, 1843), I, 310.

repeatedly over coarse matting until most of the skin of his back was removed. Fadhl recovered, to die of cancer of the mouth five years later.
When Harun heard of his death, he said: 'My fate is near to his,' and in
fact he died a few months later, having surrendered to one last feverish
bout of brutal murder.

Harun was thirty-nine when he gave orders for the execution of Ja'far.
He looked like an old man, was slow in his movements, and his hands
trembled. One day his half-sister Ulayya, famous for her poetry and her
singing, said: 'I never saw you enjoying a single day of happiness since
you put Ja'far to death. Then why did you kill him?' 'If I thought even
my inmost garments knew the reason,' Harun replied, 'I would tear them
apart!' His reply seems to pause on the edge of a revelation of almost
unbearable intimacy with the dead man. When Ja'far died, a part of
Harun died with him.

The most succinct account of the tragedy was given by a visitor to the
treasury who found in one of the ledgers the entry: 'For a robe of honour
for Ja'far ibn-Yahya—400,000 dinars.' A few days later he noted another
entry: 'For naphtha and shavings for burning the body of Ja'far ibn-
Yahya—10 kirats.' A kirat was one twenty-fourth of a dinar.

Six years of life remained to Harun after the murder of Ja'far, but
during most of those years he gave the impression of a man going through
the processes of kingship like a sleepwalker, barely conscious of what he
was doing, fearful of what would happen after his death and still more
fearful about the present. In the past he had always treated the Byzantine
Emperor Nicephorus with contempt, sending him insulting messages—
'From Harun, the Commander of the Faithful, to Nicephorus, the dog of a
Roman'—but as the years passed, the tide of war began to turn in favour
of the Byzantines in Asia Minor. Revolts in the provinces were suppressed
ruthlessly, but rarely effectively: they would spring up again the moment
the pressure was removed. In Syria, North Africa and Khurasan there
were continual revolts which were only put down at the cost of enormous
losses in men and treasure.

The empire of Harun could well afford such losses. Not since the time
of Augustus Caesar had so much wealth and power been at the disposal
of one man. Harun, says Ibn Khaldun, followed in the footsteps of his
grandfather except in parsimony, for no Caliph exceeded him in the
magnificence of his gifts. He was especially liberal to poets, and himself
wrote verses to his Greek concubine Helen, for whom he built on the
shores of the Euphrates a palace called Heraclea in honour of her birthplace. During his reign, and largely at his own expense, there was constructed a large number of academies and universities where scholars were
given the task of translating Greek scientific works captured from the
libraries of Ancyra (Ankara). The historian Waqidi, the protégé of Yahya
ibn-Khalid, wrote during his reign the classic account of the campaigns of
Muhammad and the wars of conquest. Jabir ibn-Hayyan, the alchemist
known to the west as Geber, was another protégé of Yahya, and for a while
a confidant of the Caliph, who showed an unusual interest in alchemical

experiments. Jabir was forced to flee from Baghdad when Yahya was arrested. Ibn Khaldun says that it was in Harun's time that the first commentaries on the Quran were written. It is clear that Harun paved the way for the great flowering of cultural activity which came during the reign of al-Mamun.

Harun's fame reached the courts of China and of Charlemagne. Eginhard, the chronicler of Charlemagne, speaks of envoys sent to Baghdad and returning home with a number of elephants and a cunningly contrived water clock of bronze that marked the time by means of little figures on horseback which paraded through little doors, one horseman for every chime. Curiously, the Arab chroniclers have left no record of this embassy from the holy Roman Emperor.

Towards the end Harun's spirit failed him completely. He slept badly. He suspected everyone of harbouring secret plans against him. He believed his sons Muhammad and Abdallah were plotting against him and against each other, and would inevitably lead the empire to ruin. Muhammad was his favourite, and accordingly the succession was granted to him, but he was aware of the superior talents of Abdallah, his son by a Persian slave girl, and did his utmost to prevent him from seizing power. When in 808 there occurred one more of the innumerable revolts which plagued Khurasan, Harun gathered an army and marched against the rebels, leaving Muhammad as regent in Baghdad and taking care that Abdallah should go with him. He reached Sanabad, then a small village, when he heard of the capture of the rebel leader Rafi ibn-Layth. He was already dying, but he had strength enough to order that Rafi be brought into his presence. Resting from the sun in a garden tent, he examined the rebel attentively, and then, remembering how he had been exhausted by the long journey, he decided upon an exemplary punishment. 'You have brought me here, and you must pay for it,' he said. 'You shall be killed as no man was ever killed before.' Rafi was hacked to pieces, slowly, and one by one the pieces were thrown at the Caliph's feet. He died a few hours later, still gazing at the remnants of the defeated rebel. He had reigned for twenty-three years, and during the last six of them he knew no happiness at all.

When the news of Harun's death reached Baghdad the following week, Muhammad assumed the Caliphate. Harun's fears seemed to be unfounded. Abdallah was in Khurasan, far from the sources of power, unable and perhaps unwilling to dispute his elder brother's authority. Muhammad became Caliph under the name al-Amin, and immediately set about enjoying his new-found powers. He was big-boned, broadshouldered, very tall, with a hooked nose and small eyes, and gave the impression of a man completely in command of himself. He possessed immense physical courage. Once a caged lion was brought to him, and everyone in the audience chamber fled when the lion broke through the door. The Caliph was drinking, and he continued to drink while the lion approached the throne. When the lion sprang, he simply held up a cushion as a shield and quietly dispatched it with his short dagger. He had a pleasant manner, laughed easily and possessed a keen intelligence, but once in power he abandoned himself to dissipation and luxury. We hear of immense sums spent on dancing girls who were trained to perform in ballets, wearing ropes of pearls and rivers of diamonds. He spent money prodigiously on soothsayers and jugglers, and on the building of palaces which were abandoned after he had lived in them for a single night.

The empire could perhaps afford such prodigality—Harun al-Rashid had left a hundred million dinars in the state treasury—but it could not afford al-Amin's ignorance of political realities. Abdallah was governor of Khurasan, and the best army was under his command. Al-Amin decided to destroy the army of Khurasan and sent a picked force of 40,000 troops against his brother. At Rayy, near Teheran, his entire army was wiped out by 4,000 men under Abdallah's general Tahir, who reported after his victory: 'The general's head lies before me; his ring is on my finger; his army is under me.' The story is told that when news of the defeat was brought to the Caliph al-Amin, he was fishing on the Tigris. 'It is a small matter,' he said, and went on fishing.

It was not a small matter. The defeat at Rayy was the prelude to a series of catastrophic defeats, culminating in the siege of Baghdad. Abdallah had decided to wrest the Caliphate from his brother by force. Half of the Caliph's generals went over to the enemy. With his capital encircled al-Amin continued to live as though he had no care in the world. Masudi describes the strange army which helped to defend Baghdad after the siege had lasted more than a year. Few of the defenders had any sound garments. They went to battle naked to the waist, but wearing on their heads sham helmets of palm fibre, and their shields were made of palm leaves, and their clubs were no more than matted rushes covered with tar and stuffed with gravel and sand. The half-naked officers directed operations from the backs of half-naked soldiers. While al-Amin amused himself in his harem, his soldiers fought with the courage of despair. Baghdad was in ruins; food prices rocketed sky-high; the corpses choked the streets; the mosques were closed and there were no more public prayers. Abdallah had only to wait, and the fruit would fall to his hands.

After the siege had lasted fourteen months and more than half the population of Baghdad had been killed, al-Amin seems to have decided that a state of emergency existed, and began to negotiate with the generals attacking the city. He dismissed as unprofitable a plan to slip out of the besieged city at night with 7,000 loyal troops and make his way to Egypt, where there was the possibility of building up a huge army. Tahir, who was one-eyed but made up for the defect by being ambidextrous, heard of al-Amin's negotiations, asking permission to kill the Caliph on his surrender, and received from Abdallah a shirt with no opening for the head—the sign that permission was granted. Another general, Harthama, was inclined to accept al-Amin's surrender and arranged a secret meeting with the Caliph, who was ordered to cross the Tigris at night in a boat sent for him. The boat was being rowed away from Baghdad when some skin divers sent by Tahir succeeded in rocking it, thus throwing the Caliph into the river. He swam ashore, hid in a house on the Street of the Anbar Gate, and was discovered by some Persians, who recognized him by the scent of musk and perfumes which still clung to his naked body. Some time later the Caliph, wearing only drawers and some scraps of cloth over his shoulders, was cut to pieces by Tahir's guards, and his head, wrapped in cloth soaked in resin, was sent to Abdallah in Khurasan.

Of all the Abbasid Caliphs, Abdallah, the son of Harun al-Rashid, was the most brilliant, the least corrupted by power, the most solicitous of the welfare of others. To him, rather than to his father, belongs the credit of inaugurating the golden age of Baghdad. His mind moved cautiously towards vast conclusions. Among those conclusions was one which outweighed all the others—his rejection of the legitimacy of his own house. Half-Persian, he possessed the Persian affection for the descendants of Ali, and the most distinguished living member of this house was a certain Ali ibn-Musa, great-great-great-grandson of Husayn, a man of saintly character and magnetic personality, believed by many to be the living representative of God on earth. Abdallah, who assumed the title al-Mamun, fell under the spell of Ali and announced that the succession would pass from the house of Abbas to the house of Ali on his own death. In the year 823, Ali was publicly acknowledged as the heir apparent to the Caliphate under the title ar-Rida, meaning 'the acceptable one'. Al-Mamun and Ali became inseparable companions, ruling the empire jointly.

Such a profound change in the nature of the Abbasid state inevitably alienated many of the governing officials in Baghdad. Al-Mamun's right to dispose of the empire to a hereditary enemy of the Abbasids was questioned. The Iraqis rebelled, and sought to put one of the sons of al-Mahdi on the throne. For a brief while civil war flared across the empire. The enemies of Ali were being won over when al-Mamun and Ali visited Sanabad to arrange for the building of a splendid tomb over the grave of Harun al-Rashid. Rumour, legend or deliberate malice spread the story that the young heir apparent was given a bunch of poisoned grapes by the Caliph. All we know for certain is that al-Mamun was inconsolable and immediately set about building a great shrine worthy of the young saint who had accompanied him on all his travels. The name of Sanabad was changed to Mashad, meaning 'the place of martyrdom'. Today this small city in northeastern Persia, close to the borders of Afghanistan, is accounted by the Persians the most sacred spot on earth after Karbala, where Husayn met a martyr's death. The shrine at Mashad, lovingly and exquisitely designed, contains the bodies of Harun al-Rashid and Ali ar-Rida, known as the Imam Rida. Harun al-Rashid lies somewhere beneath the pavement in an unmarked grave, while the Imam Rida lies in a sumptuous tomb covered with a carpet of emeralds. Pilgrims to Mashad spit when they think they are in the presence of Harun, while to the Imam Rida they show the utmost adoration.

By the fourteenth century Mashad had become the richest, the most splendid and the most highly endowed of Persian shrines. In 1601, the Emperor Shah Abbas did not think it beneath his dignity to walk the entire distance between Isfahan and Mashad in order to trim the thousands of candles in the sacred courts and to acquire at immense cost the Quran said to have been inscribed in the Imam's own hand. The gravest claims were made for the pilgrimage to Mashad. A *hadith* of dubious authenticity quoted Muhammad as saying: 'A part of my body is to be buried in Khurasan, and whoever goes there on pilgrimage, God will surely destine for Paradise, and his body will be *haram*, forbidden, to the flames of Hell: and whoever goes there with sorrow, God will take his sorrow away.' Ali is supposed to have said of pilgrims to Mashad: 'Though their sins be as many as the stars, as the leaves of trees, they will all be forgiven.'

Al-Mamun waited until 819 before entering Baghdad, and then there began the long and fruitful renaissance of the sciences and arts which is the chief glory of his age. Culture flowered, as never before. For the first time in Islamic history a ruler identified himself with the cultural aspirations of his people and celebrated the native genius of the people he ruled. He established a great Hall of Science at Baghdad with a library and astronomical laboratory; organized a college of translators who were set to work on a regular salary to translate from Greek, Syriac, Persian and Sanskrit; and showered artists and poets with his munificence. Believing that knowledge should not depend upon the occasional acts of munificence by Caliphs and nobles, he created permanent endowments for the support of colleges; and at his Tuesday audiences he encouraged theologians and scholars to discuss with him the most dangerous and heretical doctrines, saying that he wanted only to discover the truth and that everyone must be free to speak openly. For a brief while he endowed Islam with the ornament of freedom; and though this freedom was never granted again with so much largesse or greatness of mind, Islam herself never recovered completely from the shock.

Al-Mamun was more than the symbol of the times; he was the man who brought a new civilization into being. The shadow of the apostolic Imam Rida lay over him; his keen intelligence, sharpened by debate, refused to be limited by orthodoxy, even by the orthodoxy represented by the Imam Rida. In a hundred different ways he opened the floodgates and attempted to emancipate men from their fears, their dogmas, the servility of their minds. He modified the absolute autocracy of the Caliphate by bringing into existence a Council of State with representatives from Jewish, Christian, Sabaean and Zoroastrian communities sitting in equality with Muhammadans. He modified justice by continual acts of clemency, and went on to modify Islam by maintaining, in a crucial edict issued in 827, the doctrine of 'the creation of the Quran' against the fundamentalists who believed that the Quran was uncreated, being the eternal word of God transcribed for everlasting on golden plates in Heaven. Following the philosophy of the Mutazila sect, the Caliph insisted that man was endowed with free will; that God could not be seen with mortal eyes, for otherwise He would be comparable to any of His creatures; and that the divine ordinances which regulate the conduct of men are the results of growth and development: there were no supreme, permanent, irrevocable laws of the universe. All things were subject to change; and by implication he suggested that the Quran itself was far from being the final verdict on human progress. God was just, not responsible for the crimes of men. Before God man was free to do as he pleased, and his burden of freedom was also a delight.

Such liberating doctrines were not to the taste of the stern moralists who professed to believe that the Quran must be read literally, with every word divinely appointed in its exact setting on the page. They objected strenuously against an interpretation which permitted the human mind to adventure boldly in uncharted regions; and around the sternest moralist of them all, Ahmad ibn Muhammad ibn Hanbal, there gathered a group of fanatics who rejected the middle path and prepared to fight to the death on behalf of traditional interpretations. Al-Mamun was so convinced of the justice of his cause that he felt compelled to punish the traditionalists, and Baghdad was presented with the strange spectacle of the most liberal of Caliphs holding inquisitions at which the traditionalists were forced either to admit the error of their ways or to accept brutal punishment. Doctors and jurists were ordered to acknowledge 'the creation of the Quran', or lose their jobs. The traditionalists, who were continually causing street riots, were hounded down. Al-Mamun was learning the hard lesson of the liberators who discover to their surprise that the greatest freedom merges insensibly into the greatest tyranny.

The trap was sprung, but it was not entirely of the Caliph's making. Himself half Persian, he tended to view the world through Persian eyes, clearly and without any great liking for dogmatics. The followers of Ali, of whom the Imam Rida had been the living embodiment, were traditionally opposed to the harsh and threatening philosophy of the early Caliphs, whose judgment of the world was based upon the sterner edicts of the Quran. Finally, there was the liberating influence of Greek philosophy with its gentle insistence upon man as a creature living in his own light, with no nightmares of Judgment Day to cloud his imagination. Al-Mamun had embraced Greek philosophy with a full heart, until he was almost more Greek than the Greeks.

Something of the temper of the man can be seen in a story told by the contemporary historian, Masudi. Al-Mamun was sitting in his throne room when a man in a coarse white gown stood at the gate, begging to come in. The Caliph gave orders that the man should be allowed to enter the presence, and soon he came shuffling in with his shoes in his hand, stopping only when he reached the edge of the carpet in front of the Caliph.

'Am I permitted to speak?' the man said, and the Caliph answered that he could speak as he pleased, as long as his words were pleasing to God.

'I have this question,' the man went on. 'Tell me about your throne—do you sit on it by common agreement and consent, or by violence and force?'

The Caliph replied in words which showed the fairness of his character and the sincerity of his belief in his own right to rule. He said:

I am on the throne neither by the consent of the True Believers nor by my own violence. Before my time there was one who governed the affairs of the faithful, and they bore with him, perhaps willingly, perhaps unwillingly; and he appointed me and another to succeed him, calling upon the faithful to witness the deed of succession, and so at the holy place in Mecca he took an oath of allegiance from all those on pilgrimage to me and to my brother; and they gave their oaths, perhaps willingly, perhaps unwillingly.

Then it happened that my brother followed his own way, and there came a time when I succeeded to the throne, and I knew I needed the common consent of the people, of east and west. I pondered the matter, and I saw that if I abandoned the government, the security of Islam would suffer, the highways would be infested with robbers, and public affairs would fall into confusion, while God's commands would no longer be obeyed. I saw there would be strife and disorder, and Muhammadans would be prevented from going on pilgrimage and doing their duty in war, and so I arose in defence of the people until they should be of accord upon one man whom they should approve. To that man I propose to resign my authority. I shall become his subject. Take this message from me to the people, and tell them the moment they have selected a chief I will abdicate to him.

The man in the coarse white gown moved away and vanished in the crowd outside the palace. The Caliph sent someone to find what he was doing, and at last he was tracked down to a mosque where he was quietly reciting the Caliph's words to fifteen men garbed like himself in coarse white cotton. Such men were often leaders of the riots, but they were unusually quiet as they listened to al-Mamun's declaration of conscience.

'What did they do after they listened?' the Caliph asked.

'Oh, they all went quietly about their way,' he was told. 'They wandered off in different directions.'

If the story is true, and there is no reason to doubt it, this was perhaps the supreme moment of al-Mamun's career as the Prince of the True Believers.

While he worshipped justice, al-Mamun also possessed the Persian gift for magnificence. His marriage in 825 to the beautiful eighteen-year-old daughter of his Vizier, al-Hasan ibn-Sahl, was celebrated with more pomp and luxury than any marriage known to history. At the nuptials the bride's grandmother showered upon the Caliph and his bride, as they sat on a golden mat studded with pearls and rubies, a thousand pearls, which were afterwards gathered and formed into a necklace for the queen. At the banquet balls of musk were showered on the guests—each ball was wrapped in a ticket naming an estate, a slave, a blood horse, or some such gift, to be redeemed by the princes and nobles who attended. For the lesser guests there were showers of money, balls of musk, eggs made of ambergris. When night fell, the bride received a gift of a thousand rubies to match the thousand pearls she had already received, and the bride chamber was lighted with candles of ambergris weighing a hundred pounds. Ibn Khaldun, who tells the story of the nuptials in wide-eyed amazement, adds that 140 mule loads of wood were brought for a whole year to feed the kitchen furnaces, so great was the amount of food that had to be cooked for the guests, and all the wood was consumed on the wedding night. Rather less convincingly he adds that 30,000 boats were employed to take the guests to the palace on the further side of the river.

The Caliph's munificence to scholars and artists, and his displays of magnificence, depended upon a thriving economy and a state of peace within the empire, but the frontier wars continued. The Byzantines over-ran large parts of Asia Minor, and were thrown back during a series of summer campaigns. The most dangerous revolts came from the southern shores of the Caspian, where the schismatic Barbak had resuscitated the doctrines of al-Muqanna, 'the Veiled Prophet of Khurasan'. Barbak formed an alliance with the Emperor Theophilus and threatened to cut off the approaches to the west: his guerrilla armies continued to plague the armies of the empire for many years. So, too, did the armies of Theophilus, whose frontier post at Tarsus had become a huge fortress and supply dump, only to be captured during a campaign in the last year of al-Mamun's life. In 833 the Caliph was camping beside the river Buden-dun, not far from Tarsus, when a huge fish was brought to him, still alive. The fish wriggled out of the servant's hands and fell into the water with such a splash that the Caliph's neck, shoulders and chest were drenched; and he is said to have died a few days later as the result of a fever brought on by the drenching. He was forty-nine, and he had ruled for twenty-one years. Abu Bakr was the most saintly of the Caliphs, Ali the most gifted, Husayn the most heroic, Muawiya the cleverest; but of al-Mamun alone could it be said that he was truly magnificent.

Al-Mamun was a heavy man, broad-shouldered, with a great beard and an imposing manner. His brother Muhammad, who came to the throne under the title of al-Mutasim ('the steadfast'), was altogether weaker, completely devoid of moral character, famous for his fresh com-plexion, beautiful eyes, square blond beard and immense physical strength —he had muscles like iron and could carry enormous weights on his head while walking a straight line. His mother was a Turkish slave, he spoke Turkish in preference to any other language, and distrusted Persians. As a prince his passion had been for Turkish slaves bought in the markets of Samarqand; he had collected 3,000 of them before he became Caliph. These youths became his bodyguard, and were free to commit whatever enormities they pleased in the streets of Baghdad. The Arab historian Yaqubi says that the guards 'used to gallop about and collide with people right and left', and soon they were inspiring so much terror that gangs of Baghdadis went out to waylay them; and if one of the Turkish bodyguard was killed, no one ever gave evidence against the perpetrators of the crime and everyone was secretly delighted.

Al-Mutasim decided on extreme measures to punish the people of Bagh-dad: he would move his capital elsewhere. In 836 he established his

entire court in a new capital built on the cliffs overlooking the Tigris some
seventy miles above Baghdad. A great complex of buildings was erected
at fabulous cost, with the palace of the Caliph facing the river, reached
by an immense flight of steps two hundred feet wide. The Christian
churches of Egypt were plundered for columns and pavings to decorate
the new city, known as Samarra—the name is said to have meant 'He
who beholds rejoices'. Soon the people of Baghdad were regretting their
treatment of the Turkish guards, for Samarra was paid for out of their
taxes.

Built on the site of a Christian monastery, Samarra was occupied by
eight Caliphs over a period of fifty-eight years. Today the traveller in an
aeroplane can see the outline of the city, the avenues and parks, houses,
palaces and mosques, very much as it must have looked from the air
eleven hundred years ago. But those who enter on foot see only ruins.

By leaving Baghdad, al-Mutasim placed himself at the mercy of his
Turkish praetorian guard. As long as he satisfied them with booty and
honours, as long as he was able to direct successful wars from his new
capital, they permitted him to do as he pleased. Determined to bring the
schismatic Barbak to heel, he sent out an army under the great general
Haydar ibn-Ka'us, known as Afshin, a descendant of the Turkish princes
of Urushana in central Asia. After a series of quick campaigns Afshin
captured the rebel stronghold and brought Barbak in chains to Samarra.
Like Harun al-Rashid on another occasion, al-Mutasim decided upon an
exemplary punishment: Barbak was forced to wear imperial robes of red
brocade and a tall Persian hat as he rode on an elephant between rows of
soldiers in full armour stretching for five hours' march from Afshin's camp
to the palace. Afshin was given the place of honour in the throne room,
while Barbak was paraded up and down before the Caliph. When the
Caliph said: 'So this is really Barbak?' there was no answer, only a dread-
ful silence broken by the hissing of Afshin, who leaned forward, saying:
'The Commander of the Faithful has spoken, and thou sayest nothing!'
At last Barbak said: 'I am Barbak!' and soon afterwards the Caliph
prostrated himself in prayer, and when he arose he ordered that Barbak
should be stripped naked. The executioner sliced off one of Barbak's
hands and flung it in the man's face, and did the same with the other hand.
Then Barbak's feet were cut off, and he twisted and kicked in his own blood
on the leather carpet, shouting for mercy and beating against his face with
his stumps. Al-Mutasim, a hardened warrior, delighted in torture and
prolonged Barbak's agony as long as possible. Finally Barbak's head was
cut off, to be displayed on the bridge at Baghdad as a warning to the
rebellious Baghdadis, until the Caliph decided to send it to Khurasan,
where Barbak had enjoyed fame among the people. To Afshin went a
jewelled crown, a gold tiara set with emeralds and rubies, and two
jewelled girdles set with pearls.

The fame of Afshin rivalled the Caliph's, especially after a victorious
campaign against Theophilus in the west. It was rumoured that he had
failed to make the Emperor prisoner, when the Emperor fell in his power,

saying: 'One does not capture kings.' Later he put down a rebellion instigated by Abbas, the son of al-Mamun, as mercilessly as he put down the
rebellion of Barbak, and he might have gone on to further honours if he
had not made a private peace with Maziyar, the prince of Tabaristan, a
Persian rebel who believed in Zoroastrianism as much as Afshin believed
in the tribal gods of the Turks. When Maziyar was captured by another
general and brought to Samarra, the story of Afshin's apostasy came out.
Afshin was forced to admit that he possessed a library of books 'written
in strange characters', and secretly kept idols in his house. He was a
prince of the empire, and therefore once again an exemplary punishment
was needed. The proper punishment for apostasy was crucifixion. Instead Afshin was permitted to starve himself to death.

Ungrateful and ungracious, strong as a horse, glorying only in his army
and especially in his regiments of light cavalry equipped with sword, lance
and bow, al-Mutasim represented the sword of Islam in its most naked
form. No principles drove him, and his religion meant no more to him
than it meant to his unruly Turkish guards. He died at the age of forty-six
after a reign of eight years, and his last words are supposed to have been:
'If I had known it would be so short a reign, I would have done differ-
ently.' He meant perhaps that he would have been even more brutal,
more demanding, more determined to wield a naked sword.

With his death, convulsively, the Abbasid empire began to break apart.
There followed in quick succession a series of incompetent Caliphs,
many of them insane, all of them at the mercy of their Turkish guards, or
of their own sons. A few died in bed; most of them were murdered in
their own palaces or along the road between Baghdad and Samarra.
They lived in a delirium of fear, not knowing whether their enemies
would spring out of the sky or from beneath their feet. Only the ceremonies remained. The real power was in the hands of whatever freebooter
had become mayor of the palace or whatever doctor possessed a poisoned
lance.

L

THE COMING OF AL-HALLAJ

IN THE fourteenth century an Arab philosopher, Ibn Khaldun, from his castle in the Little Atlas, looked out upon the desolate prospects confronting the civilization which had begun when Muhammad first announced himself as the Messenger of God. He saw that the civilization around him was sick unto death, and that it had been sick many times, and very often in the same way. He was a cultivated aristocrat with little sympathy for the nomadic tribesmen who set out from Arabia and conquered large areas of the known world, but he nevertheless recognized their primitive force. He saw that they possessed a quality which he called *asabiyya*, an instinctive social cohesion, which enabled them to move like a knife through all obstacles to create an empire; but this quality, generated in the desert, lacked staying power, and was soon dissolved by luxury, by all the temptations of city life, and by the very nature of conquest itself. Of all men, he said, the nomadic Arabs were perhaps the least capable of rule, if only because they were naturally ferocious, and were happiest wandering from one grazing ground to another: they possessed none of the patterns of behaviour which go with a settled urban existence. The empire would never have come into being without the tremendous shock supplied by the revelations of Muhammad, who had harnessed the natural *asabiyya* of the Arabs to divine ends. Suddenly, but only for a brief while, the Arabs saw themselves as godlike, daring the impossible, hurling themselves against the powerful enemies surrounding them with the sense of inevitable victory. But what happens when the drunkenness wears off?

No one has ever studied the processes of corruption inside civilizations with so much art as this fourteenth-century Berber, who wandered over North Africa in search of the laws by which civilizations are born to flourish and then to perish. He examined minutely the reasons which led to the decay of the Abbasid empire. His conclusions, as true then as they are now, can be stated simply. Corruption is a complex process, following clearly defined stages, which can be charted almost mathematically. The process is irreversible and strangely inhuman, for it rides roughshod over the individual courage of men. Once the disease has set in, no man or group of men can prevent it, and only the divine spirit possessed with the desire to rekindle the fire in men's hearts has the power to cure the disease. What is needed in times when civilization fails is neither military strength nor a brilliant political programme, but a divine revelation.

As Ibn Khaldun made his way from one court to another, studying the various dynasties of the past and the other dynasties which had grown up more recently in North Africa, he found no reason to alter his sombre conclusions. He noted the strange contortions and spasms of civilizations as they go down to their deaths. Towards the very end, for example, a civilization will usually show an extraordinary regeneration, a sudden awakening of all its vital energies, but this is only the last flicker of the candle before going out. He noted the deadly similarity of the men who preside over a culture in decay. He showed how rising prices, vast expenditures in buildings, laxity of morals, more and more dazzling uniforms, and a curious heightening of consciousness are all involved in the decay of a culture. He worked out a complete philosophy of corruption, demonstrating how the process is invariable, infallible, predictable. According to the theory, there was no hope, no hope at all. And yet he was not completely convinced by the theory. The civilizations of Persia and Iraq, Syria and Egypt, declined, showed all the symptoms of necrosis, and yet somehow, by some unidentifiable miracle, they survived. They did not, of course, survive entire. The Umayyad civilization collapsed, but it did not perish completely, for many elements of it were incorporated in the new civilization of the Abbasids. It seemed that civilizations could sometimes survive their own deaths by a strange process of parthenogenesis and the divine revelations were not always needed. But confronted by the miracle of civilizations prolonging their existences long after they had lost all reason to exist, Ibn Khaldun remained silent. There were, as he proclaimed often, mysteries which only God could explain.

Only God could explain how the Abbasid Caliphate endured for four more centuries. The reckless and drunken al-Mutasim, the first Caliph to surround himself with Turkish guards and to become their prisoner, and the first to remove his capital outside Baghdad, died in 842, and was succeeded by his reckless and drunken son al-Wathiq, on whom William Beckford modelled the character of Vathek, the sensual Caliph who made a pact with the devil and who possessed an eye so terrible that no one could bear to behold it—'for the wretch upon whom it was fixed instantly fell backwards, and sometimes expired. For fear, however, of depopulating his dominions, and making his palace desolate, he but rarely gave way to his anger.'

According to Ibn Khaldun, the *asabiyya* of the Arabs had come to an end about the time of al-Mutasim and al-Wathiq, and it was for this reason that the Caliphs found themselves dependent upon their Turkish guards. Henceforth they ruled without divine sanction and with no popular support, but by 'royal power' (by which Ibn Khaldun means 'naked strength') alone. In a sense they did not even rule, but were themselves ruled by their guards or by the tribesmen, Persian, Turkish, Seljuk, Daylamite, or others, whom they called to their assistance. 'The influence of the dynasty,' said Ibn Khaldun, 'grew so small that it hardly extended beyond the environs of Baghdad.'

In fact Ibn Khaldun underestimated the influence of the Caliphs: if their power had extended only over the capital, it is unlikely that they would have endured for so long. The Caliphate answered a deeply felt need. Like the British monarchs the Caliphs symbolized the traditional virtues of the empire and were attended by ceremonies in which they occupied the central place accorded to half-divine characters. They were the successors of Muhammad, and therefore mediators between earth and Heaven. It was not necessary that they should be good, or even that they should be sane: for many millions of believers it was enough that they existed.

Al-Wathiq was almost certainly insane, and made no pretensions towards goodness. He was fair-haired, and half Greek, and famous as a lute player and as the composer of a hundred melodies, but he showed no gift for ruling, and he was murderous to those who refused to believe in the created Quran. The traditionalist Ahmad ibn Nasr Khuzai was brought before him and interrogated. The Caliph was displeased and shouted for a sword, saying: 'I put the burden of my sins on this unbeliever! Headsman, bring the mat!' Then he calmly strode across the throne room and cut off the man's head. The body was gibbeted at Samarra, and the head impaled in Baghdad with a guard set over it to see whether it would turn in the direction of Mecca. According to popular report, it turned one night and recited a whole sura of the Quran.

Al-Wathiq died mysteriously one hot summer day in 847, and the court attendants were in such a hurry to swear allegiance to his brother Ja'far that his corpse was left unattended and a lizard came and pecked out his eyes. Ja'far, who took the title al-Mutawakkil, meaning 'He that putteth his trust in the Lord', was made of sterner stuff. He fought in secret against the Turkish guards; he fought the doctrines introduced by al-Mamun; and he fought the Greeks. He was successful in changing the state religion: henceforth the Quran was uncreated. Hating the memory of the martyred Husayn, he ordered that the mosque at Karbala be destroyed. But though the mosque was razed to the ground and a watercourse was turned over it, the bones were carefully removed before al-Mutawakkil's agents reached the place, and he was never able to punish the offender.

For himself he built a mosque so grandiose that it rivals the works of the Pharaohs. The Great Mosque at Samarra has walls nearly ten feet thick, and is 800 feet long and 500 feet wide, a floor space nearly three times as large as that of St. Peter's in Rome. Forty-four towers once decorated the walls, and the minaret, unlike any other minaret in any existing mosque, was shaped like an ancient Babylonian ziggurat with a winding ramp on the outside, which the Caliph was accustomed to mount on a donkey. The ruins of this incredible mosque remain to this day to testify to the Caliph's megalomania, his contempt for his people, and his strange affection for ancient Babylon.

Not content with building the Great Mosque and a vast number of palaces at Samarra, al-Mutawakkil built a new city a few miles to the north, which he called after himself—Ja'fariya. On the day when he first sat in audience in the new city, he declared: 'Now I know I am indeed a king, for I have built myself a city and live in it!' He did not live in it for long. Nine months later he bought an Indian sword of beautiful workmanship and presented it to the trusted Turkish guard who customarily stood behind him. In the early hours of the morning of December 11, 861, during a drunken orgy, the Caliph was hacked to pieces with this Indian sword. According to the Abbasid tradition, his body was buried secretly in a remote region, where no one would ever find it.

For fifteen years al-Mutawakkil had reigned without ever ruling, pouring money without stint into the creation of his two cities, caring little for his army, which suffered devastating defeats at the hands of the Greeks, and thinking only of his own glory. Yet the glory had departed. None were so servile or so helpless as these Caliphs who reigned for a brief space and then sank into obscurity.

In the space of ten years, from 861 to 871, four Caliphs reigned in Samarra, and all were killed by the Turkish guards—al-Muntasir by a surgeon's poisoned lance, al-Mustain by the sword, al-Mutazz by the rope, and al-Muhtadi by being pressed between boards. They had become the playthings of the soldiers, to be murdered at leisure.

With the accession of al-Mutamid, the son of al-Mutawakkil, in 871, there occurred a pause in the long process of decay which was afflicting the empire. Al-Mutamid, an exquisite poet and incompetent ruler, was kept a prisoner by his brother, Abu Ahmad, who became the real ruler of the empire. Abu Ahmad was a man of considerable military talent. He reorganized the army, and put his chosen companions in charge of the government. Almost his first task was to deal with a revolt of the Negroes working in the saltpetre mines of the lower Euphrates, who had gathered round the standard of Ali ibn-Muhammad, who claimed to be descended from Ali. On September 7, 871, the Negroes poured into Basrah during the Friday services and put nearly everyone in the city to the sword. A quarter of a million people perished in a single day. More perished as the Negroes went on to capture city after city. At last, in 882, this strange rebellion came to an end when the citadel of al-Mukhtarah was stormed and the rebel leader killed.

The rebellion owed its strength to the mysterious power of Muhammad's name. By claiming descent from Muhammad, a hundred rebels had sprung up and gathered armies around them. For the most part these rebels were pretenders, whose claims were disputed and whose aims were strangely at variance with the principles of Islam. Here and there the true descendants of the flesh lived out their lives quietly, studying the Quran and practising good works. Those who were most highly honoured by the faithful, the Imams, who were believed to be the vice-regents of Muhammad on earth, were usually kept close to the court, watched over by the Caliphs, who feared their spiritual power. Usually the Imams suffered violent deaths. Hasan al-Askari, the eleventh Imam, died in 873 of a draught of poison administered by the order of the Caliph al-Mutamid, leaving his young son Muhammad to become the twelfth Imam. Five years later the boy, then aged about seven years, wandered down a flight of steps leading to the cellar of his house within the walls of the Great Mosque at Samarra, and was never seen again. He may have been murdered by the Caliph. Millions of Muhammadans, however, believe that he vanished only in order to gain immortal life, and will appear again as the Mahdi to bring righteousness to an evil world and to restore the golden age. He is 'the hidden one', 'the awaited one', alive but withdrawn from human sight in a temporary state of occultation, blessing the earth and guiding the fortunes of his people, the Muhammadan equivalent of Jesus at the Second Coming. Ibn Khaldun, writing five hundred years later, tells how the followers of the Mahdi would come every night after evening prayers to the entrance of the cellar, bringing a horse for the Mahdi to ride on. They would call his name and beg him to come forth, and when the stars came out they would go on their way, only to return the next evening with the same hopefulness.

Nothing in the age of the 'mad Caliphs' so impressed the Persians as the disappearance of this boy. They held firmly to the belief that 'the Man of the Hour' was the invisible mediator between God and man, who continued while absent to communicate with his chosen ones among the faithful. In the midst of darkness and uncertainty they continued to appeal to him as the future deliverer and restorer and the source of all blessings.

About the time that the twelfth Imam vanished in the Great Mosque at Samarra, an Iraqi peasant called Hamdan Qarmat, belonging to a sect that believed in the divinity of the seventh Imam, Ismail ibn-Ja'far, read in the stars that the Abbasids were about to fall in favour of a purely Persian empire. Qarmat possessed astonishing gifts of organization, and carefully prepared an uprising of dedicated followers. The movement showed its Persian origin from the beginning—it was at once theocratic and communistic, aristocratic and plebeian. The genius of Qarmat, who gave his name to the Qarmatian movement, was revealed in his capacity to weld so many contrary ideas together. His followers, like the ancient Zoroastrians, worshipped 'the Supreme Light', but they also worshipped the seventh Imam. They were admitted into the movement only after passing through complicated initiation ceremonies, and each man was given a rank corresponding to one of seven degrees, but they aimed for justice based on social equality and encouraged the community of wives. Such a movement, well-led and well-organized, with its secret rituals, its promises of immediate revolution under the banner of the mysterious *sahib an-naqah*, 'the Man with the She-Camel', and its cultivation of immeasurable ruthlessness, was calculated to attract followers from the poorest and the richest. After proving their strength during the Negro revolt, the Qarmatians marched to Bahrayn on the Persian Gulf, which became a strongly fortified base of operations against the Abbasid empire. The movement grew rapidly. The raided Basrah, which they occupied for seventeen days, and they went on to attack Damascus. By 929 almost the whole of Arabia had fallen into their possession, and they were able to hold up the trains of imperial pilgrims for ransom. On January 12, 930, they occupied Mecca itself, after a rapid march across the uplands of Najd. The swords of the Qarmatians struck mercilessly at the unresisting crowds of Meccans who thronged the narrow streets, and the slaughter did not cease until 30,000 corpses were littered over the sacred city. The holy well of Zamzam was choked with the bodies of the dead. They removed the *kiswa*, the cloth covering the Kaaba, and smashed the Black Stone, removing the pieces to their capital at al-Ahsa. The terrified Abbasids were powerless to prevent the Qarmatians from destroying whatever they desired to destroy.

Again and again in the history of the Abbasid empire there had sprung up, usually in Khurasan, revolutionary movements by leaders who claimed descent from Ali or who looked forward to the coming of an Imam from the seed of the martyrs. Of all these movements the Qarmatian was the longest-lived, and the most successful. From them sprang the great Fatimid dynasties which conquered North Africa, and many years later they were represented by 'the old Man of the Mountains', who organized his legions of Assassins from Mount Alamut. Today the influence of the Qarmatian movement survives among the Ismailis, a sect numbering twenty million Muhammadans who follow the Aga Khan.

During the last years of the ninth century the entire Abbasid empire seemed about to break apart. Vast areas of Khurasan had fallen under the control of Yaqub ibn-Layth, a former coppersmith (*saffar*), who established an independent dynasty with the help of his brother Amr, a former donkey driver: the dynasty came to be known as the Saffarid. A Samanid dynasty —its name is derived from Saman, a Zoroastrian nobleman of Balkh— ruled over Transoxiana. Egypt had fallen to the power of the governor, Ahmad ibn Tulun, whose father had been presented as a slave to the Caliph al-Mamun. The Qarmatians roamed where they pleased, and the Greeks were threatening to drive against Baghdad. In this extremity there was need for a powerful and resourceful Caliph with sufficient authority to prevent the further collapse of the empire. Such a Caliph appeared in al-Mutadid, the nephew of al-Mutamid. He was the son of a Greek slave mother, a stern, thin man with a white mole on his head which he dyed black, forceful and energetic, and when occasion demanded completely ruthless. He restored the capital at Baghdad, reconquered Egypt from Ibn Tulun's son Khumarawayh, hurled his armies against the Qarmatians, and succeeded in being both a forceful Caliph and a complete libertine. He built dungeons and torture chambers with the same careless ease as he built palaces—his Pleiades Palace, the most beautiful of all the Abbasid palaces, cost 400,000 dinars. He was pitiless, energetic and bloody, and would leave the arms of one of his concubines in the middle of the night to attend the execution of one of his prisoners—he particularly liked to watch the death agonies of prisoners who were blown up with bellows. Inevitably he suffered from sleeplessness, nightmares, hauntings and the last years of his life were sombre, with intimations of the Caliph's terror and bewilderment, as he continued to commit more and more crimes upon the palace servants to drown the memory of the crimes he had already committed. Characteristically, his last act as he lay dying of fever was to kick his doctor across the palace bedroom. A few moments later both the Caliph and the doctor were dead.

His successor, al-Muktafi, proved to be the exception to the general rule.

Quiet, confident, remarkably handsome, he had none of his father's ferocity. His first act on his arrival in Baghdad was to open the prisons, his second to destroy the underground dungeons. No other Caliph since al-Mamun had been received with such wild acclamations by the people, and none deserved the honour so well. Al-Muktafi fought against the Qarmations, inflicted heavy punishment on the Byzantines, brought Egypt under his direct control, and seemed about to bring the Abbasid empire back into its former state of glory when he died after a short reign of five years, leaving the empire to his son Ja'far, who was thirteen years old.

There is a sense in which Ja'far, who reigned under the title al-Muqtadir, 'the powerful in the Lord', was the last of the Caliphs. From time to time this short and stunted man with the little black eyes and pink cheeks would arouse himself and perform acts of startling courage. There were fifteen million dinars in the treasury when he came to the throne. He chose, or had chosen for him, viziers of remarkable quality, among them the 'wise vizier' Ali ibn-Isa, a Persian who ruled the empire 'as though he were nursing a baby'. For twenty-five of the most dangerous and exhausting years of the Caliphate, al-Muqtadir watched and prayed and looked out from the palace windows at the creeping decay sweeping over the empire, completely unable to understand what was happening, drowning his fears in wine, growing impossibly fat and careless, until in the end the power of the Caliph passed into the hands of his former chief of bodyguard Munis al-Muzaffar, a eunuch upon whom he bestowed the title *amir al-umara* ('the commander of the commanders'), and of his mother Shaghab, a woman of remarkable strength of will, who held court and received petitions as though she were herself the Caliph. Ali ibn-Isa once remarked of al-Muqtadir that if he had been five days sober, he would have shown himself as sagacious as his father.

Al-Muqtadir had all the talents, and threw them away. He set himself against Muhammadan tradition by striking coins in his own honour, which showed him sitting in state with a wine bottle in his hand. He was so much under the sway of his mother that he would defer to her during audiences and murmur a spate of childish endearments in her honour. During his reign he was twice deposed, both times for brief periods. The Qarmatians sacked Mecca, while their allies the Fatimids succeeded for a brief while in occupying Alexandria and the Fayyum, and the Hanbalites rioted in the streets of Baghdad. Al-Muqtadir showed neither dignity nor astonishment, and the best that can be said about him is that he rarely lost his temper and showed no particular interest in the palace torture chambers. Only on the very last day of his life did he show any spirit. Munis, the commander of his armies, had decided to depose him, and brought up an army against him. A sober Caliph marched out to the camp of his enemy at the head of his palace guards. He donned over his silver kaftan the black band of the Abbasids, and over that the mantle of Muhammad, and girded around Muhammad's sword with the red sword belt. He mounted his richly caparisoned horse, and held his son Abu Ali on the saddle before him. Beside him walked readers who intoned verses of the Quran, and lancers rode with copies of the Quran roped to their lances. In full armour came his escort of Hujari guards, and all the princes of the court. His progress through the streets of Baghdad was cheered by the people glad to set eyes at last on the strange fat Caliph with the thick brown beard who had never in living memory passed through the streets in such panoply.

Munis's camp was established on the shores of the Tigris a few miles from Baghdad. The Caliph took a position on high ground, surrounded by his escort, and threw his guards into battle. Neither side gave any quarter. So the battle continued for some hours on a hot October day, until a message came to the Caliph begging him to show himself to the troops to give them courage. The Caliph refused. Finally, he was assured there would be no danger, and he cantered down the hill. A young officer in Munis's army saw him as he rode through some open ground, and immediately sprang from his horse and kissed the Caliph's knee, saying: 'My Lord, Prince of the True Believers——' The Caliph smiled, pleased to receive the salute, and never smiled again. The kiss had been the signal to some Berber horsemen hidden nearby. They sprang upon the Caliph. One struck him with a sword on the shoulder so that his armour broke in pieces. They tore the sword which had belonged to Muhammad from his hands, and the signet from his finger. One blow from a sword cut his forehead in two, another cut off his left thumb, a third fell across his throat. When the body fell to the ground, the Berbers leaped upon him, cut off his head and fixed it on a spear; and while some of the Berbers stripped the body of its scented clothes and undergarments, others raced off to inform Munis that the Caliph was dead.

That night a man with a load of thorns drove his donkey across the battlefield and saw a headless body lying among the dead. In pity for the man's nakedness the labouring man covered the body with thorns, and then hurried to Baghdad to tell what he had seen.

Nineteen more Caliphs, each wearing the mantle of Muhammad and girding themselves with the sword, went through the pretence of ruling from Baghdad, but all of them were ciphers. The terrible game of kings had been played until it lost all meaning. Historians of a later age would amuse themselves by attempting to discover at what precise moment the Abbasid dynasty had become extinct as a living force, and perhaps the historian Hamza of Isfahan was right when he declared that it died in 921, the thirteenth year of al-Mustansir's reign. Previously there had been catastrophes, vast upheavals, the sense of things splitting asunder on the frontiers, but these periods had been rare and of short duration, and always a great soldier, a capable Vizier or a stern Caliph had emerged in time to prevent the destruction of the empire. According to Hamzah of Isfahan, the Abbasid empire died in 921, never to arise again. For more than two hundred years the pages of history were to be littered with the twitching fragments of its corpse.

The empire died, or was dying, but men went on living. Strangely, they lived better and reached greater heights of civilization during those decaying years when the empire was falling apart. Since the time of al-Mamun, no Caliph had shown any great discernment in the arts or any affection for the sciences, but the chieftains of the small principalities which arose on the frontiers of the empire were men who prized the arts and sciences. It was the time of Tabari, the great historian, famous for his bushy beard and exquisite table manners and for his practice during a long life of writing forty pages a day. It was the time, too, of the great doctor Abu Bakr Muhammad ibn-Zakariya, known to the West as Rhazes, meaning that he was a citizen of Rayy, who worshipped Plato almost as much as he worshipped Muhammad, and wrote voluminously about medicine and philosophy with a quiet detachment. He believed in a reasonable God, regarded Socrates as his master, and wrote with a dry wit: a man who seems to belong to an age far removed from the treacheries and miseries of the caliphal courts.

Something of that sense of embattled calm in the midst of disorder can be seen in the one great architectural monument of that age which has survived. This is the Mosque of al-Maydan, built by Ahmad ibn Tulun in 876–79, when he became an independent ruler of Egypt. This red-brick mosque is all simplicity and nobility. Nothing simpler can be imagined: a great square like a parade ground 500 feet long and 500 feet broad, surrounded by cloistered arcades and ornamented with a delicate tracery of windows. In the centre of the great courtyard was a marble basin covered by a dome, and just outside the mosque there rose a strange minaret, not unlike the corkscrew minaret at Samarra. The story is told that Ibn Tulun designed the minaret himself after toying with some paper, which he rolled round his finger; and then he ordered the minaret to be constructed on the model of the little roll of paper. But it is more likely that the minaret was derived from Samarra and modified by Ibn Tulun to suggest an even greater appearance of strength. The mosque imposes upon the imagination by its calm strength and casual nobility, at once fortress, place of worship and monument to its founder, who was particularly concerned that it should possess 'holiness and felicity', and takes care to mention these requirements in the dedicatory inscription he carved on marble. The dedicatory inscription should be quoted at some length, for it suggests the Augustan qualities in the worship of the time, of which there is no hint in the court annals of the Caliphs:

In the name of God, the Merciful, the Compassionate!

The Emir Abu'l-Abbas, Ahmad ibn-Tulun, client of the Commander of the Faithful, whose might, honour and perfect favour God prolong in this world and the next, commanded that this holy, happy mosque be built for the Muhammadan community, out of the legitimate and well-gotten wealth granted him by God.[1]

Desiring thereby the favour of God and the future world, and seeking

---

[1] Accused of using ill-gained money for the construction of the Mosque, Ibn Tulun was able to point out that the total cost came from treasure-trove.

that which will conduce to the glory of religion and the unity of believers, and aspiring to build a house for God and to pay His due
and to read His book, and to make perpetual mention of Him; since
God Almighty says: In houses which God has permitted to be raised,
wherein His name is mentioned, and wherein praise is rendered unto
Him morning and evening by men who are distracted neither by merchandise nor by selling from making mention of God, reciting prayers
and giving alms, fearing a day wherein the hearts and eyes shall be
troubled, that God may reward them for the good that they have
wrought, and may give them yet more out of His bounty.

In the month Ramadan of the year 265.

Exalt the Lord, the Lord of might, over that which they ascribe to
Him. And peace be on the messengers and praise unto God the Lord of
the worlds. O God, be gracious unto Muhammad, and Muhammad's
family, and bless Muhammad and his family even according to the
best of Thy favour and grace and blessing upon Abraham and his
family.

Verily Thou art glorious and to be praised.[1]

Like the mosque itself, this strangely moving dedication speaks with a
kind of calculated austerity about the things of the spirit, reflecting its
time. We are made aware of a man uttering words of devotion with the
full breath. The inscription composed by the Umayyad Caliph Abd-al-
Malik for the Dome of the Rock in Jerusalem is far shorter, but its brevity
conceals the implacable pride of a man who built a mosque of grave and
serene beauty in order to turn men's minds away from Mecca. Here there
is no *parti pris*—only the continuing act of devotion, the name of God
perpetually on men's lips.

Islam survived its rulers. For 350 years the descendants of Abu Sufyan
and those who claimed descent from al-Abbas had made war on the descendants of Muhammad's flesh, and shown themselves for the most part
incompetent and incapable of understanding the roles they were required
to play. The Islamic empire had come into existence as a result of the
momentum given to it by Muhammad: it was built on the bones of the
faithful. The faith remained, growing deeper and more assured as the
years passed, changing course slightly as it received other influences,
blazing with the irridescent colours of Syria when the capital was in
Damascus, lit by the colours of the golden deserts of Iraq and Persia when
the capital was in Baghdad, but never changing in its fundamental beliefs.
High above the Caliphs and the Emperors there was the stern, full-
blooded and visionary figure of Muhammad, to be remembered in dreams
and during the daily acts of worship, warning men about the littleness of
the earth and the splendours of the life to come.

Devotional life continued untouched by the continual wars. It was a
simple thing, based upon the daily reading of the Quran and men's

[1] D. S. Margoliouth, *Cairo, Jerusalem and Damascus* (New York: Dodd, Mead and
Company, 1907), pp. 19–20.

wonderment before some of the more startling utterances of Muhammad. From the beginning there had been a mystical element in Islam, which found nourishment in the famous Throne verse, in the beautiful description of the niche for the lamps, and in such texts as 'Wheresoever you turn there is the face of God', and 'A people whom He loveth and who love Him'. Among the followers of Ali and among those who held themselves aloof from the struggle there appeared people who came to be known as Sufis, from the simple woollen robe (*suf*)[1] worn by these spiritual wanderers as they meditated upon the nature of God. And if the Caliphs with their raised swords represented one aspect of Muhammad, another and perhaps more enduring aspect was represented by the Sufis with their downcast eyes.

We know very little about the early development of Sufism, or whether indeed there was any development. During Umayyad times, and especially during the short reign of Umar II, we hear of monkish ascetics who despised the world and sang the praises of poverty and mortification, but the true Sufis rejoiced in the world as evidence of God's greatness and they sang the praises of the God who seemed to be very close to them in the calm of contemplation. Just as we recognize the authentic voice of Muhammad in the Quran, so we recognize the authentic voice of the Sufis in the utterances of the saintly woman Rabi'a al-Adawiyya (717–801), who lived through the period of savage wars which followed the collapse of the Umayyad dynasty. Born in Basrah to poverty, and sold into slavery, she won her freedom by her evident sanctity, and soon gathered a small group of disciples around her, at first in the desert and then at Basrah. Among her prayers is one she was accustomed to say at night when standing on the roof:

> O Lord, the stars are shining and the eyes of men are closed and kings have shut their doors, and every lover is alone with his beloved, and I am alone with Thee.

Throughout her long life she wrote passionate verses concerning her overwhelming love for God and her indifference to all things that were not God. One day at springtime she entered her house and bowed her head. 'Come out,' said a woman servant, 'and behold what God hath made.' Rabi'a answered: 'Come in, and behold the Maker.' She never married, saying that she lived permanently in the shadow of God and the contract for marriage would have to be asked of Him. For her it was always enough to be in the company of God:

> Dear God, give to Thine enemies whatever Thou hast assigned to me of this world's goods, and to Thy friends whatever Thou hast assigned to me in the world to come; for Thou Thyself art sufficient to me.

---

[1] Ibn Khaldun suggested three other possible derivations: from *soffa* (sofa), *sof* (rank), and *safa* (purity); but he preferred the derivation from *suf* (wool). At this late date it is no longer possible to be sure of the exact derivation.

It was the same astonishing woman who wrote in a mood of fierce exhilaration:

O God, if I worship Thee in fear of Hell, burn me in Hell; and if I worship Thee in hope of Paradise, exclude me from Paradise; but if I worship Thee for Thine own sake, withhold not Thine everlasting Beauty.

A contemporary of Rabi'a was the famous ascetic Ibrahim ibn Adham, descended from one of the princes of Khurasan. He is said to have died during a naval expedition against the Greeks, and to have spent his happiest years as a beggar in Syria. Once he was asked why he left Khurasan, and answered: 'I find no joy in life except in Syria, where I flee with my religion from peak to peak and from hill to hill, and those who see me think I am a madman or a camel-driver.' Like St. Francis he believed that poverty was a gift of God, and he said once that one of the few moments of pure joy he ever experienced occurred when he looked at his fur garment and could not distinguish the fur from the lice. There was more of the ascetic in him than the mystic, but he belongs to the Sufis if only for his indifference to Paradise and the sweetness of his prayers:

O God, Thou knowest that Paradise weighs not with me so much as the wing of a gnat. If Thou befriendest me by Thy recollection, and sustainest me with Thy love, and make it easy for me to obey Thee, then give Thou Paradise to whomsoever Thou wilt.[1]

Strange tales were told about the early Sufis. There was the saintly Bayazid (Abu Yazid), the first of the 'God-intoxicated' Sufis, who was transported on the wings of mystical fervour and suddenly announced to his disciples: 'Behold, I myself am become God! There is no other God but Me! Glory to Me! How great is My Majesty!' The story is told that his disciples refused to be embarrassed by these ecstatic utterances, interpreting them as innocent of blasphemy; but when Bayazid was told what he had said, he answered: 'If you hear me speaking like this again, then kill me instantly!' The disciples sharpened their swords, and when they heard him saying: 'God is beneath my garments!' they stuck at him, only to have their swords curl back in their hands. Such at any rate is the story which was believed by the Sufis, who worshipped Bayazid this side of idolatry.

The stories about Bayazid are legion, and it would be easy to disbelieve them if his own writings did not confirm them. He is among the best, and most authoritative, of Sufi theologians. He declared that he had seen God many times, and, reading his own account of his ascent towards God's shining face, it is hardly possible to discredit him. He speaks quietly and calmly about things one would have thought impossible to describe. It was to him that the Sufis owed the doctrine of the annihilation of the self (*fana*), which from this time assumed a central position in Sufi thought.

[1] A. J. Arberry, *Sufism: An Account of the Mystics of Islam* (London: George Allen and Unwin, 1956), p. 37.

To Bayazid, too, belong the famous words: 'I am become the wine-drinker and the wine and the cup-bearer.'

A little later than Bayazid, who died in 909, came Junayd, a native of Baghdad, who lived obscurely and of whom few stories were told, though he was more deeply revered than any other Sufi of his age. Of his own mystical experiences he wrote once that it was like 'a continual burning, a continual shaking to the foundations, a continual emptiness in which nothing familiar is ever seen, unimaginable and unbearable in its fierce onslaughts'. Around the year 880 there came to his school in Baghdad a young mystic who was to become the most famous of them all, at once the most reckless, the most superbly intelligent and the most tragic.

Husayn ibn-Mansur was a Persian, the grandson of a fire worshipper and the son of a wool carder, from whom he derived the name by which he is known—al-Hallaj, 'the wool carder'. When he first appeared in Junayd's school, it was noted that he was unusually handsome, wore two gowns and seemed to be lost in his own dreams. It is related that after their first meeting Junayd said of him: 'His blood will stain the gibbet.' He spent about six years in the company of Junayd and broke with his master, believing that he could obtain greater mastery over himself and approach closer to the Vision of God by wandering alone on pilgrimage to Mecca. He spent a year in the shadow of the Kaaba without moving except for the prescribed ablutions and the ritual circlings round the Kaaba. He never slept, but sometimes dozed, and he seemed not to care whether it was day or night, or whether the sun was shining, or whether it was raining.

After a year of meditation he broke his silence and became a wandering preacher, travelling across Iraq and Persia to Kashmir and down into India, and later to the frontiers of China. In India he is reported to have seen the famous rope trick performed by a woman, and from the Chinese he was able to buy paper, which was then very rare: afterwards this Chinese paper was used by his students, who copied his sermons in gold ink. One day shortly after his journey to India he stretched forth an empty hand in the air and produced an apple from an invisible tree, saying he had plucked it from the tree of Paradise. One of the disciples pointed out that the apple was full of maggot holes, and al-Hallaj laughed, saying: 'How could it be otherwise? I plucked the apple from a tree in the Mansion of Eternity and brought it into the House of Decay, and that is why it is touched with corruption!'

His strange sermons and poems, written with fire, were filled with such paradoxes. He could say the simplest things in the simplest words, and terrify his friends because what he said possessed a blinding clarity. One day when he was wandering through the market-place, a scribe took down the words he uttered in an ecstasy of weeping:

O hide me from God! God has ravished me from myself, and will not give me back to myself, and so I cannot praise Him—I am fearful of being abandoned by Him!

For God made men out of simple charity, and if He shines before men and sometimes wears a veil before men, it is always so that men may be helped. And if He did not shine, all would deny His existence, and if He did not veil Himself, all would be spellbound! And that is why He changes from one to the other. As for me there is now no longer any veil, not so much as a wink, between me and God! And now is the time of my peace, when my humanity will perish in His divinity, my body consumed in the raging flames of His Omnipotence—and then there will be no trace of me on earth, no relic of me, no face, no word.[1]

More and more as he grew older he desired to lose himself completely in God, to become wholly man and wholly God. He was nearly fifty when he went into the Mosque of al-Mansur and sought out his friend Shibli, a Turkish nobleman, and a well-known poet, and announced simply: 'I am the Truth' ('*ana 'Haqq*'). At the time Shibli was surrounded by his disciples, and many people heard the words with a shudder, for al-Hallaj was announcing in the simplest possible terms that he had become God or that God had so penetrated him that there was no difference between them. Men feared that al-Hallaj would be arrested for blasphemy.[2]

Ecstatic, al-Hallaj continued to wander through the streets of Baghdad, delivering sermons, speaking quietly and authoritatively about the nature of God. No one dared touch him, for the Queen Mother and many of the high officials at court favoured him. But his long meditations had led him into the belief that it was necessary to 'die into God', to offer himself as a sacrifice, following the example of Jesus, and so entering into the Godhead at a moment of the highest ecstasy. Once again he entered the Mosque of el-Mansur and said to the people: 'God has made my blood lawful unto you, therefore kill me!' When they asked him why he wanted to die, he answered: 'So that you may be rewarded and so that I may have peace, and so that you may be fighters for the faith and I a martyr!' But no one desired to kill him, except the Hanbalites, those followers of the fundamentalist Ahmad ibn-Hanbal, who regarded the doctrine of *ittihad*, the identification of God with man, as the highest form of blasphemy.

In those last years the faith of al-Hallaj took on the colours of his Persian character. It was not only that he was an ecstatic, but he was ecstatic in the Persian manner, in love with fire and flame, seeing all life as a continual 'dancing into God'. He made a model of the Kaaba and walked round it, saying that the model was as good as the original in bringing one to God; and though he had made three pilgrimages to Mecca, he spoke of Mount Sinai, where Moses vanished into the Light, as a holier place. Step by step he seemed to be moving towards the inevitable cirsis, looking forward to the time when God's finger would be 'stained with the lover's blood'.

[1] Louis Massignon, *Al-Hallaj, martyre mystique de l'Islam* (Paris: Paul Geuthner, 1922), II, 123.

[2] Jalalu'l-Din Rumi, the great mystical poet of Persia, pointed out in a poem dedicated to al-Hallaj that it is less presumptuous to say, 'I am the Truth' or 'I am God' than to say, as Muhammadans continually do, 'I am the slave of God.' By saying, 'I am God' the mystic has surrendered to God unequivocally, assuming for himself no stature, not even the stature of a slave, in an extremity of humility and tenderness.

There is a sense in which the whole Abbasid epoch culminates in the figure of the handsome and superbly gifted ascetic as he appears to run dancing to his death, protesting the glory of God and the worthlessness of his age. He asked for no forgiveness. 'The perfume of Thy coming,' he wrote, 'suffices to make me despise all creation, and Hell is nothing to the void within me when Thou deserted me: forgive others, do not forgive me.' At another time he wrote: 'The way to God is two steps: one step out of this world, and then one step out of the next, and then thou art in God's holy presence.' And when he spoke about his desire to die for the sake of God, he suggested not one but many motives, as though all his senses and his intelligence had separately fused into a single shattering desire:

Kill me, my zealous comrades, for my death is a coming into life.
My life is a dying, my death an awakening,
My greatest gift the annihilation of my being.
To live a little while longer is the worst of crimes.
Among these crumbling ruins I despair over my life:
Therefore kill me and burn me in the fire until my bones perish.
And then if it should happen that you pass close by my remains,
You will find the secret of my Friend in my ghostly spirit.
I became a Patriarch of the highest rank,
And then I became a child wandering in the skirts of his nurse.
And all the time I lay on my tomb in the salty earth.
My mother gave birth to her father: such is the miracle!
And the daughters of my loins have become my own sisters,
Nor were my ways adulterous, nor did these events occur in time.
And all the scattered fragments of my being shall become air, fire and pure water,
To be thrown by the seedman into the dry soil,
And let the dancing girls pour wine and water on my fields.
In the space of seven days a perfect flower will come to birth! [1]

So in a mood of paradox, hinting at rebirth, al-Hallaj announced his coming end with no thought of how it would be brought about. He seems to have hoped that someone would strike him down with a knife, but this mercy was refused to him. Suddenly, in 908, orders were given for his arrest, and he escaped to Susa. Some of his followers were arrested, but no serious effort was made to discover his hiding place until 911, when the police pounced upon him, brought him to Baghdad in chains and threw him into prison without bringing any charges against him. At last in 913 'the good vizier' Ali ibn-Isa was ordered to inquire into the charges of heresy brought against al-Hallaj by the Hanbalites. Ali ibn-Isa was a man of high principles, judicious and unimaginative, perfectly capable of condemning al-Hallaj if he felt that the crime of blasphemy had in fact been committed, but he refused to have the blood of the saintly ascetic on his hands. To satisfy the Hanbalites, Ali ibn-Isa concluded that a token punishment was required, and accordingly al-Hallaj was condemned not as a heretic but as a charlatan, and he was ordered to have his beard cut off, to be beaten with the flat of the sword, to be exposed for four days on the pillory and to be kept in prison in chains. Al-Hallaj was as far removed as ever from the death he desired.

In prison he was treated with every mark of respect. A special building

---

[1] *Hocein Mansur Hallaj, Diwan*, tr. Louis Massignon (Paris: Editions des Cahiers du Sud, 1955), p. 27.

was erected for him just outside the prison wall, with a gate leading to a courtyard where al-Hallaj could preach to the prisoners. The walls of his new house were covered with carpets; he was allowed to receive visitors, and to keep servants. Two years later, when the Caliph al-Muqtadir seemed to be dying of a fever, al-Hallaj was brought to the palace and lodged in a room next to the Caliph's; and it was widely believed that the Caliph's recovery was due to his intercession. The Queen Mother visited him, to learn from his lips the secrets of *hulul*, by which al-Hallaj meant the incarnation of God in the human body. A host of visitors came to marvel or listen to the sermons he preached quietly, with downcast eyes, while sitting cross-legged on the floor, or in moments of ecstatic excitement, leaping about the room. Strange stories were told of how he swelled out until he filled the whole room; of how a handkerchief he had dropped walked back to his sleeve; of how he was able to foretell the future and knew all the secrets of the past.

In the court he was feared. So many legends gathered about his name that he seemed to be larger than life, and there were many who believed he was the representative of the hidden Lord of the Age. But the Caliph, his Vizier, and Munis, the Greek eunuch who had risen to the command of the armies, feared the growing power of the Hanbalites, who were threatening revolution, and quite suddenly, at the end of a feast given in honour of Munis, the drunken Caliph signed the order of execution.

On the night before the death he desired above everything else, al-Hallaj went through his customary ritual of prayers, performing the two prostrations in the direction of Mecca. Afterwards he was silent. Some who were present heard him repeating the word 'illusion' half the night with a look of despair written over his face, as though he felt that his sacrifice were in vain, but towards dawn he bounded to his feet and shouted: 'The Truth! The Truth!' He put on his turban, donned his cloak, stretched out his arms, and, while facing Mecca, he fell into an ecstasy and talked with God.

He spoke of the splendours awaiting him, and how his human body had been made in the shining image of God, and how at last he was being tested in the furnace of his desire. He gave thanks to God for having permitted him to utter the sacred words by which he had entered creation. 'Surely,' he said, 'I who have been Thine incense shall rise again,' and then he went on to speak in verse:

I cry to God: Sorrow over thy witness who now departs into the Beyond to welcome the Witness of Eternity.
I cry to God: Sorrow over the hearts bedewed in vain with the waters of revelation and the oceans of wisdom.
I cry to God: Sorrow over the Word which is lost and whose meaning is a void in the mind.
I cry to God: Sorrow over Thy love and for the goodness of Thy servants, whose mounts were continually ready to obey:
For all have passed away across the deserts, leaving no footprints nor any watering places, And the abandoned herd runs behind, blinder than the beasts, blinder than a flock of sheep.[1]

[1] *Hocein Mansur Hallaj, Diwan*, tr. Louis Massignon (Paris: Editions des Cahiers du Sud, 1955), p. 14.

M

When his servant Ibrahim asked him for a keepsake, he answered: 'I give you yourself.' When morning came, all his bitterness against 'the blind beasts' had gone, and he went laughing to the execution ground, not far from the prison, on the right bank of the Tigris. Asked why he was laughing, he answered: 'From the caresses of Infinite Beauty.' When he saw the gibbet he laughed still louder: he was like a man running to his beloved.

The news that he was about to be executed was known throughout Baghdad, and a huge crowd had gathered. To some people in the crowd he announced calmly: 'I shall return in thirty days.' Standing below the gibbet, he saw his friend Shibli and asked whether he had brought a prayer rug, and when this was given to him he prostrated himself and performed the offices which are performed by all those about to be executed, and then he said very calmly:

> Those who adore Thee, O God, have assembled here to kill me out of
> their love for Thee, so that they may come closer unto Thee. Pardon
> them, O Lord! If Thou hast revealed to them what Thou hast revealed
> to me, they would not have done what they have done; and if Thou
> hadst concealed from me what Thou hast concealed from them, I should
> not have suffered this tribulation. Power and glory unto Thee in what-
> soever Thou doest, and power and glory unto Thee in whatsoever Thou
> willest![1]

Such was his last prayer, the most beautiful he ever uttered and perhaps the most beautiful ever uttered by a Muhammadan, and a moment later he rose to face the executioner, who dealt him a blow between the eyes which smashed his forehead and sent the blood streaming out of his nose. Shibli cried out, tore at his clothes, and fell in a dead faint; and the crowd howled at the sight of the martyr's blood.

Punishment in medieval times was complex, prolonged, formed of many diverse passions. A criminal sentenced to death must die many deaths. First, his skull was smashed; then he was scourged; then his hands and feet were cut off; then the body was roped to the gibbet and tar was applied to the bleeding stumps to prevent him from bleeding to death. All day he hung there, saying nothing, and it was observed that his face was still ruddy. When night fell, a messenger came from the Caliph giving permission for his head to be struck off, but one of the officers present said that it was already too late and the final act could wait until morning. At sunrise the next day, March 26, 922, al-Hallaj was lifted barely conscious from the gibbet and deposited on a leather mat a few feet away. Someone heard him saying 'All I have longed for . . . The loneliness of God . . .' It must have been at this time that Shibli threw him the red rose which was mentioned in many poems written later. Then the sword descended, and his head was struck off. The body was thereupon rolled up in a strip of reed matting, soaked in naphtha and burned. Later the head was ex-

---

[1] Massignon, *Al-Hallaj, I,* p. 303.

posed on the bridge at Baghdad, and the ashes were taken up to a minaret and scattered to the winds.

Afterwards they remembered many strange things that happened during the long execution: how there had almost been a riot when the executioner, Abu al-Harith, struck the martyr, and how the body had writhed and twisted in the flames, and how his words seemed to echo on the air long after he was incapable of speech. Some of his followers believed, as Muhammadans believe of Jesus, that he was not crucified, but a semblance or image of him was crucified instead. And all, for different reasons, remembered him. The Caliph remembered the curse that lay upon him; Munis, too, remembered, and was to die only a few years later in the palace prison, held over the gutters while his throat was slit; the Queen Mother remembered, and she kept the embalmed head of the saint in that special treasury in the palace which was reserved for the heads of great saints and great criminals. The Sufis wrote about him endlessly, and the great poet Jalalu'l-Din Rumi celebrated him in many poems. The philosophers al-Ghazzali and Ibn Arabi wrote about him at length as though he were another Muhammad come to earth. In lands which al-Hallaj had never known, in Java and Bengal and Ottoman Turkey, his devotees built temples in honour of the man who declared quietly and confidently, 'I am the Truth,' and who wrote once in words which seem to be an invitation to a perpetual feast: 'If the sun should rise at night, the dawn of hearts will have no setting.'

THE RAGE OF KINGDOMS

THE DEATH of al-Hallaj marked the end of an era. Almost alone he had hoped to bring men into a direct awareness of the divine, that sense of a luminous divinity which had been present in the time of Muhammad; but it was already too late. Henceforward, as the poet Rainer Maria Rilke said of the years following the First World War, 'affairs were no longer in the hands of God, but in the hands of men'. Soon the Abbasid empire would split asunder; a thousand sects and a hundred contending kingdoms would arise; but such was the genius of Islam that it produced some of its greatest artists and philosophers in its time of troubles. Men were to learn that Islam could survive the Muhammadan empire.

In Baghdad the wide-eyed Caliphs, their Arab blood watered by the mingled strains of their slave mothers, still sat on their thrones in robes stiff with gold, crept about their palaces like glittering ghosts, and on state occasions held in their hands the holy sword of Muhammad, but they were no more than shadows.

The four successors of the Caliph al-Muqtadir died without honour. Al-Qahir, the half-brother of al-Muqtadir, reigned for two years until his soldiers wearied of him, and when he refused to abdicate they put out his eyes with hot needles. Al-Qahir was luckier than his successor, al-Radi, who was smothered to death at the end of a six-year reign, and al-Muttaqi and al-Mustakfi, who were both blinded. At one period three former Caliphs, all blind, were wandering like beggars through the streets of Baghdad.

Since the Caliph was the repository of both spiritual and temporal power, directly related to the family of Muhammad, there were advantages in painting the corpse and pretending there was life in him. These advantages were employed by Ahmad ibn-Buwayh, the chieftain of a rebellious tribe of Daylamites from the southern shores of the Caspian, who in December, 945, conquered Baghdad, put the Turkish guards to flight, and assumed full power, granting himself the title of Sultan, inscribing his own name on the coinage and ordering that his title of Muizz ad-Dawlah, meaning 'He who gives power to the state', be mentioned along with the Caliph's in the Cathedral services. Henceforth for a hundred years the Buwayhids ruled over the empire, giving high positions to their sons, marrying into the caliphal family, making and unmaking Caliphs at will. They destroyed the last vestiges of rule by the Turkish guards, instituted public mourning on the anniversary of Husayn's death, and abandoned Baghdad for their own capital in Shiraz, at the heart of the ancient Achaemenian empire, not far from Persepolis. For centuries

Persian influence had been in the ascendancy; now for the first time the real rulers of the empire were Persians.

The Buwayhids ruled wisely, endowed hospitals, created libraries. They had the Persian love for splendour, and the Persian carelessness with money, with the result that the treasury was often empty and there were periods when the economy broke down. They were cultivated men with an instinct for the good things of life, and they chose good viziers. Shiraz became a city as beautiful as Baghdad. Under Adud al-Dawlah, the nephew of Ahmad ibn-Buwayh, Shiraz became 'the sweetest fruit of the empire', a city of blue-tiled mosques and great rose gardens and many parks, with libraries, academies and hospitals for the welfare of the people, who were said to be so proud of their city 'that they looked down their noses at Baghdad, saying it was but a small village in the provinces'. It was not true; for the Buwayhids took care to embellish the capital city of the empire with as many great buildings as they built in Shiraz, and the first great university hospital, in which all diseases were examined, as distinguished from the small private hospitals, was built by them in Baghdad.

Under Adud al-Dawlah the real ruler of the empire was Abu Fadhl ibn-Amid, who seemed to revive in himself all the glories of al-Mamun's reign. People with bated breath spoke of his knowledge of languages, his skill at war, his understanding of the arts and sciences. He could remember every poem he ever set eyes on. He was as learned in Aristotelian philosophy as in the commentaries on the Quran. He was one of those rare universal geniuses who appear on earth from time to time, filling lesser men with inextinguishable envy. He was gentle and unassuming, and the Buwayhid prince sat at his feet and marvelled and thanked God daily that the affairs of state were in the hands of the wisest man in Islam.

Abu Fadhl needed to be wise, for already the empire was crumbling. The historian Miskawayh, who was Adud al-Dawlah's treasurer, has left a strange picture of the empire during those years when Shiraz and Baghdad were great centres of learning, crowded with gleaming buildings tiled with faïence, with trade coming from all the ends of the earth. Men spoke of their presentiment that this prosperity could not last: somewhere beyond the frontiers lay an invisible enemy, hiding in clouds of darkness, but where he was or what face he would show remained unknown to them.

The edges of the empire were breaking off, new principalities were coming into existence, rival Caliphs were proclaiming their independence, but the empire continued to flourish in an uneasy balance with all the hostile forces gathering on its frontiers. What is astonishing to the modern historian is that this slow disintegration produced so much exquisite art.

A minor princeling who called himself Sayf al-Dawlah ('the sword of the state') carved out for himself a principality in the northwestern corner of Syria, with Aleppo as his capital. He fought brilliantly against the Byzantines, and surrounded himself during the twenty-three years of his reign with a court almost as brilliant as that which surrounded al-Mamun, distinguished especially by the poet al-Mutanabbi, who is still considered by the Arabs to be the greatest of all Arab poets. Al-Mutanabbi described the wars of his sovereign with astonishing relish. The son of a poor water-carrier in al-Kufah, he was completely at home in the court, and was treated with so much tolerance by the prince that he sang his poems before the throne while sitting comfortably and without making any prostrations, one hand on the hilt of his sword, as though he was determined to proclaim the primacy of poetry. His poems are full of conceits: the teeth of lovers melt in the embrace, the king's sword hews through a hundred bodies in an instant, and a single pearl cast by a prince will put his enemies to flight. He writes best of the desert, with his portraits of the Bedouin women in scarlet robes riding their camels over the desert towards the darkness and the hills, and even to our modern ears, weary of warlike conceits, his descriptions of battle are exhilarating. In the end al-Mutannabi broke with his patron and visited Egypt, but he was too hot-tempered to take kindly to the treatment he received; he was making his way towards Persia in search of a new patron when he was set upon by a marauding band of Bedouins and killed.

Al-Mutannabi had a rival in the prince's cousin, Abu Firas, who also wrote of war, but with greater tenderness, perhaps because he knew war only too well, having fought against the Byzantines and been taken prisoner. He was one of the few great poets who have died on the battlefield, for on the death of Sayf al-Dawlah he declared himself Prince of Hims and fell fighting against his cousin's son.

Poets and historians and philosophers flocked to Sayf al-Dawlah's court. Among them was al-Farabi, a Turk from Farab in Transoxiana, who devoted himself to the study of Aristotle and whose writings on the nature of God influenced St. Thomas Aquinas. His ambition was to harmonize the different Greek systems and then harmonize these with the Quran; and it is to him that we owe the classic statement on the nature of time: 'Time is the movement which holds all things together.' No other sovereign of a small principality ever surrounded himself with so many talents.

Sayf al-Dawlah's principality was a wedge introduced between the Byzantine and Abbasid empires, and could be left safely to its own devices. It was another matter when Egypt was conquered by the Fatimids, who claimed descent from Fatima, the daughter of Muhammad, and assumed the title and spiritual prerogatives of the Caliphate, which they asserted to be theirs by divine right. The conquest had been planned during the previous century by Abdallah ibn-Maymun, a Persian oculist with visions of imperial grandeur, who established himself in Tunisia with the help of the Qarmatians and inaugurated a widespread secret society with the aim of destroying the Abbasid empire. He died in 875, but the movement he had brought into being continued under the leadership of his descendants. In 970 the Fatimid armies under Jawhar al-Katib, formerly a Christian slave from Sicily, conquered Egypt and Syria, founded the city of Cairo (al-Qahirah, 'the triumphant'), and obtained the submission of the Hijaz; and prayers were recited in the name of the new Fatimid Caliph al-Muizz in the holy cities of Madinah and Mecca. There were now three Muhammadan empires: the Umayyad Caliphs ruled over Spain, Iraq and Persia remained in the hands of the Abbasids, and North Africa, Egypt, Syria and Arabia were in the hands of the Fatimids.

The Fatimids inherited all the panoply which accompanies Arab conquerors in their progress. With startling suddenness they introduced an era of widespread peace in lands which had known only perpetual war. In a ferocious battle outside the gates of Cairo, they destroyed the armies of the Qarmatians, and settled down to enjoy the power which had come to them with so little effort Artists and poets flocked to their courts. A new art coloured by the climate of Africa emerged in their workshops. Under the second Caliph al-Aziz the Fatimid empire reached its furthest limits, extending from the Atlantic to the Red Sea.

The third of the Fatimid Caliphs who reigned from Egypt appeared to have modelled himself on the character of Nero. Tall, fair-haired, with blue eyes—his mother was the sister of the orthodox Patriarch of Jerusalem—he raged like a whirlwind through his trembling court. From the time when he came to the throne at the age of eleven in 996, he performed one atrocity after another. He issued strange and contradictory orders. He would have a Vizier executed for omitting to address him with all his titles. He suffered from bouts of intense melancholia, and at such times he wandered alone through the countryside, gazing at the stars and howling like a wolf. In his lucid moments he was intelligent and charming, and was a generous patron of the arts, but as he grew older the lucid moments became rarer. He invented stringent laws for the pleasure of punishing offenders. In 1009 he forbade pilgrimages and ordered the destruction of all churches and synagogues throughout the empire, except the Church of the Nativity at Bethlehem, but including the Church of the Holy Sepulcher at Jerusalem. He ordered all the vineyards of Egypt to be uprooted; prohibited banquets, music and chess, and even promenades along the banks of the Nile. He made Christians and Jews wear black clothes as a sign of their inferior status in comparison with Muhammadans. He set older women to spy on young women, and they were empowered to report on all love affairs. He invited the famous mathematician and physicist al-Hasan ibn-al-Haytham, known to the West as Alhazen, to his court. Alhazen was the author of a vast and compendious work on optics, which influenced medical treatment of the eyes throughout the Middle Ages, and he was the first to employ a magnifying glass. He was an engineer, geometrician and surgeon as well as a mathematician and a physicist, and when he came to Egypt he was asked to regulate the Nile's floods, from which the entire economy of Egypt derived. Unhappily, his theoretical calculations were at fault, he was unable to regulate the floods, and the Caliph ordered his arrest. For the rest of al-Hakim's life the greatest scientist of the time remained in hiding or in flight.

The unlimited power at the disposal of the weak Caliph sapped his strength. He became completely mad. Fearing the darkness, he ordered that no one should go out at night; and being in love with the grey ass which took him on his solitary wanderings, he ordered that anyone found beating an ass should be beaten almost to death. Towards the end of his life missionaries sprang up in Cairo teaching a strange new religion, the divinity of the Caliph. The submissive people of Cairo, alarmed by this new and terrifying claim, murdered several of the missionaries, and al-Hakim, who was disposed to believe in his own divinity, avenged himself by taking the Jews and Christians into favour and permitting their churches and synagogues to be rebuilt. At more bloodthirsty moments he set his Sudanese mercenaries, who performed the same function as the Turkish guards of the rival Caliph, against the Muhammadan population. Civil war flared up, to break the long midnight silences in which the Caliph communed with the stars.

He was communing with the stars when he was killed one February evening in 1021. With two attendants, riding his grey ass, he had ridden out to his observatory on the hill of Muqattam. They said afterwards that ten tribesmen approached him threateningly, saying they had often waited in vain outside his palace door, but had received no money from him. The Caliph laughed, ordered them to be paid 10,000 pieces of silver from the treasury, and offered to send one of the attendants back with them. The tribesmen suspected treachery, and asked for a safe-conduct, which the Caliph gave them. Then the tribesmen went away, only to return a little later when they learned that the Caliph had given orders for them to be murdered when they arrived in Cairo. They killed the Caliph, and then vanished. A search party was sent out. They found the ass on top of the hill with its forelegs hacked off. Blood marks on the ground led to a hollow, where they found the Caliph's clothes pierced by daggers and carefully buttoned up. There was no sign of his body.

Many Caliphs had died mysterious deaths, but no one had left his clothes so neatly behind. He seemed to have dematerialized himself, and some said he had become a Christian monk at Sketis in Egypt. A Persian, Muhammad ibn-Ismail al-Darazi ('the tailor'), announced that al-Hakim would return in good time, more godlike than ever, to destroy Jerusalem and Mecca, being absolute God and therefore to be worshipped with complex rites and secret initiations. At the last trumpet the veil covering his divinity would fall away, and all men would set eyes on that strange long-haired and blue-eyed Caliph who died near his observatory.[1] The Druses, who take their name from al-Darazi, still live in Lebanon and in the neighbourhood of Damascus and continue to believe in the second coming of al-Hakim.[2]

The mad Caliph was followed by a sane fourteen-year-old boy, who

[1] The claim of divinity had already been made by al-Muizz, who declared that his ancestors and his own person were 'the eternal world of God, His perfect names, His dazzling lights, His brilliant signs and the ineluctable decrees of fate.' See H. Lammens, S.J., *Islam: Beliefs and Institutions* (New York: E. P. Dutton and Company, n.d.), p. 162.

[2] Benjamin of Tudela, who visited the Druses in 1163, says: 'Their dwellings are on the summits of the mountains and in the ridges of the rocks, and they are subject to no king or prince. This people live incestuously; a father cohabits with his own daughter, and once every year all men and women assemble to celebrate a festival, upon which occasion, after eating and drinking, they hold promiscuous intercourse.'

took the name al-Zahir. During the fifteen years of his reign he fought a series of successful wars in Syria, which had been the prey of usurpers, but his most notable act, one most often forgotten by historians of the Crusades, was to allow the rebuilding of the Holy Sepulchre. He died of the plague in 1036, and was succeeded by al-Mustansir, who was only seven years old at the time of his accession. Power accordingly fell into the hands of his mother, once a Negro slave, and her former master, a Jewish curiosity dealer. Such an unlikely beginning might have presaged ill fortune on the dynasty, but al-Mustansir lived to be the longest reigning Caliph of all time—he survived through sixty years of war, famine and plague. During his reign Baghdad was briefly conquered, and so it happened that the treasury of the Abbasid Caliphs, which included the mantle of Muhammad and the two-pointed sword Dhu'l-Faqar won at the battle of Badr together with the cuirass of Husayn and the shield of the great warrior Hamza, fell into the hands of the Fatimid Caliphs, remaining with them until Saladin returned them to the Caliph of Baghdad.

In the intervals of war al-Mustansir gave himself up to unexampled luxury. Fatimid Egypt in the eleventh century possessed the gift of luxury, and the means to satisfy it. The handsome clean-shaven Caliph, who dressed simply in a white silk kaftan with a white turban, concealed under the mask of reserve an intoxicated delight in the splendour of his power. He was continually building palaces and pavilions. One of his palaces contained a jewelled reproduction of the Kaaba, and he liked to amuse himself by drinking in front of it, while slave girls and dancing girls attended him. He is said to have remarked: 'It is more pleasant sitting here than looking at the Black Stone, listening to the ugly voice of the muezzin and drinking rank water.' He commissioned pictures of dancers from Persian artists, built mosques and saw to it that the streets of Cairo should be lighted by oil lamps at night; and he ordered that the main streets should be roofed against the sun, a sensible device which has rarely been followed. The island of Sicily had fallen to the Fatimids, and 30,000 pieces of fine Sicilian embroidery were found in the wardrobes of one Fatimid princess.

The exquisite art of the Fatimids is still too little known, perhaps because the greater part of it has remained in Egypt. It is the art of a people who have learned how to enjoy luxury and are not afraid to express their enjoyment. The austere Kufic inscriptions in the Fatimid mosques suggest that luxury never imperilled the core of their religion; and their delicate ceramic bowls suggest an impassioned delight in colour and texture for their own sake. The most revealing of the surviving Fatimid works of art is the bronze griffin forty inches high, now in the Campo Santo at Pisa, with its superb mingling of delicacy and strength. The griffin's haunches and legs, the full expanded chest and the powerful upflung wings which would slice the air with short and savage thrusts have about them the imperious strength we associate with conquerors. Neither Persian nor Coptic influence can be felt. The bronze griffin represents Fatimid power in all it luxury and glory, four-square, with feet planted firmly in the earth, pausing for a few moments to regard the world with an imperial gesture before soaring into the dark Egyptian night.

While the Fatimids showed a superb sense of their mastery in bronze, in weaving and in ceramics, they demonstrated little taste for literature. The one great poet of the period, Abu al-Ala al-Ma'arri, was a blind Syrian with a bitter tongue who concealed his horror of the world and fears of coming disaster under a mask of perfect orthodoxy until towards the end of his life he was overwhelmed by the inanity of things and lashed out against the pilgrims and commentators of the Quran indifferently, reserving his most bitter blasts for the sacred Kaaba itself. Rage filled him, but it was like the rage of the elder Yeats, blowing like an autumn gale. 'I live in a cursed time,' he wrote once, but he seemed to have enjoyed life in spite of his bitterness and he lived to be eighty-four.

In Spain, too, Islam had passed the zenith of its power, falling into that state of decay which Ibn Khaldun detected as the inevitable consequence of luxury. Abd-ar-Rahman I, the Umayyad prince who conquered Spain and defied the Abbasid Caliph, was a man of simple tastes who waited until the end of his life before deciding to build the mosque which came to be known as the Great Mosque of Cordova. Luxury came in with his grandson Abd-ar-Rahman II, who made his Spanish eunuch his Vizier and spent his time with his Persian music master, Ziryab, who had wandered into Spain from the court of Harun al-Rashid. The Umayyad Caliph was so delighted with the talents of the young and handsome Ziryab that he would seat him beside him and share meals with him, and listen for hours to his songs. Ziryab was said to know a thousand songs, each with a different tune. Ja'far ibn-Yahya was an exquisite, but Ziryab was more exquisite still. He was Beau Brummell, the artificer of court ceremonies, the amused spectator of a thousand follies, many of which he introduced. He taught people at court how to wear their hair, how to prostrate themselves before the Caliph, how they should ride their horses during parades. He taught them to eat asparagus, suggested the advantages of crystal over metal drinking cups, of sleeping on leather beds, dining off leather mats and of wearing clothes according to the gradations of the seasons: a courtier was expected to wear the lightest of silks in summer and the heaviest furs in winter. Ziryab was the very symbol of exhausted effeminacy; and he appeared at a time when the Christians of Cordova, exasperated by the fecklessness of the Arabs, were taunting their conquerors with demands for martyrdom, denying the flesh as the Arabs satiated themselves with the refinements of luxury. An ascetic priest, Eulogius, led the movement against Muhammadanism, and was decapitated at the orders of the Caliph for having entered a mosque and denied Muhammad. There were many others. In Paris men trembled with the hope of a new age of martyrdom, and the priests of St. Germain-des-Près became the willing servants of the martyrs, stealing secretly into Spain to bear witness that the martyrs had not died in vain and returning to Paris with their bones.

Not all the Christians were prepared to die for their faith. In 850, during the last years of the reign of Abd-ar-Rahman II, the priest Alvarez of Cordova reproached the Christians for their preference for Arab speech and Arab books. 'They neglect the Bible for the Muhammadan scriptures,' he said. Arab eloquence, Arab refinement, Arab luxury had conquered Spanish hearts, and they were never to free themselves completely from these toils.

Under the reign of Abd-ar-Rahman III (912–961), who came to the throne at the age of twenty-three, Cordova reached its greatest heights. Tall, handsome, ruddy-faced and blue-eyed, his mother a Christian slave, Abd-ar-Rahman set about imposing his will upon the country as soon as he came to the throne. There had been constant rebellions; he gave orders that rebellion should cease, and when the orders were disobeyed he marched at the head of his army and demanded the immediate surrender of the rebel fortresses, saying that he was not interested in tribute, only in complete submission, and he would pardon all who would submit freely. He subdued the Christians of León and Castille; destroyed an uprising of the Basques; occupied Toledo, which had enjoyed its freedom for eighty years; took Ceuta from the Fatimids; and built in the shipyards of Almería a fleet of two hundred ships to ward off the threatened blows from the east. In all these military adventures he was assisted by mercenaries known as the *Saqalibah*, or Slavs, captives and slaves from all parts of Europe. Many were captives from the German marches bought in the great slave market at Verdun. Others came from Byzantium, whence the slave ships sailed along the northern coast of the Black Sea; Spanish privateers raided the coasts of Italy and southern France. These mercenaries, like the Turkish guards employed by the Abbasid Caliphs, were a potential danger to the state, but while he was alive he dealt with them firmly. One of these Slavs was placed in command of the army in a campaign against León and Navarre.

For eighteen years Abd-ar-Rahman III waged a series of wars through the length and breadth of Spain, and then he rested. He was powerful enough to fear no one. In 929, defying the Fatimid Caliph al-Muizz, he proclaimed himself Caliph, taking the title of al-Nasir, 'the Defender of the Faith'. He had good reason to rest. Andalusia was now the most civilized province on earth, with annual revenues of more than 6,000,000 dinars. The Caliph decided upon a simple division of expenditure: a third was spent on current expenses, a third was deposited in the treasury, a third was spent on buildings.

All the Umayyad princes had helped to build the Great Mosque at Cordova, which had been built on the grounds of the Visigothic church of San Vicenzo, overlooking the river. This immense and battlemented mosque remains today the chief glory of western Islam, though no Muhammadan prayers are ever uttered there. With its hundreds of columns, its strange horseshoe arches painted with red and white bands surmounted by a higher register of similar arches, its infinitely complicated perspectives along jewelled arcades, it somehow suggests an orange orchard in full bloom: not such an orchard as one might see with human eyes, but as it would appear in Paradise. Today, shorn of its magnificence, it is still magnificent. Once the sanctuary was paved with silver and inlaid with mosaics, and the *minbar* (pulpit), which Muhammadans liked to decorate with woods of many colours arranged in complex patterns, consisted of strips of ivory interspersed with 36,000 separate strips of wood; and the forest of columns, which in the end numbered altogether 1,293, was set with gold and lapis lazuli. The hanging lanterns were made from the bronze bells of Christian churches, and every chandelier, according to the chronicler, held a thousand lamps. All round the walls there were, and are, mosaics designed by craftsmen from Byzantium. Gone was the essential simplicity of the Mosque of Ibn Tulun. Once more at Cordova we are back again in the Great Umayyad Mosque, with its suggestion of almost feminine luxury. Quite deliberately the designers intend to suggest the vision of Paradise in all its fullness and in all its finery. There was no attempt at height, for the ceilings are low—height would come later when the Turkish architect Sinan designed his mosques in the soaring image of Santa Sophia. It was, after all, a very human Paradise which they wanted men to enter; and they deliberately planted orange trees in the courtyard to prolong the vista of the columns.

Not content with embellishing the mosque and adding a magnificent new minaret which became the model for the Giralda in Seville, Abd-ar-Rahman decided to build a royal city of his own, which he called az-Zahra, 'the shining one', after a favourite concubine. The new city was built on the spurs of the Sierra Morena overlooking the Guadalquiver. For the twenty-five remaining years of his reign, and fifteen years of the reign of his son, 10,000 workmen with 1,500 beasts of burden laboured on it. The chroniclers say that 6,000 blocks of stone were cut and polished every day. There were 15,000 doors, all coated with iron or polished brass. The city was built on three terraces, with gardens below, the houses of the court functionaries in the middle, and the Caliph's palace, with 400 rooms and apartments, standing high above them all. The throne room had a roof and walls of marble and gold; the eight doors rested on pillars of marble and crystal, under gilded arches of ebony and ivory set with jewels. Altogether 4,300 columns imported from Africa and France were employed in building the palace, and the rarest of them decorated the throne room. In the middle of the hall was a marble fountain, and above it, resting in a golden cup, was a solitary pearl. It was the largest pearl anyone had ever seen, a present from the Byzantine Emperor. In the fountain there was no water, only quicksilver. When the sun shone on the quicksilver, the whole throne room blazed with sudden silvery lights.

From the accounts of the chroniclers it is impossible to discover the slightest element of the grotesque in az-Zahra. Abd-ar-Rahman was consciously employing his wealth to create deliberate splendour, a palace worthy of a living king, as the Taj Mahal is worthy of a dead queen. The Great Mosque of Cordova resembled an orange orchard, sanctified and infinitely more desirable than any orchard, while the royal city flowing down the hillside suggested a waterfall, flashing in the sun, blinding the onlooker. Today on the slopes of the Sierra Morena there is only rubble.

While the Caliph spent money royally on az-Zahra, he was also spending huge sums on Cordova itself. It was a large city with half a million inhabitants, with 113,000 houses, 3,000 mosques, 70 libraries and 900 public baths. Travellers said you could walk ten miles through the streets of Cordova at night, and always there would be a lamp from one of the houses to light the way. The nun Hroswitha, in her Saxon convent at Gandersheim, told of the martyrdom of St. Eulogius, but could not prevent herself from exclaiming upon the beauty of Cordova, calling it 'the jewel of the world'. The arts flourished; the lecture rooms were crowded; embassies came flocking from the four corners of the earth to see the wonderful city; there was more trade than men had ever known before; and there was peace in the land. The Caliph however was not satisfied. As he lay dying at the age of seventy-three, he wrote out in a shaking hand a list of the days in his long reign which had been free from sorrow: he could count only fourteen. 'O man of understanding,' he added, 'observe how small a portion of unclouded happiness the world gives even to the most fortunate!'

None of the Arab chroniclers have disputed that he was the most fortunate of Caliphs. His son Hakam II, known as the Caliph al-Mustansir, was perhaps almost as fortunate. He is said to have collected a library of 400,000 books, and this at a time when there were probably not more than 10,000 books in England, France and Germany. He was a gentle scholar who was never more pleased than when one of his agents in Cairo, Damascus or Baghdad sent him a book he wanted. He founded free schools, paid the salaries of the professors of the University of Cordova, founded by his father, and ordered the mosque which housed the university to be decorated with Byzantine mosaics. He led his armies against the Christians of León, but showed no particular delight in war; during the last years of his reign he seems to have surrendered his power to his mother, a beautiful Basque princess, and to her lover, Muhammad ibn-abi-Amir, who began life as a professional letter writer at court. In time Muhammad ibn-abi-Amir became the virtual ruler of the Cordova Caliphate. When Hakam II died and was succeeded by his twelve-year-old son Hisham II, the letter writer assumed all the privileges of a reigning emperor, issuing rescripts and proclamations in his own name, inscribing his name and titles on coins, ordering prayers to be said on his behalf in the mosques, and he even wore the imperial garments of gold tissue, with his name woven into the borders—the privilege reserved for the Caliph alone.

Muhammad ibn-abi-Amir rose from being an insignificant student at the University of Cordova to the highest office in the land. There was nothing unusual in his rise to power—such usurpers have arisen in all the ages of Islam. But he possessed qualities which were needed to replenish the vigour of the Caliphate. He was harsh, puritanical and generous to his soldiers. He suppressed a conspiracy of palace 'Slavs' and went on to destroy the Christian armies on the northern marches, always taking care to give donatives to his soldiers and to stage splendid triumphs. He sacked

Barcelona, and razed to the ground the famous shrine-cathedral of Santiago de Compostela; and when he died in 1002 after partaking in fifty campaigns, a monkish chronicler who knew him by the name of Al-manzor (Al-Mansur, 'the victorious') wrote: 'In this year died Al-manzor, and was buried in Hell.'

The brilliant letter writer had been the kingpin; without him all Andalusia was in danger of falling apart. For a brief while the Caliph Hisham emerged from the harem where he had hidden for thirty years, but he soon abdicated, escaping at last to Asia or Mecca or an underground dungeon, no one knew where. An impostor who closely resembled him set himself up as Caliph in Seville, but was soon dethroned. The unhappy Umayyads suffered the fate of the Abbasids: they lived or died at the whim of their guards. Hisham III was thrown into a dungeon attached to the Great Mosque at Cordova, and the wretched Caliph sat there in total darkness, surrounded by his wives, clutching his only child, a girl, to his breast. The guards had forgotten to bring him food, while they debated what should be done with him; and when at last one of the jailors came in to inform him that the council of regency, which was in effect a council of jailors, would soon come to a conclusion on the matter, the Caliph was heard to say: 'Let them decide as they please, but bring me a little bread, for my daughter is dying of hunger.' They brought the bread, and a little later another deputation appeared in the dungeon to inform him that a castle had been selected for his imprisonment and he would be taken there at daybreak. The Caliph seemed not to be listening. He said: 'Please give me a lantern, for it is very dark here.' The spiritual and temporal ruler of Andalusia was begging for bread and a candle.

It was dark in the dungeon, but it was dark all over Islam. From Spain to Persia a general disintegration was taking place. In Spain the process was quickened by the sense of failure which followed the easy victories of Almanzor. There was no one strong enough to weld Moslem Spain into a united power. In the first half of the eleventh century, twenty independent dynasties arose, ruling over as many cities; and soon every city in Andalusia became a state in itself.

An exactly similar process of fragmentation was coming about in the Near East, where the Abbasid Caliphs were incapable of preventing the local governors from exercising their autonomy. The Seljuk Turks had conquered Khurasan in 1040, and this ruthless tribe under its leader Toghrul ('the falcon') seemed determined to assume the power once possessed by the Abbasids. Two alternatives confronted the Seljuks: they could destroy the power of the Caliphate, or they could inherit it by peaceful means. They chose the latter. One day in 1055 the Seljuk army appeared outside the walls of Baghdad. The Caliph al-Qaim had been warned, and knew exactly what was expected of him. He received the Seljuk prince in his palace, and there followed one of the strangest of all acts of abdication.

The Caliph sat on his golden throne, wore the famous black mantle of the Abbasids and grasped the staff of Muhammad in his right hand.

Following the pattern which existed in Sassanian times, and perhaps went back to the Archaemenian period, the Caliph was hidden from the court by a hanging curtain, but this was lifted when the Turkish prince appeared. Toghrul sat on a throne directly facing the throne of the Caliph. An interpreter stood between them. At great length Toghrul explained his undying loyalty to the Caliph, and at equally great length the Caliph explained his undying friendship for the prince. Thereupon Toghrul was invested with seven robes of honour, and presented with seven slaves, representing the seven provinces of the empire. Over his head was placed a golden musk-scented veil and two fillets were bound around it, to represent the Arabic and Persian crowns. He was girt about with two swords as ruler of the East and the West, and at this moment he attempted to prostrate himself before the Caliph, as though he felt unworthy of the honour he had received; but servants and ministers hurried forward to prevent him. Then he kissed the hand of the Caliph, and his name and titles were publicly proclaimed by the heralds.

The Seljuk Turks, who only a hundred years before had been a tribe of horsemen fighting their way through Central Asia, had inherited the empire.

Toghrul died shortly after coming to power, and was succeeded by the brilliant and handsome Alp Arslan ('heroic lion'), his nephew. Alp Arslan was famous for his moustaches, which were so long that they had to be tied up when he went out hunting, for his skill at archery and for his devotion to the arts. He enjoyed the distinction of capturing the Byzantine Emperor, Diogenes Romanus IV, who fell into his hands at the battle of Manzikert. According to Persian historians, the Byzantine Emperor had taunted the Seljuk monarch, saying: 'If this barbarian really desires peace, let him come over to my camp and solemnly surrender his palace at Rayy as a pledge of security.' Alp Arslan was enraged; and some time later, remembering the efficacy of prayer, he fell to his knees and prayed for victory. Afterwards he donned a white gown, perfumed himself with musk, surrendered sword and spear for mace and scimitar, and promised he would not leave the field alive until he had destroyed the enemy. There was a hard-fought battle, and by nightfall the Emperor Romanus, his horse dead, himself wounded, his army destroyed, waited for whatever might befall him. He was seen by a slave and by a deformed soldier, who led him to Alp Arslan's tent, where he prostrated himself before his conqueror. Alp Arslan seems to have been amused.

'I would like to know what you would do, if you were in my place,' he said.

'I would beat you to death with whips,' Romanus answered.

The honest answer pleased Alp Arslan, who had the satisfaction of being able to remind the Christian Emperor about the quality of mercy. At the cost on an enormous bribe, the surrender of all Moslems in Greek hands, and an annual tribute of 360,000 pieces of gold, Romanus was allowed to go free.

Alp Arslan was not always so generous. He was leading a punitive expedition against some tribes in Transoxiana when he met his death. The captain of a captured fortress addressed him insolently. Alp Arslan ordered the man to be impaled, and the captain suddenly began shouting curses which continued even when Alp Arslan drew his bow and fired an arrow at the unfortunate man. The arrows went wide. The captain sprang forward and struck at the prince with a dagger, fatally wounding him. Four days later Alp Arslan died. The captain was cut to pieces by the guard.

It was a time of splendour, of wide-ranging conquests, of a curious marriage between Persia and Turkestan. Alp Arslan had succeeded in regaining Mecca and Madinah for the empire. He recovered Aleppo. Above all he cherished artists and poets, and the pottery and architecture of his time have a wonderful glowing spontaneity. From the kilns of Rayy came the delicate pottery painted with Persian princesses riding on horseback, with feathers in their hair, holding bridles of silk, their faces lit with a serene sweetness; the horses are drawn with power, but the riders are filled with a subtle enjoyment of life. The Seljuks had come just in time. Out of their enjoyment in life came the amazing development of the arts which characterized the comparatively brief period of their rule in Persia. Their mosques and memorial towers suggest the same qualities which appear in their pottery: strength, a dancing gaiety, an absorbed wonder at all the passing events of life.

Alp Arslan reigned for only nine years. When he died, he asked that he should be buried in Merv. He had already written his epitaph: 'O ye who have seen the glory of Alp Arslan exalted to the skies, repair to Merv and behold it buried in the dust.'

He was succeeded by his son Malik Shah, who extended the boundaries of the empire as far as the mountains of Georgia and the walls of Constantinople, Jerusalem and all Arabia. Austere and tolerant, he ruled benevolently, patronized Omar Khayyám and built hospitals for the poor and spent immense sums on caravanserais. 'During his reign,' says Ibn Khallikan, 'all the roads were safe, and places of danger no longer inspired terror.'

To safeguard his dynasty Malik Shah married the daughter of the Caliph, and for a while thought seriously of abolishing the Caliphate, which had long since outlived its usefulness. In his reign the Seljuks entered their golden age, and in this same reign the forces which began to emerge from obscurity to destroy the Seljuks were preparing their engines of destruction. These forces were the Assassins, the murderous Mongol horde and the Crusaders.

In any study of the Arab empires the Crusaders can have little place. Those waves of Frankish and German armies which descended upon the coast of Palestine changed little. They quarrelled ceaselessly among themselves and possessed no pronounced gifts of government. Their chosen battlefield lay on the frontier between Seljuk and Fatimid power, in a no man's land ruled by semi-independent local governors who were often only too content to watch their neighbours fall before the crusading armies.

If it had not been for a poisoned toothstick there might have been no successful crusades at all.

The greatest contributing cause to the success of the early crusades was the death of Malik Shah in 1092 of poison administered in a toothstick. Following his death, the empire was divided between his three sons, Bartyaruk, Sinjar and Muhammad. By this division the strength of the Abbasid empire was broken. No Abbasid army ever went to assist the hard-pressed local governors, and none of Malik Shah's sons was worthy of the father.

Western historians have always felt uncomfortable when contemplating the strange half-savage man who is responsible for the First Crusade, but Arab historians would have understood him perfectly. Throughout Arab history 'the man on a donkey' has created revolutions and ordered men into battle. Peter the Hermit was short and swarthy, with a long lean face and lantern jaws, and they said of him that he resembled the donkey he was always riding. He believed he heard voices from Heaven, and there was an air of compelling sanctity about him. 'Whatever he said or did,' wrote a contemporary, 'it looked like something half-divine.'

When Peter forsook the service of his feudal lord, Eustace de Bouillon, and set out from Picardy to arouse the nobility of the Rhenish provinces against the Arabs, he set in motion a long chain of events from which the world is still suffering. The First Crusade produced the greatest effect upon the Arabs. With stunned amazement they learned that the Crusaders had fought the Seljuk Sultan of Iconium and completely defeated him, and then some 40,000 of them passed through Asia Minor and along the coast of Syria, with nothing more than a few skirmishes to delay their progress. In the summer of 1099 they were outside the walls of Jerusalem. They were unprepared to take the city by assault, but a hermit on the Mount of Olives promised them that God was fighting on their side—'If God wills, he will storm the walls even if there is only one scaling-ladder.' The Crusaders had little faith in the hermit, and spent some weeks building siege engines; then they marched in procession round the city, prayed, fasted, gave alms, and attacked with all their strength, only to be driven back. A second assault three days later proved more successful. Firebrands were shot into the city. Treachery, or stupidity, permitted the Franks to seize the citadel and the great courtyard of the Dome of the Rock. The Crusaders were merciless. They rode in blood up to their knees and bridle reins, and amused themselves by butchering everyone in sight, Jews and Moslems alike. Raymond, the venerable chaplain of Count Raymond of Toulouse, described the scene. 'When our men had possession of the walls and towers, wonderful sights rewarded our eyes,' he wrote. 'Some of our men, and they the more merciful, cut off the heads of the enemies; others shot them with arrows, so that they fell from the towers; others tortured them longer by casting them into the flames. Piles of heads, hands and feet were to be seen in the streets of the city.' The acknowledged ruler of Jerusalem was now Godfrey of Bouillon, the thirty-nine-year-old Duke of Lower Lorraine, a descendant of

N

Charlemagne. He refused the crown, and called himself simply 'Baron of Jerusalem and Defender of the Holy Sepulchre'. When he died a year later, he was succeeded by his younger brother Baldwin, who was crowned king in Bethlehem. Godfrey was tall and yellow-haired, and looked like a Viking. Baldwin was short, dark-haired, with a strange pallor of the skin and a ferocious haughtiness of manner. Unchaste, rebellious, driven by an inner fury, he ruled over a thin sliver of land which stretched from Aqabah to Beirut. The Arabs hated him.

They had reason to hate him. It was not only that Baldwin represented to an almost exaggerated degree the peculiar cold vindictiveness of the Crusaders at their worst, but he lacked nobility. There was something disquieting in his mere presence. He seemed to attract evil to himself: he had a magician's power of terrifying at a distance. His unchastity might be pardoned, his ruthlessness might be forgiven, but the Arabs feared the gleam of insanity in his eyes and recognized in him an enemy almost impossible to destroy. Ekkehard speaks of the 'delirium' of the Crusaders. Baldwin was delirium in the seat of power.

To the Arabs Baldwin represented a threat of vast magnitude, but with his death in 1118 the danger of a great explosion of Christian energy in the Holy Land vanished. The Christians settled down to live amicably with the Arabs, in the small sea-girt kingdoms of Jerusalem, Tripoli and Antioch. The Franks took to wearing Arab dress; they learned Arabic, intermarried with the Arabs and joined forces with their former enemies against marauding tribes. In the long history of the Crusades the periods of peace were longer than the periods of war.

But the memory of the massacre at Jerusalem rankled. It rankled especially in the hearts of the Persians, who owed allegiance to the Abbasid Caliph. Salah-al-Din Yusuf ibn Aiyub, known to the western chroniclers as Saladin, came from a Kurdish family long resident in Azerbaijan in northwest Persia. He had spent his youth in Baalbek, where his father was governor. Graced with a commanding presence, with liquid dark eyes and a thick black beard, he enjoyed theology almost as much as he enjoyed fighting; and his theology was of the strictest and most puritanical kind. He detested Sufis, and he particularly detested the inventors of *hadiths*. But this greatest detestation was reserved for the Franks, who broke their oaths at will and whose presence in the Holy Land he regarded as an affront to the Caliph, the descendant of the house of Muhammad.

During the time when Saladin was rising to power the Assassins were waging war against the orthodox Moslems. They derived their name from the hashish which they smoked or drank to make them reckless in war. They formed a heretical sect, holding that the succession belonged to the descendants of Ali, and the last of those descendants worthy of reverence was the seventh Imam, whose name was Ismail. Several mountain strongholds in Persia had fallen into their hands, the most important being Alamut, 'the Eagle's Nest', north of Kazvin. Their terror was felt throughout the empire, and reached into Syria: and among the enemies they hoped to assassinate were Saladin, the Fatimid King of Egypt and

the leaders of the Frankish principalities. Saladin laid siege to the stronghold of 'the Old Man of the Mountains' at Masyad, and lifted the siege
only when he received a promise of immunity from attack. He had conquered Egypt and received from the Abbasid Caliph a diploma of investiture over Egypt, Nubia, Palestine, most of Syria and the western part
of Arabia. The way was now open for a concerted attack against the
Franks.

On July 1, 1187, Saladin captured the Crusader base at Tiberias, and a
few days later the Crusaders suffered a decisive defeat near the Horns of
Hattin, a few miles away from Magdala and Mahanayimi, where David
defeated Absalom. On the night before the battle the soldiers of both sides
slept on the ground, for both were afraid of night attacks. Guy de Lusignan, King of Jerusalem, fought with the courage of despair, but he was no
match for his adversary on an ill-chosen battleground: Saladin with his
back to the lake, and the Franks on the parched uplands. The battle was
soon over. Among the captives was the King of Jerusalem and Raynald de
Châtillon, the lord of the Kerak fortress in ancient Moab to the east of the
Dead Sea, which dominated the caravan highway from Damascus. Ray-
hald de Châtillon had sent raiding parties against the caravans, murdered many pilgrims and held others for ransom; and Saladin, who regarded the pilgrimage as a sanctified rite, was determined to make an
example of his prisoner. In a calm rage he prepared to murder his enemy.

The scene has been brilliantly described in Ibn Sheddad's account of
Saladin's life. Raynald and the King of Jerusalem were brought into
Saladin's tent. The King was suffering from thirst, and so Saladin offered
him a bowl of sherbert made with iced rose water. The King drank a
little, and then handed the bowl to Raynald. Saladin was watching closely,
and observed quietly that he was being placed at a disadvantage. By
immemorial custom he could not kill a man who was his guest and who
had accepted food from him. He had not himself given the sherbet to
Raynald, and was therefore free to kill. He ordered the interpreter to explain to Guy de Lusignan that the sherbet was a gift of the Sultan to the
King, and this gift must not be interpreted as a pardon for Raynald. And
when this legal interpretation had been conveyed, Saladin dismissed his
prisoners and they were taken to a place prepared for them: there, outside
the Sultan's tent, they were permitted to eat and drink to their heart's
content, before being summoned once more into the presence of the Sultan.
Here is Ibn Sheddad's account of the interview:

At this time there were only a few servants in the tent. The King was
ordered to stand at the tent-gate, but the prince [Raynald] was summoned into the presence, and thereupon Saladin reminded him of what
he had previously said, adding: 'Behold, I will support Muhammad
against thee!' He then called upon the prince to embrace Islam, and
when the prince refused, he drew a sword and struck him a blow which
severed the arm from the shoulder. This was the signal for the servants
to dispatch the prisoner, and God hurled his soul into hell. And when

the corpse was dragged away and thrown out of the tent-gate, the King saw how his companion had been treated and thought he would be the next victim, but the Sultan brought him into the tent and calmed his fears.

'It is not the habit of kings,' said Saladin, 'to kill kings. That man transgressed all bounds, and that is why he was killed.'

And all that night the conquerors rejoiced and chanted the praises of God until the dawn came, and then the Sultan went down to Tiberias.[1]

For Saladin the victory was complete: from this disaster the Crusaders never completely recovered. The tide was running against the Franks. In the following weeks one fortress after another fell—Acre, Nablus, Haifa, Caesarea, Sephoriya, Nazareth, Beirut. Failing to capture Tyre, Saladin marched on Ascalon, which the Franks had conquered thirty-five years before, and after a brief siege Ascalon fell. Saladin at once turned his attention to Jerusalem, receiving the capitulation of the defenceless city on October 2. The Christians expected to receive the same treatment which was meted out to the Jews and Moslems when the Crusaders conquered it, but Saladin was unexpectedly lenient and allowed them to ransom their lives—each man paid ten Tyrian dinars, each woman five dinars, and each child one dinar. The penniless Saladin allowed to go free. The huge gilded cross which surmounted the Dome of the Rock was hurled down, and in its place there rose the crescent of Islam.

The wars continued. Though they had lost most of their towns and fortresses in Syria and Palestine, the Franks still held to a scattering of isolated forts, while Antioch, Tripoli and Tyre were still defended by their garrisons. Acre, in particular, became the *point d'appui* by which the Crusaders hoped to regain their lost territories. The Pope urged the Christian nations to regain the Holy Sepulchre, and the largest of all the Crusades set out under the magnificent auspices of three kings, Philip of France, Frederick of Germany and Richard of England. Acre was invested and captured: once again the Christians permitted themselves the pleasure of a general massacre of Moslems. By this time Saladin was too weak and too sick to manoeuvre his forces successfully, and a few months later, in February, 1193, he died of fever in Damascus and was buried in an ornate tomb near the Great Umayyad Mosque.

History has dealt kindly with Saladin. It is remembered of him that he was often chivalrous, gentle and kind. On one occasion he sent snow from the mountains around Damascus to cool the tent of Richard the Lionhearted, who was stricken with fever. The Franks who met him reported on his superb dignity and imperial presence, which did not in the least conflict with his natural warmth. The Arab chroniclers were even louder in their praises, and his friend Ousama said he was 'the Sultan who restored the tradition of the righteous Caliphs'. It is forgotten that he was a soldier

---

[1] Beha Ed-din ibn Sheddad, *The Life of Saladin* (London: Palestine Exploration Fund, 1897), p. 115.

of limited skill whose passion for orthodox theology led him to execute all those he regarded as heretics, and his rage against the heretics, as recounted by Ibn Sheddad, is not pleasant to watch. When he died, the sword he carried in the wars was placed beside his body and buried with him. 'His sword,' says the pious chronicler, 'accompanied him to Paradise.'

For a brief while Saladin had united the western borders of the Abbasid empire under a single ruler, but with his death the irreversible process of fragmentation was resumed. His brothers, his eldest son and an uncle inherited the territory he had conquered, and were soon fighting among themselves, while the Crusaders rejoiced. One after another the towns captured by Saladin were reconquered by the Franks, who retained their small strip of coast for another century.

In theory there was still an Abbasid empire ruling from Transoxiana to the Mediterranean. Saladin's devotion to the ghostly Caliph who reigned in Baghdad was undisguised. It happens that we possess a contemporary account of this Caliph written by a Jewish rabbi from Navarre, Benjamin of Tudela, who visited Baghdad about the year 1170. He describes the palace with its parks and menageries and ornamental pools, a place provided with every imaginable luxury; and through these enchanted gardens walked the pious and gentle Caliph, who earned his living by making bedcovers with his own hands and stamping them with the caliphal seal before selling them to the nobles in the land. He lived in mysterious isolation, appearing in public only once a year at Ramadan, when he rode in procession through the city on a mule, wearing robes of gold and silver cloth, a turban ornamented with precious stones, and a black veil, which hid the brilliance of his face from the sight of the crowd. Benjamin of Tudela goes on to describe the strange procession and its stranger aftermath:

As he rides in procession, the Caliph is accompanied by a numerous retinue of Muhammadan nobles, arrayed in rich garments and riding on horseback, princes of Arabia, of Media, of Persia, even of Tibet, a country distant three months journey from Arabia. The procession goes from the palace to the mosque at the Basrah gate, which is the metropolitan mosque. All who walk in the procession, both men and women, are dressed in silk and purple. The streets and squares are enlivened with singing and rejoicing, and by parties who dance before the great king, called Caliph. He is saluted loudly by the assembled crowd, who cry: 'Blessed art thou, our lord and king.' Thereupon he kisses his garment and by holding it in his hand acknowledges and returns the compliment.

When the procession enters the court of the mosque, the Caliph mounts a wooden pulpit and expounds their law unto them. The learned Muhammadans rise, pray for him, and praise his great kindness and piety; upon which the whole assembly answer, 'Amen!' The Caliph then pronounces his blessing, and kills a camel, which is led thither for that purpose, and this is their offering. It is distributed to the nobles, who send portions of it to their friends, who are eager to taste of the meat killed by the hands of their holy king, and are much rejoiced therewith.

After the ceremony the Caliph leaves the mosque and returns alone, along the banks of the Tigris, to his palace, the noble Muhammadans accompanying him in boats, until he enters this building. He never returns by the way he came: and the path on the bank of the river is carefully guarded all the year round, so as to prevent anyone treading in his footsteps.

The Caliph never leaves his palace again for a whole year.[1]

Benjamin of Tudela provides another glimpse of the Caliph at the time of the pilgrimage. The faithful crowded outside the palace, calling him by name and asking for blessings, imploring him to grant them the honour of letting them gaze on him. In reply, the Caliph permitted a part of his garment to be thrust out of a window, and the faithful were permitted to kiss it. Then one of the palace servants was heard saying: 'Go in peace, for our Lord, the Light of the Muhammadans, is well pleased and gives you this blessing.' It was, however, a light that shone rarely, and then only with a flickering radiance.

The prodigious death of the Caliphate, delayed over so many centuries, is frightening to contemplate. That a symbol could have survived so long without any fresh accretions of strength, that it could have maintained itself by its own dying momentum against all reason and continually prolonged its existence by recourse to its own weakness and the very insignificance of the person who wore the sumptuous robes of office, suggests a fact which is often hidden from historians: robes of office possess the power to command. The Caliphate died many deaths, but the robes of office survived. In the history of Islam there are few moments stranger than the moment when we see the Caliph, weighed down by his heavy garments, while he totters alone along the towpath to his palace in full view of the nobles lying at their ease in boats. In that moment we are made aware of the loneliness and misery of the caliphal existence. Beyond that loneliness, beyond that misery, it was impossible to go.

Yet in spite of the Crusades and the fragmentation of the empire under the perpetually dying Caliphate, these were times of magnificent achievement. The spiritual life survived, growing greater as earthly life lost its significance. Al-Hallaj had not lived and died in vain. Others came after him who fed at the springs, to be revived by the freshness flowing from his memory. Gradually and imperceptibly it became clear that al-Hallaj, like Muhammad, had been a Messenger of God. In the eyes of the great philosopher al-Ghazzali three men had walked the earth bathed in the light of divinity. They were Jesus, Muhammad and al-Hallaj; and the last was not the least.

Abu-Hamid al-Ghazzali was born in 1058 at Tus in Khurasan, the son

---

[1] Thomas Wright, *Early Travels in Palestine* (London: Henry Bohn, 1848), pp. 95–6.

of a spinner of wool, who died when he was young, and he was brought up by a Sufi. Though living in a Sufi environment and practising spiritual exercises, he seems to have had no taste for mysticism. He had a quick brain and a longing for fame. He was about sixteen when he decided that the quickest route to preferment lay in the law, and accordingly he set out to be the most learned exponent of canon law in his time. In religious matters he remained a sceptic, but it delighted him to improvise on the subject of the religious laws of Islam before admiring students: he became the most brilliant theologian of his age without the least belief in theology. At thirty-three he was professor of theology at Baghdad, with 300 students. He enjoyed his growing fame, and he enjoyed the exercise of his mind, and he might have continued indefinitely increasing his vast knowledge of canon law if he had not suddenly felt a profound revulsion against himself and everything he stood for.

Exactly what happened to make him change his life is unknown. As reported by his friend and biographer Abd-al-Ghafir al-Farisi, 'a door of fear was opened to him, which diverted him from everything else and compelled him to ignore all but God'. For six months, from the summer to the winter of 1095, he fought a losing battle with himself. He was ill, and shut himself up alone in his rooms, uncertain of everything except his uncertainty. He lost his power of speech, and could no longer give lectures. For a while he was unable to eat, and the doctors despaired of his life, and when he asked them what had happened, they answered: 'The trouble arises from the heart, and from there it has spread through the whole system: the only cure lies in allaying the anxieties of the heart.' His friends, observing the strangeness of his manner, said he had 'clothed himself in a garment of pretence'. But it was no pretence. Suddenly he gave out that he intended to go on pilgrimage to Mecca, although he had already resolved to become a wandering dervish in Syria. These precautions were taken because the Caliph and the high officials in Baghdad would probably have prevented him from leaving the city if they knew he never intended to return. No one knew he was about to enter the religious life and to abandon the law for ever.

He went to Damascus and stayed there for two years in complete retirement and solitude, sometimes climbing the minaret of a mosque and remaining there alone. Then he went to Jerusalem, where he spent his days within the Dome of the Rock, and afterwards journeyed to Mecca, only to return to the solitudes of Damascus, living on dried bread and dressed in rags. He wrote voluminously, but did not publish his writings. His days were spent in the endless contemplation of the glory of God, as he followed the Sufi practices he had learned as a child and then abandoned.

What he had discovered was something very simple. He had learned with certainty that the mystics walk the road of God; their life was the best life, their character the purest. The learning of scholars was as nothing compared with those 'who bring illumination from the lamp of prophetic revelation'. The mystics alone can speak with angels and behold the spirits of the prophets; to them come the miraculous graces, and the knowledge of God. Unlike most of the Sufis, he respected the religious ordinances and commented upon them at length.

He had spent eleven years in tranquil seclusion in Damascus when he was summoned by 'the Sultan of my time' to teach at Nishapur. It was a summons he could hardly disobey, and so for a few months he was to be found teaching again in a style so unlike his previous style that his friends could no longer recognize him. When his strength failed, he returned to Tus, where he lived quietly, surrounded by his disciples. He was only fifty-three when he died. Dying, he performed his ablutions and prayers; then he turned to his brother, and said: 'Bring me my shroud.' He kissed the shroud, laid it over his eyes, and said: 'Most gladly do I enter into the presence of the King.' A little while later he stretched out his feet and lay still. He was buried at Tus close to the grave of the poet Firdausi.

It was not perhaps the death that al-Ghazzali had hoped for. He had half-hoped for martyrdom. He had Origen's fierce intensity, and Origen's desire to lay down his life for others, and Origen's vast scholarship, and Origen's gift of style, and like Origen he was to be known as 'the father of the church', the only father that the Islamic church has ever had. During those eleven years of seclusion in Damascus he changed the course of Muhammadanism by compelling Islam to come to terms with the Sufis. Mysticism became orthodox, at the behest of an orthodox believer who became a mystic.

Al-Ghazzali's greatness lay in his power to see Islam whole, unfragmented, filled with the energy of God. For him Muhammad and the early Caliphs were living presences, and al-Hallaj was like a neighbour to whom he talked on familiar terms even when the subject of conversation was that extraordinary statement: '*ana 'l-Haqq*' ('I am the Truth'). Indeed, he speaks interminably about this statement, analysing it from all possible angles, suggesting all possible interpretations, and always coming at last to the conclusion that al-Hallaj meant precisely what he said, though sometimes he will raise a warning finger and suggest that it were better for some things to be left unsaid.

For al-Ghazzali the task of man was to know God and to live fully. He had no aversion to the human condition, and some doubt about whether theologians go to Heaven. In his famous *Ihya* he tells the story of the Israelite who wrote 360 books on all subjects which might commend themselves to God, only to receive the admonition: 'Thou hast filled the world with hypocrisy. I will have none of it!' Then the Israelite went into a cave and mortified himself, and God again cast him out. Finally the Israelite went among men and feasted with them, and God said: 'Now thou hast attained to my good pleasure.' He thought marriage eminently desirable, and liked to recall Muhammad's well-known saying: 'I have loved three things in the world: perfumes, and women, and refreshment in prayer.' He enjoyed telling stories, and his works are full of stories told for no particular reason except his own delight in them. His attitude towards all human preoccupations is one of intense understanding and delight in them, while realizing the deceitful character of the world, 'which pretends she will always be with you and continually bids you farewell'.

But though knowledge of this world was desirable, the knowledge of God was still more desirable, since it was for the purpose of knowing God that man was created. So he wrote in his introduction to *The Alchemy of Happiness*:

> Know, O beloved, that man was not created in jest or at random, but marvellously made and for some great end. Although he is not from everlasting, he lives for ever; and though his body is mean and earthly, yet his spirit is lofty and divine. When in the crucible of abstinence he is purged from carnal passions he attains to the highest, and in place of being a slave to lust and anger becomes endued with angelic qualities. Attaining that state, he finds his heaven in the contemplation of Eternal Beauty.[1]

Such was the aim, but how was this desirable state to be brought about? Al-Ghazzali begins his examination of the mystic's ultimate experience of God by developing an idea already present in the famous verse, *The Niche for Lights*. Man sees a light which is like unto God, but is not God. There is a patch of light on the floor which is reflected down from a wall, and the light on the wall comes from a mirror reflecting the moon, which itself reflects the light of the sun. So there are four lights ranged one above the other, each one more perfect than the other. The task of man is to reach out beyond all the reflected lights towards God, 'the source of all splendour'.

But this is only the beginning of the strange odyssey upon which al-Ghazzali embarks with limitless courage. The 'ascent of the soul' is a commonplace of mystical belief: saints of all periods have winged their way upwards to God, and some have described God's face. But al-Ghazzali seems to have been the first to suggest that this is in itself not a sufficient goal. It is more wonderful to descend from God than to rise into the Presence. Some indeed, like al-Hallaj, seem to have made 'the Descent into the Lower Heaven', to have moved from rapture in God to the sharing of divine powers. Muhammad, too, according to some of the more mysterious *hadiths*, had partaken of the divine splendour during his descent and had become one with the angels, not those angels of whom it was said in the Quran that they bowed before men, but the great guardian angels like Gabriel who hold the keys to Heaven and Paradise. God descends, moves among the 70,000 veils which surround his throne, and becomes man, and the saints also descend, becoming God. In this mysterious and blinding landscape there are no signposts, no pathways: here the mind reels at the edge of the precipice, and only a few men have ever described that landscape convincingly. Among Christian theologians perhaps only St. Gregory of Nyssa spoke about it with complete authority in the *Vita*

---

[1] Al-Ghazzali, *The Alchemy of Happiness*, tr. Claud Field (Lahore: Muhammad Ashraf, n.d.), p. 17.

Moysis. Al-Ghazzali speaks about it with no less authority in a passage of amazing complexity, putting the words in the mouth of al-Hallaj:

Immersed in the divine Oneness, he spoke of God as 'descending into the lowest heavens', and said that this descent was His descent, in order to use physical senses and to set in motion bodily limbs; and that He is the one indicated in the tradition in which the Prophet says: 'I have become His hearing whereby He heareth, His vision whereby He seeth, His tongue whereby He speaketh.'

Now if the Prophet was God's hearing and vision and tongue, then God and He alone is the hearer, the seer, the speaker; and He is the one indicated in His own word to Moses: 'I was sick, and thou visitedst me not.'[1] And so it follows that the bodily movements of this Confessor of the Divine Unity are from the lowest heaven; his sensations from the heaven next above; and his intelligence from a heaven next above that. From that heaven of the intelligence he fares upwards to the limit of the Ascension of created things, the Kingdom of Absolute Unity, the seven-fold way. Thereafter he 'settleth himself on the Throne' of the Divine Unity, and therefrom 'taketh command' throughout his storied heavens. And looking upon such a one, well might we apply to him the saying: 'God created Adam in the image of the Merciful One'; and so at last, contemplating these words more deeply, we become aware that these words mean the same as: 'I am the Truth' and 'Glory be to Me!' and also those sayings of the Prophet, that God said: 'I was sick and thou visitedst me not', and 'I am His hearing, and His vision, and His tongue'.[2]

Al-Ghazzali's purposes in this passage are manifold. He is describing, as succinctly as words permit, the downward passage of the soul after being embraced by God, but he is also attempting the task of reconciling the Quran and the traditions with the words of the God-intoxicated Sufis, and at the same time he is suggesting that the wildest leap of the human spirit might be the most orthodox of all spiritual movements. For many years it had been an article of faith among the Sufis that a mysterious vice-regent of God existed on earth. He was al-Mutah, 'the administrator', 'he who commands the whole universe'. The Caliphs, who thought themselves invested with divine powers as successors of Muhammad, did not share this belief, for good reason. But what if al-Mutah were a man like al-Hallaj, in full possession of the transcendent flame of God? And what if al-Hallaj possessed in himself the archetypal image of Muhammad, the Heavenly Man created in the image of God? All these things are hinted at, without ever being concretely expressed, and sometimes al-Ghazzali will suggest that all these suppositions are no more than the ravings of lovers:

For those who returned from their Ascent into the Heaven of Reality confess with one voice that they saw nought existent there save the One

[1] A *hadith*, which echoes Matthew xxv. 46.
[2] Al-Ghazzali, *Mishkat al-Anwar*, tr. W. H. T. Gairdner (London: Royal Asiatic Society Monograph, XIX), pp. 114–15.

Real. Some, however, arrived at this scientifically, and others experimentally and subjectively. From these last the plurality of things fell away in its entirety. They were drowned in the Absolute Unitude, and their intelligences were lost in Its Abyss. Therein they became as dumbfounded things. No capacity remained within them save to recall God; yea, not so much as the capacity to recall their own selves. So there remained nothing with them save God. They became drunken with a drunkenness wherein the sway of their own intelligence disappeared, so that one exclaimed: 'I am the Truth' and another, 'Glory be to Me! How great is My glory!' and another, 'Within this robe is nought but God!' But the words of passionate lovers in their intoxication must be hidden away and not spoken of.[1]

But in fact al-Ghazzali *had* spoken of those words at length, and with grave understanding, without ever completely identifying himself with them, leaving always a loophole by which he might escape into orthodoxy. But the damage was done. Henceforward the wildest claims of the Sufis were to be listened to with attention. *Al-Mutah*, 'the Descent to the Lowest Heavens', the mysterious qualities of the great saints who quietly concealed their divine powers, all these were matters which were to engage the attention of the most orthodox theologians. Al-Ghazzali's greatest contribution, at a time when the empire had already fallen into decay, was to re-define man. Man was no longer the abject slave of an all-powerful God, but a being imbued with divinity, capable of assuming a divinity within himself. Man was divine.

Al-Hallaj had opened the way; al-Ghazzali had explored the possibilities of taking Heaven by storm and returning with a fragment of it in one's hands, and it was left to Ibn Arabi to inquire at length into the nature of man seen as a divinity walking the earth.

Muhiyuddin Muhammad ibn-Ali ibn-al-Arabi, known as Ibn Arabi, was born in Murcia in Andalusia in 1165. His father seems to have been a man in affluent circumstances, who spared no pains to give the boy a sound education. At the age of eight he was taken to Seville, where he attended the theological seminary and became a teacher. Men observed a strangeness about him from the beginning. He liked to sing, and often fell into a trance while singing. He seemed to acquire knowledge through sources not available to ordinary mortals, and stories were told of his powers of clairvoyance and telepathy. He said once: 'It is especially necessary that men should be the masters of their dreams, so gaining all the fruits which come to those who enter the intermediary world.' For two years he lived in a reed hut with Fatima bint al-Waliyya, a female mystic renowned for 'having the sight of God in everything in the world'. She was nearly a hundred years old, but hale and hearty, and Ibn Arabi acquired from her a delight in associating with female mystics which never left him. He was thirty-seven when he left Seville and took up his

---

[1] Al-Ghazzali, *Mishkat al-Anwar*, tr. W. H. T. Gairdner (London: Royal Asiatic Society Monograph, XIX), pp. 106-7.

residence in Ceuta. One night he dreamed he had wedded all the stars and
moons in the sky, and when he mentioned the dream to a famous interpreter of dreams, he was told: 'Immeasurable bounty will flow upon you.'
Shortly afterwards he left Spain, and travelled across North Africa, Egypt
and the Hijaz. He made two pilgrimages to Mecca; wandered through
Iraq, visiting Baghdad, Aleppo and Mosul; and settled down in Damascus,
already famous, praised by many, hated by others for his heretical views,
the recipient of many gifts from members of the princely houses, known for
his charities, a quiet, simple man possessed of an inner fire and a ruthless
determination to express his beliefs, even when they outraged conventional
morality and orthodoxy. He never returned to Spain.

The dream at Ceuta was followed by visions in Mecca. For days on end
he walked around the Kaaba, meditating upon Muhammad. In his
enormous work, the *Futuhat al-Makkiya*, or *Meccan Revelations*, he relates that he saw Muhammad seated on a throne amidst angels, prophets
and saints, and he was summoned into the presence and received the command to discourse on the divine mysteries. He was permitted to climb
the pulpit where Muhammad was sitting, and he observed some strips of
cloth on the ground: he stood on these, so that his feet might not touch the
place trodden by the Prophet. On another occasion, while circumam-
bulating the Kaaba, he met a celestial spirit in the form of a youth who
showed him the living Temple concealed beneath the bare walls; and as he
penetrated the splendours of the Temple, he fell into a swoon, blinded by
all the majesty he had seen. Afterwards the mysterious angelic youth appeared on a three-legged steed, breathing fire into his breast, and once
more he was commanded to describe the heavenly mysteries. So he wrote
down in 560 chapters the revelations which he received from Muhammad and the Angel.

When he reached Damascus, men flocked to him as they flocked to the
courts of a king. Gifts poured on him; he was continually pouring them
back into the hands of the poor. When a beggar complained he had nowhere to live, Ibn Arabi simply offered him the house he was living in and
went out of the door, never to return. Strange stories were told by his
disciples of his psychic powers, and how he had summoned the long-dead
prophets and even God Himself into his presence. He wrote voluminously
—altogether 289 books were listed in a catalogue he drew up when he was
seventy-three—and he seems to have enjoyed life to the full, for he was well
past sixty when he married a girl of eighteen. He died in 1240 at the age
of seventy-eight, while talking to his students: he had completed all the
work he wanted to accomplish except an unfinished commentary on the
Quran. He was buried at the foot of Jabal Qasiyun, and some three hundred years later his bones were transferred to the Mosque of Sultan Selim,
which the Sultan had erected in his honour. Even in his lifetime he was
known as *Shaykh al-Akbar*, or 'the greatest Shaykh'. It was an age of imposing titles, and others followed after his death. He was called 'the Outward Proof of God' and 'the Astounding miracle of God'. It is unlikely
that he would have disapproved.

Repeatedly in his works al-Ghazzali shook a warning finger at the proud, but Ibn Arabi seems to have been able to consort pleasantly with his own heaven-storming pride. Once a puzzled student was invited to have breakfast with him. The student said: 'Sir, who is the greatest saint of our time?' Ibn Arabi answered sternly: 'You should pay more attention to your breakfast.' But the student was unable to eat, and begged Ibn Arabi to tell him the name of the greatest living saint. There was a momentary pause, and then Ibn Arabi smiled and said: 'The greatest saint is Shaykh Muhiyuddin Ibn Arabi.'

His extraordinary gifts were matched by his extraordinary style, full of allusions and abstruse metaphysical conceits. He could write simply when he wanted, but preferred to throw veils of mystery over his most intimate thoughts. Like al-Ghazzali he combined an outward orthodoxy with an inner ecstasy and the rejection of all authority. He dared to say that there was mischief in Muhammad's statement that 'there is no God but God'. He wrote once: 'The Creator is the creature and the creature is the Creator,' and went on to illuminate some of the startling consequences of this doctrine. 'How can God be entirely independent?' he asked, and answered: 'God is not independent, for I help Him and make Him good.' He believed that if there were no prophets the whole universe would come to an end, for they were the food by which the universe maintained its existence. He had Blake's way of looking at the world, and sometimes Blake seems to echo him; and he would say very simple and mysterious things as though he possessed some secret knowledge denied to those who came after him, as when he said: 'The Throne of God is on water, and water guards it from below and from within.'

But it was with his doctrines on the nature of man that Ibn Arabi made his most startling discoveries. God worships man. God and man are necessary to each other: without man, God cannot exist. God's dependence on man is so great that He is like a beggar continually seeking man's mercy. On behalf of God the whole universe is preserved by the existence of man. When Ibn Arabi first announced these claims in Egypt, they were regarded as so heretical that attempts were made to assassinate him.

His most complete statements on the nature of man appear in his *Fusus al-Hikam*, or 'Bezels of Philosophy', which he completed in Damascus in 1230. In the opening chapter he asserts that man is quite simply the successor (*kalifah*) of God:

Man is to God as the pupil is to the eye, since sight is effected through the pupil, and so it is through man that God is able to contemplate his creation and dispense His justice. Man is at once ephemeral and eternal, created in perpetuity and graced with immortality, the Word distinguishing and uniting all things together.

Through man the world came into existence. He is to the world as the bezel to the ring, for the bezel bears the seal which the King uses to guard his treasure-chests; and therefore men are called the successors and representatives of God, preserving the safety of His creation.

As long as the King's seal remains on the treasure-chests, none will dare to open them without His permission. Thus man is entrusted with the safety of creation, and as long as man remains in the universe, so long will it be preserved.[1]

Ibn Arabi refers often to the seal, that badge of honour which is worn most visibly by the prophets and the saints, and sometimes he will use the word exclusively to refer to the greatest among them: thus Muhammad becomes the Seal of the Prophets; and the Seal of the Saints, the most perfect manifestation of sanctity, was worn by one who was 'born in my time, and I have encountered him and observed the signs upon him'. There is little doubt that Ibn Arabi regarded himself as the Seal of the Saints.

It is possible to love al-Hallaj to distraction as one loves St. Francis, and for the same reasons, but it is not possible to love Ibn Arabi. He hides from us behind that secret smile of savage superiority. The close-wrought pages of *Fusus al-Hikam* give the impression of being hammered out of rock. Here, he seems to be saying, is the ultimate answer to all the questions which have ever perplexed the human spirit. Would you know whence Jesus derived his power? Would you know the true meaning of the floor of Solomon's palace, which shone like a sea of glass? Are the stars the names of God, and is the face of God perceived by human eyes? He knows all the answers, and only occasionally does he descend to human levels. His tenderness is reserved for his love poetry, which was always admirable, deeply felt and intensely metaphysical; and though he wrote endless commentaries to show that his love poems were expressions of his love of God, there is altogether too much passion in the verses to suggest that he was always thinking about God when he wrote about love.

According to Ibn Arabi, man is the mirror in which God contemplates himself, and woman the mirror in which man contemplates God. He believed that the most perfect vision of God is enjoyed by those who contemplate Him in woman. Between human love and divine love there was only a hairbreadth of difference:

For when a man loves a woman, he finds the most complete union in the act of love when all his senses are pervaded by desire. Therefore the holy law demands that he should perform the ablution of his whole body after love, and this purification of the body corresponds to the annihilation of the man within the woman at the moment of his most intense enjoyment. For God is jealous of his servant, and He will not permit man to enjoy anything save Himself. Therefore God purifies man so that he returns in vision to Him in whom he was annihilated, for there is only Him.

So it comes about that the contemplation of God in woman is the most perfect there is, for in woman man sees God in His active and passive principles, while when a man contemplates God in himself, he

[1] Muhyi-d-din Ibn Arabi, *La Sagesse des Prophètes*, tr. Titus Burckhardt (Paris: Editions Albin Michel, 1955), p. 25.

sees God only in his passive principle. It is for this reason that Muham
mad loved women, seeing in them the most perfect means to contemplate God.[1]

With such views it was no wonder that Ibn Arabi was regarded as a
heretic by some, and as 'the saint of saints' by others. There was nothing
essentially new in his attitude towards human and divine love, for such
statements had been hinted at before; but no one until his time had spoken
with such authority. His influence was vast, and not least among esoteric
Christian circles; and the fierce explosion of spiritual energy in Damascus
was felt by a Christian poet who was born only a few years after Ibn
Arabi's death. The enormous debt of Dante to Ibn Arabi has been proved
conclusively by Miguel Asín y Palacios in his work *El Islam christianizado*.
To the surprise of Christians, the *Divine Comedy* is seen to have its roots in
the visions of a Spaniard in Mecca.

There is a sense in which all Ibn Arabi's works are a commentary on
the famous *hadith* which states that when David expressed to God his intense desire to know Him, God answered: 'How much greater is my intense desire to know man.' No one ever expressed so brilliantly God's dependence upon man or the strange burden of that singular love affair in
which it is man, not God, who is pursued. For him God, man and woman
formed a trinity, and if one member of the trinity had been lacking, all of
creation would have perished.

Ibn Arabi celebrated the divinity of man at a time when Islam was preparing to receive one of the most terrible of all the blows ever inflicted on it.
Sixteen years after Ibn Arabi's death, on January 1, 1256, Hulagu, the
grandson of Genghiz Khan, crossed the Amu-Darya and received the
allegiance of the petty princes of Persia and the Caucasus. Hulagu had
intended to march straight on Baghdad, but was delayed by a campaign
against the Assassins. For two years he waged war across the length and
breadth of Persia, and then he sent envoys to the Caliph, demanding his
surrender. The incautious Caliph sent a haughty reply, and permitted the
rabble to insult the envoys. Hulagu decided to delay no more. In January,
1258, all the heights dominating the city and all the towers and palaces
commanding it were fitted out with mangonels and flame throwers, and
the long siege began, to the surprise of the Caliph al-Mustasim, who seems
to have believed that the city would be protected by the sanctity of his
presence. Baghdad was already in flames when the Caliph sent 300 high
dignitaries from his court to negotiate with Hulagu, whose answer was to
massacre them. At last on the fortieth day of the siege the Caliph himself,
attended by his brother and his two sons, and all the remaining officials of
the court, left Baghdad and proceeded to the tents of Hulagu.

Among Muhammadans it was believed that if the blood of the Caliph
was shed the world would be overspread with darkness and all his enemies
would be swallowed up in an earthquake. But in fact many Caliphs had

[1] Muhyi-d-din Ibn Arabi, *La Sagesse des Prophètes*, tr. Titus Burckhardt (Paris: Editions
Albin Michel, 1955), pp. 186–7.

been killed, and their enemies had usually survived. Hulagu had long ago determined to destroy the Caliph. He treated the Caliph with honour, fed him well, spoke of peace, and suggested that the people of Baghdad should throw away their arms and assemble before the gates so that a general census might be taken. The Caliph agreed. The people of Baghdad flocked through the gates, to be plundered, raped and massacred by Hulagu's warriors. For ten more days Hulagu permitted the Caliph to remain alive, and then he ordered him to be beaten to death. More than three-quarters of the inhabitants of the city, which previously numbered two million people, were massacred, and only a few buildings were left standing. Baghdad perished, its libraries and schools destroyed, its great history as the cultural centre of Islam at an end. So strong was the smell of decaying corpses that Hulagu ordered his soldiers to retire from the city, for fear they would be destroyed by the pestilential vapours.

It was perhaps a fitting end for the proudest and greatest city on earth. The death of Baghdad was quick and terrible, coming like the whirlwind; and for a month the smoke hung about the city. Afterwards men remembered that there had been many warnings, many portents. A furious rushing wind had torn away the curtain from the Kaaba, an earthquake had shaken Muhammad's pulpit in the mosque at Madinah, and fire issued unaccountably from a hill in Aden. Fire, flood and plague had swept through the Muhammadan countries to mark the approach of the Mongolian hordes.

On Friday following the death of the Caliph, the remnants of the faithful gathered in the great mosque at Baghdad to lament the fate which had come over them. They prayed for the soul of the Caliph: 'Praise be to God who has caused such exalted personages to perish, and with them so many people of this city. O God, help us in our misery, for assuredly Islam has never witnessed such misery as this. Woe to Islam and her children . . .' And then they added the cry which all good Moslems whisper at the moment of death: 'We are God's and unto God do we return.'

Islam was dead. For three and a half years there was to be no Caliph on the throne. To Muhammadans everywhere it was as though the sun had gone out and there was no moon. The next great upsurge of Islamic energy came from a quarter which no one expected—from a handful of slaves on the banks of the Nile. These slaves saved Islam; and in saving Islam they saved Christendom.

(*Left*) Persian building reached its highest achievement at Isfahan. Madraseh Chahar Bagh is among the world's finest works in tile mosaic. (*Right*) The Tower of Victory in the Red Fort, Delhi, commemorates the victories by which the Muslim empire was established in India

The famous mosque at Samarqand in which the Tatar conqueror Timurlane (1336–1405) is buried

The throne of the great Shah Jehan in the Red Fort, Delhi

THE FALL OF EMPIRES

WHEN HULAGU set fire to Baghdad and went on to ravage all the surrounding territory, he put an end to medieval Islam. The shock was an
enduring one, felt throughout all the lands conquered by the Arabs, even
those lands which had been spared the Mongol invasions. Arab savagery
had broken against the greater savagery of Hulagu, and the sword of Islam
bowed before the more merciless sword of the Mongol conqueror. Henceforward Islam was to change direction. Never again would Muhammadans regard themselves with complete conviction as the possessors of the
God-given right to rule the world, for the evidence of their failure was all
around them in the ruins of three empires.

Around the year 1260 an observer in Cairo would have seen very little
to suggest that Islam had the strength to survive. Arabia had become a
backwater, remembered only because it contained the Black Stone and
the mortal remains of Muhammad, and because the whole splendid drama
had its origins among the desert wastes. The Crusaders were still entrenched along the coast of Syria and Palestine. Persia, Iraq and parts of
Asia Minor were under the rule of Hulagu, whose religion was a form of
shamanism common among the wandering tribesmen of the Asiatic plains.
Byzantium was still powerful, capable of putting to sea a fleet of a thousand
ships. The Muhammadan princes of Spain were at one another's throats;
Cordova, Seville and the larger part of Andalusia were in the hands of the
Christians, and Sicily had long since been abandoned by its Muhammadan
overlords. But while the Christians were victorious in Spain, Pope Alexander IV, trembling before the power of the Mongols, was addressing to
all the princes of Christendom a desperate appeal for unity against the
common danger. In the bull *Clamat in auribus*, issued from Rome, he urged
a general crusade against the Mongols:

> There rings in the ears of all the terrible trumpet of dire warning,
> rousing to vigilance all those whose minds are not completely be-
> fuddled. We observe every day the evidence of events which proclaim
> with unmistakable voice the coming of wars of universal destruction.
> The scourge of Heaven's fury in the hands of the merciless Tartars arises,
> as it were, from the secret depths of Hell, to oppress and crush the people.
> No longer is it the task of Christians to listen for surer tidings of these
> events, as though there was still any doubt about them. No: the need is
> to forewarn against the impending peril so clearly approaching. . . .

Both Christians and Muhammadans saw the year 1260 as one of impending disaster. Only the Polos, setting out that year on their great

o

journey which was to take them across the whole of Asia, seem to have felt
no fear at the approach of the Tartars.

For Muhammadans and Christians alike the fear was real, palpable,
mysteriously present like a cloud of doom. Hulagu was depicted as a
monster of unparalleled cruelty, a man with enormous eyes and scaly skin
whose greatest pleasure was to toss children into the flames: the portrait
was not far from the truth. Men searched for a ray of hope, and very few
of them could have guessed that salvation would come from Egypt.

At that time Egypt was in the first years of that perpetual palace
revolution which was to endure for two hundred and fifty years. The
dynasty founded by Saladin had come to an end; in its place there was the
rule of any local bandit or army commander with the strength to seize the
throne. These usurpers, rarely related to one another, often sprang from
the ranks of former slaves, and it pleased them to call themselves members
of the Mamluk ('Slave') dynasty. In 1260 the ruler of Egypt was a former
slave and military adventurer who had seized the throne by force. He was
the third Sultan of his dynasty, and was called al-Muzaffar Qutuz. It was
this Sultan, who ruled for only one year and of whom almost nothing is
known, who saved Europe and North Africa from the Tartars.

At a moment in history fraught with terror and uncertainty the Sultan
made a decision of such magnitude that we are still deeply indebted to him.
The Tartars were driving everything before them. They had massacred
the people of Aleppo, Nisibin and Edessa, and were preparing to destroy
Jerusalem and Cairo. An ambassador from Hulagu arrived in Cairo to
demand the surrender of all Egypt. Infuriated, Qutuz killed the envoy
out of hand, and then summoned a council of state to decide on the proper
course of action now that he had invoked the wrath of the most murderous
prince on earth. There was nothing else to do but to equip an army hurriedly and send it against Hulagu. Money for the army was raised by
ruthless extortions, and the command was given to Baybars al-Bunduq-
dari, a former Turkish slave. Baybars was a native of Kipchak, a district
between the Caspian and the Ural Mountains, magnificently built, tall
and broad-shouldered, with a resonant voice and a swarthy complexion.
He had been sold in the market-place at Damascus for 800 dirhems, a sum
which was later returned when his new owner discovered that he had a
cataract in one of his eyes. His eyes were blue, very bright and steely. It
was this fanatically brave soldier who led the vanguard of the Egyptian
army against the Tartars in a furious battle at Ayn Jalut ('the Pool of
Goliath') near Jerusalem on September 3, 1260. The Tartars fought
well, but they were no match for the Egyptians, who were far more
numerous and who were able to conceal their numbers until the time
came for the last devastating charge. The Tartars were pursued beyond Aleppo, and swept out of Syria. Baybars seems to have hoped
that Aleppo would be given to him as a reward, but no reward was
given to him. He decided to kill the Sultan, and gathered together a
small band of conspirators. One day, when the Sultan's attention was
distracted, a conspirator begged for the honour of kissing his hand. At

that moment Baybars leaped behind the Sultan and stabbed him in the neck.

It was the beginning of one of the longest reigns ever enjoyed by a Mamluk sovereign. Baybars assumed the title al-Malik al-Zahir ('the conquering king'), and for seventeen years acted with commendable forthrightness in ruling the kingdom. He had nerves of steel; he was always on the move; and he worked tirelessly through the night. The story is told of how Baybars arrived before Tyre one evening; a tent was immediately pitched by torchlight, and seven secretaries and the commander-in-chief of the army were summoned into the presence. For hours the secretaries wrote down orders as they were dictated by the king: letters, diplomas of rank, instructions to minor officials followed one another in a steady stream, all of them beginning with the proper invocations to God and concluding with the seal, which the Kind affixed with his own hand. One of these letters has been preserved. It is addressed to Bohemond, Prince of Antioch, who had been absent from the city when Baybars took it by assault. The letter gently commiserates with the Prince on his loss, ironically compliments him on his change of title from Prince to Count, as a result of losing his city, and then goes on to describe the siege and capture of Antioch, sparing no horrors. It concludes with a happy commentary on the delights of absence: 'This letter holds happy tidings for thee! It tells thee that God watches over thee, inasmuch as in these latter days thou wast not in Antioch! As not a man has escaped to tell thee the tale, we tell it thee: as no soul could apprize thee that thou art safe, while all the rest have perished, we apprise thee!' Nothing else that has survived from the time of Baybars gives us so well the flavour of that remorseless man.

Baybars was more than a military figure: he was also a superb administrator and a consummate politician. In the intervals of making war against the Crusaders, the Armenians, the Seljuks and the Assassins, he built mosques, dug canals, improved harbours and arranged a fast postal service between Egypt and Syria. Letters dispatched from Cairo were delivered in Damascus four days later. The roads were so good that the King was able to play polo in Damascus and Cairo in a single week. He built an enormous bridge over the Great Canal and decorated it with stone lions, because there were lions on his coat of arms. He invited Turkish colonists into Egypt, and when he discovered a pocket of Mongolian horsemen among the Syrian hills, abandoned in the retreat, he invited them to Cairo, pardoned them for any crimes they might have committed, and ordered houses built for them and for their families, thus adding three or four thousand good workmen to the labour force of Cairo. He was a firm believer in the *jihad*, or 'holy war', and he never lost a battle.

When the last Abbasid Caliph was murdered, Islam lost its spiritual head. However incompetent the Caliph had been, he represented in his living person the tradition which went back in a straight line to Muhammad. For three years Muhammadans had lamented the absence of a spiritual ruler who could legitimately wear the mantle of Muhammad. Baybars decided to remedy the situation. In June, 1261, an uncle of the murdered Caliph who had escaped the massacre was brought from Damascus to Cairo in great state, escorted by the royal guard and accompanied by Jews bearing the Torah and Christians bearing the Gospels. After his genealogy had been formally approved by the *qadis*, he was acknowledged as Caliph under the name al-Mustansir; and playing his comic role to the end, Baybars solemnly swore allegiance to the Caliph, who would never be allowed to rule and who was shortly afterwards put to death. From the new Caliph, who was remarkably dark in colour and suspected of being no descendant of Muhammad, Baybars received a robe of honour and a diploma of investiture giving him authority over Egypt, Syria, Diyar Bakr, Hijaz, Yaman and the land of the Euphrates. The diploma should be quoted at some length and compared with the memorial inscription by Ibn Tulun:

Praise be to God who has displayed upon Islam the robes of glory, and has made the brightness of its pearls shine forth, that aforetime were hidden under a thick veil; and has so firmly established the edifice of its prosperity that thereby He has caused all record of all that went before to be forgotten . . .

There has come a ruler who sets his hand to generous deeds with might and main, and, sword in hand, never destroys the hiding-place of error, without giving it over to the flames and drenching it in blood. Since all these noble qualities are the special characteristics of His Sublime Highness, Sultan al-Malik al-Zahir Rukn-al-Din[1] (may God ennoble and exalt him!), the High Chancellery of the descendant of Muhammad, the Imam Mustansir (may God exalt his power!) has been pleased to extol the lofty merit of this prince and to proclaim his good offices, which even the most eloquent language would fail adequately to express or fittingly commend, for it is he who has raised up against the Abbasid dynasty after it had been crippled by the blows of ill-fortune and robbed of all its welfare and blessings. . . .

Therefore the Commander of the Faithful gives you thanks for such kindness, and makes known to all, that but for your watchful care, the ruin would have been beyond repair. He therefore confers on you authority over Egypt, Syria, Diyar Bakr, the Hijaz, the Yaman, the land of the Euphrates and whatever fresh conquests you may achieve, on plain or mountain. He entrusts to you the government of them and the control of their troops and their population, so that you may become for them a paragon of generosity, and he makes no exception of any single city or fortress or any object, great or small. Then keep a watch over the interests of the whole body of the faithful, since this burden has been laid upon you.[2]

---

[1] Rukn-al-Din means 'pillar of the faithful'. Rulers had quite naturally taken over such titles since the time of the Buwayhids.

[2] Sir Thomas W. Arnold, *The Caliphate* (Oxford: Clarendon Press, 1924), pp. 90–2.

It is in the nature of things that in a time of decadence the language should become sterile, the words as meaningless as the emotions they are intended to convey. The pompous proclamation gave Baybars rule over lands which he had not conquered and which were to remain forever outside the jurisdiction of the Mamluk sultans. But the formalities had to be observed, and the Caliph who went on to speak of the Caliphate regaining 'its ancient glory' and 'the need to be ever watchful that the victory of Islam is secure' was so evidently a puppet that it is surprising that Baybars, with his acute sense of reality, permitted the imposture. When the ceremony was over, there was a solemn procession through the streets of Cairo, with one of the officers of state holding the diploma of investiture aloft, exactly as the Torah and the Gospels had been held aloft during the journey from Damascus.

The Sultan soon wearied of his Caliph. A few weeks after the investiture, Baybars suggested that the Caliph should lead a *jihad* against the enemies of Islam in Baghdad. The Caliph seems to have been overjoyed and set out with a small army provided by the Sultan for Damascus, which was to become his base. Here Baybars was warned that the re-establishment of the Caliphate in Baghdad would inevitably endanger his own independence, and he therefore abandoned the Caliph to his fate. He was killed when making his way across the desert by a small force sent out by the governor of Baghdad; and nothing more was ever heard of the handful of troops who accompanied him.

The experiment, however, was successful. Caliphs being expendable, there was nothing to prevent Baybars from attending the inauguration of a new Caliph whenever he pleased. In the following year another prince of the Abbasid house, Abu'l Abbas Ahmad, made his way to Cairo and was installed in the Caliphate with pomp and ceremony, taking the name al-Hakim. Once again there was the careful examination of his genealogy, with the learned *qadis* sitting in judgment and pronouncing on the legitimacy of the new incumbent; once again there were gifts; once again Sultan and Caliph marched through the city in triumph. By this time the Caliphate had become no more than a meaningless title, the shadow of a shadow of a shadow. A long succession of Caliphs continued to be proclaimed in Egypt, until the Turks conquered the Mamluks and carried back to Constantinople the supposed relics of Muhammad. The Turks saw no reason to subscribe to the devious ways of the Mamluks; the Sultan himself assumed all the rights and responsibilities of the Caliphate.

Baybars had hoped to found a dynasty, but on his death—he is said to have died from drinking out of a poisoned cup intended for one of his enemies—his two young sons were quickly deposed by another Turkish slave who had risen to military power. The new Sultan came from Kipchak, and had been sold in the market-place of Damascus. Having two good eyes, he was sold for a thousand dinars. His Turkish name, Qalawun, was exchanged readily for the more high sounding al-Mansur, whom he resembled only in his passion for building. The new Sultan was as ruthless as Baybars in attacking the Crusaders and the Mongols. An excellent diplomat, he maintained friendly relations with Michael VIII Palaeologus, the Emperor of Byzantium, and he had so little respect for Muhammadam opinion that he dispensed with the ceremony of investiture by the Caliph. When he came to the throne the Crusaders, who had once controlled the whole length of coast from Gaza to Cilicia, were reduced to their citadels at Acre, Tyre, Sidon, Tripoli, Jebayl, Tortosa and the isolated town of Latakiyeh; and he proceeded to prepare the ground for their final eviction. When he died at the age of seventy in 1290, and was succeeded by his son al-Ashraf, the Crusaders may have known they had only a few more months to enjoy their possessions. Under a sovereign of a 'Slave' dynasty, whose mother was a Mongol, the last remnants of the Frankish power in the Holy Land were destroyed.

The Crusaders died in pools of blood, betrayed by their conquerors, alone in a land where they had never struck deep roots. The last act of the drama took place in the spring and summer of 1291, as the Mamluk army swept along the coast of Syria. In May, after a siege of forty-three days, Acre surrendered: the survivors were offered a safe-conduct, only to be massacred when they came out of the fort. Acre itself was reduced to smoking ruins. There followed a brief campaign in which all the cities held by the Crusaders fell one by one to the invaders until nothing was left except the obscure island of Arwad off the Syrian coast, and this too fell eleven years later.

Al-Ashraf returned in triumph to Cairo. A jewelled parasol was held over his head; trumpeters filled the air with songs of victory. In front of the Sultan rode the Mamluk cavalry, bearing on their lances the bloody heads of dead Crusaders, while behind him in fetters came the living remnants of the once-great army which had hoped to make the Holy Land a part of Christendom. The conqueror carried the banner of the Cross reversed, as a sign of his triumph over the West. And when the triumphal march through the city was over, al-Ashraf visited his father's grave, and for a long time prostrated himself, before returning to the citadel to give rewards to his soldiers. For two hundred years his predecessors had vainly striven to defeat the Crusaders; the knowledge of so great a triumph drove him almost insane.

His triumph was brief. On December 12, 1293, while out hunting without an escort, some soldiers in the pay of the Viceroy Baydara fell on him and hacked him to pieces. Baydara had already made plans to assume power, and was making his way to Cairo when the aroused guards and ministers of the dead Sultan met him on the left bank of the Nile. There was a short battle, most of al-Ashraf's assassins were slain, and Baydara was cut to pieces. As an added refinement, his liver was cut out of his body and eaten by those who were loyal to al-Ashraf, and for three days the body of Baydara was left in the desert, to be gnawed by wolves. Finally the body was removed to a mausoleum which the Viceroy had built and completed only a few months before.

The savagery of the Mamluks did not prevent them from creating exquisite art. It is an art without character, yet never decadent; filled with intelligence, yet lacking in directed passion. In such an age it could hardly be otherwise. They were conquerors without responsibility, men of immense daring, who saw that life was brief and therefore to be enjoyed to the uttermost. In their wars against the Mongols they were as successful as they were against the Crusaders. In some strange way they seemed to retain their primitive *asabiyya*; and so for 250 more years the Mamluks remained in power. The individual sultans nearly always died miserably: they were thrown down wells, poisoned, cut in two, or smothered in their beds. Plagues swarmed over Egypt, famine raged, earthquakes shook Cairo to its roots; but this dynasty of usurpers, which began shortly after the death of Saladin, continued uninterruptedly until 1517, when the Ottoman Sultan, Salim I, conquered Egypt.

The Mamluks destroyed the Crusaders, but they saved the West. The last great battle between Mamluks and Mongols took place at Marj al-Suffar south of Damascus in 1303, but by this time the Mongols themselves had been weakened. The leader of this expedition was Ghazan Khan, the great-grandson of Hulagu, a small, withered, tireless man who had embraced Buddhism and discovered Islam on the eve of his succession to the Persian throne. Under the pressure of Islam even the Mongols had become civilized.

No one could have recognized in Ghazan Khan the ferocity of his forebears. He was stern in battle, but gentle in time of peace. 'Among his soldiers,' wrote a chronicler, 'scarcely one could be found as small and ugly as he is, but he surpassses them all in virtue and integrity.' Ghazan Khan decorated his capital at Tabriz with a magnificent mosque, two colleges, a hospital, a library and an observatory. He encouraged poets and scientists, and he was especially concerned with reviving the economy of his small and powerful empire. He encouraged settlements in the lands through which the Mongols had swept like a whirlwind, and decreed that taxes should be announced publicly 'on wood or on stone or written in chalk'. He listened to the complaints of poor peasants, and spoke gravely about the need for good government. Persian became the language of his court. Once more the Persians had tamed their barbarian invaders.

Those years when the Crusaders were fighting a battle for survival and the Mongols were roaring like a whirlwind towards the Mediterranean seem in retrospect to be years of confusion and disaster. But in fact confusion and disaster were localized. Cities in the path of the Mongol invaders were put to the flames, but life went on in the villages, which were rarely worth setting on fire. Here and there, in the broad swath cut by the Mongols, we find communities untouched by the wars. The farmers continued to till their fields, the maids went to the wells, and the poets sang their songs.

The poet Sa'di of Shiraz (1184–1291) lived out his long life in the shadow of the wars. The painting over his tomb shows him as a small wiry man, with a fraying moustache, and an air of gentle bewilderment. He tells the story that when he was a child he was given to long vigils at night and earnest prayers on behalf of erring humanity, but one night, when his father found him on his knees, he was asked what he was doing. 'I am praying for the sins of mankind,' he answered. 'You have better think of your own sins first,' his father answered, and packed him off to bed. Sa'di spent the rest of his life thinking of his own sins only at rare intervals. He delighted in erring humanity, and travelled over the known world to contemplate ordinary human beings at their toils. He wandered to India, settling down long enough in Delhi to learn the language. He wandered to Arabia and seems to have had a child by an Arabian girl. When the child died, he decided to drown his grief by undertaking an expedition to Abyssinia. He travelled over North Africa, and for a while lived in Damascus and Baalbek, where he became a famous pulpit orator. Growing weary of civilization, he withdrew into the desert near Jerusalem, enjoying, like John the Baptist, the company of wild beasts until, as he says, 'the time came when some Franks took me prisoner and kept me with Jews in a trench at Tripoli, digging clay.' A leading citizen of Aleppo chanced to see him working at the fortifications, took a fancy to him, ransomed him for ten dinars, and offered a further hundred dinars if Sa'di would marry his daughter. Sa'di agreed, but soon wearied of his shrewish wife, divorced her, and went wandering again. He travelled all over North Africa and Asia Minor, and he was fifty when he finally returned to his native Shiraz. Baghdad was in ruins, but the south of Persia had been left more or less untouched by the Mongols, and he lived quietly and contentedly in this city famous for its roses, and not far from Persepolis, the heart of ancient Persia.

In Shiraz he wrote his famous *Gulistan*, or *Rose Garden*, partly in prose, partly in verse, and filled with innumerable wry stories concerning the fate of kings (usually bad) and of gentle peasants (usually good). He compiled his long storybook lightheartedly and without heroics; and if it never achieved the fame of Firdausi's *Shahnameh* it nevertheless represented an important aspect of the Persian character, for he told of their laughter, their quick wits, their lightly held loyalties, their love of majesty.

Where Sa'di is of the earth, earthy, Jalalu'l-Din Rumi (1207–73) is of the spirit, and so deeply immersed in the spirit that for him the earth hardly exists. He was born at Balkh, the son of a well-known teacher and theologian, and he was twelve when his father, fearing the onrush of the Mongols, moved with his family to Konya, at that time the capital of the Western Seljuk empire. For the rest of his life he remained at Konya, becoming a religious teacher; surrounding himself with disciples, who called him *Mawlana*, or 'master'; writing poetry on the theme of mystical love; and introducing certain techniques into the worship of God, apparently never used before, among them a dance performed by the devotees wheeling in circles corresponding to the orbits of the heavenly bodies, at a pace so dizzy that the dancers lost consciousness and came to believe they were in the presence of God. In time these dancers were known as the 'whirling dervishes', and were considered by foreigners to be members of a strange and ludicrous sect, but in fact the dance of the dervishes was an inevitable development of Sufi beliefs. For them God was a holy dance, and how better to imitate God than to dance in holiness? So they danced barefoot, wearing their high camel's-hair hats and their long blue plaited robes which perhaps represented the skies, at first dancing gravely round their leader, then spinning like a top in one place with eyes closed and arms outstretched, the right palm turned up, the left down, until their skirts ballooned out, giving them so much momentum that they could whirl uninterruptedly for half an hour to the music of flutes from the musicians' gallery until at last, streaming with sweat, they gradually slowed down, and an attendant threw a robe over their shoulders; and then after a short interval they would resume the dance.

Jalalu'l-Din Rumi sometimes led the dance and composed music for it; but he was more famous for his poetry. He wrote voluminously, composing a flood of mystical odes and the huge compendium of mystical lore known as the *Mathnawi* in six books. Like Blake he wrote unevenly: the most authentic descriptions of the joys of Heaven are followed by rigmarole. Yet he remains the greatest of Muhammadan mystical poets.

He was thirty-seven when there arrived in Konya a strange sixty-year-old dervish, said to be the son of a cloth merchant and known by the name Shamsi Tabriz. Infatuated by his utterances, Jalalu'l-Din Rumi took the old man into his house, and for two years they were inseparable. The disciples complained that their teacher was paying no attention to them. They resented the intruder and threatened violence against the favourite, who always wore a gown of coarse black felt and was known as 'the far-flying one' because he had journeyed widely. At last Shamsi Tabriz fled to Damascus. Jalalu'l-Din sent his own son to bring the old man back. There was peace again, but only for a short while. Suddenly Shamsi Tabriz vanished. According to a story told several years later, he was set upon one night by seven conspirators, all heavily armed. Though without weapons, Shamsi Tabriz fought them off and escaped, leaving a few drops of blood on the earth as a sign of his victory; then he vanished from the world. Jalalu'l-Din, overcome by grief, wrote in his honour the huge collection of lyrical poems known as the *Diwani Shamsi Tabriz*. Among them are the verses which the poet Sa'di regarded as the greatest written in Persian:

> Forever and ever the voice of love is calling.
> Our ship sails for Heaven: who are the voyagers
> Who do not share our desire for the journey?
> We have been to Heaven: we are companions of angels.
> So let us journey together, there is our country.
> We are even higher than angels and closer to Heaven.
> The end of our journey is a most perfect majesty.

It is a note we hear again and again in the poetry of Jalalu'l-Din Rumi. Heaven is close, almost we can breathe the scents flowing from it, almost we can rest in its shade:

> Lovers, O lovers, it is time to abandon the world:
> The drum of departing is heard on my spiritual ears.
> Behold, the camel-driver is surely preparing his train:
> And shall we blame him when the travellers are asleep?

Listen! The clanging of the camel-bells can be heard,
And every moment a soul is setting out to the Frontier.
From these inverted awnings, from these blue candles
There comes a marvellous people, to share in the mysteries.
A heavy sleep falls from the circling spheres.
Alas, that life should be like a feather and slumber so heavy!
Dear one, seek the beloved: he is close by your side.
Watchman, awake! Never should a watchman sleep!

No poet ever spoke of the heavenly mysteries with more assurance or more grace. Like the great Andalusian poet, Ibn Arabi, he speaks of Heaven as though he had been there and mapped out its pathways. So he says in one of the poems of the immense *Diwan*:

I have circled with the Nine Fathers in the Heavens,
For years I have followed the stars in their revolutions,
And always I was secret, dwelling in Him.
I touched the walls of the Kingdom, and my eyes were open.
I received nourishment from God, as a child in the womb.
Men are born once: I was born many times.
And wearing a coat of flesh, I have gone about spiritual affairs,
But often I have slit my coat wide open with my own hands.
Long nights have I passed with the priests,
And I have slept with pagans in the market-places.
I am the green eyes of jealousy, the fever of sickness.
I am cloud and rain, I have swept down over the meadows,
Yet never did the dust of mortality touch the hem of my garments.
I have gathered a treasure of roses in the Field of Eternity.
I am not water nor fire: there is no pride in me.
I am not fashioned in clay: I am the voice of mockery.
I am not Shamsi Tabriz: I am the pure Light!
Beware, if thou seest me! Tell no one I am here!

In this poem, where humility fights with pride, and the most assured wisdom is concealed in a cry of pain, Jalalu'l-Din Rumi seems to be attempting to describe the heart of the mystery. Death was never far from his thoughts, and he was half in love with it. He wrote once:

Illness is a treasure, for it contains mercies:
The kernel is soft when the rind is scraped away.
O brother, the place of darkness and cold
Is the fountain of life and the cup of ecstasy!

Once, when he ordered music and dancing to accompany the funeral of one of his disciples, he was told he was behaving improperly. 'How should I do otherwise?' he asked. 'Surely when at last the spirit is free from the dungeon of the body and wings its way to the source from which all things come, it is an occasion for rejoicing.' Like al-Hallaj, he could tell stories which make the head whirl. He believed that even evil contributes to the glory of God. He wrote once: 'I die as a stone and become a plant. I die as a plant and am raised to the rank of an animal. I die as an animal, and am reborn as man. I die as a man, and come to birth as an angel. I shall die as an angel and become something that no man has seen, and then I shall be the Nothing, the Nothing!' It was as though in a few lines he was attempting to suggest the entire cosmology of the Sufis.

His greatest work was the *Mathnawi*, which he wrote at intervals over a period of forty-three years. He called it 'the path of the ascetics and the garden of the initiated', 'the river of divine love', and 'the mirror held up to the face of God'. At once epic and textbook, the book claims to cover the entire field of love in all its multitudinous and divine aspects, and if it can be compared with any poem at all, it must be compared with Dante's *Paradiso*.

He died amid his beloved dervishes and was buried close to the dancing floor, not far from the musician's gallery, in a tomb shrouded in green embroidered velvet, crowned with the long dervish cap shaped like the vase of light which contained Muhammad's soul. Here too his successors, the hereditary heads of the order of Mawlawi dervishes, known as Chelebi, were also buried. In time the authority of the order grew so great that the Chelebi had the right to gird the sword of Osman on the Sultan at the time of his coronation.

When Jalalu'l-Din Rumi died in 1273, the Seljuk princes of Asia Minor were already suffering from the weaknesses which come with luxury. So it happened that the wise old sultan of Iconium, Jalalu'l-Din's friend and protector, Ala-ad-Din II, found himself at war with an army of marauding Mongols and sought the help of some fierce Turkish tribesmen camped near the battlefield under their leader Ertoghrul. The tribesmen offered to fight if they were given land; the battle was won; and the Turks were allowed as a reward for their assistance to occupy the border marches in the Karasu valley, where their only neighbours were Byzantine Christians. Only four hundred families of Turks took part in the battle, but they began to see themselves as the inevitable inheritors of the crumbling Seljuk empire. Ertoghrul died in 1288, and was succeeded by his son Osman, who in a reign of thirty-eight years succeeded in extending his dominions until they reached the Bosphorus and the Black Sea. In the next two centuries the Osmanli Turks were to spread their conquests into the heart of Europe, through southwest Asia and across North Africa, nearly to the Atlantic Ocean; and the dynasty founded by Osman ruled for six centuries, twice as long as the longest Greek or Roman dynasty, longer than the Abbasid dynasty and therefore longer than any other dynasty which has ever ruled on earth.

In the beginning the Osmanli Turks possessed all the virtues which, according to Ibn Khaldun, were necessary to the founders of empires. Embracing Islam with the fervour of converts, merciless to their enemies, persistent in their desire for conquest, puritanical and despising luxury, they won every battle they fought, and fought continuously. When Osman propounded to his ministers a scheme for further aggression against his enemies, his ninety-year-old uncle, who had taken part in all his campaigns, objected: the uncle was immediately murdered. In all its long and checkered history the Osmanli dynasty continued to reserve the harshest treatment for those close to the throne.

When Osman died at the age of sixty-eight, he had already established most of the rules by which his successors were to reign. He was a heavy-set man, with a thick black beard, dark features and the look of an emperor, though he called himself *amir*. He dressed simply and despised luxury: at his death his wealth consisted of a wooden spoon, a salt bowl, a braided coat, a white linen turban, his battle flags, a yoke of oxen and a few droves of sheep. With rare exceptions the Turkish sultans of the next three centuries lived just as simply.

As time passed, there was less and less Turkish blood flowing in the veins of the sultans. Osman married his younger son and successor to the daughter of the Greek lord of Yar Hissar in Bithynia, the celebrated Nilaufer ('Lotus Flower'), renowned for her beauty. The elder of Nilaufer's sons was Sultan Murad I, from whom all subsequent sultans were descended. Yet the characteristic Turkish features persisted: the hawk nose, the heavily lidded eyes, the curling lips and the perpetual look of hurt surprise can be seen on the portraits of the sultans up to the time of the last Sultan Muhammad VI, exiled by Kemal Atatürk.

Urkhon, who inherited the throne from Osman, was deeply attached to his brother Ala-ad-Din, and at one time suggested they should share the throne. Ala-ad-Din refused, but became Grand Vizier, devoting himself to the reorganization of the army. It is largely due to the gentle and saintly Ala-ad-Din that the Ottoman Empire owes the introduction of the Janissaries, Christian mercenaries trained from childhood to guard the Sultan and protect the imperial standards.

The first detachment of Janissaries, numbering a thousand youths, was raised about 1330 and immediately put into training. Thereafter, every fourth year one-fifth of the young Greek youths were rounded up by the local inspectors and sent off for training. They were the physical property of the Sultan. They were given the traditional uniform of green and yellow cloaks with high plumed bonnets and taught the traditional marching steps—three paces forward, then a pause, then three paces forward again. They were affiliated into the Bekhtashi order of dervishes, and could therefore be regarded as a priestly army. According to a legend, the first recruits were led by Urkhon himself into the presence of a famous dervish, Hajji Bekhtash of Khurasan, for his blessing. The dervish stretched his arm over the nearest boy so that his long white sleeve trailed down, and he said: 'Let them be called *Yeni Cheri*, the "new strength", and may their countenances ever be bright, their swords keen and their hands victorious.' The loose sleeve of the dervish was remembered in the flowing white pendants worn by the Janissaries from their grey woollen caps.

In theory the Janissaries were attached to the royal household, and the titles of their officers, *Chorbaji* and *Kahwaji* (Soup-maker and Coffee-maker), bore witness to the fact that they were privileged members of the Sultan's household. In fact their privileges were minimal. They drew no pay, they were not allowed to marry, and they slept in long dormitories with a watchman continually walking up and down, making a vast amount of noise. They were allowed to carry a long slender reed as a mark of rank, and their standard was a flag of pure white silk ornamented with horsetails. Their chief object of affection was the soup kettle, which they employed as a drum, beating it with wooden spoons—hence 'kettle-

drum'. When the Janissaries overturned their soup kettles it meant
revolution. But revolution was rare, and the Sultan usually took care to
be on good terms with them. The first act of each Sultan on his accession
was to go to the Janissary barracks and drink to their health 'and to our
merry meeting at the Red Apple' (Constantinople).

The Red Apple was already ripening on the stem. In 1341 the Emperor
Andronicus III died, and with him died the hope of a united Byzantine
empire free of doctrinal quarrels under a single ruler. He was succeeded
by the nine-year-old John V Palaeologus, his son by his second wife, Anne
of Savoy, who became the regent. The boy had been entrusted to the care
of the Grand Domestic, John Cantacuzene, who had always feared the
Empress for her undisguised meddling in the affairs of the Byzantine
Church. John Cantacuzene decided to raise the banner of revolt against
the Empress, escaped to Thrace, gathered an army and proclaimed himself Emperor. Shortly afterwards the boy Emperor was crowned in
Constantinople. Then there were two emperors, and the country was
plunged in civil war. By this single act John Cantacuzene, a deeply religious man of great resourcefulness, signed the death warrant of the
thousand-year-old empire founded by Constantine.

To survive, it was necessary for him to seek help wherever it could be
found. In 1346, when the civil war was going in favour of the Palaeologi,
John Cantacuzene offered Urkhon the hand of his daughter Theodora in
return for military assistance—6,000 Ottoman troops entered Thrace.
For the first time the Turks poured into Europe. They were to increase
in numbers with every passing year, and were to become a European
power long before the fall of Constantinople.

In the following year the Byzantine empire enjoyed a brief moment of
peace when the civil war came to an end, with the coronation of both
emperors in Santa Sophia followed a week later by the marriage of the
fifteen-year-old John V Palaeologus with Helena, the daughter of John
Cantacuzene. For a few more years the Byzantine emperors went through
the motions of government, signed treaties, and attempted to conceal
their weaknesses from their enemies; but their thrones were tottering, and
they had little heart for empire.

When the Turks crossed over into Europe, they came casually, almost
carelessly, with the effrontory of a people who knew their own strength.
Urkhon's eldest son Sulayman simply crossed the Hellespont one night
with eighty followers on three rafts, and attacked the castle of Tzympe.
The castle fell. During the following days reinforcements arrived and the
castle was put in a state of defence. The Byzantine army was still powerful,
and when the Byzantines offered a ransom for the castle, Urkhon was prepared to withdraw. When an earthquake destroyed the neighbouring
town of Kallipolis (Gallipoli), the Turks decided that Kallipolis had been
destroyed by the hand of God and all the auspices were favourable. Afterwards no inducement would lead the Turks to surrender this strategic site
at the mouth of the Sea of Marmora. It was the first European town occupied by the Turks: there were to be many more.

Three years later Sulayman died after falling from his horse, and when the news reached Urkhon he died of a broken heart. He was seventy-two. During a reign of thirty-three years he had enormously increased the Ottoman dominions and driven the Byzantines from their remaining possessions in Asia Minor. He had secured a foothold in Europe, and reduced the Byzantine Emperor almost to vassalage. Few of the Ottoman sultans who came after him had his presence. He was tall and thickset, with bright eyes and beetling eyebrows, a reddish face and thick moustaches and beard. He looked like an Emperor; his successors, even the great conqueror Muhammad II and Sulayman the Magnificent, looked like imitators.

Urkhon's second son Murad, who followed him to the throne in 1359, strove to enlarge his empire at the expense of the Byzantines and the Balkan princes. Adrianople fell; and this city, so close to Constantinople, became the capital of the Ottoman empire. In vain did Pope Urban V summon Christians to the defence of Constantinople. An army of knights under Amadeus of Savoy occupied Kallipolis for a brief space, but nothing came of their intervention. The Turks were on the march, relentlessly hammering at the frontiers of the empire.

From Thrace, Murad set out to conquer Bulgaria, Macedonia and Serbia, until in time they all fell to his power. The defeated armies melted into the mountains, to resume their campaigns when the Turkish army had passed; there were constant rebellions. He fought his last battle on the Field of Blackbirds (Kossovo Polye) against Lazar, the Serbian king, on June 15, 1389. The battle was fiercely contested, with the decision wavering backwards and forwards, now in favour of the Turks, now of the Christians. For the first time cannon, recently invented in Europe, were being used by the Turks. Murad was in his tent when a nobleman, Milosh Kobilich, who proclaimed himself a deserter from the Serbs, was introduced into his presence. Kobilich offered to reveal important secrets to the Sultan, and he was kneeling in homage when he was asked what the secrets were. In answer Kobilich drew a dagger, killing Murad with a single blow.

They said of Murad that he was 'a man of few words, and he dissembled deeply'. For twenty-four years he had led his armies in the field, increasing fivefold the extent of his empire, bringing his armies to the Danube. Henceforth Thrace, Macedonia, Bulgaria, Serbia and almost the whole of Asia Minor were to belong to the Turkish empire; already the greater part of the empire, which was to last for nearly five and a half centuries, had been won.

His son Bayazid, married to a Greek princess, sent a shudder through the heart of Europe. He was feared as the Mongols had been feared. Pope Boniface IX granted plenary indulgence on all those who would join the Crusade against the Turks, and a vast army set out under the command of Sigismund, King of Hungary. The flower of the French and German chivalry met at Buda, and marched down the Danube to Nicopolis. The Turks were accustomed to throw their irregulars into battle at the beginning. These irregulars were expendable, and the purpose of sending them into battle was to weaken the enemy and slow down his advance. The army of King Sigismund had no difficulty in dispersing the irregulars, but when confronted by the main body of the Ottomans, 60,000 strong, together with the Serbian troops who had joined the Turks as allies, they were defeated with great slaughter. The battle lasted only three hours. When it was over, the captives, wearing only their shirts, were led before the Sultan with the Ottoman army drawn around him in the form of a great semicircle. There were 10,000 captives. Roped together in small groups, they were brought before the Sultan, who examined them briefly, decided on the spot whether they were worth a ransom, and gave permission to his Janissaries to pound to death those who could not be ransomed. For a whole day, from daybreak to four o'clock in the afternoon, Bayazid watched the procession with the expression of a man enjoying the visible evidence of his triumph. It especially delighted him that the very greatest lords of France and Germany were brought stark naked before him. He spared the lives of the most handsome Christian youths and later enrolled them in his bodyguard. Not since the time of the Mamluk Sultan al-Ashraf had a Muhammadan monarch enjoyed so great a victory over the West.

To repeat the triumph Bayazid determined on the conquest of Constantinople. For this purpose he erected on the Asiatic coast of the Bosphorus, six miles from Constantinople, a fortress which came to be known as the Anadolu Hissar, 'the Anatolian fortress', which still exists. He was preparing to besiege the city when great events in Asia compelled him to turn eastward against an enemy far more powerful and far more merciless than any he had yet confronted.

Timurlane—the name comes from Mongol root-words meaning 'iron' and 'lame'—was threatening the West, employing the same tactics which Hulagu had used before him. Born in 1336, he had been a shoemaker until he led a small raiding party against the Jaghatai amir of Khurasan and Transoxiana. He overthrew the amir and inherited the least distinguished of the dynasties founded by Genghiz Khan, from whom he was descended on his mother's side. He made his capital at Samarqand and invited Persian artists and architects to his court. He was an obscure prince of a remote territory in the heart of Asia, and nothing about that dark-featured, spade-bearded man suggested that he was to become a world conqueror. At the age of forty-four he set out to conquer the world.

His first conquests were in Afghanistan and Persia, where he captured Isfahan and feasted his eyes on the spectacle of a pyramid of 70,000 skulls. He sacked Baghdad, massacred most of the inhabitants and took what treasure he could—not very much treasure, for Baghdad had never recovered from the wounds inflicted by Hulagu. He overran Mesopotamia, swung north to Moscow, which he held for over a year, and three years later he was outside the walls of Delhi, admiring a still more extravagant pyramid of skulls. In 1401 he swept through Syria, pausing three days at Aleppo to build a comparatively small tower of skulls: according to the Arab chronicler it was thirty feet high, and all the faces were turned outwards. Hims and Baalbek fell, and then it was the turn of Damascus, which held out for a month. The city was sacked, and the Great Umayyad Mosque was left an empty shell. From Damascus he returned to Baghdad to avenge the deaths of his officers murdered by an enraged populace—he built 120 towers of skulls in their memory. During the following year he prepared an invasion of Asia Minor. It was this threat which drew Bayazid from the walls of Constantinople. With 120,000 men he marched to meet the enemy. Timurlane had an army of 800,000 men. The battle, which lasted a day and a night, was fought on the plain of Angora (Ankara) on July 20, 1402. It was a broiling hot day. Bayazid's army was cut off from water. Some 18,000 Tartars in his employ went over to the enemy, and the Janissaries and the Serbian auxiliaries were no match for the invaders. Trying to fly from the battlefield, Bayazid was captured, brought before Timurlane, and for the remaining eight months of his life he was transported from place to place in a cage slung between two horses. The Tartars went on to destroy Brusa and Smyrna, and might have gone on to destroy all of Europe, but Timurlane had already decided to march on China. Europe was saved, but the Ottoman empire was in turmoil: for eleven years a succession of Sultans attempted to seize power. Civil war flared up. At last in 1413 there came to the throne the first of the two Ottoman sultans who possessed any mildness of manner. This was Muhammad I, known as *Chelebi*, 'the gentleman', who said to the ambassadors of Hungary, Serbia, Wallachia, Venice, Ragusa and Epirus who came to congratulate him at Adrianople: 'Tell your masters that I send peace to all and accept it from all, and may God punish the violators!' It was a strange statement to come from the lips of a Sultan.

Everything one knows about Muhammad I suggests a man of great moral dignity and religious feeling. He was the first to send an annual expedition bearing imperial gifts to Mecca. He was on friendly terms with the Byzantine Emperor, whom he visited during a royal progress, and he treated his Christian subjects well. He built superb mosques and wrote excellent poetry, and set the intellectual tone of his reign. Almost saintly and incapable of deceit, his death was attended by a strange and deceitful ruse which was to be imitated many times in the future. He suffered a stroke while riding through Kallipolis, fell from his horse, and died a few days later, after begging his Vizier to place his two minor sons under the protection of the Byzantine Emperor. The heir to the throne, Prince Murad, made it his first task after his accession to kill off his brothers. But while the Sultan lay dead and before Murad could reach Kallipolis, the Janissaries threatened to take matters in their own hands. To appease them, and to prevent them from coming out in open revolt, it was arranged to prop up the Sultan's body near the windows of a darkened kiosk; and while a page hidden behind the corpse passed his arms through the Sultan's cloak, the Sultan was seen to be waving his arms. A few days later the body of Muhammad I was transported to the Green Mosque at Brusa;

The Taj Mahal, Agra, erected by Shah Jehan in memory of his wife,
Mumtaz Mahal

Ivory horn decorated with roundels containing representations of a variety of animals; Egyptian, eleventh century

Ivory casket made by Abd-ar-Rahman III (A.D. 912-961), the Umayyad emir of Cordova, for his daughter. Abd-ar-Rahman was the first Spanish ruler to take the title Caliph of Cordova

Decorated ewer of hammered brass damascened with silver and inlaid with black composition; Mesopotamian, thirteenth century the pantomime was over; and in the place of the gentle Muhammad came the conquering Murad.

Murad II was all fire and venom, happiest with the sword, treacherous and vindictive. He was eighteen when he came to the throne, but he had an old man's cunning and a mature man's delight in conquest. The Byzantine Emperor Manuel II Palaeologus made the mistake of advancing the cause of a certain Mustapha, who claimed to be the son of Sultan Bayazid and the rightful successor to the throne of the Ottoman Turks. Mustapha raised an army, crossed the Hellespont, and was about to attack the young Murad when his soldiers arrested him and summarily committed him into the hands of his enemy: he was tortured and hanged. Murad concluded that there was no safety in Constantinople and vowed its destruction.

From that moment the fate of Constantinople was sealed. Murad was nineteen, and he had been on the throne less than a year when he brought his army up against the walls of Constantinople. Wave upon wave of Turks were hurled against the ramparts of the greatest city in Christendom, and the Byzantines had almost given up their cause in despair when they observed that the Turks had vanished—Murad had called off the assault to put down the rebellion of his thirteen-year-old brother in the rear. For a few more years Constantinople was spared, but her days were numbered.

Murad never again felt himself sufficiently strong for a frontal assault on Constantinople, but he devised other plans to reduce the hated city to insignificance. He would conquer all eastern Europe, capture all the outlying bastions of Constantinople, isolate it completely. He marched against Hungary, captured Salonica from the Venetians, invaded Macedonia and engaged in constant raids across the Danube. He was not always successful. When invading Transylvania in 1439, his armies were met by the Hungarians under John Hunyadi, the natural son of King Sigismund. At the battle of Hermannstadt, north of the Danube, 20,000 Ottoman Turks were killed, and the heads of the defeated generals were thrown like cabbages into wagons, which were then sent to the neighbouring allies as an inducement to them to join in the battle. In the following year, with reinforcements from Serbia, Wallachia, Poland and Germany, John Hunyadi brought about more victories against the Turks, who panicked and fled, with Hunyadi in pursuit. For twenty years the fearless and handsome Hunyadi was the terror of the Turks.

Murad bided his time. Most of the advantages were on his side. He had a greater army than any that could be mustered in Europe, and it was not commanded by rival princelings who contended among themselves. His opportunity came when King Ladislaus led a combined army of Poles and Hungarians across Bulgaria to Varna on the Black Sea. Murad hurriedly organized an army in Asia Minor and arrived in front of Varna unexpectedly, before the Christians knew he was on his way. In the ensuing battle the forces of King Ladislaus were routed, and the King's head was struck off by an aged Janissary; John Hunyadi fled, to fight again, but the tide was now working in favour of the Turks.

P

There was no mercy in Murad. His aim was to destroy eastern Europe; and when he had disengaged his forces from the Hungarians and the Poles, he set about reducing Greece. He conquered the Peloponnese, sacked Corinth and took all the captured young Greeks into slavery. The Peloponnese never recovered from that fatal invasion. Then he resumed his attacks on the combined forces of Hungary, Serbia and Bosnia, led by Hunyadi, and defeated them at the battle of Kossovo; and so Serbia fell finally into the power of the Ottoman Turks. At his death—he died of apoplexy as the result of drinking too much wine during a feast—the Turkish empire reached towards the Adriatic and northwards along the coast of the Black Sea. The heavy, dark wedge of Ottoman power was aimed towards the heart of Europe.

Murad had prepared the ground for the capture of Constantinople; his son Muhammad II, 'the Conqueror', merely consolidated the conquest. Muhammad was twenty-one when he came to the throne, a stern, severely intellectual monarch who spoke five languages fluently and behaved at all times with cruelty and studied arrogance. His first task when he came to the throne was to capture Constantinople, and he set about it with characteristic caution. He knew he had only to shake the tree, and the ripe plum would fall into his hands. A few heavy cannon, another fortress overlooking the city, bribery, infiltration into the enemy ranks—this would be enough. He began the siege on April 6, 1453, with 160,000 men, among them 12,000 Janissaries, and a fleet of 150 ships. The defenders were outmanned and outgunned. When the Emperor Constantine XI ordered a census of the males of military age in the city, he learned that there were only 4,973 men with military experience. Muhammad II had brought up a sledgehammer to squash a fly.

The Byzantines defended themselves brilliantly and with honour under the dual command of the Emperor and Giovanni Giustiniani, who broke through the Turkish blockade with 700 well-equipped Genoese soldiers. Constantinople itself was so well-fortified that in spite of the vast disparity in numbers it is possible that it would have beaten back the Turkish attacks if there had not been treachery in high places. John Hunyadi, so long the terror of the Turks, sent a messenger to the Sultan with detailed instructions on how to breach the walls; a Serbian hermit had prophesied that there would be no peace in Christendom until the Greek Church and Santa Sophia were destroyed. There were turncoats among the *condottieri* paid to defend the city. The orders of the Emperor were often disobeyed. A handful of men fought off the massive Turkish attacks. On March 20, when the siege had already lasted a month and a half, four Genoese warships again broke the blockade, pushing their way through the entire Turkish fleet and entering the Golden Horn in full view of the Sultan, who raged like a maniac, summoned his admiral, had him spread-eagled on the ground and beat him unmercifully with a cane; and he would have had the man impaled if his generals had permitted him.

While the Sultan roared like a madman, the Emperor Constantine went about his affairs quietly and impassively. He showed emotion only when he was begged to flee. He answered: 'How can I leave the churches of our Lord, and His servants the clergy, and the throne, and my people?' He superintended every detail of the defence, refused all offers of surrender, and very nearly succeeded in making the Sultan raise the siege. The Turks stormed the walls under the protection of huge wooden towers, from which they poured a murderous fire into the city, but Giustiniani succeeded in blowing up the towers with gunpowder. The Turks thereupon resorted to the use of mines, but a German engineer, Johann Grant, who constructed counter-mines, blew up the Turkish miners with gunpowder or smoked them out with stinkpots or drowned them by letting water in. There were battles in the mines fought with knife, axe and spear. A good deal of the battle for Constantinople was fought underground.

Constantine had no illusions about being able to hold out. Every day the Sultan threw fresh troops against the walls until the defenders were weary beyond endurance. Without sleep, with little equipment and with their food running out, they could hope only for a miracle or the intervention of a vast European army; and neither was forthcoming. The Sultan ordered 2,000 scaling ladders to be brought up. He held a review of his troops, inspected his fleet, ordered bonfires to be lit, and behaved as though he was about to launch a vast expedition against a powerful enemy, at a time when the defenders of Constantinople numbered no more than three or four thousand men. On the night of May 28 the Emperor attended divine service for the last time in Santa Sophia, promising the defenders honour and glory in Heaven and a martyr's death on earth; then he went out to inspect the defences. Towards midnight he observed from the ramparts that all the Turkish fires had suddenly been put out. It was a dark night, with patches of mist in the fields, and a few heavy drops of rain were falling. He knew the Turks were about to attack. The first massive assault came at half past one in the morning, but was beaten back. But all night the attacks went on, wave upon wave without pause, and when dawn came the walls were already breached in places. At nine o'clock in the morning the Emperor galloped towards the Roman Gate, through which the Turks were pouring. He shouted: 'God forbid I should live an Emperor without an empire! If my city falls, I shall fall with it!' A moment later he was cut down.

For the rest of the morning the Turks ravished and murdered and desecrated to their hearts' content. Santa Sophia was crowded with refugees who hoped for asylum within its walls, but the Turkish soldiers burst through the gates and plundered at will. At noon the Sultan entered by the Adrianople Gate and ordered an end to the massacres, and he killed with his own hand a drunken soldier who was attempting to break up the marble floor of Santa Sophia; for was not the church his own possession? He ordered the capture and arrest of the Byzantine officials who had taken part in the defence of the city, and offered a reward to the discoverer of the body of the dead Emperor. When at last the body of Constantine XI was found under a heap of dead near the Roman Gate—

he was recognized only by the double-headed eagles embroidered on his buskins—Muhammad II ordered the head to be cut off and placed between the feet of the bronze horse which bore the bronze figure of Justinian. Such deeds of traditional piety continued throughout the early days of the occupation, for the Sultan was perfectly aware how such actions would be interpreted. He dipped his hand in blood and left his imprint on one of the marble columns of Santa Sophia, as a sign of his perpetual ownership of the great cathedral, and afterwards he ordered an *imam* to ascend the pulpit and proclaim that the church was dedicated to Allah, and he was heard to mutter the famous elegy of the Persian poet Firdausi:

> The spider's curtain hangs before the gate of Caesar's palace;
> And the owl stands sentinel on the towers of Afrasiab.

But though the blood streamed, and Constantinople was reduced to desolation, the young Sultan was in a mood to enjoy his conquest to the last drop. There were small imperial massacres to be added at the appropriate moment to the general massacres. The Grand Duke Notaras, the highest surviving functionary of the Byzantine court, was executed together with his whole family; and the Sultan celebrated the occasion by ordering the heads to be placed like oranges on his dining table. The Venetian and Spanish consuls, who had actively assisted in the defence of the city, were also executed.

The Sultan, however, could show mercy when it suited his purpose. Tolerant in religious matters, he had no intention of proscribing Christianity. Having heard that the scholarly George Scholarios was universally respected by the Christians, he gave orders that a search should be made for the man, who was found in a small village near Adrianople, the slave of a Muhammadan merchant. Scholarios was ordered to appear in Constantinople. In the Church of the Holy Apostles he was at once invested with the rank of Patriarch in the presence of the Sultan and the assembled bishops, the ceremony following the lines of the ceremony performed by the Byzantine emperors. After the election Scholarios accepted an invitation to dine with the Sultan, who entertained him royally and presented him with a pastoral staff studded with diamonds, and conferred on him in token of his temporal dignity the rank of *Beyler Bey*, which meant that the Patriarch was henceforth preceded by a standard-bearer holding a pole from which three horsetails hung. The Sultan is supposed to have declared during the investiture: 'The Holy Trinity, which has bestowed upon me the Empire, promoteth thee to be the Patriarch of the new Rome.' It was a strange alteration in the Muhammadan character of the monarch that he should display so great an interest in Christianity, but there were stranger things to come.

Muhammad II claimed descent from the Comneni through John, the elder brother of Andronicus I, and he possessed the peculiar Byzantine flair for ruling with imperious irresponsibility. The conqueror was soon conquered. All that was perverse, otiose and evil in the Byzantine court was imitated by this weak Emperor, who laid down the traditions that were to continue during the surviving years of the Ottoman empire. Yet with him the empire reached its greatest heights, and thereafter there was only the long road downhill.

The attempt to conquer Europe went on unabated. In 1456 the Sultan marched against Belgrade with 150,000 men and 300 cannon, together with some 200 galleys which were rowed up the Danube and moored outside the city walls. Muhammad boasted that he would reduce the city in fifteen days, but the Franciscan friar John Capistrano and the ageing John Hunyadi were determined to put an end to the invasion. The Turkish fleet was destroyed. The friar led a thousand Crusaders against the Turkish batteries, captured them and turned the guns against the Turks, who fled. Muhammad fought with his troops, but could not stem the advance of the people of Belgrade. In the rout the Sultan was carried off by his attendants, and 24,000 of his army were left dead on the battlefield. A few weeks later John Hunyadi died, leaving to his son Mathias Corvinus the task of keeping Islam at bay.

Muhammad had been wounded in the battle for Belgrade, and was more than ever determined to inflict punishment on the Europeans. He sent armies into Greece, to put down the constant rebellions in the Peloponnese, and against Trebizond on the Black Sea coast, where the vast library of King David Comnenus was put to the flames. In a single year he engaged in wars against the Venetians, the Princes of Caramania and the Bosnians. Treacherous always, he promised to 'spare the head' of the Venetian governor of Euboea, when he attacked the island; and when the governor surrendered, his head was untouched but he was sawed in half. With such pastimes did the conqueror of Constantinople amuse himself.

Merciless as he was, Muhammad II concentrated in his own person the entire intellectual range of his own period. As a poet who modelled his verses on the heroic odes of Perisa, he was not to be despised; and he was aware of the intellectual renaissance in Italy, and anxious to borrow from it. He built magnificently, employing the Greek architect Christodulos to design the great mosque, the Mehmediye, which bears his name, and he was responsible for the erection of nine other mosques. In the intervals of bouts of drunkenness and vanity he was capable of exercising intelligence and self-restraint. He was very short, and called 'the Parrot' from his beaked nose, but he was every inch an Ottoman Sultan. It was characteristic of him that he should die while preparing a campaign against Egypt, in the midst of his soldiers, at the moment when he was about to give orders for the expedition to start.

He was succeeded by a saint, a lunatic warrior, an epicurean and a drunkard.

The saint was Bayazid II, who followed in the gentle footsteps of Muhammad I. With little taste for war, he concluded peace with Mathias Corvinus, withdrew his troops from Otranto in Italy, and maintained excellent relations with the Pope. A fat man who moved lethargically, he spent his years superintending the building of mosques. Towards the end of his reign civil war flared up, with the Janissaries demanding his abdication in favour of his son Selim. The Sultan gracefully assented to the request and asked his son for permission to go into exile. Selim accompanied his father on foot to the gates of the capital, made a long speech praising his father's virtues and gave orders that he should be poisoned during the journey. Then he mounted the throne, and for eight years ruled as though he were another Timurlane.

Selim I, 'the Grim', rarely belied the title that was given to him. His instinct was to murder everyone who crossed his path. He strangled his brothers and nephews, carefully considered the advantages and disadvantages of strangling his own son, and beheaded his grand viziers so frequently that for centuries anyone wishing the death of another would say: 'May you be as the Grand Vizier of Sultan Selim.' He had thick black eyebrows, protruding eyes, a shaven chin and a look of placid imbecility; and he liked to wear a jewelled crown on his thick turban.

Selim had hardly mounted the throne when he decided to make war on Persia, then ruled by the young Shah Ismail, the founder of the Safavid dynasty, who claimed descent from Muhammad and the Sassanian King Yazdagird. Shah Ismail had the instincts of gentleness, and was in every way the opposite of Selim. 'He is fair, handsome and pleasing,' said the Venetian Angiolello, who visited him. 'He has a light and well-built appearance, his hair is reddish and he wears moustachios. He is as brave as a gamecock, and stronger than any of his lords.'

Selim and Ismail were well-matched, but the Turk had the advantage in fire power. Selim advanced on Baghdad, massacred the inhabitants, and went on to Tabriz, leading his army across the desert. Shah Ismail confronted the largest army of the time, composed of cavalry and artillery divisions and the famous Janissaries, on the plain of Chaldiran outside Tabriz on August 14, 1514. The Persians attacked on both flanks of the Turkish forces, hoping to win by surprise; but were beaten back. The Shah killed the commander of the Janissaries, but was himself seriously wounded and forced to leave the battlefield. A route followed, with the Turks employing muskets for the first time in history. The Turkish victory was complete: so complete indeed that the Persians, recognizing their own weakness in the face of the foreign adversary, set their house in order and for the first time in centuries united behind their ruler.

With Persia defeated, Sultan Selim advanced into Syria, defeated the Mamluks at Aleppo and carried the war into Egypt as a punishment for Mamluk incursions into Palestine and some small Mamluk assistance to the Persians. In Aleppo the captured Caliph was brought into the presence of the Sultan. Selim asked where he had come from. 'From Baghdad,' answered the Caliph. 'Then I shall see that you return to Baghdad,' Selim said; and to the long list of his own titles—'Sultan, Son of the Sultan, King of the Two Lands and the Two Seas, Destroyer of the Two Armies, Sultan of the Two Iraqs, Servant of the Two Holy Sanctuaries, Victorious King, Sultan Selim Shah'—he added that of

Caliph.[1] For the first time since the end of the Abbasid empire the spiritual power of the Caliphate reposed in the hands of a terrestrial Emperor. Like Muawiya, Selim assumed the Caliphate by right of conquest.

Together with the Caliphate went the outward symbols of spiritual power—Muhammad's signet ring, his cloak, his staff, and a host of minor objects which may or may not have come down from the ancient treasuries of the Umayyad Caliphs who scrupulously preserved the relics of the Prophet.[2] By this time the famous two-pronged sword Dhu'l-Faqar seems to have vanished, and the most important relics were the signet ring and the mantle. The jeweller Tavernier reported that the signet ring was kept in 'a little Ebony box, about half a foot square, enchas'd with Crystal with a Bordure of Ivory', and every three months the ring was solemnly raised from the box and held in the smoke of incense rising from a blinding goblet of gold sparkling with diamonds and blue sapphires. When Tavernier asked about the nature of the ring, he was told that no one had ever been able to see it clearly, so thick was the smoke pouring around it; and though some letters were thought to be engraved on the ring, no one had ever been able to see them.

Tavernier tells an equally strange story about the mantle, which was supposed to be the one given to Ka'b ibn Zuhayr for reciting his famous poem, the *Qasida-i-Banat Su'ad*. The mantle was kept in a chest in the same room as the signet ring: the chest was opened once a year by the Sultan. The mantle was of white mohair with large sleeves. Removed from the chest, the mantle was 'placed in a golden cauldron, soaked there, then wrung out hard, and the water from the cauldron fills a great number of Venice-crystal bottles'. On the next day the bottles were solemnly presented to the high officials of the empire, and the very highest were permitted to touch the mantle with their forheads, while the Sultan himself, according to some reports, donned the mantle on the fifteenth day of Ramadan. Accounts of the mantle are confused. It has been described variously as green, black, cream-coloured and striped. There seems to be little doubt that a mantle belonging to Muhammad survived into Abbasid times, but it is unlikely that it survived the nine hundred years which separated Muhammad from Selim the Grim.

One other relic of doubtful authenticity is also said to have survived— the sacred standard. The original standard was the curtain over Ayesha's door, and appears to have been purchased by Muawiya from Ayesha and kept in a special enclosure within the Great Umayyad Mosque in Damascus. This, too, fell into the hands of the conquering Abbasids. When the

---

[1] There is some doubt about the date upon which Sultan Selim assumed the Caliphate. Sir Thomas Arnold in *The Caliphate* (Oxford: Clarendon Press, 1924), pp. 139–58, argues that the Sultan refused the honour, while bringing forward convincing evidence that he accepted it. Selim's official historian called him 'Kalifah of God upon Earth'.

[2] The relics still preserved in the Topkapee at Istanbul are said to include a tooth of the Prophet, his clogs, his shirt, his prayer rug, his banner and the hilt of his sword, the turbans and swords of Hasan and Husayn, some water in which the Prophet had washed, the prayer rug of Abu Bakr, the Quran which Uthman was reading at the time of his assassination, the sword of King David, Noah's cooking pot and Abraham's caldron.

Turks acquired the sacred standard, they regarded it with a special veneration, exhibiting it only at moments of national crisis. It accompanied the
armies to Hungary in a special tent with a guard of a thousand Janissaries;
it was unfurled again when the Sultan Mahmud II ordered the massacre
of 100,000 Janissaries on June 10, 1826; and was seen briefly for the last
time in 1915 when the Ottoman empire declared a *jihad* against the
West.

Selim's brief reign—he ruled for only eight years—was characterized by
the crudest violence: a long series of causeless murders and massacres. At
the same time there arose a mysterious flowering of the arts; and while the
looms of Shah Ismail were producing the most magnificent carpets that
the world has ever seen, the Sultan's architect Sinan built the most magnificent mosques. Of Sinan almost nothing is known. We do not know
whether he was Greek, or Albanian, or Armenian. This mysterious per-
sonage appears to have been at one time a Janissary, and later a military
engineer. Between his fiftieth and ninetieth year he built more than a
hundred mosques in different parts of Turkey, and the greatest of them is
the Mosque of Sultan Selim in Damascus with its quiet enclosures and
brooding peace among the cypresses. The ferocious Sultan died on his way
to Adrianople, close to the place where his father had been poisoned by
his orders, and was buried in the Mosque of Sultan Selim near the Edirne
Gate in Constantinople. He lies among translucent tiles of springlike
greens and yellows. A Turkish inscription over his tomb compares his
reign to 'the afternoon sun which, though it casteth long shadows, is but
fleeting'.

The reign of his son, Sulayman I, the Magnificent, lasted forty-six years.
He was the last of the great Sultans, the tenth of the House of Osman,
called to rule at the dawn of the tenth century of Islam; and throughout
his long reign he showed by every gesture that he enjoyed himself. He had
Muawiya's gift of finding prolonged pleasure in the art of government.
He enjoyed the pleasures of the table, of the harem, of the hunt. He liked
to compose poetry, and he liked to pore over books of mathematics. He
especially liked war.

It was the custom of the Sultans to embark on great military campaigns
shortly after reaching the throne; Sulayman was no exception. He decided
to conquer the island of Rhodes, which under Pierre d'Aubusson had successfully resisted the fleet and army of Muhammad II in 1480. He aimed
to destroy the power of the Knights of St. John, who were openly aiding
the Christian corsairs raiding the coasts of Asia Minor. The siege of
Rhodes, which began in June, 1522, continued for more than six months.
Under the Knights the huge fortifications of Rhodes had been designed
for just such an emergency, with the result that the siege became an endurance contest, and the Turks were never able to penetrate far beyond
the huge outer walls and glacis. The Grand Master of the Knights,
Philip de Villiers de l'Isle-Adam, proved himself a cautious and willing
defender, but when winter came, with food and ammunition running out,
he was forced to accept an honourable surrender; and the Knights marched

out of Rhodes to the amazement of the Sultan, in good order, with their flags flying.

In 1526, Sulayman resumed the war against the Hungarians, who had hitherto prevented the Turks from driving into the heartland of Europe. He set out at the head of a quarter of a million men, and at the battle of Mohacs on August 29, 1526, the Hungarians were finally routed. The twenty-year-old King of the Hungarians was killed, a hundred thousand Christians were taken into captivity and the treasures of the palace of Mathias Corvinus went to decorate the Seraglio in Constantinople. The floodgates were opened; and there was nothing now to prevent the Turks from invading Europe in strength.

Three years later Sulayman marched on Vienna, fixing his headquarters near the village of Simmering. From the top of St. Stephen's Tower the white tents of the Turkish army resembled a white sea stretching for miles, and the Danube was crowded with Turkish ships. The defenders could command no more than 20,000 infantrymen and perhaps 2,000 cavalry; they had altogether 76 small cannon against the 300 powerful guns of the enemy. The Viennese, however, were determined to resist. Men and women constructed earthworks behind the walls. After three weeks of fruitless assaults Sulayman decided to raise the siege, and returned to Constantinople. He possessed Hungary; Austria could wait.

The typical pattern of Turkish conquest had long since been worked out: an invasion of the West would be followed by an invasion of the East, and then of the South. Sulayman hurled his armies at the Persians, hoping by a show of force to bring about the surrender of Shah Tamasp. The Persians simply withdrew. It was November, and the rain falling in the passes was freezing into ice. Sulayman led his armies through the defiles of the Zagros Mountains. Swollen streams swept part of his artillery away. Gun carriages had to be burned to prevent them from falling into the hands of the enemy. Cannon were spiked and buried underground. In despair of overtaking the Persians, Sulayman ordered his army to turn west, and when the hills of Luristan fell away and the plains of Mesopotamia lay before him, he sighed with relief. He had been defeated, not by the Persian army, but by the misery of a Persian winter. The rains were his perpetual enemy: it was the rain falling on the plains of Vienna which had forced him to raise the siege.

Once again in 1532 Sulayman marched into Austria, sending his fleet up the Danube as far as Pressburg, and devastating the province of Styria. But the western powers were beginning to strike back. Admiral Andrea Doria led his fleet against Greece, capturing Patras and Nauplia. Malta held out against a Turkish fleet. The Hungarians, subdued so often, rose in revolt, and once again Sulayman had to lead an expedition against them; and Buda, sacked twice before in living memory, was sacked a third time. And while Barbarossa plundered the Neapolitan coast, Italian pirates raided the Greek islands and advanced close to Constantinople.

It was a time of strange alliances: Sulayman at war with all Europe, the Europeans at war among themselves. Charles V, Emperor of Austria,

Spain, the Netherlands and great parts of Italy, fought against François I; and so it happened on one occasion that a combined Ottoman and French fleet attacked the Italian coastal town of Nice. The celebrated Turkish corsair Torghut (Dragout) found shelter in the harbour of Marseilles after his raiding expeditions, until the French grew weary of his habit of sending raiding parties into France. Over all Europe there hung the thread of a Turkish victory which would bring the power of the Ottoman Sultan beyond the Brenner Pass, Yet strangely there was no concerted plan to rid Europe of the Turks: the main burden rested upon the indomitable Hungarians. The days had long since passed when John Hunyadi could lead a crusade composed of armies from five nations against a common enemy.

Sulayman continued to hammer against Europe to his last breath. He died at the age of seventy-four, in the town of Szigetvar in Hungary, having only the previous day mined its fortress and seen the defenders blown sky-high. He had reigned for forty-six years, and the Turks could not bring themselves to believe he was dead. For more than seven weeks, while his armies made their way slowly back to Constantinople, it was rumoured that the man who was swathed in linen garments and carried in a litter was suffering from fever and the fatigues of the journey. In fact he had died before the army set out on its homeward march, and all the orders given in his name were forgeries. There is a sense in which all the Sultans who followed him were dead men sitting on thrones: drunkards and murderers, perverts, fear-ridden maniacs, who spent the greater part of their lives in the dubious security of their seraglios.

No one like Sulayman came after him. Henceforward the tortuous history of the Ottoman empire moves faltering to its decline. Islam, imposed upon eastern Europe, failed to dig deep roots. Turkish armies conquered the plains of Hungary and their fleets dominated the eastern Mediterranean, but from the beginning the Turks on European soil gave the impression of being interlopers. They were freebooters, and those massive armies composed of hundreds of thousands of men were no more than raiding parties. They brought no new ideas; even their faith was weak. They were not a united people moved by the passionate desire to conquer for the sake of saving souls. They were not even a nation, but a host of peoples, an imperial family and a system. The Sultan's subjects belonged to many diverse races, and his invincible Janissaries were all originally Christians, and most of his sea captains were renegades from the Christian faith. His military advisers, technicians, financiers, merchants were Christians or Jews. Muhammad Sokolli, his Grand Vizier, the father of another Grand Vizier, was descended from a Christian slave. The Sultan, descended from the Comneni, cared for neither Christianity nor Islam: all he desired was the enjoyment of the chase in its most elementary form— the military expedition.

The Turks brought no new wealth to Europe; and as they failed to impose their religion on the conquered races, so they failed to impose a workable social system on the conquered territories. In the end the Europeans, who had failed to unite against a merciless enemy, observed with horror the decay of the Turkish empire; and then for the first time they united in support of the tyrant who had become 'the sick man of Europe'.

While the sun was setting over the Ottoman empire, it rose again over Persia. The fearful Shah Tamasp was succeeded by Shah Abbas the Great, whose handsome clear-cut features have been preserved in a hundred miniatures. Sir Anthony Sherley, who equipped his army with cannon, described him as 'excellently well-shaped, of a most well-proportioned stature, strong and active; his colour somewhat inclined to a man-like blacknesse, is also more blacke by the Sunnes burning; his furniture of mind infinitely royal, wise, valiant, liberall, temperate, merciful, and an exceeding lover of Justice, embracing royally other virtues, as farre from pride and vanitie as from all unprincely signs or acts'.

In 1598 Shah Abbas moved his capital to Isfahan, and at once set about making it worthy of a man who claimed descent both from Muhammad and from the Sassanian emperors. During his reign Isfahan was at the height of its prestige and importance, and it was larger than Paris. It was said to have 600,000 people, 162 mosques, 48 religious colleges, 1,802 caravanserais and 273 public baths. It was so magnificent that the Persians coined the saying 'Isfahan is half the world'—*Isfahan nisf-i-jahan.* Though much of the glory has departed, enough remains to take the breath away.

No one ever constructed a more splendid parade-ground than the *maidan-i-shah* in Isfahan, with its royal palace on one side facing the delicate blue mosque of Shaykh Lutfallah, while between them there stands the most beautiful of all Persian mosques, known simply as the *Masjid-i-shah,* the mosque of the Shah. Here at last the Persian imagination came to terms with Islam. Dignity and grace, gentleness and tranquillity are all reflected in this building which glows in blue magnificence: to the Persians alone was given the gift of depicting magnificence in a state of peace. There is no reaching out, no strain, no sense of pride. All that the Umayyad Caliphs accomplished in building the Dome of the Rock is repeated here, but with the addition of a new and unexpected element of towering glory. To come upon the Mosque of the Shah on a cloudless summer day is to know Paradise. Here, unequivocally, in a building which gives the impression of having risen effortlessly at the bidding of a magician, a Persian Emperor stated the utmost limits of the Persian dream.

There is no end to the treasures around the parade-ground. The royal palace, known as Ali Qapu, combines delicacy and strength in exquisite proportions. Above the heavy brick archway, slender wooden columns arise, forming a kind of roof patio, but the columns are so wonderfully shaped and so intimately related to the surrounding minarets of the mosques that everything about the palace appears inevitable and at the same time it seems about to float away into thin air. On the patio the Emperor held audiences, and from the balcony looked down on the games and processions and markets below. Here, sitting cross-legged on a low-lying couch of gold, he received ambassadors and administered his empire.

Here the dancing girls danced at night with oil-lamps in their hands, the harpists played, and the wine flowed freely. Thomas Herbert speaks of 'the Ganimed boys in vests of cloth of gold, rich spangled Turbans, and embroidered sandals, curled hair dangling over their shoulders, with rolling eyes and vermilion cheeks, carrying in their hands flagons of best Metal; and they went up and down, proffering the delight of Bacchus to such as were disposed to take it.'

The Ali Qapu is full of small rooms and alcoves, bright with tiles and painted hunting scenes and lovers wandering in haunted gardens. There is hardly a square inch on the walls which does not suggest a vision of Paradise. But it is important to observe that the palace was not given over to the utmost license: it is no more than a toy for the occasional amusement of a deeply religious Emperor. The Mosque of Shaykh Lutfallah, facing the palace, gleams with the colour of blue grapes when the sun's shadow falls on them, but the calm austerity of the interior speaks of an assured faith. In the dome chamber, the words of the Quran decorate the walls in characters which gleam and tremble like spring leaves when the wind touches them; but the decoration is deliberately designed to lead the onlooker into contemplation of the peace of God. Shah Abbas built superbly, but his faith was far removed from the puritanical faith of Muhammad. Persia transformed Islam, and in the process of transformation was herself transformed. The word 'Paradise' is a Persian word, and the entire history of Persian art during the time of Shah Abbas is a commentary on the possibilities of Paradise on earth.

So it is with the Persian carpets fashioned on the imperial looms during the reigns of the early Safavid emperors. These carpets are nearly always deliberate portraits of Paradise, with running streams and singing birds and shady trees, always stylized and deliberately removed from the world of the senses to a mysterious other world, where there is no passing of time and no sun ever sets. The same resourcefulness which permitted the Persian artist to fill the interior of a mosque with a delicate arabesque of abstract designs permitted him to design carpets filled to overflowing with symbols representing the glory of God—leaves, flowers, animals, trees, all caught in the timeless wind of God. The great Ardebil carpet, which hangs in the Victoria and Albert Museum in London, paints a garden in springtime with huge sprays of blossom lit by the great yellow sun in the centre, which symbolizes the majesty of God. The sun is flanked by two delicately fashioned mosque lamps, and in a corner of the carpet are the words:

> I have no refuge in the world other than Thy threshold,
> My head has no protection other than Thy porchway.

A deep religious feeling swept over Persia during the time of the Safavid emperors: it was as though once again the Persians were enjoying the religious dominance they exercised during the early years of the Abbasid dynasty. Outside the Mosque of the Shah in Isfahan there used to hang, on ceremonial occasions, the bloodstained shirt reputed to have been worn by the martyred Husayn, grandson of the Prophet, and within the mosque was the Quran supposed to have been written by the hand of the sainted Imam Rida, whose shrine was at Mashad. Shah Abbas did not think it beneath his dignity to walk the entire distance of 800 miles from Isfahan to Mashad to light candles for Imam Rida in the sacred courts, and he deposited the great bow, which had helped him win his victories, in the same mosque. He swept out the tomb of his ancestor Ali at Najaf. He surrounded himself with philosophers and poets, and talked learnedly about religion. When he died at a ripe age, the Persians remembered him with the saying: 'When the great Prince died, all prosperity died with him.'

With the death of Shah Abbas in 1629, Persia went into a decline. The arts still flourished, but the life had gone out of them. A new dynasty arose, led by a tribal chieftain, Nadir Quli, born in Mashad, and for a few brief years it seemed that the days of imperial glory had returned. The armies of Nadir Shah raged across Afghanistan and India, and once again Delhi was sacked and robbed of its treasures, including the famous Peacock Throne, removed to decorate a Persian palace. But by this time the great days of the Mughal emperors were over, and the British were already preparing to inherit the crown of Hindustan.

For century after century Islamic warriors had swept into India. Shortly after the death of Muhammad, traders from Arabia reached the Makran coast and sent raiding parties against the army of the Hindu ruler of Sind. These trials of strength were inconclusive. More massive raids came later, usually from the north and through the Khyber Pass. The first invasion of magnitude came when Mahmud of Ghazni, after conquering Rayy, Hamadan and Isfahan, swept through northern India and captured Muttra, the birthplace of Krishna, and bore away the great gates of Somnath to decorate his capital in the Afghanistan highlands. He hated the Hindus, and massacred them at his leisure. A slight man with slanting eyes and a scant beard, which betrayed his Turcoman ancestry, he ruled for a brief space over an empire which included Persia, Afghanistan and northern India, but died too soon to consolidate his gains. A second and more successful invasion occurred in 1193, when Muhammad Ghuri defeated Prithviraj, King of Delhi, at the battle of Tarain. Prithviraj was captured and put to death; his queen, accompanied by her handmaidens, mounted the funeral pyre. It was a battle to be remembered ever afterwards in the annals of the Hindus, who had never been defeated so decisively. For mile upon empty mile the battlefield was strewn with discarded banners, spears and shields, plumed casques and jewelled swords, exquisitely moulded and damascened gauntlets, and gaily coloured scarves. The flower of Hindustan had fallen, and the Moslems were henceforward in the ascendant.

Muhammad Ghuri consolidated his Indian empire by destroying everything in his path. Benares fell in 1194, Bihar fell four years later and the last flicker of Indian Buddhism expired when he destroyed the great

university of Nalanda. The Rajputs did not lack valour, but they were un-
trained in fighting massive wars of manoeuvre. By 1203 all of upper India
lay in the hands of the conqueror, who died like so many conquerors before
him—by an assassin's knife.

With the Rajputs in perpetual revolt, the Sultans of Delhi ruled com-
plaisantly over their Indian empire, rarely attempting to extend their hold
over the subcontinent. For some ninety years there was peace interrupted
only by minor skirmishes. Then in 1294, with some 8,000 dedicated followers, Ala-ad-Din Khilji, the nephew of the reigning Sultan, set off on a
private expedition to the Deccan far to the south, conquered Deogiri,
which he renamed Daulatabad, 'the place of victory', and returned to
Delhi in triumph, his first act being to cut off the head of his seventy-year-
old uncle, the Sultan. Ala-ad-Din, who never learned to read or write,
became the undisputed master of northern India and the first to send
armies into the Tamil and Telinga countries in the south. He conquered
Guzerat, routed a Mongolian invasion by trampling the Mongols under
the feet of his elephants, and died in 1316 when about to embark on the
conquest of the whole of India.

Ala-ad-Din was the first of the great Muhammadan emperors of India
to show a peculiar intolerance of Islam. He married a Hindu princess,
and seems to have been secretly converted for a while to Hinduism, which
he abandoned only to preside over a new religion, of which he was the
founder. He regarded himself as a prophet, and drew up a long list of
religious ordinances, Like Hakim, the ruler of Fatimid Egypt, he demonstrated a ruthless intolerance by proscribing the majority of human joys.
His new religion was harshly puritanical. He forbade all visiting, feasting
and meetings of any kinds, and punished anyone found drinking wine or
beer, or playing with dice. He especially frowned on dancing.

India was no better served by his successor, Muhammad ibn Tughlak,
who was civilized, learned, well-versed in Arabic and Persian literature,
but suffered from the defect of believing that he was a god. On a whim
he debased currency, with the result that the entire merchant class was
ruined. On another whim he sent off an expedition to conquer China—
the entire expeditionary army was annihilated in the Himalayan passes. A
more dangerous whim occurred when he discovered that the people of
Delhi were writing scurrilous verses on the walls against his government: he decided to abandon Delhi and to remove all its inhabitants to
Daulatabad 600 miles to the south. Accordingly, the population was given
three days to move out of the city, and when the capital was completely
evacuated, and no fire or smoke could be seen, he was heard to say: 'Now
my soul is content, and my heart at peace.' Ibn Battuta, the great traveller, who stayed at his court for five years, described him as a pure sadist.
'He delights most,' he wrote, 'in giving presents and shedding blood.
At his door there is always some pauper on his way to wealth and some
corpse which has just been executed.'

The rule of the intolerable Muhammad ibn Tughlak was followed by
the reign of his cousin Firoz Shah (1351–88), who for nearly forty years

administered the conquered territories of India with justice and gentleness. He dug a series of great canals and surrounded Delhi with gardens; and when he died at the age of seventy-nine, they said of him, as the Persians said of Shah Abbas, that 'prosperity ended with him'. After the gentle Firoz Khan came Timurlane: instead of the saint came the savage, and all of northern India trembled at his coming.

There were moments when Timurlane saw himself as a Muhammadan prince. He declared that he had two objects in mind when he attacked Hindustan. 'My aim,' he wrote, 'is to make war upon the infidels, who are the enemies of the Muhammadan religion, and by waging religious war I hope to achieve some merit in the life to come.' His second aim was simpler: ' I believe plunder in war to be lawful as mothers' milk to Muhammadans fighting for their faith.' In the autumn of 1398 he crossed the Indus with 90,000 cavalry, plundered unmercifully, massacred to his heart's content, and might have gone on to destroy the whole subcontinent if it had not occurred to him that there were richer fields in the west. He called off the invasion of India and swept into Syria.

He was the fourth of the great Muhammadan invaders. The fifth was an obscure Jaghatai Turcoman named Zahir-ud-din Muhammad, who employed the *nom de guerre* of Babur, meaning 'tiger'. He was a distant descendant of Timurlane, and the chieftain of a small tribe near Ferghana. At the age of twenty-two, with 250 of his followers, most of them armed only with clubs, he attacked and captured the important city of Kabul. Then he determined upon the conquest of India. He wrote in his famous diary: 'On Friday, the first of Safar 932 [November 7, 1525], when the sun was in Sagittarius, I set out on my march into Hindustan.'

The conquest of India took him only a little more than a year, for on February 11, 1527, the Rajputs under Rana Sanga were decisively defeated. For the remaining three years of his life Babur consolidated his empire and demonstrated a remarkable taste for painting, continued to write a diary which from the beginning had shown an exquisite sensitivity to nature, and cultivated scholars. From him descended the great Mughal dynasty of India, which did not end completely until the Mutiny of 1857.

Babur represented an attitude of mind which was perpetuated throughout his dynasty: a harsh warrior, he was also a just administrator and dedicated aesthete. He possessed a Persian sense of colour and a Persian delight in life, and his Muhammadanism was only skin-deep. Akbar, his grandson, who called himself on his gold coins 'the great Sultan, the exalted Caliph', was even less inclined to insist upon the overwhelming supremacy of Islam, and studied Brahmanism from learned Hindu priests, gave close and admiring attention to the arguments of Roman Catholics and acquired a special sympathy for the sun worship of the Parsis, those modern descendants of Zoroastrians. He was a heavy man, broadshouldered, with very bright eyes, and was bandy-legged from much riding; he looked like a general. But his overriding passion was the pursuit of the truth, wherever it could be found. Married to a Rajput princess, he refused to regard Hinduism as the belief of a deluded people and he detested the

rancour of the orthodox believers as they disputed among themselves. It
was a time of intense intellectual striving. A contemporary of Elizabeth
of England, Shah Abbas of Persia and Henry IV of France, Akbar saw
himself as the destined leader of a religious movement which would somehow embrace a synthesis of all existing religions.

As always, India was conquering her conquerors. Throughout the history of Muhammadan rule in India, there had been a peculiar slackening
of the Islamic fibre, for the Indian imagination, bred among mountains
and tropical valleys, did not take easily to the stern commands of an Arab
teacher, who spoke of the One God, when they demanded an infinitude of
gods; who spoke of God as the masculine principle, when they saw their
greatest gods always as Mothers; and who insisted that death led to a final
paradise, when they believed in endless cycles of rebirth. The Aryan invaders had failed to impose their religion on India. Buddha, too, arising
from the foothills of the Himalayas, had failed to impose his beliefs on
more than a scattering of Hindus. So the Muhammadans remained in
India as strangers to the Hindus, and the great poet Kabir, who wrote:
'God is one whether we worship him as Allah or as Rama,' remained to
the end of his days essentially a Hindu. The story is told that when he died,
his Muhammadan and Hindu disciples were discussing where to bury
him when they lifted his shroud and discovered only rose petals.

On one level only could there be a marriage between Muhammadanism
and Hinduism. The mysterious rose petals which descend from Heaven
on all mystics, whether Christian, Muhammadan or Hindu, suggested
that there was a realm where the quarrels of the faithful could be laid at
rest. A strange passion united the mystics of all lands. They spoke, and
still speak, a common language. Here, for example, is Kabir speaking in
a language which would have been immediately understood by al-Hallaj,
Jalalu'l-Din Rumi or Ibn Arabi:

> I hear the melody of His flute, and I cannot contain myself.
> The flower blooms, though it is not spring; and already the bee has received the
>   invitation.
> The sky roars and the lightning flashes; the waves rise in my heart.
> The rain falls, and my heart longs for my Lord.
> Where the rhythm of the world rises and falls thither my heart has reached:
> There the hidden banners are fluttering in the air! [1]

In this spirit of lucid mysticism Akbar pronounced his own faith to be
'the search for the divine in all things', and to the end of his days surrounded himself with Sufis and Hindu *sunyasis*.

So it was with his successors Jehangir and Shah Jehan, who retained the
outward forms of Muhammadanism while filling them with the sense of
the sanctity indwelling in all things; and these emperors, who were also
mystics, saw no reason to despise the world, but instead created monuments to the divine spirit wherever they travelled. Their palaces were
temples. No one who has travelled through Delhi, Agra and Lahore can

---

[1] *One Hundred Poems by Kabir*, tr. Rabindranath Tagore (London: Macmillan and Co.,
1926), p. 71.

fail to perceive that these superbly decorated palaces of the Mughal emperors are attempts to portray Paradise, as the Taj Mahal is an attempt to
portray a moment of illumination.

The saintly Shah Jehan had hoped his eldest son, Muhammad Dara
Shikoh, would inherit the throne. Prince Dara grew up to be one of those
rare creatures gifted with all the talents. A superb soldier and excellent
administrator, he devoted his days to the earthly empire and his nights to
the heavenly kingdoms. He practised austerities, read widely, translated
the *Bhagavad Gita* and fifty chapters of the *Upanishads* into Persian, and was
constantly visiting the shrines of the Muhammadan saints in the company
of his father. He was twenty-four when an angel cried out to him in a
dream that he would receive from God a reward which had not been
bestowed on any previous prince, and a year later he was introduced by a
famous mystic, Miyan Mir, into an order of Sufis which claimed to have
direct correspondence with God through visions. The Prince had reached
the height of his ambitions. But he did not retire from the world. He
continued in his offices, and in the intervals of wars and journeys through
the empire he read the whole of the Old and New Testaments and became
the devoted commentator of Ibn Arabi's *Fusus al-Hikam*. Continually
smiling, splendidly handsome, he seemed to pass through life like someone
graced with angelic qualities. He said once that he had succeeded in
spending his nights 'in the calm of two breaths, one breath to ascend to
God and one to return'. At the age of forty-two he wrote his most famous
work, *The Mingling of the Two Oceans*, in which he attempted a synthesis
of Muhammadanism and Hinduism. Here is Dara speaking on the nature
of the heavenly light:

> This light is of three kinds, for when it is seen with the attribute of
> Majesty, then it is sun-coloured, ruby-coloured, or fire-coloured; and
> when it is seen with the attribute of Beauty, it is moon-coloured, pearl-
> coloured, or water-coloured; but when it is seen as the Light of the
> Essence, then it is devoid of all these attributes, and is visible only to
> the eyes of the holy men in whose favour God (the Most High and Holy)
> has declared: 'Allah guides to His light whom He pleases.'
>
> This is a light which appears to a man in sleep or with his eyes closed,
> who neither sees with his eyes nor hears with his ears nor speaks with
> his tongue nor smells with his nose nor feels with his sense of touch, but
> performs all these functions in sleep with only *one* faculty and does not
> require the aid of his limbs, nor the use of his faculties, nor the light of
> a lamp; and the senses of sight, hearing, taste, smell and touch become
> one sense—such is the Light of the Essence, which is the Light of God.[1]

In his determination to bring about a synthesis between Muhammadanism and Hinduism, Dara was forced to rely heavily on the *hadiths*. When
he came to discuss *karma* and the endless cycles of existence, he remembered
a *hadith* traditionally connected with Muhammad's Night of Ascent. It

[1] Prince Muhammad Dara Shikoh, *The Mingling of the Two Oceans*, tr. M. Mahfuz-ul-
Haq (Calcutta: The Asiatic Society of Bengal, 1929), pp. 48–9.

Q

appears that the Prophet saw an endless line of camels passing before him, and each camel had two saddlebags, and in each of them there was an entire world. Muhammad asked Gabriel the meaning of the procession of camels. 'O Prophet of God,' replied Gabriel, 'since my creation I have been witnessing this line of camels with their saddlebags, and I also am unaware of their significance.' On this note, believing that he had discovered a correspondence between *karma* and Muhammadan belief, he brings his work to an end, signing it, as he signed all his works: 'the unafflicted and unsorrowing *fakir*, Muhammad Dara Shikoh.'

He was not left unsorrowing for long. In the war of succession which followed his younger brother Aurangzeb's rise to power, Dara was arrested, brought before the court of the *ulamas* and sentenced to death for heresy. With his death and the passing of Shah Jehan the Mughal dynasty went into its decline.

For two more centuries Mughal emperors sat on their thrones in Delhi. When the Mutiny of 1857 broke out, the mutineers swore allegiance at Patna to Bahadur Shah II, the last of the Mughal emperors. The rebels unfurled the green flag of the Prophet and proclaimed a *jihad*, led by Mughal princes, against the British. But the old order had already perished, and with the victory of the British over the rebels there died the last hope of establishing Moslem sovereignty over India.

While it lasted, the Mughal empire had shown a way by which Muhammadanism might have been placed at the service of all the people of India. Especially under the early rulers Islam had demonstrated a brilliant tolerance. Beauty and majesty had been the concern of those emperors who consorted with saints and lived more splendidly than the Caliphs of Baghdad. In the end they failed, because the strength of Islam lay in its uncompromising logic. As always, strength came from the savage puritans, not from the mystics who saw the fullness of the earth as a foretaste of Paradise.

THE AWAKENING

ONCE more Islam was slowly dying. All through the Middle East the springs were drying up. The muezzins still cried from the minarets that Muhammad was the Prophet of the One God, but Islam itself seemed to have lost its savour. There was no art, no religious feeling, only the interminable and empty recitation of the Quran. The great thinkers of the past were no longer read, their books gathering dust in the libraries. The greatest Islamic power was Turkey, which maintained a remote suzerainty over Egypt, Arabia and Iraq, but the Ottoman Turks had failed to fertilize the Arab genius. The sun had gone down, and there seemed no hope of a dawn.

The shock which revived Islam came from an unexpected quarter—from the armies of Napoleon. On July 1, 1798, the people of Alexandria saw 300 ships standing out to sea, preparing to invade Egypt and cut the British lifeline to India. Napoleon had no illusions about the nature of his task. The whole of the East lay before him, and he was already drawing up plans for marching on Mecca, Delhi and even Peking.

Napoleon arrived in Egypt with a staff of expert geographers, surveyors, architects and archaeologists. To the Egyptians he proclaimed that he was a Muhammadan. 'There is only one God,' he declared, 'and He is the God of victory.' He destroyed the Mamluks within sight of the Pyramids, to discover that Nelson had destroyed his fleet at the Battle of the Nile: only two men of war and two frigates escaped to France. He had an army, no ships, an invincible faith in his destiny; and when the Ottoman Sultan Selim III sent a small army to wrest Egypt from the conqueror, Napoleon had no difficulty driving the Turks into the sea. Among the Turkish troops sent to Egypt was an obscure pockmarked Albanian, the son of a tobacco merchant, a small, illiterate, brutal officer with a bulging forehead and quick bright eyes. He called himself Muhammad Ali, and he was to become the greatest ruler of Egypt since the time of Baybars. Napoleon had awakened the sleeping lion; Muhammad Ali set it on the path of conquest.

He was born in Kavalla, a small town in Macedonia, about the year 1769. His father died when he was young, and he entered the service of the local governor as a ruthless tax collector. On one occasion, when some villagers revolted against paying taxes, he invited them into a mosque, closed the doors, suggested that they should pay their taxes on the spot, and when they refused he beckoned to some cut-throats he had previously hidden in the mosque and had the villagers trussed up and carried off to the governor's palace. It was a trick he was to use many times in the future: the gentle invitation followed by swift threats, and these in turn followed by the appearance of his private army of cut-throats. The governor was pleased, married him to a rich niece, gave him a post in the local militia and advised Constantinople about his abilities. When Napoleon invaded Egypt, Muhammad Ali was given command of a troop of irregulars, and served so conspicuously that he was raised to the rank of colonel. He fought again with the Turkish irregulars who served under Abercrombie, and when the French were finally evacuated from Egypt, he was an obscure officer on the staff of the Turkish governor of Egypt, Khosrev Pasha, who was recalled in 1803. Muhammad Ali saw his opportunity. With a regiment of highly disciplined Albanian guards under his command, he held the balance of power in the struggle between the Turks and the Mamluks, siding now with one, now with the other, and playing his hand so well that by 1805 he was the undisputed master of the country. In the following year the Sultan bowed to the inevitable and raised him to the rank of viceroy.

There remained the Mamluk officers, who had ruled Egypt as their private preserve for centuries and were seething with discontent against the obscure Albanian, who modelled himself on Napoleon and introduced French officers into his army. Muhammad Ali was in no hurry to destroy the Mamluks. He waited until 1811 before putting into effect a long-prepared plan for annihilating them. On March 11 he invited the Mamluk officers to a reception at the citadel in honour of the approaching campaign against the Wahhabis, a puritanical sect in Arabia which had proclaimed its independence of the Sublime Porte. The officers came in their most brilliant uniforms. There were speeches; immense supplies of food were served; and Muhammad Ali behaved like a discreet, generous and convivial host. But when the reception came to an end and the officers were riding down the avenue cut in the solid rock which leads away from the citadel, Albanian guards mounted on the walls opened fire with cannon and musket shot. It was a massacre. None escaped; and the bodies of nearly five hundred officers with their dead horses were left for some days beneath the high walls, and the people of Cairo were allowed to witness the fate of the Mamluks, who had ruled Egypt for nearly seven centuries. The heads of the principal officers were carefully embalmed and sent to the Sultan in Constantinople.

Muhammad Ali had shown himself capable of treachery, but this was the least of his vices. He was avaricious, sensual, mean and incompetent to rule except by the sword. He introduced a permanent reign of terror into Egypt, while showing to the West only the affable side of his character; and foreigners flocked to Egypt, as later they were to flock to the Soviet Union, to see a primitive country being modernized by decree. He imported education, architecture and military sciences from the West, built canals, established schools and public works, created a civil service, fostered native industries and behaved in his dealings with his French advisers like an enlightened monarch. Cairo and Alexandria became modern cities. The price was high. The Egyptians were reduced to servitude. In 1815 the Viceroy was claiming as his exclusive property the yield of all the cotton, hemp and flax produced in Egypt, and two years later he was claiming all the indigo. Because cotton got better prices on the London market, he ordered that large areas which had been producing flax and sugar cane should be transformed into cotton fields; and since most of the land was soon producing cotton, the economy of Egypt was dependent on the whims of the London stock exchange. The whole of Egypt became his private farm. When he dug canals, he simply ordered the fellahin to go to work, and forgot to pay them or give them medical services, with the result that thousands died of malaria. He fought the Wahhabis and freed the holy places of Arabia from the heretic sect, and then, more daring, when Turkey was weakened by the Greek War of Independence, he sent his son Ibrahim Pasha to overrun Syria and Asia Minor; and he was threatening Constantinople itself when Russia intervened to prevent him from dealing with the Sultan as the Seljuks had dealt with the Caliph of Baghdad. Russia sent warships to the Bosphorus. Ibrahim Pasha retired to Syria, where a peace treaty was concluded with the new Sultan, Mahmud II, later to be known as 'the Reformer'. By this treaty Muhammad Ali was confirmed in the government of Egypt and Crete, and in addition was given Jerusalem, Tripoli, Aleppo, Damascus and Adana, while still remaining in theory a vassal of the Sultan. He had conquered for Egypt very nearly the same territory which had been conquered by Saladin.

For forty years Muhammad Ali consolidated his power as the unchallenged ruler of Egypt. He could not read Arabic until late in life, but he knew how to impress his own energy on the country he had adopted and ruled. Significantly, the first institute of learning opened during his reign was a school of mathematics. He built a fleet, employed an army of foreign engineers and attempted to make Egypt a manufacturing nation, taking the fellahin off the land and putting them to work in factories: Egypt became a vast military camp and a great factory, so that the energies of the people were strained to breaking point. Before he died in 1848, Muhammad Ali had single-handedly changed the face of Egypt. It was no longer an ancient and somnolent land at the mercy of the army, but had become the most progressive of the Muhammadan states. Though ruined by his exactions, the people were wide awake and in touch with the blessings of civilization.

What Muhammad Ali had done was something of incalculable importance to the Muhammadan world. It was not only that he shook the tottering throne of the Sultan, conquered the greater part of the Sudan, forced the Wahhabis to surrender the cities they had captured, transformed Egypt into a vast cottonfield dotted with factories; but he had shown that there were springs of energy which could be tapped. He was not an Arab, but more than anyone else he was responsible for the Arab renaissance. He had no thought of Arab nationalism, and never regarded himself as the ruler of an Arab empire. His greatest service was to throw the gates wide open to Western learning, with the result that the Egyptians until the time of Kemal Atatürk were the acknowledged leaders in the fight to transform the ancient Middle Eastern states into modern nations.

There were to be other leaders of the revolution later, whose rise was less quixotic. Muhammad Ali was squat, ugly, brutal and insanely avaricious: he brought about the Egyptian renaissance by the accident of his greed. He accepted help from the West, never fought against a European power and employed all his resources to transform Egypt into a crude imitation of a western state.

Abd-al-Qadir, who was born in 1807, was in every respect the contrary of Muhammad Ali. This rapier-thin, nervous and handsome warrior with the luminous dark eyes and the gift of bringing the best out of everyone he met was closer to Saladin than anyone of his time. He was more scholar than warrior. Son of a famous ascetic teacher, he could read and write at the age of five and graduated in theology at the age of twelve. In his youth he made two pilgrimages to Mecca, and on his return from the second pilgrimage, it was assumed that he would enter the religious life. It was said of him that he walked with a grave nobility and most of his thoughts were concerned with God.

In April, 1827, Pierre Deval, the French consul in Algiers, quarrelled with the Dey of Algiers over some financial matters, and the fiery-tempered Dey burst into the consulate, charged Deval with being 'a wicked, faithless, idol-worshipping idiot', and struck him three times with a peacock-feathered fly whisk. The consequences of that blow were disastrous. The story of the meeting between the Dey and the consul spread rapidly through Algeria, and Abd al-Qadir was one of those who foresaw the trouble ahead. In 1829, when he was twenty-two, two important tribes, the Hashim and the Amir, weary of their perpetual feuds, placed themselves under his command. The following year, after brooding over the insult for three years, the French sent a fleet across the Mediterranean to conquer Algiers. Altogether there were 600 ships in the fleet, twice as many as Napoleon needed for the conquest of Egypt.

On June 14, 1830, the French landed off Algiers, and within a month the Dey had capitulated, and the French began to push southwards towards the Lesser Atlas. The Algerian tribal chieftains were unconcerned with the capture of Algiers, whose Dey they had detested, but Abd al-Qadir knew enough about western history to know that the French were in earnest in their attempts to conquer the whole of Algeria. Frantically he rode from village to village, calling for an end to feuding and a united stand against the invaders. The chieftains laughed at him, and one of them, Abu ibn-Duri, told him to 'go back to your books, teacher'.

The French wasted their strength on skirmishes with the tribesmen, never coming into open battle, but proving themselves to be ruthless and hard-bitten. The army fighting against the Arabs consisted of the first units of the newly created Foreign Legion, specially created by King Louis Philippe for the conquest of Algeria. They were the dregs of Europe, who thought nothing of wiping out a tribal settlement to the last child.

In a single lightning swoop the Legion destroyed the settlement of the Ouffiya tribe until none were left alive. In a later *razzia* the Legionaries found nearly 500 Algerian men, women and children hiding in a cave: they simply lit fires at the mouth of the cave until everyone inside was asphyxiated. The western tribesmen proclaimed Abd al-Qadir their commander in chief and give him the title Amir al-Muminin, 'the Commander of the Faithful': it was a title first borne by Abu Bakr and by most of the Caliphs after him. Soon all Algeria was united behind Abd al-Qadir.

Plans were made for an all-out counter-attack, but at the last minute Abd al-Qadir refused to allow his chief forces to march against the Legionaries. The French remained close to their ships and their lines of supply. The harbour cities of Oran and Bougie fell, but Abd al-Qadir waited. The tribesmen accused him of being timid, but instead he was being cautious, waiting for the opportunity to strike to the best advantage. Such an opportunity came in October, 1837, when 12,000 Legionaries marched inland and stormed the fortified city of Constantine in a surprise attack. In revenge Abd Al-Qadir proclaimed the *jihad*, and all Algeria was up in arms. The Legionaries were merciless; Abd al-Qadir could be equally merciless. The white-robed desert horsemen struck against the enemy wherever they could be found. At Guelma he surprised a camp of enemy engineers. Without a sound the tribesmen slit the throats of the sentries, and were in the camp before a single bugle could sound the alarm. Within twenty minutes 150 Frenchmen died. When the relief column arrived next morning, it found a camp of corpses.

No one could have recognized Abd al-Qadir as the religious scholar he was. He was in the saddle for forty-eight hours at a stretch, living on a handful of boiled rice and a bowl of milk a day. He seemed to have a charmed life. Once he led 2,000 horsemen to attack a French regiment marching on Setif. Five times the French hurled back the assault, killing two horses under Abd al-Qadir, riddling his flowing cloak with their bullets. The sixth charge broke the Legion square, and the desert was suddenly full of fleeing soldiers. Only fifteen thirst-maddened Legionnaires reached the safety of an encampment two days later.

Step by step the French were being forced back to the coast, where they barely managed to control a thin strip of territory, and were twice in danger of losing Algiers. Two-thirds of Algeria was now in the hands of the tribesmen. In 1838, when both sides were exhausted, Abd al-Qadir signed a peace treaty at Tafnah. For a few months there was peace. Abd al-Qadir rode among his tribesmen, warning them that there was worse to come, and with stern severity he banned wine and prostitution, and even discouraged smoking. His task was to prepare the tribesmen against the coming invasion. He drank only milk and lived on boiled rice.

The French were arming rapidly. They had assembled 58,000 men on the coastal strip and equipped them with the finest artillery of the time. Against them Abd al-Qadir could bring only four ancient cannon, one of them a Dutch field-piece cast in 1620.

Among his warriors was a renegade young Frenchman named Léon Roches, who had been converted to Muhammadanism, married an Algerian girl and adopted native ways. When news came that the French had broken the treaty and were marching into Algerian territory, Roches denounced the new faith and shouted at Abd al-Qadir: 'Kill me if you like, but while there is life in me I shall do my utmost to return to my own people and fight against you.' For a moment there was silence, then Abd al-Qadir wrote out the orders to allow Roches to return to the French.

There was, however, little chivalry shown by either side in the remaining years of the campaign. Abd al-Qadir swept down on the advancing French in the Mitijah plain, and hurled them back almost to the gates of Algiers. Louis Philippe dispatched 108,000 men—a third of his army— to put an end to the revolt. These troops were placed under the command of General Thomas-Robert Bugeaud, a veteran of Napoleon's Spanish campaign, where the word guerrilla was invented: he decided to throw guerrillas against guerrillas. He was the most ruthless of army commanders, and his motto was: 'I know no civilians.' Soon his troops were shooting on sight virtually every male Arab or Kabyle they encountered.

In the spring of 1842 Bugeaud occupied Tlemsen, and early the next year he took the fortress of Sebhu, which had been Abd al-Qadir's supply base. While Abd al-Qadir roved the country with his followers, 50,000 strong, Bugeaud's flying cavalry columns were stabbing deep into Arab territory, killing every head of cattle, burning every patch of corn in their path. This meant slow starvation for the tribesmen. They retaliated by butchering French prisoners, and the French butchered their Arab prisoners. Once the Duc d'Aumale surprised Abd al-Qadir's camp, capturing 4,000 Arabs and seizing the treasury, but Abd al-Qadir himself escaped with a handful of followers into Morocco. Bugeaud followed him across the frontier, fought the army of the Sultan of Morocco, who refused to surrender the leader of the Algerian forces. Secretly, Abd al-Qadir slipped back into Algeria, to collect his scattered tribesmen. Through the winter of 1845–46, eighteen flying columns were pursuing him, and he evaded them all. He had put his trust in the Moroccans, who were themselves hard-pressed. Towards the end of 1847, Abd al-Qadir was in Morocco when he learned that orders had been given by the Sultan to expel him by force. He crossed the frontier under Moroccan fire, to find himself encircled by French troops. After a campaign which had lasted more than fifteen years, on December 23, he surrendered to General Lamoricière, after receiving the promise that he would be allowed to go to Acre or Alexandria. Instead he was taken to the fortress of Toulon, and later held captive at Amboise. In the following year Algeria became formally a part of France.

Abd al-Qadir's conduct during the war had aroused the sympathy of the British, but though the French Foreign Office received repeated requests to free him, he was kept in captivity for five years. Napoleon III ordered his release after he signed a promise never to set foot on Algerian soil again. He settled quietly in Brusa, the old Turkish capital, and later in Istanbul. The scholar who had fought the French returned to scholarship, and set about editing the works of the great mystical philosopher Ibn Arabi, who was buried in Damascus. Accordingly he went to live in Damascus to further his studies. There one day in the spring of 1860 some Muhammadan and Christian children were playing in the street, when one of the Muhammadan boys drew a cross on the sand and ordered a Christian to trample on it. The children began fighting. Soon Muhammadans and Christians everywhere in the city were at one another's throats. The Druses came down from the mountains, to cut the throats of the Christians. The massacre went on until 30,000 Christians had lost their lives, and many thousands more would have been killed if Abd al-Qadir had not invited as many as possible into his house and, with the help of his two sons and 300 Algerians who had followed him into exile, with a naked sword in his hand drove off the mob.

When the massacres were over and Damascus was at peace again, Abd al-Qadir was the most unpopular Muhammadan in the city; but he hardly cared. He was content to work on his edition of Ibn Arabi and wrote a treatise on Sufism. He received some strange rewards for his courage, including the cross of the Legion of Honour encircled with emeralds and diamonds and surmounted with a gold crown, but liked best of all a brace of revolvers, a present from the United States. As he grew older, he put on weight: a tall man with a soaring forehead and large black eyes and a wisp of beard, who cared very little for the things of the world. He died in May, 1883, and was buried in the Mosque of Sultan Selim at Damascus, close by the tomb of Ibn Arabi, whom he had loved almost to distraction.

The story of the renaissance of Islam in the nineteenth century is the story of failure—of many kinds of failure. The quick and brilliant Muhammadan mind seemed incapable of dealing with problems of the modern age. Their roots were in the ancient past, and they were baffled by the vast forces in the service of the western powers.

Two years before the death of Abd Al-Qadir, Colonel Ahmad Arabi became the acknowledged leader of the Egyptian Nationalist party. He was forty years old, a thickset, broad-shouldered man with a bulging forehead and thick curling moustaches. He was the son of peasants and in his youth he had studied at al-Azhar University, but he had little formal education and spoke only Arabic. Like Abd al-Qadir he was to throw his Muhammadan army against the invader, but where Abd al-Qadir fought a continual battle over a period of fifteen years, Ahmad Arabi, with even deeper roots among the people and with every prospect of victory, fought a battle which lasted only twenty minutes and retired defeated.

By the eighties of the last century Egypt had lost the important position acquired during the reign of Muhammad Ali. A succession of incompetent khedives had reduced the country to a state of near anarchy.

Egypt was being ruled by a governing body composed almost entirely of Turks. Ahmad Arabi's rise to power, first as leader of the Egyptian Nationalist party, then as minister of war and finally as dictator, reflected the growing determination of the Egyptians to be ruled by one of themselves; and when in the early part of 1882 Great Britain sent a fleet to manoeuvre outside Alexandria with a show of force, Ahmad Arabi took the part of the fellahin who rebelled against the foreigners.

The massacre in Damascus arose as a result of a quarrel between children in the street. The massacre at Alexandria began at one o'clock on November 11, 1882, as the result of an argument between an Arab donkey-boy and a Maltese, who was a British subject. It was a bitter argument; blows were exchanged; hundreds of spectators gathered; passions were aroused; and soon knives were flashing. By five o'clock in the afternoon the massacre had spread through the city and 200 Europeans had lost their lives. Towards evening arrangements were made to evacuate the European population. Then for many months there was an uneasy truce. On July 5, after making careful inquiries about the situation, Sir Charles Dilke announced in the House of Commons that the British Government could not tolerate the possibility of renewed massacres in Egypt, and the fleet had accordingly been given orders 'under certain circumstances to act in a certain way'. In fact an ultimatum had been delivered to Colonel Arabi demanding that he abandon his forts, or the guns of the Royal Navy would open fire.

Colonel Arabi refused to capitulate. On July 11 the British naval guns bombarded Alexandria. It was expected that the Egyptians would be brought to their knees, but nothing of the sort happened. Colonel Arabi rallied his followers. He proclaimed that any landing by foreign troops would be resisted. The Khedive, who allied himself with the British, was ignored. The Marines went ashore at Alexandria, and almost simultaneously there came ominous reports that tribesmen, under orders from Colonel Arabi, were beginning to make their way towards the Suez Canal, presumably to cut the canal if any attempt was made by British troops to disembark at Ismailia. He argued that the British would attempt to safeguard the canal, and to use it as the base for the conquest of Egypt.

In his interpretation of British intentions Colonel Arabi showed considerable acumen. He had not, however, counted on Mr. Gladstone's determination to suppress what he called 'a military revolt' in Egypt. The British, angered by the massacre, were up in arms. Towards the end of July the reserves were called to the colours, and a cheering House of Commons was voting £2,300,000 for the expedition. At once 15,000 men were ordered to Malta and Cyprus in preparation for the campaign, and Sir Garnet Wolseley—W. S. Gilbert's 'model of a modern major-general' —was placed in command. At the War Office he had studied the war maps and concluded that everything depended upon reaching Ismailia before the Egyptians cut the canal.

Though perfectly aware of British intentions, Colonel Arabi made two miscalculations. It had not occurred to him that the British would reach Egypt so quickly, and he had not counted on the influence of Ferdinand de Lesseps, the builder of the Suez Canal, who sent him a stream of telegrams insisting that the British would never dare to use the canal for war-like purposes. 'Make no attempt to cut *my* canal,' De Lesseps wrote. 'I am here. Not a single English soldier shall disembark.' Fatally for Colonel Arabi, no attempt was made to cut the canal until it was too late.

On the night of August 19, thirty-two British warships and troopers steamed silently and with doused lights past Port Said and down the canal. At every strategic point small landing parties went ashore to secure the barges and dredgers. Realizing what had happened, Colonel Arabi sent telegrams to his forces on the banks of the canal, ordering them to scuttle all available ships to prevent the passage of the warships; but the telegrams arrived fifteen hours too late. The British were in Ismailia; they had secured the canal banks; it remained to be seen whether they could be dislodged.

Long before he left England, Sir Garnet Wolseley had made two prophecies. Pointing to a map of Egypt, he placed his finger on Tell al-Kabir, and said: 'The decisive battle of my campaign will be fought here.' He added that he intended to arrive in Cairo on September 16. Only the second prophecy proved inaccurate: he did in fact arrive in Cairo a day earlier.

The Egyptian troops were no match for the British. Once they were in possession of the canal, Colonel Arabi's only hope lay in cutting the sweetwater canal which brought fresh water to the banks of the Suez Canal. Without fresh water the British would die of thirst. He dammed the sweetwater canal at a place called Tell al-Mashuta: the dam was made of piled sand and reeds bound with telegraph wire. He went on to make another dam, but Sir Garnet Wolseley sent raiding parties, and both dams were destroyed. Then for a brief while both sides rested, seeking out each other's strength, waiting for the inevitable moment when they would be locked together, quietly disposing their forces.

In the early days of September spies and prisoners brought information that Colonel Arabi had arrayed some seventy guns, 18,000 infantry and three regiments of cavalry at Tel al-Kabir. The colonel himself was in command.

Sir Garnet Wolseley advanced to Kassassin, five miles from Tel al-Kabir, where Colonel Arabi's forces were entrenched. Between them there was only flat, open ground. On the night of September 12 the British, leaving their camp-fires burning as a blind, made their way in the dark, guided only by the stars, until they were within a mile of the enemy. The army moved without lights and in absolute silence, except for a drunken soldier who started shouting and had to be silenced with chloroform. The attack was timed for the first light. Just before dawn the British hurled themselves against the enemy lines. The battle was all over in twenty minutes, with 1,500 Egyptians killed against 75 British, and the rest in full flight. That morning Colonel Arabi was a refugee in a train taking him to Cairo.

The battle was over, and the occupation of Egypt had begun. The cavalry division arrived at the gates of Cairo the next afternoon, worn out after riding eighty miles through the heat of the day. There was no opposition. They entered Cairo to find that the soldiers in the garrison had thrown down their arms and melted into the surrounding countryside, resuming their long blue shirts and skullcaps. Colonel Arabi made no effort to escape. He handed over his sword and awaited the vengeance of the conquerors.

The conquerors were in a quandary. They could, of course, execute him out of hand; they could send him into exile without troubling themselves with anything more than a drumhead court-martial; or they could put him on trial on charges of rebellion and complicity in the massacres. The Khedive refused to allow Colonel Arabi to go free, and the British military refused to permit him to be executed. It was therefore arranged to put him on trial, and the best lawyers from London were sent out to Cairo to defend him, their fees being paid for out of a defence fund, to which half the members of the House of Commons subscribed. The farcical trial ended with the prisoner being sentenced to death, pardoned and exiled to Ceylon, where he remained until 1901, when he was allowed to return to Egypt. When the death sentence was passed, an Englishwoman, the wife of a junior counsel, thrust a bouquet of white roses in his arms. The enemy of England had become the favourite of the English.

Colonel Arabi's rebellion was the last for half a century. The British assumed virtual control of Egyptian finances, foreign affairs and the comman of the Egyptian army; and the real ruler was the consul-general who stood beside the throne of the Khedive and whispered orders which were then announced with khedival authority. By the historic decree of December 1882—'The Egyptian army is disbanded'—Britain assumed the responsibility for creating a new army, whose task was to defend the Suez Canal. So matters remained until another colonel, Gamal Abdal Nasser, came to power.

Colonel Arabi's failure was one of nerve, indecision, a strange lack of caution. He possessed in himself all the resources which make for a popular leader. He had roots among the fellahin; his officers were fanatically loyal to him; he was clever and unscrupulous. If he had not failed at Tel al-Kabir, the history of the Middle East would have been vastly different.

Colonel Arabi never saw himself as the destined leader of an Arab renaissance and a new striving towards the Arab empires of the past. He regarded himself as a nationalist leader, and was without any exalted opinion of himself or any *mystique*. He lacked the strength which comes to a man who makes overwhelming demands on history and who sees himself as the destined triumphator, clothed with religious and moral sanctions.

Such a man was Muhammad ibn-Abdallah, born in the middle of the last century, the son of a poor carpenter, who proclaimed that he was a descendant of Muhammad and had come on earth to bring righteousness to Sudan and to the world. The governor of the Sudan, appointed by the Khedive, heard that a man who called himself the Mahdi was living quietly on the island of Abba on the White Nile, about 200 miles south of Khartum; but his quietness was delusory. The whole country was being flooded with the agents of the self-styled Mahdi. The governor made inquiries. He learned that Muhammad ibn-Abdallah came from Dongola, the riverine province in the north, and that some rich merchants supported him. Nothing else of importance could be discovered about this obscure Sudanese who on June 29, 1881, suddenly proclaimed himself as the Mahdi at Abba.

Quite sensibly, knowing the explosive power of those obscure men who from time to time have claimed divine status, gathered armies and changed the course of history, the governor decided to nip the rebellion in the bud. Accordingly, he sent a small detachment of 200 men by steamer to the island. The attack failed. The Mahdi and his followers hid in the tall grass, waited until darkness fell, and then with only their long knives they threw themselves on the Egyptians, killing nearly all of them and capturing their rifles. The few survivors swam to the steamer. The victory was so complete that thousands flocked to the Mahdi's banner, believing him to be the divinely commissioned deliverer of Islam.

The first engagement possessed all the characteristics of a classic encounter between unarmed rebels and a well-armed army, and the Mahdi might have remained on the island of Abba indefinitely if it had not been that he possessed an instinctive knowledge of strategy. Near Abba there were nomad tribesmen who were resentful of any government interference and who could be counted on for assistance, and there were wealthy Sudanese merchants who could be trusted to provide financial help, but the Mahdi was already determined to capture the whole of the Sudan. He therefore decided to march to Kordofan and to establish his base at Qadir, a hill in the south of the province. Egyptian troops attempted to head off his march, but were routed when they failed to take the elementary precaution of protecting their night encampment with a barricade of thornbushes. The Mahdi's forces swept down on the camp and killed nearly all of them.

The Mahdi's strength came from his fanatical belief in his own destiny, and his speeches to his followers were couched in the language of Islamic mysticism. To them he was Muhammad *redivivus*, an august and godlike person who resembled the popular image of Muhammad, full-bearded and heavy set, attired simply in *jubbah* and linen trousers, with a cord round his waist, humble in manner except when anyone suggested doubts about his divine role; then, like Muhammad, the Mahdi was merciless, and ordered the culprit to be put to death. He shared with Muhammad a great passion for women and a determined opposition to those who refused to pay their taxes. He called his followers the *Ansar*, or 'helpers', and discovered in most of his battles correspondences with the battles fought in the early years of

Islam. He punished drinking, smoking and theft with a heavy hand, and forbade the reading of any books except the Quran and a selection, carefully chosen by himself, of the *hadith*.

On January 19, 1883, his forces surrounded al-Ubayd, the capital of Kordofan, and compelled it to capitulate. He now possessed a strong base some 200 miles southwest of Khartum, and when in November 10,000 Egyptian troops under Hicks Pasha attempted to invade Kordofan, the Mahdi was able to choose his battlefield and hurl his fanatical warriors at the Egyptians at a time convenient to himself. The Egyptians, who comprised the remnants of Arabi's army, panicked and fled, and all of the Sudan now lay at the mercy of the Mahdi.

When Gladstone heard of the defeat at Shaykan in Kordofan, he sent General Gordon on an ill-defined mission to save the Sudan for Britain. Egypt was a British colonial possession, and British public opinion demanded that the Sudan be safeguarded from the Mahdi, who had spoken of sending his warriors to Cairo and Alexandria. Gordon, fresh from his victories against the Taiping rebels in China and a sojourn in the Holy Land, where he had discovered the exact sites of Golgotha, Gibeon and the Garden of Eden, arrived in Khartum with the knowledge that he was facing almost certain defeat. He had never underestimated the Mahdi's fanatic power, for he was himself a fanatic and understood only too well the nature of the enemy. Reinforcements and relief supplies failed to reach him in time, and when the Mahdi's army approached Khartum, food was already low and ammunition was running out. Gordon was completely brave and completely dedicated. Urged to sandbag the palace windows, he refused. Instead he ordered a lantern with twenty-four candles to be placed in one of the windows, and declared: 'When God was portioning out fear, it came to my turn, and there was no fear left to give me. Go, tell all the people of Khartum that Gordon fears nothing!' But the Mahdi was just as fearless, and he could call upon all the Sudanese to help him.

On the night of February 3, 1885, the Mahdi and his dervishes approached Khartum. By sunrise they were pouring through the city. Gordon was waiting for them on the palace steps. Sword in hand, he fought magnificently, and died amid a heap of corpses at the foot of the palace steps. His head was cut off, wrapped in a cloth and presented to the pitiless Mahdi, who gave orders for the head to be hung from a tree for the hawks to peck at.

For the next few years the British were forced to abandon the Sudan to the Mahdi and his successors. Muhammad ibn-Abdallah survived his victory by only a few months, dying of typhus in the following June. Once, shortly after the victory at al-Ubayd, he had foreseen in a vision the conquest of the Muhammadan world. The vision was not fulfilled, but he had shown during the few years of his rule that all the vast reaches of the Muhammadan world were ripe for conquest by a dedicated warrior.

All the advantages were on the side of the Mahdi, whose power arose from popular belief in his status as one who receives special guidance from

God. Such men had arisen before, but they had rarely possessed his skill in strategy or his deep sense of a divinely appointed mission. He died at the height of his victorious career; his successor was less fortunate.

As his successor the Mahdi had appointed his leading follower Abdallahi ibn-Muhammad under the name of Abu Bakr. The dead Mahdi was to be followed by a Caliph, and the Mahdi appears to have seen a complete repetition of the Islamic odyssey with himself as the eponymous founder of the new dynasty. Abdallahi was plagued with civil war, famine, continual quarrels among his closest supporters. He raided Egypt and Abyssinia, but, possessing none of the personal authority of the Mahdi and little of his military genius, he failed to unite the country behind him. Yet the Sudan remained a theocratic Moslem state for thirteen more years. Then at last Kitchener, with a military railway and machine guns enabling him to extend his long supply lines from Wadi Halfa, confronted the Caliph's army at Kerreri, a few miles north of Omdurman, on September 2, 1898. When evening fell, the flower of the Mahdists had fallen to the machine guns and Abdallahi was in full flight. For twelve months he held out on the western bank of the White Nile with the remnants of his forces, not far from the place where the Mahdi had begun the movement which brought him to power. The final battle was fought at Umm Diwaykarat on November 24, 1899, south of the island of Abba. When the battle was over and a search was made among the dead, his body was found lying on the sheepskin which served as his prayer rug, with the bodies of his devoted followers all round him.

The Mahdist movement in the Sudan, carefully prepared and sometimes brilliantly led, had failed. It was their misfortune that they began their movement at a time when the European powers were in the full tide of their expansionist policies in Africa. If the British had not been in occupation of Egypt, nothing could have prevented them from extending their power over North Africa, and perhaps over Arabia. In time their programme bore fruit. Gamal Abdal Nasser studied the campaigns of the Mahdi and the Caliph Abdallahi, and the vision at al-Ubayd was vividly remembered by him when he in turn put forward his expansionist policies in Africa. There had been many Mahdis in the past, but none gave so much promise as the obscure son of a boat carpenter in the Sudan, and no Egyptian or Sudanese ever possessed a tithe of the power which Nasser employed in his attempt to institute an Arab empire.

The visionary element remained, when all others had failed. The strength of Islam throughout its history has lain with the visionaries who could summon out of the people the latent vigour and disciplined fervour which alone brings new nations into existence. Sometimes the visionaries occupied thrones; at other times they fell by the wayside. But all of them in their various ways have added to the white-hot core of Islam something of their own peculiar fire.

Sometimes, too, the very fervour of the visionary becomes self-defeating. A certain Ali Muhammad, the son of a grocer, born in Shiraz in 1821, announced that he was the long-promised Bab or 'Gate', by which

mankind would be united with the twelfth Imam. He appeared at Shiraz
on May 23, 1844, exactly one thousand years after the disappearance of
the twelfth Imam. He claimed to be even greater than Muhammad: he
called himself 'the Highest' and 'He who arises from the House of the
Prophet at the end of time'. He described himself as the mirror in which
men might see God. With astonishing astuteness he combined elements of
Zoroastrianism with elements of Islam. He issued edicts as though he
were King, Emperor and Archpriest. All Persia trembled before the
power of this man who seemed possessed of supernatural gifts. Women
flocked to him. His followers spread over every city in Persia, announcing
the new law of equality between men and women, the efficacy of the
mystical number 19 and the need to blow a kiss to the sun every Friday
morning. His power came precisely from his encouragement of ancient
Persian customs which Islam had sometimes attempted to destroy. So he
ordained that burial should be in stone coffins and the great New Year
celebration of Nauruz should be regarded as the principal festival of the
new cult; and both of these derived from Zoroastrian sources. The Shah
feared for his throne and issued orders to stamp out the movement. Jailed,
the Bab succeeded in escaping, and the governor of Isfahan offered him
hospitality. There were battles near Mashad. By August, 1849, the Shah
realized that the movement was so strong that he possessed no physical
means of putting an end to it. Accordingly, he induced the followers of
the Bab to surrender on the promise of an amnesty, then massacred them.
The Bab was captured. In the great square of Tabriz the man who
claimed to be God was blindfolded, bound hand and foot and set up
against a wall. When the smoke cleared after the first volley of the firing
party, there was no sign of him—the shots had cut his ropes and he had
fled. The miracle of his disappearance was explained a few days later
when he was found in a guardroom by one of his own followers, who shot
him out of hand.

For two years after the Bab's death the movement went underground and little was heard of his followers; then in 1852 three of
them made an attempt on the life of the Shah. There followed a
wave of persecution such as Persia has rarely seen. Captured Babis
were put to death by being buried upside down or immolated within
stone pillars where they suffocated to death. Martyrdom only increased
the number of the Bab's followers. Before his death he had assigned the
succession to a youth called Mirza Yahya, upon whom he conferred the
title 'the Dawn of Eternity'. Gradually the movement began to lose its
impetus within the borders of Persia; the surviving Babis escaped to
Baghdad, where they remained until 1864, when the Persian Government, alarmed by their proximity to the Persian frontier and the shrine
at Karbala, put pressure on the Sublime Porte to have them removed.
Accordingly they were transferred as political prisoners to Constantinople
and then to Adrianople, where the half-brother of Mirza Yahya, who had
slowly been displacing the appointed leader of the movement, declared
that he was the Mahdi and even asserted that the Bab was merely the

herald of his advent. The new leader called himself Baha Allah, or 'Glory of God'. The Babi community was now rent in twain; violent quarrels broke out; there were threats and counterthreats; finally the Turkish Government stepped in to separate the antagonists. Baha Allah and his followers were sent to Acre, while Mirza Yahya was exiled to Famagusta in Cyprus, dying in austere poverty in 1912 at the age of eighty-two, having survived his half-brother by twenty years.

The Babist movement, with its headquarters on Mount Carmel, survives to this day, still powerful and aggressive, though the last descendant of Baba Allah is dead and the church is governed by a board of directors. Originally an expression of a characteristically Persian desire to revive elements of Zoroastrianism within Islam, the movement later embraced a new form of religion without ritual, without priests and without laws. Universal peace was to be brought about by universal humility. Austerities were forbidden. People were to be taught to do good and to devote themselves to healing the sick. Finally all trace of Islam and Zoroastrianism vanished, and in their place there was only a general benevolence.

The Babists represented the centrifugal tendency which had been present in Islam from the beginning. But the contrary tendency towards a hardening of the Islamic fibre had also been present, and this was represented during the last century by the growth of the puritanical Wahhabi movement, a revival of the strict Hanbalite movement which first appeared under the Abbasid dynasty. A certain Muhammad ibn-Abdal Wahhab preached against the veneration of Muhammad and the saints, forbade the use of rosaries and silken clothes, ordered the destruction of the minarets of mosques and frowned on all singing and music. He refused to accept any laws except those prescribed by the Quran and the earliest *hadiths*. His followers allowed their dislike of the cult of saints to lead them on strange errands: they plundered the tomb of Muhammad at Madinah. After a period of warlike successes they were curbed by the Egyptians and retired to their desert homes in the Najd. But the tradition continued. In the heart of Arabia there remained throughout the last century a solid core of fervent puritans. Their leaders were the amirs of Najd, and from their ranks came Abdal Azis ibn-Abdal Rahman al-Faysal ibn al-Saud, known to the world by the name of King Ibn Saud.

When Ibn Saud was born in November, 1880, the family fortunes were in decline. His father Abdal Rahman bore the title of amir of Najd, but his three brothers were attempting to undermine his position in his capital at Riyadh. While the Najd was in a perpetual state of civil war, Muhammad ibn-Rashid, the amir of Hail,[1] waited for a favourable opportunity to attack Riyadh, which fell in 1884. Abdal Rahman escaped with his family to Kuwait, planning vengeance on the house of Rashid, and hating

---

[1] Charles Doughty gives a wonderful portrait of this murderous scoundrel in *Travels in Arabia Deserta*. He was lean and yellow-skinned, with enormous feminine eyes, and he had a habit of jerking his head when talking. His birdlike looks, said Doughty, were 'like the looks of one survived out of much disease of the world'.

R

the Turks, who claimed suzerainty over the whole of Arabia, until at last, disgusted by Kuwait, he rode off to join the Bedouin in the desert called al-Rab al-Khali, the Empty Quarter, which stretches across five hundred miles of sand and empty desolation to the Indian Ocean. There Ibn Saud grew up, his companions being the wild Murra tribesmen, unkempt and murderous men who hated all those who did not live in the wilderness. With them he learned how to read the tracks on the desert sand, how to cure camel mange, how to travel for a week on a handful of dates and a skin of curdled milk. Above all he learned how to plunder and kill.

Ibn Saud belonged to the desert; was of the desert. His loyalties were to the desert and his memories of the stories he had heard of the time when his uncles were kings. He grew up tall and straight, big-boned, his handsome hawklike head perched on heavy shoulders, his enormous sinewy hands, twice the size of normal hands, never at rest. He had an easy magnificence of manner, and the tribesmen looked to him as their leader. His closest companion was his cousin, Abdallah ibn Jiluwi, a dark, saturnine youth, who rarely spoke and was always falling into fits of melancholy, but who possessed all the instincts of a guerrilla chieftain.

With Abdallah ibn Jiluwi and sixty tribesmen Ibn Saud decided to attack Riyadh. He had no carefully conceived plan; he would simply arrive there in the night and somehow seize the governor and the garrison. It was to be like those raids he had led before, but with one difference: he would plunder the entire town and take permanent possession of it.

In January, 1901, he arrived at an oasis two hours' walking distance from the town. Here he left twenty of his men with the camels, saying that if he did not return in twenty-four hours they were to report to his father that he was either dead or a prisoner of the governor. Then with his chosen companions he made his way secretly through the gardens to the walls, arriving there about midnight. They uprooted palm trees, laid them against the walls, and climbed into the town. There were now only eight or nine men, for the rest of the raiding party was waiting outside the walls. With the help of those eight or nine men he hoped to take over all of desert Arabia.

From the beginning the plan worked well. They made their way through the dark streets to the home of the governor, a man named Ajlan, only to learn that he was sleeping at the fort under the protection of his troops. This did not disturb them. They spent the night at their prayers in the house next door to the governor's, facing the fort. Ibn Saud called for the men he had left outside the walls, climbed on to the roof of the governor's house and captured everyone in it, and when dawn broke he looked through the slit windows and saw the governor sauntering out of the fort with a bodyguard of eight men. Calling to his men to follow him, Ibn Saud raced across the square and hurled himself at the governor. When Ajlan struck at him with a sword, Ibn Saud parried with his rifle butt, and soon they were struggling on the ground. The bodyguard scattered. Ajlan jumped up. He had almost reached the safety of the fort when Ibn Saud caught him by the legs, bringing him down. Then they were all fighting confusedly. Ajlan had been wounded by a rifle shot in the arm, and Ibn Saud was suffering from a savage kick in the groin. At last the guards succeeded in dragging the governor into the fort and they were about to close the gate when Abdallah ibn Jiluwi with three men succeeded in keeping the gate open. The governor had been wounded by a knife which tore open his stomach. He succeeded in reaching the paradeground, and there Abdallah ibn Jiluwi shot him in the head. For the next two hours Ibn Saud's men grappled with the garrison. He had less than thirty men, and there were more than eighty soldiers on the parapets, but victory was already in his hands. A few weeks later Abdal Rahman rode to Riyadh from Kuwait and proclaimed his son Amir of Najd and Imam of the Wahhabis, giving him at the same time the gold-handled damascene sword which had belonged to his ancestor known as Saud the Great. Ibn Saud was twenty-one, and master of desert Arabia.

The years passed, and Ibn Saud remained quietly at Riyadh, biding his time. During the First World War he took no part in the guerrilla actions led by T. E. Lawrence against the Turks. Events, however, were working in his favour. Events had in fact always worked in his favour, and he possessed an uncanny faculty for striking only when the enemy was completely oblivious that an attack was impending. In later years they called Ibn Saud 'the lion of Arabia', but he resembled a panther, a more calculating beast.

The tides of war, moving from Arabia to Syria, left him untouched. Since none of his fanatical Wahhabis had taken part in the march on Damascus, the British saw no reason to reward him, but instead championed the claims of Husayn, Sharif of Mecca, and his four sons, Ali, Abdallah, Faysal and Zayd. Already in the spring of 1918, Husayn had proclaimed himself 'King of the Arab countries', claiming an empire which extended from the Red Sea to the Persian Gulf and from the Indian Ocean to the borders of defeated Turkey. Ibn Saud raged in his desert fastness. He raged still more when Iraq was given to Faysal and Transjordan to Abdallah, Faysal and Abdallah being the most talented of the Sharif's sons. Faysal in particular possessed a natural grace and dignity, tall and slender with the air of a man removed from human preoccupations, his dagger-sharp mind at war with his instinct for perpetual contemplation. Abdallah had little natural grace, but much charm and forthrightness. Zayd was half-Turkish, and therefore unacceptable to many Arabs, and Ali was too much the scholar to be a ruler, a man of moods, subject to sudden passionate outbursts which were caused by tuberculosis.

From his palace in Riyadh, Ibn Saud viewed the rise of Husayn with considerable detachment. He was ready to spring, but had not chosen the time or place. When the Wahhabis flocked to his court and demanded that he should proclaim a holy war against the British and drive them and Husayn into the sea, and if necessary assume the position of Caliph or at the very least call himself the Mahdi, 'the guided one', he answered sternly: 'With Mahdis and suchlike superstitions and sorceries I will have no dealings. As to the Caliph, the question does not arise. I am a simple preacher. My mission is to spread the faith, if possible by persuasion and if not by the sword.' He meant he would attack when the time was ripe, preferably at a moment when Husayn was weakest or showed himself least responsible for his actions.

Such a moment came on March 6, 1924, when Husayn proclaimed himself Caliph of Islam three days after the Turks abolished the Ottoman Caliphate. He made the claim reluctantly, largely under pressure from his son Abdallah, and he seems to have known from the beginning that he would incur the hostility of Ibn Saud. For more than three months Ibn Saud prepared his campaign. In the last week of August his armies struck at Taif, where Muhammad, the Messenger of God and ancestor of King Husayn, had once been a goatherd. Taif was a pleasant town in the uplands, where the notables of Mecca built their summer palaces. It represented the luxury and refinement which the Wahhabis despised. Some five hundred of the inhabitants were massacred, not because Ibn Saud had any particular feeling against those who were murdered; his task was to create panic in Mecca. In this he was eminently successful. Mecca suffered a panic such as it had rarely known before. Husayn hoped the British would intervene, but the British were in no mood for further adventures in Arabia: St. John Philby, long a close friend and adviser of Ibn Saud, had made it clear in his reports that the armies of Ibn Saud would carry everything before them. For a few more weeks Husayn clung to his throne in Mecca. Finally, on October 5, he abdicated, and a week later the advance forces of the Wahhabis entered the Holy City. Husayn was conveyed by a British warship to Cyprus, spending the remaining years of his life in exile in Nicosia. So ended the chapter of Arab history which began when Lawrence armed the tribesmen of the Hijaz and sent them under a cruel banner against the Turks.

Once more the theory of Ibn Khaldun, which says that kings and empires will always fall before small groups of fanatics armed with *asabiyya*, was proved accurate. It remained to discover whether the rest of the theory would also be proved true. In fact, the rise and decline of the Saudi dynasty took place with amazing rapidity, for with the discovery of oil in Arabia, unimaginable wealth poured into the treasuries of the King, who in his youth had slept under the stars, hungry and penniless. This wealth, largely divided between the King and his sons, did little to increase the native strength of the state. Private aeroplanes were purchased for the Saudi princes; millions of pounds were spent on building palaces provided with modern refrigeration, and while the social fabric of the state remained unchanged the wandering tribesmen were only a little richer than they were before. Decadence set in before there had been any visible culture, and neither poets nor artists graced the court of the richest of Arabian kings. As a youth Ibn Saud had been 'the sleuth of all the sleuths on earth, swifter than the lightning in the sky'. He had been a figure of portentous legend, brother to the Mahdis and the Veiled Prophets who in the past had emerged from Arabia and Khurasan. When he died in 1953 he had outlived his own legend.

Throughout all the centuries of Islam a strange fate had hovered over the descendants of Muhammad. It was as though that part of the world which eagerly accepted the Messenger of God had turned forever against his living descendants. The Hashimite King Husayn died in misery in Nicosia, his son King Abdallah of Jordan was assassinated while entering the Dome of the Rock in July, 1951, his grandson King Ghazi of Iraq was killed in a motor accident, and his great-grandson King Faysal II was shot to death by usurpers in July, 1958. On the day of his death the Baghdad radio urged the people to go out in the streets and see the body of Crown Prince Abdal Ilah, who had acted as regent during the minority of the King. 'Go out into the streets,' said the radio. 'See the body of the tyrant who was the enemy of God and the people, being spat on by the people and kicked by their feet!' It was the voice of medieval Islam, a voice impelled neither by hunger nor by despair of God, but by the memory of tribal feuds engendered centuries ago.

Everywhere one looks in the Muhammadan world the past impinges on the present. For the Muhammadan the past is more real than the present: the home of his imagination is still the camp, the raiding party, the worship of the Black Stone, the symbol of an ageless antiquity as old as earth. From these naked beginnings his mind can soar to the most exquisite perfection of architectural design and to the most luminous poetry, but the very nature of his religion makes him incapable of understanding the social forces which move the modern world, and he remains intolerant of all forms of government except feudalism. Only among the Shi'as of Persia, with their annual miracle play in honour of the martyred Husayn, is there a sense of the tragedy of man, and only in modern Turkey is there any understanding of democracy. For the Muhammadan life is a harsh and brittle thing under the sun, to be thrown away at a whim, unworthy of the dignity which the western world proclaims to be man's greatest possession.

The Muhammadans lack a democratic tradition. When at the end of World War II the Muhammadan states one after another obtained their freedom from the colonial powers and set about governing themselves, they found themselves in a quandary. It was not only that the colonial powers had prevented the development of a democratic tradition, but the Muhammadans themselves had no experience of thinking in democratic terms, and were by nature perhaps incapable of doing so. Almost simultaneously Egypt, Pakistan and Indonesia became free states, with houses of representatives and all the complex appurtenances of modern government. On paper there existed a free electorate; in fact, there were feudal rulers, armed with the same despotic powers wielded by caliphs and sultans. Nothing corresponding to the French Revolution had ever shaken the uninterrupted calm of Islam, which proclaims that all believers are brothers and the lowliest slave is the equal to the king in the eyes of God. But the king remains, and the slave is still a slave.

Not all the kings remain. When King Farouk of Egypt abdicated in July, 1952, as the result of a military *coup d'état* organized by Colonel Gamal

Abdal Nasser, a tolerant world assumed that the removal of a sybaritic King was long overdue, and a military government was a small price to pay for a much-needed revolution. Colonel Nasser himself, when he emerged from behind the figurehead he had installed in office, proved to be a singularly gifted ruler, audacious and intelligent, determined to put a stop to corruption, tolerant in religious matters, realistic and practical in his approach to political problems. He had schooled himself in the hardest school of all: the school of conspiracy. He had spent years organizing and maintaining the secret conspiratorial group known as the Free Officers Movement. He had no plans for managing the country when he came to power, but relied on his instincts, his knowledge of men and his wide reading in history. From a distance he seemed to be superbly equipped for the task he had given himself.

In 1952 he was thirty-four, a good age for a man embarking on a back-breaking career. He had other advantages. He was handsome and strongly built, with great physical stamina. He had no vices, worked long hours and had few relaxations apart from reading. He enjoyed simplicity, and lived in comparative obscurity in a suburban villa. He believed passionately in the cause of Egypt, and in the Palestine War of 1948–49 he had fought bravely and was wounded. During the war, when mortars and shells were dropping round him, one of his closest friends had said just before being killed: 'Listen, the greatest battlefield is in Egypt', and he had never forgotten it. He was a man of fire and immense daring, in danger of being burnt by his own fire, but otherwise not dissimilar to thousands of Egyptian officers determined to put an end to corruption and to give Egypt a place in the sun.

Some time in 1953, with the memory of the *coup d'état* still fresh in his mind, Colonel Nasser put together some notes he had written on his impressions of the 'revolution'. There had not in fact been a revolution at all, but this was a matter of little importance; there had been vast changes in the system of government, and in time those changes might be expected to percolate among the fellahin. These notes were not originally intended for publication. He was concerned, he said, to allow his ideas to explore themselves, and he liked to regard the exploration as in the nature of a reconnaissance patrol. This short book is at least as important as *Mein Kampf*, and perhaps as important as the *Communist Manifesto*, for in it he announced quietly and with conviction three theses of vast magnitude. First he announced the revival of the idea of *al Umma al Arabiya*: a united Arab nation stretching from the Atlantic to the Pacific, from Morocco to Indonesia. There was nothing particularly new in the idea, which had been first expressed by Lebanese students of the American University of Beirut about the year 1880: what was new was that he was in a position to employ all the resources of government propaganda to broadcast the idea wherever Arabic was spoken or understood. Secondly, he announced that Africa, the whole of Africa, was ripe for conquest. This, too, was an idea which had been maintained for many centuries by Muhammadans who travelled across the length and breadth of northern Africa, establishing outposts as far west as Ghana on the plain between the Senegal and Niger rivers. One such outpost was visited by the Arab geographer al-Baqri in the eleventh century. He reported that Arab colonists controlled the treasury and all the political affairs of the idol-worshipping king of Ghana, and had built a town for themselves with twelve mosques. In the thirteenth century the larger part of North Africa was controlled by the Mandingo people, whose empire extended from the Sudan across the wastes of the Sahara. Under the great fourteenth-century Emperor Mansa Musa, all the tribes were at peace with one another, and the Emperor made his annual pilgrimage to Mecca in magnificent state. Ibn Battuta, that most enterprising of Arab travellers, said that even white men could travel about this country without fear of robbers, and if they died with treasure in their hands, no one would steal it. During the sixteenth century, Goa and Timbuktu on the Niger were the centres of flourishing Muhammadan civilizations. Leo Africanus, who travelled from Morocco to the court of King Askia the Great, the ablest of the West African sovereigns, reported that Timbuktu was the headquarters of a vast trade in books, and the King was deeply respectful to men of learning. There had been great Muhammadan empires in Africa. Colonel Nasser announced that Africa was *terra irredenta*, to be returned to the Islamic fold.

His argument was simple and needed no elaboration. He did, however, elaborate on the reasons which brought him to this conclusion. Egypt had always been the protector of Africa ever since the Mamluks checked the onslaught of the Mongols at Ayn Jalut. She had exhausted herself by holding the barbarians at bay. He added justly that 'the rule of the Mamluks in Egypt was characterized by tyranny, oppression and ruin, which continued for many dark centuries. During that period our country was transformed into a jungle ruled by wild beasts'. With one hand he paid tribute to the Mamluk conquerors, and with the other he took it back. He had fallen into the dilemma which confronts all dictators, without being aware there was any dilemma at all.

Colonel Nasser made no attempt to hide his determination to bring Africa within the fold. He wrote:

> We cannot in any way stand aside, even if we wish to, from the sanguinary and dreadful struggle now raging in the heart of Africa between 5 million Whites and 200 million Africans. We cannot for one principal and clear reason, namely that we are in Africa.
>
> The people in Africa will continue to look up at us, who guard the northern gate of the continent and who are its connecting link with the outside world. We cannot under any condition relinquish our responsibility in helping, in every way possible, to diffuse the light of civilization into the farthest parts of that virgin jungle.
>
> There is another important reason. The Nile is the artery of the life of our country. It draws its supply of water from the heart of the continent.

There remained the third thesis: the need to bring within the fold the Muhammadans 'beyond the continents and oceans', all the unnumbered millions of believers living in Indonesia, China, Malaya, India, Burma, Pakistan and the Soviet Union. In some unexplained way they were to be brought into the union 'in a co-operation going not beyond the bounds of their natural loyalty to their own countries'. Yet even as he names the sovereign states there is an air of unreality in his recital of them. The third thesis is the most far-reaching and difficult to achieve, and therefore he dismisses it in a few words at the end of his book. He tells of standing beside the Kaaba at Mecca, seeing in his mind's eye all the regions of the world which Islam has reached, and how the Kaaba might become the providential symbol of the awakened unity of the Arab world.

When he asked himself how these three theses would become realities, he spoke characteristically of the role wandering in search of a hero. He had read Pirandello's *Six Characters in Search of an Author*, and it occurred to him that there was an actor living 'somewhere near the borders of our country' who might play the role of the Great Unifier. He wrote:

> The pages of history are full of heroes who created for themselves roles of glorious valour which they played at decisive moments. And in the pages of history we find, too, heroic and glorious roles which never found heroes to perform them. I do not know why it always seems to me that this role, exhausted by its wanderings, has at last settled down, tired and weary, near the borders of our country and is beckoning us to walk on to the stage, recite the lines, put on the proper costumes, since no one else is qualified to play it.

At this point, for fear that anyone might suggest that Colonel Nasser was depicting his own role, he stepped back, and in the next sentence explained that he was not referring to Egyptian leadership, but to a nebulous 'interplay of reactions and experiments with all these factors, aiming at exploding the tremendous latent energy in all the areas around us.'

By the nature of things Nasser was treading on dangerous ground, awakening forces over which he must have known he would have little control. He saw himself as another Saladin, capable of uniting Syria and Egypt as Saladin had done before him; but he lacked Saladin's nobility of purpose as he lacked the great paladin's deep religious faith. Nasser's impulses were fundamentally honest—no one can read his *Philosophy of the Revolution* without admiring his relentless efforts to understand the springs of his own actions—but the man as he reveals himself in his speeches is the child of frenzied dreams who will play the game of empire on those frontiers of the imagination which open into nightmare. Muhammad, too, had his frenzies, his dreams of empire, and the greatest of his enemies had inherited the empire he did so much to found. The knowledge of treachery is very close to the Arab mind. Wherever Nasser looks he is aware of traitors in the shadows. As the years pass, if he escapes assassination, he will inevitably grow harsher, more imperious, increasingly at the mercy of his limitless dreams; and it is unlikely that he can survive for long the pressure of his fears. Where an Augustus was needed, the world has been presented with a Caligula.

'The duty of Egypt,' Nasser wrote, 'is to create an immense power which will be able to drive the African countries into revolution.' The art of creating revolutions is well known. Trotsky and Hitler have elaborated upon the simple elements of that destructive art, and Nasser has sat abundantly at their feet. He was wiser when he was younger. He wrote in *The Philosophy of the Revolution* that what he wanted most from the endless crowds who cheered him was to hear 'but one Egyptian uttering one word of justice about another'. He rarely heard the words he desired to hear, and soon became too embroiled in conspiracy to care. Today, in full possession of his destructive art, he stands with the sword of Islam in his hand, more dreadfully imperious than any emperor before him.

To understand the danger of Nasser, one has only to compare him with Muhammad. What Muhammad tapped were elements of human consciousness which are timeless, changeless, quite without historic answer— the human need for submission, the heart's hunger for God, man's thirst for dominion over himself, over his own passions and the aimless wanderings of his mind. An ultimate and relentless faith illuminated his spirit. He was no hero searching for a role to play, but a stern taskmaster who would shape heroism to the ends of God. Nasser, employing the weapons of subversion, must subvert Islam to his own ends, becoming Caliph and Sultan, creating and ruling over an empire which in the nature of things must split apart at the moment of his death. His legions lack the *asabiyya*, the cohesiveness, which is the firm requisite of conquerors. He must trust to instinct where in the past the great sultans and caliphs trusted in their faith. And he must work alone, without friends, always with the knowledge that his most powerful adversaries in the Soviet Union are working towards his destruction. None ever walked such a tightrope before, or pretended so convincingly that he was walking on air.

With the figure of Gamal Abdal Nasser the story of Islam comes to its present end. All the forces of historic Islam bear against this strange dictator in a modern business suit. He represents the awakened fury of aroused Islam, which sees itself surrounded by enemies beyond its understanding. He must fight the 'war of the desert' in an age given over to wars which are not fought according to the law of Islamic warfare. Inevitably he makes war against those who might have been his closest allies: a shadowy war fought among shadows.

There is a sense in which the story of Islam is already over. There was a time when the power of Islam was poured into great monuments and the building of great cities, when the Masjid-i-Shah, the blue mosque at Isfahan, and the great Maidan were regarded as supreme examples of the grace of God; when a Caliph would devote his life and fortune to the creation of his library; when poets and philosophers were rewarded. With flawless taste the artisans built prayer chambers filled with the magnificence of tiles of lapis lazuli, to represent the blue meadows of Paradise in flower. But as the ages passed the glory departed. Today we see only the husk of Islam, shorn of its ancient grandeur. Always the Muhammadans were faced with a dilemma. Since 'all things are passing save His Face', what was to be gained by building earthly empires by the sword? All that was best in Islam came, not from the sword, but from the contemplation of God's peace.

GLOSSARY

Abu	Father of.
Ahl al-bait	People of the House (of the Prophet), as distinguished from *ahl al-kitab*, the People of the Book, i.e., Christians and Jews.
Allah	The supreme Being of the Moslems, from the Aramaic *alaha*, 'the god'.
Allahu Akbar	God is the greatest of all.
Amin	So be it.
Amir	Leader, chieftain.
Ansar	Helpers. The first converts from Madinah.
Ana 'l-Haqq	'I am the Truth.' The famous cry of al-Hallaj.
Asabiyya	Group feeling; instinctive social cohesion. Used by Ibn Khaldun in his study of corruption.
Bab	Gate.
Bismikka Allahummah	'In Thy name, O God.' A common invocation.
Burda	Cloak.
Dawlah	A new era.
Dervish (Darwish)	Member of a religious fraternity.
Dhu'l-Faqar	Splitter of Vertebrae. The famous two-pointed sword won at the battle of Badr.
Fana	Annihilation of the self. A technical term used by Sufis.
Fakir	Mendicant dervish.
Fatihah	The opening chapter of the Quran.
Hadith	Originally a story, then one of the sayings of the Prophet.
Hajji	One who has performed the *hajj*, or pilgrimage.
Haram	Forbidden, sacred.
Hijra (Hegira)	Abandonment, emigration. Used of Muhammad's flight to Madinah.
Hulul	The loosening: hence the incarnation of God in man.
Huri	The white ones, the maidens of Paradise.
Ibn	Son of. Corresponds to Hebrew *ben*.
Ihram	Mortification. Especially refers to the major and minor pilgrimages.
Imam	Leader in the widest sense. Leader of prayer in the mosque, or any spiritual leader in authority.
Islam	Submission. The faith of the Muhammadans.
Ittihad	Becoming one. Used of the coalescence of divine and human creatures.

Jahannam	Hell.
Jihad	Holy war.
Jinn	Intelligent creatures of air and fire.
Jubbah	A loose cloak.
Kaaba	The sacred cube in the centre of Mecca.
Khalifah	Successor, vicegerent. Caliph. The term is also used by Malays to describe a mystical rite.
Kiswa	Black curtain covering the four walls of the *Kaaba*.
La ilaha illa Allah	There is no God save Allah.
Mahdi	The guided one, hence the deliverer.
Maidan	Parade-ground.
Masjid-i-Shah	Mosque of the Shah.
Mihrab	Niche at east end of mosque giving direction of Mecca.
Minbar	Pulpit.
Mutah	Administrator: hence the secret ruler of the universe.
Nabi	Prophet.
Quran (*Koran, Kur'an*)	The discourse.
Qubbat al-Sakhrah	Dome of the Rock.
Qubbat al-Silsilah	Dome of the Chain.
Rak'a	Bending the body in prayer.
Rasul	Messenger, apostle.
Sahib an-naqah	Man on a she-camel. Said of some founders of dynasties.
Saqalibah	Slavs.
Sha'ir	Literally 'knower'. Applied to poets, soothsayers and possessed people.
Shaykh	Title of respect: used for leader of a tribe, holy men, anyone regarded with veneration.
Shi'a	Party, especially the Party of Ali. The form of Muhammadanism common throughout Persia.
souk	Bazaar.
Sufi	Probably from *Suf*, wool. Denotes the mystics whose doctrines emerged during the third century after the Hijra.
Sunna	Custom, tradition, especially the traditions associated with Muhammad.
Sunni	Traditional Muhammadanism, as distinguished from the Shi'a sectarian movement.
Sura	The chapters of the Quran.
Tawaf	The running round or circumambulation of any sacred object, used especially of running round or circumambulating the *Kaaba*.

CHRONOLOGICAL TABLE

A.D.

c. 570	Muhammad born.
c. 610	The Vision in the Cave.
617	Flight of his followers to Abyssinia.
622	Migration to Madinah. Beginning of Islamic era.
624	Battle of Badr.
625	Battle of Uhud.
627	Battle of the Ditch.
630	Conquest of Mecca. Battle of Hunayn.
632	Farewell Pilgrimage. Death of Muhammad (June 8)
632—634	Caliphate of Abu Bakr.
634	Battle of Ajnadayn.
634—644	Caliphate of Umar.
635	Conquest of Damascus.
637	Moslems take Jerusalem and Ctesiphon.
641	Conquest of Persia and Egypt.
644—656	Caliphate of Uthman.
651	Yazdagird, last Sasanian Emperor, assassinated in Khurasan.
656—661	Caliphate of Ali.
656	Battle of the Camel.
657	Battle of Siffin.
659	Arbitration at Adhruh.
661—750	Umayyad Caliphate.
661—680	Caliphate of Muawiya I.
669	Constantinople besieged.
674	Second siege of Constantinople.
680	Death of Husayn at Karbala.
685—705	Caliphate of Abd-al-Malik.
691—694	Dome of the Rock built.
711	Moslems enter Spain. Conquest of Sind and Transoxiana.
720	Arabs in Narbonne.
732	Battle against Charles Martel near Tours.
749	All Persia in hands of the Abbasids.
750—754	Caliphate of As-Saffah. Umayyads destroyed.
754—775	Caliphate of al-Mansur.
756—788	Abd-ar-Rahman, amir of Cordova.
762	Baghdad founded.
778	Charlemagne enters Spain.
786—809	Caliphate of Harum al-Rashid.

803	Execution of Ja'far.
831	Palermo seized by Arabs.
833	Death of Caliph al-Mamun.
836	Samarra founded.
847—861	Caliphate of al-Mutawakkil.
858—922	Al-Hallaj.
871	Basrah destroyed.
868—906	Tulunids as hereditary governors of Egypt.
876—879	Mosque of Ahmad ibn Tulun.
909	Death of Bayazid.
910	Death of al-Junayd.
912—961	Abd-ar-Rahman III. Cordova at its greatest glory.
923	Death of historian Tabari.
930	Qarmatians sack Mecca.
932—934	Al-Qahir.
961—976	Hakam I in Cordova.
996—1021	The Fatimid al-Hakim in Egypt. Rise of the Druses.
1027—1031	Hisham III, last Umayyad ruler of Cordova.
1040	Toghrul Beg seizes Khurasan.
1055	Seljuks capture Baghdad.
1061—1091	Normans settle in Sicily.
1063—1072	Alp Arslan.
1058—1111	Al-Ghazzali.
1066	Normans conquer England.
1071	Battle of Manzikert.
1099	Crusaders capture Jerusalem.
1138—1193	Saladin.
1147—1149	Second Crusade.
1165—1240	Ibn Arabi.
1171	Saladin overthrows Fatimids in Egypt.
1182—1226	St. Francis of Assisi.
1184—1291	Sa'di of Shiraz.
1187	Saladin defeats Franks at Horns of Hattin and captures Jerusalem.
1189—1192	Third Crusade.
1203	Muhammad Ghuri conquers northern India.
1207—1273	Jalalu'l-Din Rumi.
1227	Death of Genghiz Khan.
1254—1517	Mamluk rule in Egypt.
1258	Hulagu captures Baghdad.
1260	Mamluks defeat Mongols at Ayn Jalut.
1260—1267	Baybars.
1294	Ala-ad-Din conquers Daulatabad.
1291	Crusaders ousted from Syria.
1303	Battle of Marj al-Suffah.
1330	Janissaries first appointed.
1331	Death of Emperor Andronicus III.

1336—1405	Timurlane.
1337	Urkhon attacks Constantinople.
1389	Battle of Kossovo Polye.
1389—1402	Sultan Bayazid.
1400	Damascus sacked by Timurlane.
1402	Battle of Ankara. Defeat of Bayazid.
1439	Battle of Hermannstadt.
1453	Fall of Constantinople.
1456	Siege of Belgrade.
1481	Death of Muhammad II, the Conqueror.
1492	Fall of Granada. Moors expelled from Spain.
1514	Selim I defeats Shah Ismail at Chaldiran.
1517	Selim I conquers Egypt.
1520—1566	Sulayman I, the Magnificent.
1522	Siege of Rhodes.
1525	Babur sets out to conquer India.
1526	Battle of Mohacs.
1556—1605	Akbar.
1638	Murad IV storms Baghdad.
1628—1658	Shah Jehan.
1681	Turks cede Kiev to Russia.
1687	Turks defeated at Mohacs.
1699	Peace of Karlowicz.
1736—1747	Nadir Shah.
1739	Nadir Shah captures Delhi.
1769—1848	Muhammad Ali.
1789	Napoleon in Egypt. Battle of the Pyramids.
1801	Wahhabis raid Karbala.
1803—1804	Wahhabis capture Mecca and Madinah.
1811	Muhammad Ali destroys Mamluks.
1821—1829	Mahmud II massacres Janissaries.
1830	Algiers occupied by French.
1835	Abd-al-Qadir defeats French.
1839	Aden occupied by British.
1842	Revolt of Druses.
1843	Abd al-Qadir passes into Morocco.
1853	Crimean War.
1857	Indian Mutiny.
1860	Construction of Suez Canal begins.
1869	Suez Canal completed.
1870	The Mahdi in the Sudan.
1880—1892	Tewfiq, Khedive of Egypt.
1881	French occupy Tunisia.
1882	Battle of Tell al-Kabir. Mahdi drives Egyptians from the Sudan. British occupation of Egypt.
1883	Death of Abd al-Qadir.
1885	Khartum attacked. Gordon killed. Death of the Mahdi.

1894	French capture Timbuktu.
1898	Battle of Omdurman.
1901	Ibn Saud captures Riyadh.
1908	Revolution of Young Turks. Sharif Husayn becomes guardian of Mecca.
1911—1912	Italy conquers Tripolitania.
1914—1918	First World War.
1916	Arab revolt begins.
1917	British capture Baghdad.
1918	T. E. Lawrence occupies Damascus.
1919	Revolution in Egypt.
1920	Allies occupy Istanbul.
1921	Revolt of Abd el-Krim in the Rif. Kingdoms of Iraq and Transjordan proclaimed.
1923	Turkish Republic proclaimed.
1924	Caliphate abolished. Ibn Saud conquers Hijaz.
1925	Riza Khan Pahlavi, Shah of Iran.
1932	Ibn Saud proclaims Kingdom of Saudi Arabia.
1933	Death of Faysal I of Iraq.
1936	King Farouk comes to the throne.
1938	Death of Atatürk.
1939—1945	Second World War.
1941	Revolt of Rashid Ali in Iraq.
1947	Partition of India and Pakistan.
1948	Israel proclaims independence. Iraq, Lebanon, Egypt, Syria and Jordan invade Israel.
1951	King Abdallah assassinated.
1952	King Farouk exiled. Libya proclaims independence.
1953	Egypt proclaimed a republic, with General Naguib as president.
1954	Gamal Abdal Nasser becomes dictator of Egypt.
1956	Sudan and Tunisia become independent. Pakistan becomes Islamic Republic. Egypt nationalizes Suez Canal. Israel, Britain and France invade Egypt.
1958	United Arab Republic proclaimed.

SELECTIVE BIBLIOGRAPHY

There are in English five indispensable works for the study of Muhammadan theology, history and art. They are Alfred Guillaume's translation of Ibn Ishaq's *Life of Muhamad*, A. J. Arberry's translations of the Quran, Arthur Upham Pope's *Survey of Persian Art*, K. A. C. Creswell's *Early Muslim Architecture* and Charles Doughty's *Travels in Arabia Deserta*. These are all full and meaty books written with scholarly genius, and must stand apart in any list of books dealing with Islamic studies. The only other comparable work in a European language known to me is Louis Massignon's *Al-Hallaj, Martyre mystique de l'Islam*.

Unhappily, there are no collections of works devoted to translations of Islamic texts comparable with the great series of translations of Christian theologians. The E. J. W. Gibb Memorial Translations are numerous and excellent, but do not form a co-ordinated series. The American Council of Learned Societies published a group of ten translations of modern Arabic books, but the translations are of unequal value. Whole areas of Islamic knowledge remain closed to us. We lack a good history of the Seljuk Turks or of Fatimid Egypt; there is no dependable survey of Islamic art in Spain. Dozy's monumental study of Islamic Spain needs to be brought up to date. Only Creswell has had the patience and scholarship to knit together all the threads of early Muslim architecture, but much work remains to be done on the early origins of Muhammadan art. Monographs abound, but we are still only at the beginning of Islamic studies in this country.

Of recent works the most impressive studies made in England have been devoted to the Sufis, and those of Margaret Smith and A. J. Arberry deserve special mention. In America there is Franz Rosenthal's translation of Ibn Khaldun's *Muqaddimah* in three handsome volumes. It is a work of impressive scholarship, but does not materially add to the translation published by de Slane in Paris more than a hundred years ago.

The great standby of all those who work on Islamic studies is the monumental *Encyclopaedia of Islam*, scholarly and humane, but curiously lacking on the subject of the Islamic arts. The *Shorter Encyclopaedia of Islam* is, of course, invaluable, though limited to articles dealing with Islamic religion and law. A completely rewritten *Encyclopaedia of Islam* is now being prepared by Islamic scholars from all over the world, but unfortunately it is to be published only in Urdu. It seems a pity that the work of so many talents should be published in a language which can be read by very few scholars in the West.

For the present there is a great need for a standard collection of authoritative Islamic texts in translation. Until that time comes the task of understanding Islam will remain almost intolerably difficult. It is not only that Muhammadan patterns of thought are foreign to us, but we have the added disadvantage of knowing so little about the most elementary facts of Muhammadan history, which have rarely been analysed with the same scrupulous care that we devote to western history. Background and foreground are both legendary. So it will remain until another inspired Gibbon surveys the whole field of Islamic history and gives us the facts interpreted with imaginative truth.

s

THE SANDS OF THE DESERT

BROCKELMANN, CARL, *History of the Islamic Peoples* (London: Routledge and Kegan Paul, 1949).

GUILLAUME, ALFRED, *Islam* (Harmondsworth: Penguin Books, 1956).

HOGARTH, D. G., *Arabia* (Oxford: Clarendon Press, 1922).

PHILBY, H. ST. J., *The Heart of Arabia* (New York: G. P. Putnam's Sons, 1923).

SCHROEDER, ERIC, *Muhammad's People* (Portland: The Bond Wheelright Company, 1954).

THE MESSENGER OF GOD: THE HOLY SWORD

ALI, MUHAMMAD, *The Prophet Muhammad* (London: Cassell & Co., 1947).

ANDRAE, TOR, *Mohammed, the Man and his Faith* (London: George Allen & Unwin, 1936).

DERMENGHEM, ÉMILE, *Mahomet et la Tradition islamique* (Paris: Aux éditions du seuil, n.d.).

——, *Muhammad and the Islamic Tradition* (New York: Harper & Brothers, 1958).

DIBBLE, R. F., *Mohammed* (New York: The Viking Press, 1926).

GUILLAUME, ALFRED, *The Life of Muhammad*: a translation of Ibn Ishaq's *Sirat Rasul Allah* (London: Oxford University Press, 1955).

IRVING, WASHINGTON, *Life of Mahomet* (London: J. M. Dent and Sons, 1949).

MARGOLIOUTH, D. S., *Mohammad and the Rise of Islam* (London: G. P. Putnam's Sons, 1927).

PIRENNE, HENRI, *Mohammad and Charlemagne* (New York: Meridian Books, 1957).

WATT, W. M., *Muhammad at Mecca* (Oxford: Clarendon Press, 1953).

——, *Muhammad at Medina* (Oxford: Clarendon Press, 1956).

THE HOLY WORD

ALI, MUHAMMAD, *The Muslim Prayer Book* (Lahore: Dar-ul-Kutub, Islamia, 1957).

AL-SUHRAWARDY, Allami Sir Abdullah Al-Mamun, *The Sayings of Muhammad* (London: John Murray, 1949).

ARBERRY, A. J., *The Koran Interpreted* (New York: The Macmillan Co., 1955).

ARNOLD, T. W., *The Preaching of Islam* (Westminster: Archibald Constable & Co., 1896).

DAWOOD, N. J. (tr.), *The Koran* (Harmondsworth: Penguin Books, 1956).

LAMMENS, H., *Islam: Beliefs and Institutions* (New York: E. P. Dutton & Co., n.d.).

PICKTHALL, MOHAMMAD MARMADUKE (tr.), *The Meaning of the Glorious Koran* (New York: New American Library, 1953).

ROBSON, JAMES, *Christ in Islam* (New York: E. P. Dutton & Co., 1930).

RODWELL, J. M., *The Koran: the Suras arranged in Chronological Order* (London: J. M. Dent, 1918).

TRITTON, A. S., *Islam: Beliefs and Practices* (London: Hutchinson's University Library, 1954).

THE ARABIAN CALIPHS

ALI, MAULANA MUHAMMAD, *Early Caliphate* (Lahore: Ahmadiyyah Anjuman Ishaat Islam, 1951).

FORSTER, E. M., *Alexandria: A History and a Guide* (Alexandria: Whitehead Morris, 1902).

SHERWANI KHAN, *Hadrat Abu Bakr* (Lahore: Muhammad Ashraf, 1947).

TRITTON, A. S., *The Caliphs and their Non-Moslem Subjects* (London: Humphrey Milford, 1930).

THE CALIPHS OF DAMASCUS

BRIGGS, MARTIN S., *Muhamadan Architecture in Egypt and Palestine* (Oxford: Clarendon Press, 1924).

CRESWELL, K. A. C., *A Short Account of Early Muslim Architecture* (Harmondsworth: Penguin Books, 1958).

——, *Early Muslim Architecture* (Oxford: Clarendon Press, 1932, 1940), 2 vols.

RICHMOND, ERNEST TATHAM, *The Dome of the Rock in Jerusalem* (Oxford: Clarendon Press, 1924).

THE CALIPHS OF BAGHDAD

AMEDROZ, H. E., and MARGOLIOUTH, D. S., *The Eclipse of the Abbasid Caliphate* (Oxford: Basil Blackwell, 1920–21), 7 vols.

ARNOLD, T. W., *The Caliphate* (Oxford: Clarendon Press, 1924).

BECKFORD, WILLIAM, *Vathek* (New York: Brentano's, n.d.).

LEVY, REUBEN, *A Baghdad Chronicle* (Cambridge, Cambridge University Press, 1929).

LLOYD, SETON, *Ruined Cities of Iraq* (Oxford: Oxford University Press, 1942).

SLANE, BARON MacGuckin de (tr.), *Ibn Khallikan's Biographical Dictionary* (Paris: 1843), 4 vols.

TABARI, MUHAMMAD IBN JARIR, *The Reign of al-Mutasim*, tr. Elma Marin (American Oriental Series, vol. 35).

THE COMING OF AL-HALLAJ

ARBERRY, A. J., *Sufism* (London: George Allen & Unwin, 1956).

——, *The Doctrine of the Sufis* (Cambridge: Cambridge University Press, 1935).

MASSIGNON, LOUIS, *Hocein Mansur Hallaj: Diwan* (Paris: Cahiers du Sud, 1955).

——, *Al-Hallaj, Martyre Mystique de l'Islam* (Paris: Paul Geuthner, 1922).

SMITH, Margaret, *Readings from the Mystics of Islam* (London: Luzac and Co., 1950).

——, *Rabi'a the Mystic and her Fellow Saints in Islam* (Cambridge: Cambridge University Press, 1928).

——, *Al-Ghazzali the Mystic* (London: Luzac and Co., 1944).

THE RAGE OF KINGDOMS

AFFIFI, A. E., *The Mystical Philosophy of Muhyid-Din Ibnul-Arabi* (Cambridge: Cambridge University Press, 1939).

ALI, SYED NAWAB, *Some Religious Teachings of al-Ghazzali* (Lahore: Muhammad Ashraf, 1946).

BEHA ED-DIN IBN SHEDDAD, *The Life of Saladin* (London: Palestine Exploration Fund, 1897).

BURCKHARDT, TITUS (tr.), *La Sagesse des Prophètes, de Muhyi-d-din Ibn Arabi* (Paris: Albin Michel, 1955).

FIELD, CLAUD (tr.), *The Alchemy of Happiness by al-Ghazzali* (Lahore: Muhammad Ashraf, n.d.).

GAIRDNER, W. H. T. (tr.), *Al-Ghazzali's Mishkat al-Anwar* (Lahore: Muhammad Ashraf, n.d.).

KREY, AUGUST G., *The First Crusade: the Accounts of Eye-witnesses* (Princeton: Princeton University Press, 1921).

MARZIALS, SIR FRANK T. (tr.), *Memoirs of the Crusades: Villehardouin and Joinville* (New York: E. P. Dutton and Co., 1958).

MOULAVI, S. A. Q. HUSAINI, *Ibn al 'Arabi* (Lahore: Muhammad Ashraf, n.d.).

O'LEARY, DE LACY, *A Short History of the Fatimid Khalifate* (London: Kegan, Paul, Trench, Trubner and Co., 1923).

POTTER, GEORGE RICHARD (tr.) *The Autobiography of Ousama* (New York: Harcourt, Brace & Co., 1929).

WATT, W. MONTGOMERY, *The Faith and Practice of al-Ghazzali* (London: George Allen and Unwin, 1953).

WRIGHT, THOMAS (ed.), *Early Travels in Palestine* (London: Henry G. Bohn, 1948).

THE FALL OF EMPIRES

ARBERRY, A. J., *Classical Persian Literature* (New York: The Macmillan Co., 1958).

DARAH, PRINCE MUHAMMAD, *The Mingling of the Two Oceans*, tr. M. Mahfuz-ul-Huq (Calcutta: Asiatic Society of Bengal, 1929).

DAVIS, F. HADLAND, *The Persian Mystics: Jalalu-d-din Rumi* (Lahore: Muhammad Ashraf, n.d.).

GREY, BASIL, *Persian Painting* (London: Ernest Benn, Ltd., 1930).

HIDDEN, ALEXANDER W., *The Ottoman Dynasty* (New York: Nicholas W. Hidden, 1912).

LEVY, REUBEN, *Persian Literature* (London: Oxford University Press, 1948).

LUKE, SIR HARRY, *The Old Turkey and the New* (London: Geoffrey Bles, 1955).

MUIR, SIR WILLIAM, *The Mameluke or Slave Dynasty of Egypt (1260–1517 A.D.)* (London: Smith, Elder & Co., 1896).

NICHOLSON, R. A., *Rumi: Poet and Mystic* (London: George Allen and Unwin, 1956).

PAYNE, ROBERT, *The Splendor of Persia* (New York: Alfred A. Knopf, 1957).

POPE, ARTHUR UPHAM, *An Introduction to Persian Art* (London: Peter Davies, 1930).

——, *Masterpieces of Persian Art* (New York: The Dryden Press, 1945).

——, *Survey of Persian Art* (London: Oxford University Press, 1938–39), 6 vols.

PRICE, M. PHILIPS, *A History of Turkey* (London: George Allen and Unwin, 1956).

TAGORE, SIR RABINDRANATH (tr.), *The Songs of Kabir* (New York: The Macmillan Co., 1915).

TOBIN, CHESTER M., *Turkey: Key to the East* (New York: G. P. Putnam's Sons, 1944).

WILBER, DONALD N., *Iran: Past and Present* (Princeton: Princeton University Press, 1955).

THE AWAKENING

ARMSTRONG, H. C., *Lord of Arabia: Ibn Saud* (Harmondsworth: Penguin Books, 1938).

DOUGHTY, Charles Montagu, *Travels in Arabia Deserta* (London: P. L. Warner, 1921).

ELLIS, HARRY B., *The Heritage of the Desert* (New York: Ronald Press Co., 1956).

GAURY, GERALD DE, *Arabian Journey* (London: George G. Harrup and Co., 1950).

HASLIP, JOAN, *The Sultan: The Life of Abdul Hamid II* (London: Cassell and Co., 1958).

IZZEDDIN, NEJLA, *The Arab World* (Chicago: Henry Regnery Co., 1953).

LANE, EDWARD WILLIAM, *Cairo Fifty Years Ago* (London: John Murray, 1896).

LAWRENCE, T. E., *The Seven Pillars of Wisdom: A Triumph* (Garden City, N.Y., Doubleday, Doran and Co., 1935).

LUKASH, HARRY CHARLES, *The Fringe of the East* (London: Macmillan & Co., 1913).

MEULEN, D. VAN DER, *The Wells of Ibn Saud* (New York: Frederick A. Praeger, 1957).

NASSER, GAMAL ABDUL, *Egypt's Liberation: The Philosophy of the Revolution* (Washington: Public Affairs Press, 1955).

TWITCHELL, K. S., *Saudi Arabia* (Princeton: Princeton University Press, 1947).

GENERAL

ALI, AMEER, *A Short History of the Saracens* (London: Macmillan & Co., 1899).

ARNOLD, T. W., *Painting in Islam* (Oxford: Clarendon Press, 1928).

ATIYAH, EDWARD, *The Arabs* (Harmondsworth: Penguin Books, 1955).

BOUQUET, A. C., *Comparative Religion* (Harmondsworth: Penguin Books, 1950).

BROWNE, LAURENCE E., *The Prospects of Islam* (London: S. C. M. Press, 1944).

CHEW, S. C., *The Crescent and the Rose* (New York: Oxford University Press, 1937).

DIMAND, M. S., *A Handbook of Muhammadan Art* (New York: Metropolitan Museum of Art, 1958).

DOZY, REINHART, *Spanish Islam: A History of the Moslems in Spain* (London: Chatto and Windus, 1913).

FARIS, NABIH AMIN (ed.), *The Arab Heritage* (Princeton: Princeton University Press, 1946).

GIBB, H. A. R., *Mohammedanism: A Historical Survey* (New York: New American Library, 1955).

HITTI, Philip K., *History of the Arabs* (London: Macmillan & Co., 1946).

——, *History of Syria* (New York: The Macmillan Co., 1951).

——, *Lebanon in History* (London: Macmillan & Co., 1957).

KIRK, GEORGE E., *A Short History of the Middle East* (New York: Frederick A. Praeger, 1958).

LANE-POOL, STANLEY, *The Story of the Moors in Spain* (New York: G. P. Putnam's Sons, 1891).

MAHDI, MUHSIN, *Ibn Khaldun's Philosophy of History* (London: George Allen and Unwin, 1957).

MARÇAIS, GEORGES, *L'Art de l'Islam* (Paris: Libraire Larousse, 1946).

MARGOLIOUTH, D. S., *Cairo, Jerusalem and Damascus* (New York: Dodd, Mead & Co., 1907).

MASUDI, ABU AL-HASSAN, *L'Abrégé des Merveilles*, tr. Baron Carra de Vaux (Paris: C. Klincksiech, 1898).

NICHOLSON, REYNOLD A., *A Literary History of the Arabs* (New York: Charles Scribner's Sons, 1907).

ROSENTHAL, FRANZ (tr.), *Ibn Khaldun: The Muqaddimah* (New York: Pantheon Books, 1958), 3 vols.

PARKES, JAMES, *A History of Palestine from 135 A.D. to Modern Times* (New York: Oxford University Press, 1949).

WOLLASTON, ARTHUR N., *The Sword of Islam* (London: John Murray, 1905).

INDEX